HARD LINE

HARD LINE

THE REPUBLICAN PARTY AND U.S. FOREIGN POLICY SINCE WORLD WAR II

COLIN DUECK

PRINCETON UNIVERSITY PRESS

Princeton and Oxford

Library of Congress Cataloging-in-Publication Data

Dueck, Colin, 1969–
Hard line : the Republican Party and U.S. foreign policy since
World War II / Colin Dueck.
p. cm.
Includes bibliographical references and index.
ISBN 978-0-691-14181-7 (hardcover : alk. paper)
— ISBN 978-0-691-14182-4 (pbk. : alk. paper)
1. United States—Foreign relations—1945–1989.   2. United States—Foreign
relations—1989–   3. United States—Foreign relations—Philosophy.   4. United
States—Foreign relations administration.   5. Republican Party (U.S. : 1854–)—
History—20th century.   6. Republican Party (U.S. : 1854–)—History—21st
century.   7. Presidents—United States—History—20th century.   8. Presidents—
United States—History—21st century.   9. Conservatism—United States.
10. Nationalism—United States.   I. Title.
E840.D84 2010
327.73009′04—dc22
2010011199

British Library Cataloging-in-Publication Data is available

This book has been composed in Minion
Printed on acid-free paper. ∞
press.princeton.edu
Printed in the United States of America
1   3   5   7   9   10   8   6   4   2

CONTENTS

Acknowledgments   vii

Introduction   Conservative Traditions in U.S. Foreign Policy   1

Chapter One   Republicans, Conservatives, and U.S. Foreign Policy   11

Chapter Two   ROBERT TAFT
                    The Conservative as Anti-Interventionist   39

Chapter Three   DWIGHT EISENHOWER
                    The Conservative as Balancer   85

Chapter Four   BARRY GOLDWATER
                    The Conservative as Hawk   117

Chapter Five   RICHARD NIXON AND HENRY KISSINGER
                    Realists as Conservatives   142

Chapter Six   RONALD REAGAN
                    The Idealist as Hawk   187

Chapter Seven   GEORGE H. W. BUSH
                    The Conservative as Realist   232

Chapter Eight   GEORGE W. BUSH
                    The Nationalist as Interventionist   265

Conclusion   Republicans and U.S. Foreign Policy in the
                    Age of Obama   290

Notes   323

Index   359

ACKNOWLEDGMENTS

WHILE THE VIEWS PRESENTED in this book are my own, I am grateful to many people who helped me in the writing of it. A set of conferences at Princeton University in 2008–9 on the subject of conservatism and U.S. foreign policy, attended by a number of distinguished foreign policy experts, helped sharpen my ideas. Special thanks to the conference co-organizers, Aaron Friedberg and Jakub Grygiel, for exchanging views with me, reading pieces I sent them, and contributing to my understanding of the subject. Thanks are owed to the archivists at the Ronald Reagan Presidential Library in Simi Valley, California, and the National Archives in College Park, Maryland, for their crucial assistance with documents from the Reagan and Nixon years, respectively. My appreciation goes to David Frum, Francis Fukuyama, Richard Haass, Kim Holmes, William Kristol, Rich Lowry, Joshua Muravchik, Grover Norquist, Mitchell Reiss, Dimitri Simes, and George Will for agreeing to be interviewed for this book—interviews that gave me useful insights into recent Republican foreign policies from a variety of perspectives. Peter Beinart, Ben Fordham, James Kurth, Paul Lettow, Brian Rathbun, Gideon Rose, and Peter Trubowitz all read and commented on various chapters or essays drawn from this manuscript—my thanks to each of them. I've also learned a great deal from conversations on this subject over the years with Nick Gvosdev, Mark Lagon, Chris Layne, Daniel Markey, Henry Nau, and Ray Takeyh. Thanks to the anonymous reviewers at Princeton University Press for their very helpful suggestions on the manuscript. Particular credit goes to my remarkably congenial editor, Chuck Myers, for keeping me on track and for being so supportive of this project from the start. Sincere thanks to my fellow faculty at George Mason University's Department of Public and International Affairs, especially Bob Dudley, for providing a collegial environment conducive to research. Finally, my greatest gratitude is to my wife Kirsten, who provided loving, irreplaceable intellectual and practical support over the lengthy period of time that it took me to write this book. The result is dedicated to our son, Jack.

HARD LINE

doctrine's place in the history of American conservatism and the Republican Party. The first interpretation is that the story of right-wing foreign policy approaches in postwar America is one of radically aggressive, militaristic, and unilateralist ideas, thankfully ignored by moderate presidents such as Dwight Eisenhower but fully embraced by George W. Bush, to the combined detriment of the United States, the international community, and the Republican Party itself.[3] Call this the "radical right" thesis. The second interpretation is that a small group of neoconservatives took control of the Bush administration and drove it to war against Iraq, in contradiction to traditional Republican internationalism.[4] Call this the "neoconservative hijacking" thesis. The third interpretation is that both the Bush doctrine and the Iraq War were soundly conceived, despite certain failures of implementation, and need not be revisited or reexamined as bases for a new conservative foreign policy approach, especially since Iraq did no lasting damage to Republicans politically.[5] Call this the "tactical errors" thesis. All three of these arguments are made by sincere and intelligent people, but the more one looks at each interpretation, the less satisfying any of them are. The tactical errors thesis underestimates the seriousness of George W. Bush's early mistakes in Iraq. The neoconservative hijacking thesis overstates the policy impact of public intellectuals, as well as the philosophical break between Bush and earlier Republicans. The radical right thesis is correct in noticing some of the fundamental continuities in conservative foreign policy approaches since World War II, but exaggerates their deleterious effects.

The following pages tell a different story. First, I argue that despite apparent oscillations between internationalism and isolationism, there has in fact been one overarching constant in conservative and Republican foreign policies for several decades now, namely, a hawkish and intense American nationalism. By this I mean that since at least the 1950s, Republicans and conservatives have generally been comfortable with the use of force by the United States in world affairs, committed to building strong national defenses, determined to maintain a free hand for the United States internationally, and relatively unyielding toward potential foreign adversaries. The typical conservative Republican foreign policy approach for over half a century has been, in a word, hard-line—a long-term trend with considerable domestic political as well as international significance, especially since a majority of liberal Democrats began to abandon hard-line foreign policy views following America's war in Vietnam. Second, I demonstrate that certain particular conservative and Republican foreign policy tendencies have still been possible within the above framework, and that contrary to popular arguments centering on the importance of public intellectuals or economic interests, the crucial factor in shaping these specific foreign policy tendencies has been presidential leadership. Presidents have acted as focal points for their party, and Republican presidents have been given remarkable leeway to redefine not only conservative foreign policies but what it means to be a conservative in the United States.

These two observations, taken together, delineate both the past and the future of the Republican Party on American foreign policy. Republicans will continue to be relatively hard-line on international and military issues, as the party of a hawkish American nationalism, but the particular policy choices they make and the tendencies they reveal once back in control of the White House will depend heavily on presidential leadership. Among other things, this means that the recent obsession with "neoconservatives" is mistaken. Neoconservative ideas have been important over the past few years, but foreign policy is made by presidents, not intellectuals, and the Bush doctrine had deep roots in Republican and American foreign policy perspectives long before the word neoconservative was invented. Conservative foreign policy views and traditions are too strongly ingrained in the United States to fade away now, regardless of past furor over the neoconservatives and Iraq. The crucial consideration, therefore, is not so much the influence of neoconservative ideas but whether Republican presidents in practice have shown the prudence, pragmatism, and care to implement hawkish foreign policies skillfully and successfully. As I suggest in subsequent chapters, most Republican presidents since 1945 have done just that; in mismanaging the initial occupation of Iraq, George W. Bush was the great exception. Conservatives therefore have a history of foreign policy success to which they can turn, if they are willing to recall the examples set by previous Republican presidents.

This book tells the story of the relationship among presidential leadership, party politics, conservative ideas, and U.S. foreign policy since

World War II. As such, it can be seen as part of a current trend in scholarly political and intellectual histories that takes American conservatism seriously.[6] This is the first such work to focus on the long-term evolution of Republican foreign policy approaches. The book itself is written from a conservative point of view, although, as the reader will discover, one that emphasizes the traditional conservative virtues of prudence, balance, and tenacity. When it seems to me that conservatives or Republicans have gone wrong on specific foreign policy issues, I say so. One observation, however, that I hope readers will take to heart is that conservative foreign policy positions grow from authentic convictions regarding the nature of international politics. American conservatives generally view themselves as watchdogs of their country's security. As much as this self-image infuriates liberal critics, it is genuinely held, and flows from an intense love of country. Observers who assume that conservative foreign policy stands are simply the result of narrow economic interest or partisan calculation really say more about themselves than they do about conservatives.

Conservatives and Republicans in the United States are not entirely synonymous. Still, the Republican or "Grand Old Party" (GOP) has tended to be the more conservative of the two major American political parties on economic issues, certainly since the 1930s, and arguably since the election of 1896. Beginning in the 1960s, partisan disagreement over economic issues was gradually supplemented—although not displaced— by a new and further division between Democrats and Republicans along social and cultural lines.[7] The new social or cultural dimension of partisan disagreement was manifest in a wide range of issues, such as civil rights, criminal justice, and the implementation of traditional moral norms. Voter preferences on these matters often cut across existing alignments on economics: some voters, for example, supported increased government spending while maintaining a conservative stance on social issues. This led to an influx of social conservatives to the Republican Party and a corresponding outflow of social liberals from the GOP to the Democratic Party. As a result, today the Democratic Party is clearly the more liberal of the two major parties on social as well as economic issues, just as the Republican Party is clearly the more conservative on both dimensions. The interesting question for our purposes, then, is what exactly it means to be a conservative in the United States when it comes to foreign policy.

The traditional conservative attitude toward transformational and perfectionist political visions, whether in the domestic or the international arena, is one of skepticism. Traditional or classical conservatives like Edmund Burke point to the unintended consequences of well-intentioned political reforms and tend to be anti-utopian in their basic outlook. Yet there are central elements of the American experience that are not exactly conservative in the traditional sense. The United States was born out of a revolution based at least partly on classical liberal ideas. The leaders of that revolution held that a certain amount of progress was possible in human affairs. They believed, and indeed American citizens of all parties have commonly believed, that the United States has a special role to play in promoting popular self-government internationally—a belief that forms part of a cluster of ideas known as American exceptionalism. The prior, domestic component to this belief in democracy promotion overseas is a strong attachment to individual freedom, rule of law, enterprise, love of country, and republican self-government inside the United States as central to American national identity.[8] The founders of the United States, however pragmatic in promoting their nation's interests, certainly believed in American exceptionalism and took it for granted that the United States represented a new form of government that would have broad implications for the cause of popular self-rule worldwide. They trusted that the spread of democratic (or as they would say, republican) governments, trading with one another peacefully, would lead to the creation of a more friendly, just, and pacific international system. This is not a classically conservative but a classically liberal belief, and it has been hard-wired into the American mindset from the very beginning.

All attempts to formulate a distinctly conservative U.S. foreign policy alternative thus face an inherent tension. Any foreign policy approach that completely rejects classical conservative insights can hardly be called conservative; any foreign policy approach that completely rejects classical liberal assumptions cannot be called American. The problem is not insoluble, but it would be wrong to suggest that American conservatives have hit on only one lasting solution. In fact, if we look beyond the overarching continuities since the 1950s, there have been a variety of specific conservative foreign policy traditions or tendencies within the United States.

For the sake of simplicity, conservative U.S. foreign policy alternatives past and present can be categorized into four broad tendencies or schools of thought: realists, hawks, nationalists, and anti-interventionists. Conservative realists emphasize a balance of power, the careful coordination of force and diplomacy, and the international rather than domestic behavior of other states. Conservative hawks emphasize the need for accumulating military power and argue for armed intervention overseas, whether on pragmatic or idealistic grounds. Conservative nationalists emphasize the preservation of national sovereignty and an unyielding approach to foreign adversaries. Conservative anti-interventionists emphasize the avoidance or dismantling of strategic commitments overseas. Since each of these four categories is a pure type, few practical politicians fall neatly into only one school of thought, but even real-world conservative foreign policy leaders and advocates usually reveal a tendency toward certain archetypes over others. The overarching prevalence of a hawkish American nationalism in Republican foreign policy since the 1950s has not prevented fine-tuned adjustments, variations, and corrections between tendencies: more or less interventionist, more or less realistic, and so on. The question then becomes, why does one particular tendency win out over another at a given point in time?

A central argument and finding of this book is that the answer to that question is to be found in the possibilities of presidential leadership. Both popular and academic interpretations of U.S. foreign policy tend to fixate on external forces pushing presidents toward certain decisions over others. Economic interests, international pressures, domestic political concerns, and public intellectuals are variously said to determine presidential behavior on foreign policy matters. All of these factors are important, and considerably more will be said about them in the following chapters. But it is worth remembering that foreign policy is not made in exactly the same way as domestic policy in the United States. In comparison with domestic policy, presidents are given a greater degree of latitude by their own party, the American public, and Congress to make foreign policy decisions. That degree of latitude means that their particular beliefs, personalities, and choices make a real difference when it comes to precise foreign policy outcomes. This is not to suggest that presidents are all-powerful on foreign affairs; far from it. But even after economic, political, ideological, and international pressures are all taken into account, the triumph of one foreign policy tendency over another is crucially shaped by the president's own choices. If they are sufficiently skilled, determined, and fortunate, presidents can even reshape political constraints and use international issues to help cement and expand their party's domestic coalition. In sum, to a remarkable extent, when one party controls the White House, that party's foreign policy is what the president says it is. Consider the following examples, each the subject of a separate chapter in this book:

- Dwight Eisenhower sought to contain the Soviet Union and its allies without bankrupting the United States. He won over the bulk of Republicans to a stance of cold war internationalism while balancing that stance with diplomatic sensitivity and a keen desire for peace.
- Richard Nixon initiated multiple innovations in American diplomacy, reorienting it toward a primary emphasis on geopolitics and great power relations. In an era of collapsed foreign policy consensus, he tried to build a new center-right majority by reaching out to national security hawks and conservatives across party lines.
- Ronald Reagan pursued a bold strategy of aggressive anticommunism and indirect rollback, with the goal of weakening the USSR and reducing cold war tensions on U.S. terms. At home, he consolidated a winning coalition of Sun Belt conservatives, foreign policy hawks, evangelicals, and traditional Republicans, and by refusing to overreach either domestically or internationally, he left this coalition the most dynamic force in American politics.
- George H. W. Bush followed a temperamentally conservative foreign policy approach that emphasized caution, stability, and prudence. He locked in international changes of lasting benefit to the

United States in relation to Germany, Eastern Europe, the collapsing Soviet Union, Latin America, arms control, democracy promotion, and international trade.

- George W. Bush embraced "compassionate" or "big government" conservatism at home, and preventive warfare together with attempted
democratization in the Middle East. The resulting U.S. occupation of
Iraq was conducted with a serious lack of preparation on Bush's part—
an error corrected by him only in the winter of 2006–7.

As is evident from each of these cases, presidents play a central role in
determining their party's specific foreign policy tendencies from year to
year. Yet the history of major political parties in the United States also
reveals certain broad continuities that transcend short-term changes.
The Republicans have been the party of a hawkish American nationalism for several decades now and are unlikely anytime soon to become
the more dovish or accommodationist of America's two major parties
on international and military issues. Whatever the internal integrity of
their views, strict anti-interventionists such as Representative Ron Paul
(R-TX) are therefore probably not going to win many internal debates
over Republican foreign policy stands during the next few years. Still,
this does not mean that future GOP presidential candidates need repli-
cate exactly the foreign policy approach of George W. Bush. Indeed, if
the central findings of this book are correct, then any future Republican
president will have considerable leeway to shape the exact content of his
or her foreign policies—good reason, as I argue in the conclusion, to
learn from the mistakes as well as the successes of the past, and to devise
a foreign policy approach that is more realistic, and consequently more
rather than less genuinely conservative.

The book ends with a survey of current Republican foreign policy
alternatives, together with a recommendation for greater conservative
realism in international affairs. Conservatives are still coming to grips
with the fact that George W. Bush showed insufficient such realism in
planning for the invasion and initial occupation of Iraq. The reason why
this matters going forward is that in truth, President Barack Obama is
no more of a foreign policy realist than was Bush. Obama made great
gains in 2008 by criticizing Republicans on Iraq and by touting the vir-

tues of foreign policy pragmatism. Yet his administration has adopted an international approach that in important respects cannot be described as realistic. Obama and his most enthusiastic supporters appear to view the president as somehow capable of transcending international differences, partly through Obama's very existence and partly through what might be called the transformational power of unilateral diplomatic outreach. The president's assumption seems to be that if only the United States reaches out and makes preliminary concessions to international competitors, they will necessarily reciprocate. True realists make no such assumption. Nor do true foreign policy realists place much weight, as Obama appears to, on the possibility that an American president's personal style, autobiography, and conciliatory language might actually alter other countries' perceptions of their own vital interests. The current president's core foreign policy instincts are therefore not so much realist as accommodationist, informed in turn by an exaggerated sense of what personality can accomplish in world affairs. All the more reason for Republicans and conservatives to develop a cogent critique of Obama's foreign policy approach—not one based on a reflexive defense of every past feature of the Bush doctrine but one based on a greater dose of classical conservative skepticism and tough-mindedness regarding international relations. In other words, Republicans need to reclaim their own history, and then they will be able to reclaim mastery of American foreign policy.

Chapter One

REPUBLICANS, CONSERVATIVES, AND U.S. FOREIGN POLICY

REPUBLICANS ENTERED THE twentieth century, somewhat to their own surprise, as the party of American expansionism overseas. For most of the late nineteenth century, there had been no fundamental differences between Democrats and Republicans on issues of international expansion or military intervention. On the contrary, both parties embraced the Monroe Doctrine, strategic nonentanglement, economic opportunities abroad, and consensual ideas of American exceptionalism while arguing over trade and protection. Indeed, the presidential election of 1896 was fought primarily not over foreign policy but over issues of silver and gold currency, and over domestic economic affairs more generally. Ohio governor and Republican presidential nominee William McKinley campaigned on a platform of high tariffs and sound money, with a promise to restore prosperity in the midst of economic depression. The Democratic nominee, prairie populist William Jennings Bryan, called for a sweeping struggle against moneyed interests and an end to the gold standard, while combining this fire-breathing stance with a culturally traditional Protestant evangelicalism. In this way, Bryan won over western populists and agrarian radicals to the Democrats but lost support among northern urbanites, immigrants, Catholics, and organized labor. The result was a consolidation of Republican dominance in the Northeast and Midwest, and McKinley won the White House. In terms of foreign policy, both parties at the time stood for measured support for Cuban independence from Spain, leaving little difference between them on an issue of secondary interest to most voters. As reports leaked out to the American press of Spanish atrocities against Cuban civilians, and particularly after the February 1898 explosion in Havana Harbor on board the U.S.S. *Maine*, prominent Democrats, populists, and silver Republicans demanded military action. Conservative Republicans in Congress, alarmed by the possibility of being outmaneuvered and defeated on this issue, responded by calling on the president to declare war. McKinley handled the entire crisis with considerable care and political skill, ensuring that the exact timing and nature of hostilities corresponded with his own goals, but in the final analysis he launched the United States on a war he had hardly sought when running for president two years earlier.

Once Spain was defeated militarily, both Democrats and Republicans called for U.S. gains in the Caribbean, specifically in Cuba and Puerto Rico. Only when the question of the Philippines was raised did the war's outcome become a truly controversial and partisan issue. The acquisition of Spain's colony in the Philippines was almost an afterthought for McKinley; he had no initial intention of annexing it. But with the Spanish role in the Philippines destroyed, the president decided it would be unwise to give that colony its independence. The Filipinos, he believed, were unready for independence and subject to intervention on the part of the other great powers. If the United States took control of the Philippines, it could forestall such intervention, while securing a valuable base on the way to China and its vast potential markets. McKinley did not expect the annexation of the Philippines to be especially popular with the American public, and for this reason he went on the campaign trail in the fall of 1898 to make his case. A nasty guerrilla war between insurgent Filipinos and U.S. troops erupted a few months later. The question of the Philippines' fate triggered a significant anti-imperialist political and intellectual movement in the United States, allowing Democrats an opportunity to criticize the president on foreign policy. In the end, the treaty annexing the Philippines to American control was passed by the U.S. Senate in 1899 by just one vote over the necessary two-thirds. Believing anti-imperialism to be a winning political stance, the Democrats, with William Jennings Bryan again as their presidential nominee, decided to make it a leading issue in the election of 1900.

The annexation of the Philippines was indeed unpopular in parts of the country, especially the Northeast, and triggered intense opposition from aging GOP mugwumps along with some important economic conservatives in both parties. On balance, however, McKinley was able to make foreign policy a winning issue for himself and the Republicans in 1900. For one thing, Pacific expansionism appealed to westerners, including many populist Democrats. U.S. military victories against Spain still carried a certain luster in 1900. McKinley's Open Door policy, declaring support for the independence and integrity of China amid conditions of equal commercial opportunity for outside powers, was also quite popular at home. Moreover, the GOP was able to persuasively make the case that with the acquisition of the Philippines a fait accompli, the issue was not so much the expansion as the contraction or surrender of American power—a contraction or surrender that Republicans opposed. McKinley promised to give the Philippines independence eventually, but not prematurely. Indeed, for all the passion surrounding questions of a new American empire abroad, the practical foreign policy differences between the two presidential candidates in 1900 were quite narrow, centering on the exact timeline for Filipino self-government. Bryan, for example, had no special objection to U.S. acquisitions or dominance in the Caribbean. Voters were therefore not really presented with an unmistakable choice between one party for "empire" and another against it. Nor did Bryan stick to a consistent theme throughout the campaign. Above all, with the return of domestic economic prosperity, voters were inclined to reward the incumbent while avoiding proposals for radical change. McKinley therefore sailed to reelection, giving the appearance of a popular mandate for empire and war in the Philippines, when in fact that particular outcome was quite controversial even among many staunch conservatives inside the United States.[1]

McKinley's successor in the White House, Theodore Roosevelt, pursued a skillful, realistic, and adept foreign policy that belied his image as a bombastic cowboy. As a younger man, Roosevelt had often called for American military action, but as president he showed no interest in launching the United States on any costly wars. Roosevelt believed that the United States, along with other major powers, had a moral obligation to extend orderly and humane government abroad. He also believed that in an age of intense great power competition, the United States would be outmaneuvered internationally unless it acquired a stronger navy, control over maritime trade routes, and new naval bases overseas. Roosevelt's most famous saying with regard to foreign affairs, "Speak softly and carry a big stick," was not an admonition to strut and swagger but rather the opposite. The phrase captured many of his central ideas and practices regarding effective statecraft, namely, avoiding commitments that could not be kept, being firm, tactful, and patient in negotiations, and not expecting diplomacy to be effective unless backed by sufficient military power. Roosevelt operated under conditions of general popular indifference to international affairs and intense skepticism from Congress regarding new foreign commitments. Any enthusiasm for empire had long since dissipated. Specific business interests associated with the Republican Party sometimes had clear preferences on certain foreign policy issues, such as the construction of a trans-isthmian canal in Central America, but generally had little interest in costly or risky imperial adventures. In any case, Roosevelt was contemptuous of the notion that American diplomacy should be dictated by narrow or private economic concerns, and there is no evidence that he made important foreign policy decisions primarily to satisfy the pecuniary interests of particular banks or corporations. Roosevelt's time in office saw the expansion of a significant progressive faction within the Republican Party that was suspicious of moneyed interests. The president tried to straddle the conservative-progressive divide, gradually moving toward a more interventionist stance on issues of domestic political economy—a move that brought him into increasing conflict with his own party's dominant congressional and conservative wing. These intraparty tensions had little impact on American diplomacy at the time, however. GOP conservatives appreciated Roosevelt's foreign policies; GOP progressives such as Senator Robert LaFollette (R-WI) liked Roosevelt's domestic policies, deferred to him on foreign affairs, and had not yet embraced anti-imperialist ideas. Indeed, some GOP progressives, such as Senator Albert Beveridge (R-IN), were avid American expansionists. Consequently, Republicans were generally united behind Roosevelt on foreign policy matters, and party loyalty remained effective.

The United States in Roosevelt's time was an immensely wealthy country that had not yet converted its potential into a major diplomatic role or usable military power with regard to the European and Asian mainland. Even in much of Latin America, the economic and political influence of European powers was often still greater than that of the United States. Roosevelt's special concern—and it was not an unrealistic one—was that major outside powers, such as Germany, would take advantage of political and financial disorder in states in and around the Caribbean to intervene and establish new military bases there. This overarching geopolitical concern motivated him to engage in some reluctant and small-scale but generally effective military and diplomatic interventions in the Dominican Republic, Cuba, and Venezuela. It was also the strategic context for his autumn 1903 support of Panama's rebellion against Colombian rule, a rebellion that allowed the United States to secure a permanent lease as well as titular sovereignty over a canal zone ten miles wide. In East Asia, Roosevelt supported a regional balance of power by first welcoming Japanese resistance to Russian expansion, then mediating a peace agreement between Russia and Japan in 1905. He refused to issue toothless declarations against Japan's subsequent expansion into Manchuria because he knew the United States had little military ability to back up such declarations or defend the Philippines from Japanese attack. Instead, he signed a sphere-of-influence agreement with Tokyo that recognized American influence over the Philippines and Japanese influence over Manchuria. In Europe, Roosevelt's ability to check German power was very limited, but he interceded at the Algeciras Conference in 1906 to side with Britain and France against Germany on the issue of Morocco, while somehow maintaining cordial relations with Berlin. Even this very limited and successful diplomatic intercession was viewed by the U.S. Senate as implying dangerous foreign entanglements. Between 1904 and 1907, Roosevelt helped organize a second Hague Conference on international peace and disarmament, and he was open to arbitration efforts on matters of secondary importance. Fundamentally, however, he believed that the best guarantee of peace was military strength, and he had modest expectations for what disarmament talks could accomplish. Indeed, when it came to America's own navy, Roosevelt's focus was not on disarmament but on building up U.S. naval power to support a more active role from the Pacific to the Caribbean—a buildup that finally ran into congressional resistance from fiscal conservatives during his last years in office.

Overall, the Republican Party benefited politically from Roosevelt's image as a strong, successful leader in foreign affairs, a benefit of which he was well aware. Yet for the most part, domestic political pressures at the time ran against rather than toward the kind of foreign policy he would have liked: global, active, and engaged. Roosevelt understood these constraints and managed them quite skillfully, but ultimately he hit the limits of public and congressional tolerance on the question of America's international commitments. His response to these limits as president was to work as effectively as he could to promote U.S. national interests under the conditions of existing public opinion. In this sense, domestic political and partisan incentives acted for Roosevelt not as a stimulus to an ambitious foreign policy but as a constraint.[2]

The next Republican president of the era was William Howard Taft, a leader with a very different foreign policy approach from Theodore Roosevelt's. If Roosevelt was attuned to traditional patterns of great power politics, Taft believed in the creation of a more peaceful and prosperous world order through the promotion of international law, trade, and investment. The spread of economic interdependence, Taft suggested, would encourage stable governments in the developing world and give the various major powers a strong material incentive to keep the peace. International arbitration treaties could also be relied on to adjudicate differences between countries. Above all, finance and commerce, rather than armed force, would be the preferred instruments of international order and U.S. foreign policy, both for moral and for practical reasons. Taft's resultant "dollar diplomacy"—a term coined by the American press—was easily misinterpreted as nothing more than a crude attempt at profits for U.S. banks and corporations overseas. But while such profits were certainly sought with great vigor, the basic goals in Taft's mind were also much broader, transformational, and idealistic. Dollars were not so much the primary end as the primary means of a foreign policy based on the classical liberal assumption that the international system could be modernized and pacified through the benign effects of commerce and investment. Taft's dollar diplomacy played itself out in two main geographic venues, Latin America and East Asia. In Latin America, Taft tried to encourage U.S. investment, along with governments open to such investment, but the tactlessness of the effort alienated its supposed beneficiaries. In the end, like Roosevelt, Taft felt bound to intervene militarily in the region several times—notably, in Nicaragua—in order to promote financial and political stability. In East Asia, Taft rejected any notion of a sphere-of-influence arrangement with Japan and instead focused on trying to win international support for a new U.S.-led financial consortium with the aim of developing new railways in the Chinese province of Manchuria. Since Manchuria was already the subject of intense great power rivalry, however, with Japan and Russia in the lead, those powers naturally viewed Taft's proposal as an attempt to muscle them out while muscling the United States in. Indeed, the proposal was so alarming to both Russia and Japan that it led them to reconcile many of their differences and draw together diplomatically. The Chinese, for their part, resented the American proposal as another foreign infringement on their national sovereignty and dignity. Nor were American bankers entirely convinced that the proposed railway project was creditworthy. The Taft administration's well-intentioned proposal therefore came to nothing, and succeeded only in alienating every other major power, as well as the Chinese themselves, who soon collapsed into violent nationalist revolution. Meanwhile, Taft deemphasized any U.S. naval buildup, one of the few practical mechanisms of American influence across the Pacific, since military power did not form an especially important part of his foreign policy philosophy.

The Taft years saw a growing and climactic split between the progressive and conservative wings of the Republican Party. Taft initially tried to straddle this divide but soon sided with the conservatives, encouraging rebellion on the part of GOP progressives. The intraparty divide was reinforced by the overshadowing figure of Theodore Roosevelt, who had moved further left on domestic issues while out of office and decided to run for the White House again in 1912. In the presidential election that fall, the Democrats put forward a timely and credible candidate in Governor Woodrow Wilson of New Jersey, leaving Taft and Roosevelt to split the normally Republican electoral majority. Wilson consequently swept to victory, although GOP conservatives at least had the satisfaction of confirming their own control over the Republican Party. Foreign policy was not a primary concern either for rebellious progressives or for American voters in 1912. Nevertheless, GOP progressives had begun to develop their own distinct foreign policy critiques during the Taft presidency, and for much of the next decade Republicans would struggle to develop a united stance.[3]

U.S. foreign policymakers during the presidency of Woodrow Wilson were preoccupied, initially by violent disorder in Mexico, and then by world war in Europe. The spectacle of such conflicts abroad left Republicans deeply divided as to how to respond. Many western GOP progressives, such as Robert LaFollette, had come to believe that U.S. military interventions in Latin America served only the interests of large eastern banks and corporations. They applied the same logic to the prospect of U.S. intervention in Europe, and therefore resisted it. Other progressives, such as Senator William Borah (R-ID), generally opposed intervention abroad but were intensely nationalistic, concerned to protect the nation's honor in foreign disputes and willing to spend on the military in order to safeguard U.S. interests. At the other end of the party, ideologically, Republican conservatives often had close ties to northeastern law firms and financial and business interests, but they also had foreign policy beliefs of their own, which sometimes varied. Numerous GOP conservatives, such as Senator Henry Cabot Lodge (R-MA), favored increased defense spending, strong action to defend U.S. interests in Mexico, and intervention in Europe, the latter out of a fear that German victory would represent a massive defeat for both America's ideals and its interests. Other establishment Republicans, such as former president Taft, sympathized with Great Britain against Germany, but were also wary of military intervention and powerfully drawn to visions of international law, arbitration, and mediation. Theodore Roosevelt, for his part, soon returned to the GOP fold as a progressive on domestic issues and a hawk on international affairs—so hawkish that he alarmed even those who shared his basic foreign policy views. There was consequently a very broad variety of domestic and foreign policy issue stands among Republicans during this period, a fact that did not initially work in their favor. Wilson was able to campaign in 1916 as an incumbent who had presided over a prosperous era, kept the peace, and initiated some popular domestic reforms. The combination was hard to beat, especially in the western states. Republicans tried to straddle the issues of both peace and reform by nominating the moderate, well-respected former governor of New York, Charles Evans Hughes, but his colorless campaign failed to break through in crucial states such as California and Ohio. So, while the election was close, and covered a range of issues, foreign policy worked against the Republicans in 1916.

By the spring of 1917, unrestricted submarine warfare on Germany's part finally convinced both Woodrow Wilson and a majority of the American people that war with Berlin was inevitable. Wilson chose to lead the nation into war on the most idealistic grounds, arguing that this titanic struggle was being fought not to establish a new balance of power but to overturn all such balances and institute a revised international order characterized by democracy, open markets, and international law. The keystone of this order would be Wilson's proposed League of Nations, a global association of countries dedicated to upholding the independence and integrity of one another through a universal commitment to collective security. While foreign leaders were skeptical of this transformational vision, the American public generally liked it. In fact, a majority of Republican senators were willing to entertain U.S. entry into a new League of Nations, so long as Wilson toned down what they viewed as an excessive and unrealistic commitment to universal collective security contained in Article X of the League Covenant. This Wilson would not do, whether out of principle, pique, ill health, or some combination of the three. The result was a sustained struggle in the U.S. Senate in 1919–20 over ratification. Henry Cabot Lodge, the sardonic chairman of the Senate Foreign Relations Committee by this time, actually wanted a firm American commitment to the postwar security of Britain and France—something like an early version of NATO—but just as much he wanted the defeat of Woodrow Wilson, whose personality, domestic agenda, and foreign policy he now held in contempt. Lodge therefore skillfully rallied opposition to Wilson's league from all quarters and succeeded in preventing the president from ever attaining sufficient support to pass the treaty through. Republican progressives like Borah were happy to see the league proposal defeated, committed as they were to a general policy of strategic nonentanglement. The Republican presidential nominee in 1920, Warren G. Harding, capitalized on popular fatigue with eight years of political experimentation, war, and upheaval by promising a return to normal times while opposing Wilson's version of the league. It soon became clear, once Harding entered the White House, that he opposed new U.S. security commitments to Europe altogether. Ironically, the final result in 1921—complete rejection by an incoming Republican administration of any peacetime military alliance with France and Great Britain—was one that Lodge himself never sought, and hoped to avoid.[4]

Subsequent Republican foreign policy during the 1920s was strikingly modern, carrying as it did a strong emphasis on the pacifying effects of economic interdependence. No individual better embodied this approach than Herbert Hoover, secretary of commerce from 1921 and president of the United States from 1929 to 1933. Hoover and other leading Republicans—including private bankers and businessmen, as well as diplomats and politicians—sought to promote a peaceful, liberalized international system characterized by mutual arms reduction, nonaggression, open markets, political stability, and sustained economic growth. In this sense, the foreign policy of the 1920s was extremely ambitious and classically liberal in its goals. Simultaneously, however, Hoover and his colleagues put strict limits on the costs and obligations entailed on Americans in pursuit of these international goals. Specifically, Washington would not offer tariff reductions, war debt forgiveness, direct economic aid, or strategic guarantees to support U.S. aims in Europe and East Asia. On the contrary, it would avoid financial or military commitments of virtually any kind.

In later years, the weakness of this strictly anti-interventionist approach would become obvious, but it was extremely popular at the time. Indeed, it was one of the focal points on which Republicans were able to agree and win reelection, especially since Democrats offered no coherent alternative. Western progressives, small and import-competing businesses, peace groups, farmers, organized labor, and conservatives all agreed that the United States was best served by a foreign policy emphasizing arms control and economic opportunities but strategic nonentanglement overseas. This approach did seem to secure some impressive diplomatic victories in the early to mid-1920s. In 1921–22, a series of treaties signed at the Washington Conference instituted mutual limitations on naval construction by Japan, Britain, and the United States, as well as formalizing the commitment of the other great powers to the principles of the Open Door policy in China. In 1924, European war debts and German reparations were renegotiated successfully under American mediation with the Dawes Plan. This in turn encouraged Berlin, London, and Paris to mutually guarantee the Franco-German border at the Locarno Conference of 1925. The feeling of most Americans with regard to both Europe and East Asia was that historic progress had been made toward peaceful forms of conflict resolution, a feeling that reached its giddy apogee with the Kellogg-Briand Pact of 1928, a pompous and completely unenforceable but immensely popular document outlawing war as an instrument of national policy. In reality, U.S. foreign policymakers were leaning on a weak reed, and with the rise of profoundly illiberal forces in Germany and Japan, together with the onset of the Great Depression in 1929, that weakness was revealed. As private American loans to Europe dried up and an increasingly militaristic Japan invaded Manchuria, Hoover was left with few policy instruments to revive international economic cooperation or halt authoritarian aggression. In the case of U.S. military power, at least, he did not even look for such instruments. Hoover believed that defense spending was wasteful and retrograde; he counted on the force of international law, economic interdependence, public opinion, and moral reprobation to stop aggression. He was, however, willing to let his secretary of state, Henry Stimson, condemn Japanese behavior in Manchuria as unacceptable. In effect, this put Washington on a long-term collision course with Tokyo over China without providing the United States with the military means to do anything about it. Only with regard to Latin America, where the United States already possessed undoubted supremacy over any other major power, did Hoover and the GOP's business-minded doves of the 1920s leave a truly positive legacy by scaling back excessive military interventions, improving relations, and introducing an early form of the Good Neighbor Policy.[5]

The party in which Senator Robert Taft became prominent during the 1930s was consequently building on an immediate legacy of business-minded and idealistic anti-interventionism with regard to foreign affairs. Still, there were significant differences of opinion among Republicans over international politics, and that was part of the GOP's legacy as well. Republican foreign policy between McKinley and Hoover was characterized

lationship of party politics to conservatism in the United States. Then we can examine the relationship of both party politics and conservatism to U.S. foreign policy.

Americans claim to dislike partisan politics, but it is virtually impossible to imagine democracy in the United States without competition between political parties. Such parties serve several constructive functions in allowing a democratic form of government to work effectively. First, major political parties look to secure and maintain power through established peaceful, legal, electoral means. While sometimes derided as unprincipled, the competitive search for electoral success by each party is actually crucial to the preservation of democratic freedoms, in that each party acts as a check on the power of the other. Parties also play a central role in aggregating and representing individual and group interests within the political arena. They help structure and simplify the almost unlimited number of policy alternatives that might be placed before the voters at election time. Finally, parties tend to embody certain ideological traditions, however loosely or flexibly, and in this sense they are distinct from one another in terms of the core principles they represent.[6]

Since Franklin Roosevelt's 1930s New Deal, at least, the Republican Party has tended to be the more conservative of the two major American political parties on economic issues. Beginning in the 1960s, partisan disagreement over economic issues was gradually supplemented, although not displaced, by a new and further division between Democrats and Republicans along social and cultural lines. The new social or cultural field of partisan disagreement was reflected in a wide range of issues, such as civil rights, criminal justice, and the implementation of traditional moral norms. Voter preferences on these matters often cut across existing alignments on economics: some voters, for example, supported increased government spending while maintaining a conservative stance on social issues. This led to an influx of social conservatives into the Republican Party and a corresponding outflow of social liberals from the GOP to the Democratic Party. In formal terms, the axis of cleavage between the two parties rotated to include social as well as economic dimensions. The process by which the line of division between parties shifts and rotates to include new issue dimensions is known as realignment. In its more ambitious form, realignment theory has been

rightly criticized as overly complicated and deterministic. Yet if we define realignment simply as a durable shift in the line of cleavage between
political parties, it is not only plausible but empirically true to say that
America's two major parties have realigned themselves over the past
fifty years. The Democratic Party is now clearly the more liberal of the
two major parties on social as well as economic issues, just as the Republican Party is clearly the more conservative. The interesting question, then, is what exactly it means in the United States to be a conservative as opposed to a liberal.[7]

It is sometimes suggested that conservatism is not a coherent ideology at all but simply the articulated defense of established institutions in
a particular time and place. Yet conservatives in different eras and in
different countries tend to refer back predictably to several interrelated
ideas. To begin with, conservatives believe there is such a thing as human
nature, and that it is relatively fixed and imperfect. Whether they refer
to religious concepts such as original sin or to recent insights from evolutionary psychology, conservatives believe that human self-interest
renders perfectionist political visions not only unattainable but down-
right dangerous. Conservatives therefore begin with a skeptical, limited,
or constrained vision of what government can accomplish. Conservatives are opposed to revolutionary political change. They point to the
perverse, unintended consequences that typically follow efforts at major
political or social reform. They vest considerable weight in the value of
custom and tradition, arguing that the accumulated wisdom of genera-
tions is usually greater than the expressed rationality of individuals,
however intelligent or well-intentioned those individuals. Conservatives
believe that there can be no meaningful political justice or freedom in
the absence of social and political order. They point to the central role of
civil society and intermediary social institutions such as family and
church in both supporting and buffering the individual in relation to the
state. Conservatives may support democratic forms of government, but
they do not believe that democracy should be unconstrained. They look
for filters and balances on the power of popular majorities just as much
as on the power of elites, because they mistrust unchecked power from
any direction. Conservatives stress the necessity of the rule of law, and
of abiding by traditional legal forms. They put particular emphasis on
respect for private property. They may support equality of rights before

the law, but they have no interest in equality of socioeconomic condition, or any belief that such equality is even possible. Conservatives embrace patriotism or love of country as a healthy and ennobling passion. They are traditionalists with regard to culture and education. They look to the past for instruction and inspiration. They respect the social role of religion, whether or not they are themselves believers. And they do not conceive that a free society can function or endure as free in the complete absence of public and private virtue. Taken together, this cluster of ideas and beliefs can be referred to as classical conservatism. The single best expression of the classical conservative perspective is Edmund Burke's *Reflections on the Revolution in France*. Burke wrote in defense of a particular eighteenth-century European social order that included monarchy, aristocracy, and established churches and against the spectacle of radical revolution. But the kinds of arguments he deployed against that revolution have been regularly used by conservatives against their opponents in other times and places. In this sense, we can say that there exists a set of typically classical conservative arguments, apart from the circumstance of each case. The real issue is not whether such a thing as classical conservatism exists, but what it has to do with the United States.[8]

Even a superficial glance at the above list of classical conservative beliefs reveals that several of them bear little relation to politically influential forms of conservatism in America. The United States was founded in a revolution that declared "all men are created equal." No revolution, and no such declaration, could be described as entirely conservative. To be sure, the American Revolution was as deeply influenced by a variety of premodern political ideas as by the belief that the colonists were fighting to preserve their traditional rights as Englishmen. In that sense, this particular revolution contained strongly conservative elements. Yet the national political creed that was already developing in America even before the Revolution was essentially a classical liberal one, characterized by an emphasis on liberty, popular sovereignty, individual rights, equality of opportunity, entrepreneurship, self-reliance, limited government, forward progress, and a deep suspicion of centralized authority.

Numerous observers have argued that the classical liberal roots of both the American founding and U.S. political culture leave serious doubt as to the possibility of any genuinely conservative tradition in the

United States. If America was founded on liberal principles, so the argument goes, and if the United States never experienced feudal aristocracy, then what role is there for conservatism in such a country? The stated paradox, while superficially perplexing, is less problematic than it might seem. For one thing, if classical conservatism constitutes a perennial critique of radical reform, as I have suggested, rather than simply an emission of lingering feudal or aristocratic mentalities, then the admitted absence of feudalism or aristocracy from the United States poses no especially great difficulties. One can adhere, for example, to the classical liberal principles of the American creed while also believing, as conservatives do, that new radical reforms are difficult and dangerous. Moreover, political permutations over the past century have often left conservatives the primary defenders of the classical liberal tradition, as self-described liberals have looked toward an ever-expanding role for the federal government in the country's social and economic life. In the United States, at least, it is precisely the nation's classically liberal founding order that conservatives seek to preserve against more recent liberal innovations. The powerful role of premodern influences in the American founding, including civic republican, biblical, and common law ideas, also leaves U.S. conservatives free to position themselves in defense of certain ancient Western concepts and traditions that were never rejected by America's founders. Any politically significant form of conservatism in the United States must at least nod in the direction of America's classical liberal political culture. To do otherwise confines conservatives in this country to the status of politically irrelevant malcontents. At the same time, any declared version of conservatism that completely rejects core notions of human imperfectability, limited government, tradition, or constraint can hardly be called conservative. There is consequently a healthy tension built into the very nature of conservative movements in America. As *National Review* editor Frank Meyer argued half a century ago, any such movements must skillfully fuse classical conservative with classical liberal assumptions or risk intellectual and political degeneration.[9]

In the arena of foreign policy, we might expect conservatives to be realists, as against their more idealistic left-liberal domestic political opponents. Classical conservatism, at least, leads naturally to a number of conclusions about international relations that align with realism. Such conservatives tend to take a pessimistic stance regarding the possibilities for transforming the international system. Their view of human nature leads them to skepticism regarding schemes for permanent peace through international organization, treaties, or political reform. They put great intrinsic value in their foreign policy approach on the protection of their own particular nation's interests and way of life, viewing it as entirely legitimate to do so. Indeed, conservatives believe that it is impossible to love humanity without first loving your own country. Classical conservatives look to protect the nation's freedom of action and independence against external threats or challenges. They tend to be very resistant to proposals that involve significant cessions of national sovereignty to international or transnational organizations. They hold that the use or threat of force will never be erased from the anarchic arena of international politics. They have no difficulty believing that the international political arena is a dangerous place, requiring vigilance. They consequently emphasize the importance of military strength and credibility in world politics, although they may be quite cautious in actually resorting to armed intervention. They are not inclined to use force to transform the domestic arrangements of other countries, viewing such efforts as costly and improbable. And while they are not necessarily militarists, classical conservatives have an inherent respect and admiration for the traditions and constraints of the soldier's profession.[10]

The complication regarding conservatism in the United States, of course, is that in foreign policy, just as in domestic politics, American thought and behavior are powerfully shaped by widely held classical liberal assumptions. U.S. citizens of all parties have long believed that the United States has a special role to play in promoting democratic freedoms worldwide—a belief that forms part of a cluster of ideas known as American exceptionalism. The prior domestic component to this is a strong and widespread belief in individual freedom, rule of law, popular self-government, enterprise, and love of country as central to U.S. national identity.[11] The founders of the United States, however pragmatic in promoting their nation's interests, certainly believed in American exceptionalism and took it for granted that the United States represented a new form of government that would have broad implications for the cause of popular self-rule abroad. A common assumption or animating vision throughout the history of American diplomacy has been that the spread of democracy and trade overseas will create a more peaceful, transformed international system, friendlier to U.S. interests and to the democratic way of life. This vision is not classically conservative but classically liberal. For this reason, it might be said that classical liberalism is hard-wired into the American way of thinking when it comes to foreign policy. Even conservatives in the United States do not entirely reject classical liberal assumptions in world politics, and those conservatives who do soon find themselves marginalized from national influence. There is, however, a wide range of practical policy options that might follow from any acceptance of classical liberal assumptions. In particular, Americans have always debated whether to promote democracy overseas by force or by example. The first alternative has been to vindicate the democratic cause by riding to its defense or promotion abroad, even through the use of military intervention. The second alternative has been to affirm America's special role as an example for democratic freedoms but to reject the use of force in promoting that example abroad. This is only one way in which a classically liberal political culture still allows for multiple foreign policy options.[12]

The particular challenge for American conservatives with regard to foreign policy has been to fuse or integrate classical liberal and classical conservative foreign policy beliefs in a principled and viable way. This is essentially the same challenge that conservatives in the United States face with regard to domestic politics. Any foreign policy approach that completely rejects classical conservative insights cannot be called conservative. Any foreign policy approach that completely rejects classical liberal insights cannot be called American. To suggest that conservatives in America have hit upon a single solution to this challenge would simply be inaccurate. Indeed, the most striking thing about U.S. conservative foreign policy ideas and approaches, even if the discussion is limited to the period since the 1930s, has been their sheer variety, and since the Republican Party has been during this time the more conservative of America's two major parties, the political and conceptual foreign policy challenge facing Republicans has been very much the same one as the challenge facing conservatives. Republican and conservative foreign policy traditions in the United States are therefore characterized by sev-eral recurring tensions or dichotomies that help structure our under-standing of their variety, as well as our understanding of their typical distinction from left-liberal approaches. Four such leading and recur-ring tensions are realism versus idealism, hawk versus dove, nationalism versus accommodation, and intervention versus anti-intervention.

The realist versus idealist tension has already been introduced. For-eign policy *realists* believe in the prudent and coordinated use of force, diplomacy, and balances of power to pursue the national interest, nar-rowly conceived. They are skeptical of any transformational vision based on an assumption of historical progress, and they focus on the interna-tional rather than the domestic behavior of other states. Foreign policy *idealists*, drawing on classical liberal thought, believe that the spread of democracy, economic interdependence, and international organization will ultimately change the nature of world politics and render realist methods obsolete. Idealists are generally opposed to the use of force, for both moral and practical reasons, but are sometimes willing to support military intervention for humanitarian or moral ends. They are keenly interested in the domestic behavior of other states and define their for-eign policy goals to include global as well as national interests.

Foreign policy *hawks* believe in the utility of force in world politics and the accumulation of national military power. They support defen-sive military measures and often the use of force overseas. The reasons given for the use of force by hawks may be either geopolitical or idealis-tic; this is one of the features that distinguish them from realists, who prefer geopolitical reasons to idealistic ones. Foreign policy *doves* be-lieve that the use of force is almost always either wrong or irrelevant in the modern world. They favor neither armed intervention abroad nor the accumulation of military power, and indeed they view such power as inherently wasteful and provocative. Doves and idealists are often one and the same, but the existence of idealistic hawks necessitates a distinc-tion between the two.

Foreign policy *nationalists* look to protect the country's indepen-dence and freedom of action. They oppose ceding the nation's sovereign authority to international or transnational arrangements and institu-tions. They prefer unilateralism to multilateralism in foreign affairs, and they resist diplomatic concessions to other countries. They may or may not be hawkish, just as they may or may not be realistic. Foreign policy *accommodationists* welcome national membership in a wide variety of multilateral agreements and institutions and have no objection to resulting constraints on the country's freedom of action because they view such mutual constraints as crucial to achieving global public goods such as international peace, security, and prosperity. Accommodationists also tend to see international cooperation and better relations with other countries, including potential adversaries, as worthwhile goals in themselves. They are distinct from doves, in that one can imagine foreign policy doves that prefer unilateral to multilateral approaches.

Foreign policy *interventionists* are defined by their readiness to engage in military intervention overseas. They are similar to but not identical with foreign policy hawks in that hawks may believe in the utility of force without always supporting military intervention abroad. Professional soldiers, for example, tend to be hawkish in their view of international affairs but not necessarily interventionist. *Anti-interventionists* or *noninterventionists* are defined by their opposition to military intervention overseas. They may be quite hawkish, nationalistic, and even realistic in their reasons for doing so. Anti-interventionists are not necessarily opposed to the construction of a strong national defense or to thinking in geopolitical terms, but they view military intervention abroad as risky and counterproductive.

If we consider only recent foreign policies favored by most American conservatives, such as the 2003 invasion of Iraq, we might conclude that conservatives are highly interventionist when it comes to international relations, but this has not always been so, and may not be so in the future. In the past, U.S. conservatives and Republicans have tended to prefer nationalism over accommodation in foreign affairs, but they have sometimes opted for nonintervention, for very conservative reasons. The relationship between realism and idealism in Republican foreign policy is furthermore a complicated one historically, with multiple twists and turns. The dichotomies listed above allow for multiple combinations, but for the sake of simplicity they can be reduced to four distinct archetypes most characteristic of Republicans and conservatives in

America, namely, conservative realists, conservative hawks, conservative nationalists, and conservative anti-interventionists.

Conservative realists favor the coordinated and prudent use of force and diplomacy to pursue narrowly defined national interests.

Conservative hawks believe in the utility of military power, and sometimes the necessity of armed intervention overseas.

Conservative nationalists look to preserve the nation's sovereignty and independence of action while avoiding diplomatic concessions to potential adversaries overseas.

Conservative anti-interventionists seek to avoid military entanglements abroad.

Since each of these four categories is a pure type, and since there are overlapping possibilities between them, it is unlikely that any real-world conservative would show features of only one category, but even real-world conservative foreign policy leaders and advocates will usually reveal a tendency toward certain archetypes over others. If these are the four preeminent conservative or Republican foreign policy types in America, then what explains the emergence or decline of one particular type over time? Why, for example, has the Republican Party gravitated toward hawkish idealism in foreign affairs at one moment, realism at another, and anti-interventionism at a third? Several possible explanations or answers can be drawn from existing theories in political science, referring either to (1) economic interests, (2) partisan politics, (3) international pressures, or (4) the power of policy ideas.

The first potential explanation for the rise and fall of specific foreign policy tendencies within a political party concerns the nature of the *economic interests* at the base of that party. This is an explanatory approach with a well-established pedigree in the field of international relations. A number of political scientists explain changes in the foreign policies of various countries by referring to changes in the composition of class-based sectional or sectoral interests at the foundation of existing party coalitions. In a few cases these authors have tried explicitly to account for changes in Republican foreign policy over time. Peter Trubowitz, for example, suggests that the rise of Republican foreign policy hawkishness by the 1970s was due to the concentration of defense industries in newly Republican Sun Belt states and to the export orientation of these same states, in contrast to the import-competing midwesterners who dominated the GOP during the 1930s. The key point with this approach is that the foreign policy preferences of parties are viewed as primarily the expression of particular subnational economic interests. Different parties have different foreign policy tendencies because they represent distinct and evolving sets of economic interests.[13]

The second possible explanation for changes in a party's foreign policy refers to *partisan politics*. This model owes as much to the study of American government as it does to the field of international relations. A common assumption in American politics is that each major party is primarily focused on winning and keeping office, and will pursue whatever specific politics are required to do so. If foreign policy is not exempt from such considerations, then we would expect political parties to use foreign policy as a tool to bolster their electoral and political fortunes and undermine those of their opponents. This could manifest itself in several distinct ways. A political party might hit on specific foreign policies primarily to undermine or divide the political strength of the opposing party. A party or administration might be drawn to specific foreign policies to differentiate itself from the opposing party or preceding administration. A party might use specific foreign policies to appease various intraparty factions and hold itself together as a broad coalition. A political party in power might even engage in military intervention or the show of force overseas to divert attention from domestic political or economic problems. If this explanatory approach is accurate, we might also expect to see Republicans support Republican presidents on foreign affairs and oppose Democratic ones, regardless of substantive policy content, simply for reason of party loyalty. A notable exception to this last expectation would be if supporting a Democratic president's foreign policy was deemed to be in the political interest of Republicans. If, for example, it was very popular to do so, then a "bipartisan" foreign policy approach might redound to the party's political interests.[14]

The third possible explanation for changes in a party's foreign policy refers to *international pressures*. Such an explanation would suggest that variations in the degree of military intervention, diplomatic accommodation, and so on among Republican foreign policy leaders have more to do with international conditions than anything else. For example, a country that is extremely powerful in relative terms, as the United States was in the 1950s, can afford to engage in military intervention abroad, regardless of which party is in power. A country that is threatened by a clear external danger, as the United States was by the Soviet Union during the cold war, will also be inclined to respond assertively, regardless of party. Conversely, a country that is unthreatened or relatively constrained by geopolitical conditions will be likely to follow a more restrained or accommodating foreign policy, regardless of which party is in office. According to this model, we should therefore see little variation in U.S. foreign policy due to partisan interest or ideology; the major variations should come in response to international conditions. The nature or composition of the Republican Party itself counts for little in this approach.[15]

A fourth possible explanation for changes in a party's foreign policy refers to the power of certain *policy ideas*. According to this approach, neither international nor economic nor political pressures are entirely determinate in causing policy outcomes. Foreign policy decision-makers necessarily rely on some set of assumptions or prior beliefs in order to organize and simplify an array of incoming information while under severe time constraints. These assumptions or beliefs help specify the national interest as well as the best way to pursue it. The preconceived policy ideas held by party leaders are therefore crucial in shaping precise foreign policy responses. In the case of the Republican Party since the 1930s, one can easily imagine some of the specific sets of influential ideas to which this sort of explanation would point in order to account for changes in GOP foreign policy over time, such as ideas of anti-Communist liberation or rollback in the 1950s, or neoconservative ideas beginning in the 1970s. An ideas-based approach looks to the autonomous power of such ideas to explain the emergence or decline of certain Republican foreign policy tendencies.[16]

It is worth noting that all four of these explanatory models could account for continuity as well as changes in a party's foreign policy approach. At least three of the four explanatory models could also account for intraparty divisions as well as commonalities regarding foreign policy.

For example, in analyzing the division between interventionist and anti-interventionist foreign policy factions inside the GOP during the 1940s, one might refer to differences in economic basis, immediate partisan interest, or ideology. International pressures, of course, could hardly account for such intraparty differences, but international pressures might help explain why executive officials with ties to one party faction felt constrained to follow certain foreign policies over others.

Each of the above four potential explanations for the rise and fall of particular foreign policy types is useful and plausible, but each also has difficulties and limitations. An explanation based on the impact of policy ideas, for example, still begs the question of why one particular idea and not another wins out at any given time. The success or failure of specific policy ideas is undoubtedly related to configurations of political power, even if ideas do have a certain influence of their own. An explanation based on partisan politics faces the opposite problem. Granted that party leaders look to outmaneuver one another, this is hardly the only consideration in their thoughts as they formulate their stance on the nation's foreign policy. Distinct, sincere convictions regarding the national interest do count for something, and it would simply be inaccurate to say that party leaders approach foreign policy purely on the basis of partisan considerations. An explanation based on international pressures is a very useful starting point but one limited by the indeterminate nature of such pressures in accounting for specific foreign policy decisions. On the other hand, explanations based on economic interest tend to downplay the impact of international pressures as well as policy ideas altogether. Economic explanations are also insufficiently attuned to the purely domestic political side of partisan coalition building. Such economic explanations assume that coalitions form with specific foreign policy preferences in mind. But in reality, in the United States at least, political coalitions form over a wide range of issues, many of which have little to do with foreign policy per se. There is little evidence to suggest that most Americans vote primarily to express clear, competing preferences over controversial foreign policy issues. In fact, the primary cleavages between U.S. political parties have typically been over domestic economic and cultural issues rather than international ones. Nor have these domestic economic and cultural cleavages always aligned with differences over foreign policy. On the contrary, party coalitions and political conflicts in the United States are best thought of as multi-dimensional. The implications for foreign policy are rather surprising.[17]

At the risk of oversimplification, let us say that political coalitions in the United States form over three broad, distinct, and crosscutting areas: domestic economic issues, domestic social issues, and foreign policy issues. The first, economic dimension centers on questions such as the government's role in the redistribution of wealth. Economic liberals favor such redistribution, economic conservatives oppose it. The second, social dimension centers on questions such as the implementation by government of traditional moral norms. Social conservatives favor such implementation, social liberals resist it. The third, foreign policy dimension centers on questions such as U.S. military intervention abroad. Interventionists favor such action, anti-interventionists oppose it. These various sets of issues, taken together, create a three-dimensional issue space, with a wide variety of positions possible in that space. One might be, for example, conservative on economics, liberal on social issues, and anti-interventionist on foreign policy—which is the strictly libertarian position, not represented by either major party at the moment. If we include the alternative of moderate gradations between left and right and between interventionist and anti-interventionist, then the number of potential ideological combinations becomes almost endless. Obviously, presidents and presidential aspirants want to build and sustain national political coalitions across all three issue dimensions that allow them to be elected or reelected. Some such politicians may have genuine ideological preferences on issues that exist semi-independently of electoral incentives. A degree of uncertainty also exists over the exact distribution of voter preferences on each issue dimension, and the real or actual distribution of such preferences may change over time. Voters may furthermore cast their electoral ballots on "valence" issues such as prosperity, scandal, or a candidate's charming personality, in addition to voting on "position" issues such as economic redistribution or military intervention. Given the above and entirely realistic conditions, it so happens that formal or game theoretic models tell us potentially winning political coalitions will form and re-form, cycling through various possibilities without any single stable outcome. This is an intriguing insight

comes, which interests, and which followers? If party leaders are positioned at the head of broad, multidimensional coalitions, and if their
followers have preferences of varying type and intensity across a range
of issues, then to some extent it is up to the leaders themselves to determine which particular interests and which particular followers will be
most strongly represented on any given policy decision.[19]

Leadership in a political party is important because someone needs
to determine exactly which position will be put forward as the party
stance on each of several distinct issues. There is considerable room for
choice, creativity, and skill in this effort. Even to straddle on a given
issue is itself a position with strategic uses. Party leaders can try to build
coalitions through pressure, persuasion, negotiation, and compromise
among various party factions and across multiple dimensions. They can
set the agenda by putting forward certain policy ideas and not others, by
emphasizing one issue area over another, and by shaping the choices
available to the public. This is all the more true of presidents, who are
uniquely positioned at the apex of the American political system. Presidents are the only figures in that system unquestionably at the head of
their political party. They are also uniquely positioned at the point where
the international system intersects with American government, at the
highest level. They possess unusual status and resources with regard to
the making of foreign policy, and they are given a certain amount of
latitude by their own party, the American public, and Congress to make
foreign policy decisions. This degree of latitude means that their particular beliefs, personalities, and choices make a difference when it
comes to precise foreign policy outcomes. This is not to suggest that
presidents are all-powerful on foreign affairs; far from it. But even after
economic, political, ideological, and international pressures are all taken
into account, the triumph of one foreign policy type over another is crucially shaped by the president's own choices. When it comes to precise
trade-offs between various party factions, for example, or between the
domestic political viability and the international viability of a given policy choice, it is presidents who select the final outcome. If they are sufficiently skillful, determined, and lucky, presidents can even reshape
political constraints and use foreign affairs to help cement and expand

their party's coalition. All this is to say that to a surprising extent, when one party controls the White House, that party's foreign policy is what the president says it is.[20]

The following chapters examine the role of seven Republican Party leaders in formulating distinct approaches to U.S. foreign policy since World War II: Robert Taft, Dwight Eisenhower, Barry Goldwater, Richard Nixon, Ronald Reagan, George H. W. Bush, and George W. Bush. Five of these seven figures are presidents, the other two are leading senators. The additional and exceptional case of Henry Kissinger is considered in the chapter on Richard Nixon. Every one of these eight figures can reasonably be described as conservative, as can their foreign policies, but their exact version of conservatism varies greatly from one to the next. Each chapter therefore tells the story of a specific era in the Republican Party's relationship to America's world role by focusing on a particular party leader. Each chapter also draws a sketch of the personality and policy beliefs of that leader, the patterns of partisan coalition building under his influence, the political context and consequences of his leadership, and the success or failure of his particular approach to foreign affairs. The rise and fall of various Republican foreign policy tendencies—whether hawk, nationalist, realist, or anti-interventionist— is described and analyzed over the course of these chapters. In the conclusion, I return to the more general question of how and why one specific foreign policy type wins out over another, referring back to factors such as economic interest, partisan politics, international pressures, and policy ideas. I outline my overall findings on the precise relationship between party politics and American diplomacy. Finally, I offer concluding thoughts as to the relative prospects of various Republican foreign policy factions in the age of Obama, with some recommendations for the future.

Chapter Two

Robert Taft

The Conservative as Anti-Interventionist

To THIS DAY, Senator Robert Taft (R-OH) embodies for admirers and detractors alike a foreign policy stance of conservative anti-interventionism. From the late 1930s through the early 1950s, Taft argued quite consistently that endless military entanglements abroad would endanger American traditions of limited government. He represented with integrity a distinct type of midcentury Republican: conservative, midwestern, and deeply skeptical of overseas engagements. Yet in truth, Taft's own foreign policy views changed considerably during his years in the Senate. By the time of the Korean War, Taft was calling for a worldwide strategy of anti-Communist rollback or liberation that in numerous respects was more aggressive than the existing U.S. policy of containment. It would therefore be inaccurate to describe Taft as anything like a strict anti-interventionist by the end of his career. In a sense, Taft's reluctant evolution tracked concurrent changes in his own party. Republicans as a whole became more willing to embrace activist foreign policies as a result of World War II. The question that still preoccupied many GOP conservatives after the conclusion of that war was how to halt the spread of communism abroad without abandoning limited government at home. Taft himself never hit on a successful answer to this question, either in political or in policy terms, but his attempts to find a solution had a significant impact on the Republican Party and on American foreign policy. He continued to emphasize U.S. freedom of action, and to warn of the combined dangers of strategic overextension, centralized government, and proliferating military expenditure, until the very end.

The Great Depression, the inauguration of Franklin Roosevelt as president, and the rise of fascist aggression coincided with a lengthy period during which the United States retreated into a foreign policy based on an avoidance of international commitments. Roosevelt, whatever his liberal internationalist convictions, responded nimbly to the overwhelming preoccupation with domestic economic recovery. In 1933 he took the United States off the gold standard and refused to cooperate in any efforts at international monetary stability. That same year he stated unequivocally that he would avoid direct military intervention in the internal affairs of Latin American countries—a continuation of Hoover's Good Neighbor Policy in that region. In 1935–37, Roosevelt signed a series of Neutrality Acts by which Congress imposed an embargo on U.S. arms sales to belligerent nations in case of any future foreign wars. And during the Czech crisis of 1938, he indicated that the United States would be unable to materially support Britain and France in case of war with Germany. All of these policies had broad domestic support from Republicans as well as Democrats. Indeed, throughout the mid-1930s, whatever their deep domestic differences, conservatives and liberals alike agreed that the United States needed to avoid foreign wars, or even any costly, entangling international commitments that might threaten domestic priorities. Western progressive Republicans in particular tended to be initially supportive of New Deal initiatives but staunchly anti-interventionist overseas, and since Roosevelt wanted their support on domestic matters, he dared not alienate them on foreign policy. Even Roosevelt's widely discussed speech of October 1937, in which he called for a "quarantine" against international aggression, indicated no material change in U.S. commitments overseas, as the president himself immediately made clear. The one major exception in this tendency toward international disengagement, aside from the purely rhetorical, was in the area of trade, where the Roosevelt administration initiated a striking and welcome trend toward decreased U.S. tariff barriers with the Reciprocal Trade Act of 1934. The Republican Party took a firm stand at the time against free trade and in favor of protection. The overarching pattern of U.S. foreign policy during the mid-1930s, however, was one of detachment, retrenchment, and avoidance of new international obligations. Since most Republicans, like the great majority of Americans, agreed with this overall approach, there was no really fundamental debate over foreign policy along party lines between 1933 and 1939; for the most part, politicians from both parties simply competed to see who could most convincingly promise utter disengagement from Old World conflicts and alliances.[1]

Important consequences for U.S. foreign policy also followed from the domestic political events of the early to mid-1930s, which brought a dramatic and lasting realignment in the underlying composition of both major parties. The Democrats under Franklin Roosevelt's leadership maintained the loyalty of white southerners, consolidated recent gains with immigrant and Catholic constituencies, and secured new-found levels of support from urban, working-class, lower-income, progressive, Jewish, African American, and first-time voters. Even leading banking and capital-intensive industrial interests initially lent support to New Deal initiatives. Roosevelt had not campaigned in 1932 on a particularly leftist platform. By 1936, however, it was quite apparent that the two major parties were far apart ideologically. In practical terms, Roosevelt had taken a clear stance during his first term in favor of deficit spending, increased taxes, regulation of business, organized labor, new welfare programs, and unprecedented government intervention in the economy. Republican leaders, meanwhile, denounced these trends as a revolutionary threat to traditional forms of government in the United States. The lines of partisan division on domestic economic issues were now stark. This led an increasing number of businessmen and upper-income voters to embrace the Republicans, in opposition to Roosevelt's continuing domestic reforms. A similar countermovement occurred toward the GOP among conservatives and native-born rural Protestants outside the South. On balance, these changes resulted in a Republican Party that was considerably shrunken in relative terms, but also more homogeneous socially and ideologically than before. It was now a party based, in electoral terms, in the small towns and rural counties of the midwestern, New England, and mid-Atlantic states. It was also a more

thoroughly and distinctly conservative party on domestic economic issues, at least among its representatives in Congress. The old East-West
intraparty division was temporarily gone. Western progressives such as-
William Borah, Hiram Johnson, and Robert La Follette Jr. declined in
numbers in the Republican caucus and either became independents,
converted to the Democrats, died in office, or turned against the increasingly urban, pro-labor, regulatory agenda of the Roosevelt administration.[2] Yet at the very same time, many GOP conservatives in effect
moved in the direction of Borah and Johnson on foreign policy matters,
against international commitments of any kind. For one thing, rural and
small-town midwesterners, now the heart of the party, were particularly
skeptical of entanglements abroad. More important, conservative congressional Republicans from both east and west were so distrustful of
Roosevelt and his domestic agenda by the late 1930s that many were
inclined to oppose him on foreign policy as well, especially since U.S.
involvement in overseas wars would no doubt strengthen the trend toward centralized government at home. The midterm elections of 1938
brought major GOP successes for the first time in a decade; southern
Democrats now cooperated in blocking further New Deal reforms.
As Europe edged toward war, the Republican Party in Congress was
therefore confident, conservative, and anti-interventionist, focused on
domestic economic issues and determined to avoid international entanglements.[3] The new senator from Ohio, Robert Taft, personified these
traits.

Although born in and associated with the Midwest, Taft came from a
uniquely privileged background as the son of President William Howard Taft. Robert studied at Harvard and Yale, practiced law, and during
the 1920s entered politics in Ohio at the state level. In 1938 he made a
successful run for the Senate and was recognized immediately as one of
its most promising new members. Taft's politics, like his father's, were
those of a principled economic conservative and staunch party man. He
advocated a primary reliance on market incentives, entrepreneurship,
sound credit, and a balanced budget. Moreover, he believed this approach to be most consistent with American political and constitutional
traditions of limited government, equality of opportunity, and individual freedom. Taft viewed the New Deal as wasteful, arbitrary, and "largely

revolutionary" in overturning these traditions in favor of a vast expansion of federal, executive, and bureaucratic authority. Indeed, he went so far as to say that "if we extend federal power indefinitely . . . it will not be long before we have an American fascism." Yet despite his sweeping overall criticisms of Roosevelt's New Deal, Taft was frequently open to discussion and compromise on specific legislative proposals. This was in keeping with his preferred stance as a trenchant and thoughtful critic, open to reason. With the appearance and demeanor of a stern small-town banker, Taft was hardly charismatic, but he won considerable respect across the political spectrum for his sheer intelligence, industry, honesty, and parliamentary skill. He quickly became a favored, articulate spokesman for conservative Republicans in Congress and nationwide.[4]

Taft's principal concern in foreign policy was that international political or military entanglements might threaten American traditions of limited, constitutional government at home. He was especially suspicious of new foreign commitments proposed by the Roosevelt administration, since in his view it was Roosevelt who had done more than any other figure to overturn these same constitutional traditions. Taft therefore initially embraced a "continentalist" approach to national defense, and became a leading critic of the administration's foreign policies in 1939–41. He stressed the invulnerability of the United States to foreign invasion, given U.S. control over certain nearby bases and sea routes. As Taft put it,

> I believe that the peace and happiness of the people of this country can best be secured by refusing to intervene in war outside the Americas and by establishing our defense line based on the Atlantic and Pacific Oceans. I believe that the difficulty of attacking America across those oceans will forever prevent any such attack being even considered, if we maintain an adequate defense on the sea and in the air. I believe that airpower has made it more difficult, not easier, to transport an army across an ocean and that conquest must still be by a land army.[5]

No European great power war, according to Taft, could really threaten the vital interests of the United States or justify intervention, since the United States was essentially secure and self-sufficient in its North

American citadel. On the other hand, U.S. involvement in foreign wars could do more lasting damage than any German or Japanese conquests abroad by undermining American political, economic, and legal traditions at home. While Taft certainly hoped for the preservation of free institutions in other countries, he did not view the United States as having any special obligation to promote democracy abroad by military means. Consequently, he generally opposed American military or political intervention in the Old World, especially if it seemed to threaten entanglement in European wars. He was furthermore a staunch protectionist on trade issues, believing that traditional Republican high-tariff policies had supported home markets, strong wages, national economic development, and a high standard of living in the United States. At the same time, he called for new efforts at international arbitration, and like his father sought to apply legal concepts to world politics. He also frequently supported increased appropriations in 1939–41 to the U.S. Army, Navy, and Army Air Force, viewing such appropriations as not only consistent with a continentalist approach toward national security but necessary for its successful operation.[6]

The first major foreign policy debate in which Taft and the rest of the country participated during 1939–41 was the debate over "cash and carry." In the opening months of 1939 it became abundantly clear that Hitler had no intention of abiding by the Munich Agreement or of refraining from further aggression. The Roosevelt administration therefore began to pressure Congress to revise sections of the 1935–37 Neutrality Acts, so that Britain and France would be able to purchase weapons from the United States. Anti-interventionists in Congress were able to block and delay any such revision over the spring and summer of 1939, and Roosevelt temporarily backtracked. The outbreak of war in Europe in September 1939 brought the matter to a head, and the issue of neutrality revision again came before Congress. Democratic Party leaders proposed a measure by which the arms embargo would be repealed but belligerents would have to pay cash and then carry away war materials from U.S. ports in their own ships—hence, "cash and carry." Most congressional Republicans opposed such a revision, most Democrats favored it. Taft, oddly enough, supported this particular measure, claiming to be satisfied that it did not violate a strictly neutral legal stance by the United States. Many opponents as well as supporters of cash and carry realized that the legal technicalities were somewhat beside the point. Since German ships would be unlikely to cross the Atlantic unmolested by the British navy, the measure favored the Allies. Interestingly, a bare majority of self-identified Republicans nationwide also supported revision—an indication that GOP anti-interventionists in Congress were no longer necessarily representative of their own party's membership in the country at large. The final October 1939 Senate vote in favor of cash and carry was 63 to 30. The debate set a precedent for the next two years: Roosevelt was reluctant to take political risks on the issue, allowing interventionist lobbies and congressmen to take the lead instead. Specific and limited measures were proposed, with the argument that they would keep the United States out of war and lead to no further involvement. Events overseas played into the hands of the administration, convincing increasing numbers of Americans of the need to take concrete measures to support the Allies. Anti-interventionists warned of terrible consequences should these measures pass. And in the end, the anti-interventionists lost the debate. Yet while an overwhelming majority of Americans from both parties sympathized with the Allies and hoped for the defeat of Nazi Germany, an overwhelming majority, more than 90 percent, also opposed direct U.S. involvement in the war. This meant that Republican anti-interventionists still possessed considerable potential popular support, depending on how the issue was framed. Furthermore, as of the winter of 1939–40, a great majority of Americans expected Germany to lose the war. Consequently, there was no apparent need to contemplate deeper U.S. involvement.[7]

The rapid and unexpected collapse of the French army in May 1940 was a shock to the American public as it was to the U.S. government. It suddenly appeared quite possible that Germany would secure the military domination of Europe. Republicans, and Americans in general, were deeply divided over how to respond, split between an interventionist faction and an anti-interventionist one. Anti-interventionists like Taft opposed U.S. military or financial support to Britain as likely to entangle the United States in armed conflict against Germany. Their overarching priority was to keep the United States out of war. The most famous anti-interventionist lobby, the America First Committee, was organized in September 1940 with the financial backing of midwestern businessmen such as Robert Wood of Sears, Roebuck and R. Douglas Stuart of Quaker Oats. It soon gained thousands of members and had close links to leading members of Congress. Among the general public, anti-interventionists were more likely to be midwestern than southern or northeastern, rural as opposed to urban, Catholic as opposed to Protestant, Irish, Italian, or German American as opposed to Anglo American, and Republican as opposed to Democrat. But these demographic tendencies were each rather weak, and there were certainly significant numbers of leading anti-interventionists in the Northeast, in cities, among WASPs, and among Democrats as well. Furthermore, divisions over domestic economic issues and foreign policy were crosscutting: the antiwar ranks included both conservatives and liberals, even though mainstream Democrats tended to support FDR's foreign policies. The true polarization was within the partisan representation in Congress, where most Republicans from all regions typically stood against both the administration and most Democrats. Since the Democrats held a clear majority in Congress, this gave the administration a great advantage. Yet GOP anti-interventionists were usually able to count on a significant minority of sympathetic congressional Democrats—senators such as Burton Wheeler (MT), Pat McCarran (NV), Bennett Clark (MO), and David Walsh (MA)—to break with their own party on the question of aid to Britain.[8]

Numerous organized business interests opposed war against Germany as disruptive of trade and likely to bring new domestic controls. Midwestern, import-competing, and small and medium-sized businesses in sectors such as retail, real estate, and light goods manufacturing were especially skeptical of arguments for intervention. Leading Protestant and Catholic clergy opposed war on strictly pacifist grounds. Many national newspapers and publishers also supported an anti-interventionist foreign policy stance. These included the Hearst publishing empire, the *New York Daily News*, and above all the *Chicago Tribune* under its redoubtable owner, Robert McCormick. A more unwelcome form of implicit support came from extremists on the left and right such as pro-Nazi fringe groups and (up until June 1941) the Communist Party of the United States. Such support was unwelcome because it discredited the anti-interventionist case. The America First Committee in particular, despite energetic efforts to the contrary, tended to attract vociferous anglophobes, conspiracy theorists, and anti-Semites like moths to a flame. Indeed, its most famous spokesman, the celebrity aviator Charles Lindbergh, had a knack for foolish statements such as the notion that the "greatest danger to this country" from "Jewish groups" was "their large ownership and influence in our motion pictures, our press, our radio, and our government." Roosevelt administration officials, including the president, repeatedly and publicly suggested that the anti-interventionist movement as a whole was influenced, manipulated, and led by Nazi sympathizers, spies, traitors, and propagandists. In fact, Roosevelt authorized the FBI to wiretap and investigate his political opponents on the grounds that they might be working with Berlin. Yet the greatest weight of popular or politically significant support for American anti-interventionism did not derive from anything resembling pro-fascist sentiment. Rather, it came from essentially libertarian Republicans like Robert Taft, who despised Hitler and were about as bitterly opposed to all forms of totalitarianism as one could be.[9]

The chief concern of such Republicans was that renewed entry into Europe's wars would fatally undermine American traditions of constitutional government. They literally believed, as Taft put it, that the U.S. entry would be "more likely to destroy American democracy than to destroy German dictatorship." Moreover, they suspected that this war would not only strengthen domestic tendencies toward centralized government, higher taxes, regulation of business, and executive power—tendencies embraced by the Roosevelt administration since 1933—but would also strengthen communism abroad. For these reasons, large numbers of mainstream Republicans remained bitterly opposed to war against Germany, despite their strong distaste for the Nazi regime. And in contrast to the anti-interventionists of 1914–17, opponents of war this time, such as Taft, were willing to write, speak, and think in geopolitical as well as idealistic terms. They argued that the ongoing conflict was simply another of Europe's perennial balance of power struggles; that Germany was unlikely to decisively defeat Great Britain, or vice versa; that in any case the results would not threaten the security of the United States itself; that the Axis powers could never successfully invade the North American continent; that transoceanic trade would continue regardless; and that even if did not, the United States, together with its Latin American and Canadian allies, was largely self-sufficient in economic terms. In other words, they argued that the United States had no compelling strategic interest in any war against Germany. As Taft put it, "I detest every utterance of Mr. Hitler and every action of the German Government in the last eight years, but we have no right to engage 130 million people in war, or send their sons and our own to war, except on the ground of their own interest."[10]

On the other side of the Republican Party during the great debates of 1940–41 was its interventionist wing, working in de facto alliance with the Roosevelt administration on foreign policy matters. Republican interventionists favored increased U.S. military and economic aid to Great Britain; a few even favored an outright declaration of war against Germany. Leading figures on this wing of the party tended to be disproportionately East Coast, urban, upper-income, old stock Anglo-Saxon Protestants with broad national and international experience in fields such as finance, business, the armed services, education, government, and law. Some had long favored new forms of international organization; others were hawkish realists in the tradition of Theodore Roosevelt. Many were conservative on domestic issues. Together, they were convinced that Nazi aggression posed nothing less than a deadly threat to the core values of Western civilization. They sympathized with and admired Britain's heroic defiance of Hitler under Winston Churchill's leadership. They believed that technological changes such as the rise of airpower had outmoded a strategy of strict continentalism. They also believed that German conquests in Europe would shut the United States out of vital markets, overturn the global balance of power against the United States, threaten transatlantic sea-lanes, and ultimately invite Nazi infiltration of Latin America. Republican interventionists with such beliefs helped organize a number of bipartisan foreign policy lobby groups in 1940–41, all committed to supporting Britain more energetically. These included the Committee to Defend America by Aiding the Allies, created in May–June 1940; the Century Group, created in June–July 1940; and the Fight for Freedom Committee, created in early 1941. Groups like these pressed for new legislation and public awareness in

The foreign policy debate among Republicans came to a head at the GOP National Convention in June 1940, and happened to occur the same month as France's surrender to Germany. These momentous events overseas forced Republicans to reconsider their choices for president. The leading contenders included four men who would play an important part in Republican Party politics over the next few years: Robert Taft, Thomas Dewey, Arthur Vandenberg, and Wendell Willkie. Taft, of course, took a conservative and anti-interventionist position on the issues of the day, focusing on the dangers of centralized government, and he had considerable support from party regulars but ran an uninspired campaign. His comment on May 20, 1940, that there was less to fear from Nazi conquests than from the "infiltration of totalitarian ideas from the New Deal circle in Washington" seemed particularly unsuited to the moment as German tanks rolled through France. Dewey was a New York district attorney, hard-driving, methodical, and a proven vote-getter, but disturbingly vague on specifics and inexperienced in foreign policy matters. Vandenberg was a conservative anti-interventionist senator from Michigan, a man of great self-importance and considerable political perception but little national appeal. Willkie, meanwhile, was an Indiana-born utilities executive possessed of Wall Street connections, a burly and likable figure with a reputation as a balanced critic of New Deal excesses. He was also a convinced internationalist, a registered Democrat as late as 1939, and initially the most improbable candidate of the four. In terms of their policy positions, this left Taft and Vandenberg representing Old Guard conservatives and anti-interventionists, with Willkie diametrically opposed (in intraparty terms) as a moderate on domestic issues and an interventionist on foreign policy. Dewey's chosen position was somewhere in the middle of the other candidates' as a moderate conservative with vaguely anti-interventionist leanings, and partly for this reason—his presumed ability to unify the party—he was the clear front-runner for the nomination until May 1940. The invasion and rapid military defeat of France, however, led Republicans to reconsider whether a foreign policy neophyte such as Dewey could defeat Franklin Roosevelt under the conditions of the day. The American public was shifting toward a somewhat more hawkish position against Germany. Republican interventionists mobilized and demanded a candidate ready to act energetically in the middle of this world crisis. A network of New York–based Republican editors, publishers, lawyers, and bankers rallied to Willkie and engineered an extraordinary public relations campaign on his behalf. His candidacy soon attracted genuine popular enthusiasm. In a dramatic series of ballots, Willkie outlasted his opponents, including Taft, to win the presidential nomination at the Republican National Convention. A sufficient number of party delegates had apparently decided that Willkie was the candidate most likely to beat Roosevelt in November. It was a remarkable step for a party the congressional representation of which was overwhelmingly conservative and anti-interventionist, and the first of many such disappointments for Taft and his supporters. Republican anti-interventionists rallied behind Willkie as the party nominee and one still preferable to Roosevelt, but they continued to fight against increased U.S. aid to Britain, every step of the way. They also ensured that the GOP platform that year included a strong antiwar statement, declaring that the party was "firmly opposed to involving this Nation in foreign war."[13]

Roosevelt sought to defuse political resistance and move ahead on aid to Britain with at least some support from Republicans, and for this reason, in June 1940 he appointed leading GOP foreign policy hawks Henry Stimson and Frank Knox as secretary of war and secretary of the navy, respectively. The seventy-two-year-old Stimson in particular was by this time a widely experienced and respected figure, and typically ahead of Roosevelt in pressing for intervention against Germany. The president was very reluctant in the summer of 1940 to court popular or congressional opposition through contentious foreign policy measures, especially with an election campaign approaching. Consequently, Roosevelt welcomed Willkie's nomination, since it promised to insulate the presidential campaign from any basic or politically very risky debate over foreign policy matters. Indeed, Willkie initially agreed not to criticize the administration on two controversial measures, the first the so-called destroyers for bases deal and the second conscription.[14]

On the first issue, the question was whether the United States would provide a number of aging destroyers to the British navy, hard-pressed as it was in its war against German submarines. Republican and Democratic interventionists from groups like the Committee to Defend America supported such assistance, but Roosevelt feared its domestic political ramifications, since it obviously represented another movement toward military alliance with London. He and his supporters therefore came up with a scheme by which fifty destroyers would be "traded" to Great Britain in exchange for long-term American leasing rights over several British bases in the Caribbean and Atlantic. The measure was also undertaken as an executive agreement to prevent its coming before Congress. In this way, and by portraying his critics as "appeaser fifth columnists," Roosevelt preempted and muffled political criticism. In fact the destroyers for bases deal had considerable popular support: 62 percent of the American public, according to an August 1940 Gallup poll. The same was true of conscription that year. As France fell before the German attack, an overwhelming majority of Americans rushed to support new military preparations. Conscription in particular seemed necessary to prepare for whatever eventualities followed Nazi conquests in Europe. By August more than 70 percent of Americans, including a clear majority of Republicans, favored the draft. Yet GOP anti-interventionists like Taft, while supportive of increased military expenditures, viewed conscription as an appalling departure from American traditions of individual freedom and one designed primarily, as Taft put it, to "make the country war-conscious and more inclined to enter the European war." Congressional debate over the Selective Service Act was necessarily intense over what amounted to the first peacetime draft in American history. But again, by hedging this new measure with various restrictions and concessions, by avoiding overly aggressive or unpopular initiatives, and by letting foreign policy interventionists outside the White House take the lead, the administration secured its passage through Congress in September 1940 with comfortable majorities in favor and with significant breakaway support from some congressional Republicans. By the end of June 1941, some 1.8 million men would be on active duty in the U.S. armed forces, preparing for the possibility of military involvement against Germany and Japan.[15]

The presidential campaign of 1940 proved to be a case study in convergence on foreign policy matters, as the two leading candidates took remarkably similar positions. The Democratic Party platform, like the Republican platform, promised that "we will not participate in foreign wars." Each candidate denounced Hitler, favored U.S. military readiness, and called for limited aid to Great Britain; neither proposed anything like an outright declaration of war against Germany. In this sense both candidates, whatever their private convictions, faithfully reflected the genuine ambivalence of the American electorate, torn between a desire to stay out of war and a desire to see Nazi Germany defeated. Roosevelt, meanwhile, castigated his opponents as weak on national security and allowed his new vice-presidential candidate, Henry Wallace, to declare that "you can be sure every Nazi, every Hitlerite, and every appeaser is a Republican." As the president gained and maintained a solid lead in the polls over the course of the campaign, Willkie became increasingly desperate. He reached for the peace issue, promising that "we shall not undertake to fight anybody else's war. Our boys shall stay out of Europe." Concerned by the potential impact of this attack, Roosevelt responded on October 30 in Boston with a widely publicized speech in which he too promised that "your boys are not going to be sent into any foreign war." In the end, the president for the most part neutralized the peace issue, reassuring voters that he would support the British and maintain the nation's defenses without directly involving the United States in military conflict. Diehard anti-interventionists were not about to support Roosevelt, regardless. The final election results represented a better showing than Republican presidential candidates had made in 1932–36, but it was still a solid victory for the incumbent. Roosevelt's interventionism, such as it was, appears to have gained Willkie votes among certain important constituencies, such as German Americans and rural midwesterners. On balance, however, the issue of war and peace probably helped Roosevelt win reelection, not only because he won even greater support from countervailing hawkish constituencies such as Polish, Jewish, and northeastern Anglo Americans but, more important, because a majority of the U.S. public was convinced he was simply better able to manage this crisis than the less experienced Willkie. In actuality there had been no fundamental debate over U.S. foreign policy between the two candidates. Conservative GOP anti-interventionists like Taft drew the conclusion that their party had sold its soul for a mess of pottage, and resolved not to repeat the mistake.[16]

Having won reelection, Roosevelt tacked immediately toward a more interventionist foreign policy course. The British were running out of the financial resources necessary to purchase weapons from the United States. At a press conference on December 17, 1940, Roosevelt responded by proposing that Americans "get rid of the silly, foolish old dollar sign" in providing war materials to Britain. A few days later he gave a major radio address in which he called on the United States to be "the great arsenal of democracy." The American interest in this conflict, he clarified, was that "if Great Britain goes down, the Axis powers . . . will be in a position to bring enormous military and naval resources against this hemisphere." Roosevelt's specific recommendation was that the United States loan, lease, or grant weapons and supplies to the British without the need for immediate repayment; hence, "Lend-Lease." The scale of the proposed program was massive: some $7 billion worth of war materials in the first round alone. Republican anti-interventionists were appalled, and mobilized for what they viewed as an apocalyptic showdown with the administration and its allies. Apart from the sheer cost of the initiative, it clearly amounted to another dramatic step away from neutrality and toward direct participation in hostilities. Taft was bitterly opposed. He argued that the Lend-Lease program in effect gave the executive "the power to plunge into war," arbitrarily and at the president's own discretion. It would inevitably entangle the United States in military incidents against German submarines in the North Atlantic, and such incidents would subsequently lead to more direct U.S. intervention. The central issue was therefore not sympathy for Britain, which Taft shared, but "whether we go to war or not." As he told a friend, "even the collapse of England is to be preferred to participation for the rest of our lives in European wars." Moreover, the pretense of a "loan" was, for Taft, nonsensical in relation to war materials. "Lending war equipment is a good deal like lending chewing gum," he pointed out, "you certainly don't want the same gum back." Charles Lindbergh took a position in congressional testimony that was even less supportive of the British, stating that he hoped to see a negotiated peace between Great Britain and Nazi Germany since "I prefer to see neither side win."[17]

Republican anti-interventionists had the support of some Democrats such as Senator Burton Wheeler of Montana, who suggested that Lend-Lease would "slit the throat of the last democracy still living." The America First Committee and the Committee to Defend America again squared off on opposing sides of the debate as influential lobbying groups. But a clear majority of congressional Democrats supported the initiative, as did a significant minority of mostly northeastern Republicans. Wendell Willkie, just returned from a trip to Great Britain and now able to speak his mind free from electoral pressures, provided winning congressional testimony in favor of the measure while dismissing what he himself called his own "campaign oratory" the previous year against Roosevelt's foreign policy. As with previous such measures proposed by the administration, the Lend-Lease concept had broad popular support nationwide, including 74 percent of Democrats and 62 percent of Republicans in January 1941. And Roosevelt showed his customary and manipulative political skill in accusing his opponents of "aiding and abetting the work of . . . [Nazi] agents" and insisting that the purpose of Lend-Lease was not to participate in foreign wars, but to prevent such wars from reaching America. The result was that the proposal was passed by the Senate by a vote of 60 to 31 and by the House of Representatives by an even larger margin, becoming law in March 1941. Senator Arthur Vandenberg wrote in his dairy that he felt like he "was witnessing the suicide of the Republic. . . .We have torn up 150 years of traditional American foreign policy. . . .We have taken the first step upon a course from which we can never hereafter retreat."[18]

As Taft had feared, the Lend-Lease program tended to invite and align with deepening U.S. involvement in World War II. Indeed, as Congress debated the Lend-Lease act between January and March 1941, American and British military chiefs were privately meeting in Washington, D.C., to coordinate joint strategy in case of full-scale U.S. entry into hostilities. There was also the question of how to ensure the safe passage of merchant ships on their way to Great Britain, past German submarines. The obvious answer was to have American warships escort merchant convoys across the Atlantic, but such measures were still very controversial in the spring of 1941. Roosevelt responded by initiating limited U.S. naval escort measures in secret, without asking or informing Congress. In fact, he initially denied that the U.S. Navy was engaged in escort or convoy activities at all, preferring to call them patrols. Other measures followed. An American naval security zone was extended several hundred miles off-shore, and eventually halfway across the Atlantic, in cooperation with the British navy. In April 1941 FDR extended a U.S. military protectorate over Greenland and the Azores to solidify this zone. In July he landed U.S. troops in Iceland to the same end. In August he met with Winston Churchill off the coast of Newfoundland and agreed on a broad declaration of common war aims with the British, including such Wilsonian themes as national self-determination and freedom of the seas. At this conference the president apparently told Churchill that in the North Atlantic "he would wage war, but not declare it," "that he would become more and more provocative," that "if the Germans did not like it, they could attack American forces," and that "everything was to be done to force an 'incident' that could lead to war." Over the next two months, multiple such incidents occurred as American destroyers first hunted and then were attacked by submarines. Roosevelt used these incidents to persuade Congress to repeal further sections of the 1935–37 Neutrality Acts. He also asked and won congressional approval for a new policy of "shoot on sight" against German submarines, which he termed "the rattlesnakes of the Atlantic." Most of these limited measures, with the initial exception of convoys, either possessed or gained the support of at least 60 percent of the American public. Yet FDR did not ask for straightforward U.S. entry into hostilities, knowing full well that this final decisive step was still highly unpopular. Instead, he waged an increasingly energetic and undeclared naval war against Germany in the Atlantic, hoping at least to assist Great Britain in the process. At the same time he spoke more and more directly and unequivocally to the American public over the course of 1941 about the need to act against Germany, out of simple national self-interest if nothing else. As he put it on September 11 of that year, "it is time for all Americans . . . to stop being deluded by the romantic notion that the Americas can go on living happily and peacefully in a Nazi-dominated world."[19]

Republicans remained bitterly divided over Roosevelt's foreign policies during 1941, with a majority of GOP members of Congress and their supporters in fierce opposition. Hitler's invasion of the USSR in June only renewed the determination of conservative Republican anti-interventionists to keep their country out of war, since they viewed the Soviet Union as an especially unworthy and dangerous potential ally.

Taft opposed the administration's drift toward intervention altogether, and viewed the use of U.S. naval escorts or convoys as a deliberate "means of getting us into the war" rather than a tactic based on "any concern about the arrival of our munitions." There was no reason, he argued, that the United States "should assume the burden of delivering those munitions in England, and thereby go to war in England's behalf." The senator was furthermore alarmed by the sweeping declarations of the Atlantic Charter, which seemed to imply a working wartime alliance with Great Britain. He insisted that the president had "no constitutional right to enter into any agreement to destroy the Nazi tyranny" or to "disarm any nation by force, without the consent of Congress, which alone can declare war." Indeed, the charter seemed to Taft "a declaration that the United States and England propose to run the world for the present, with some international agreement in the indefinite future." In August 1941, anti-interventionists like Taft almost succeeded in preventing a renewal of the Selective Service Act; conscription was renewed in the House of Representatives by only one vote. Such opposition indicated the continuing strength of antiwar sentiment in the United States, right through the summer and autumn of 1941. Yet the country as a whole was increasingly resigned to the idea that direct U.S. military engagement with Nazi Germany was inevitable. For the most part, Roosevelt continued to move forward successfully with incremental and aggressive steps against Berlin, carrying the support not only of most Democrats but of a critical segment of Republican congressmen, lobbyists, editors, publishers, businessmen, and party members nationwide.[20]

The final trigger for a U.S. declaration of war against Germany came in the Pacific, ironically, since the partisan and popular debate over intervention focused primarily on Europe. Republican anti-interventionists were never quite as alarmed about the prospect of war with Japan as compared to war with Germany. To be sure, they opposed war on either front, but couched their position primarily in terms of opposition to European wars and alliances. Indeed, many erstwhile anti-interventionists were willing to take a much tougher line against Tokyo than against Berlin, for example by cutting off the flow of American scrap iron to the Japanese armed forces. Economic sanctions against Japan in 1940–41 had overwhelming popular support. Nor were hard-line diplomatic, military, and economic measures against Tokyo really a focus of debate in Congress or between the two parties; for the most part, the relevant measures were taken as executive actions, and the critical debates were within the executive branch. Over the course of 1940–41, the administration attempted to pressure Tokyo and buy time through a combination of economic sanctions, deterrent military measures, and halfhearted negotiations, but this combination proved to be ineffectual and even counterproductive, as the Japanese government finally settled on a desperate course of all-out military expansion. On December 7, 1941, Japan attacked U.S. forces at Pearl Harbor. The very ease with which Roosevelt's domestic political problems were suddenly solved led some anti-interventionists, Republican and otherwise, to suspect that he had deliberately engineered this attack, a suspicion that inexplicably still lingers in some circles. There has never been any convincing evidence to support this suspicion. Apart from the improbability that Roosevelt would have knowingly encouraged a devastating attack on American civilians together with his beloved navy, he had no interest in such an event, since he was trying precisely to avert or delay war with Japan in order to focus on Germany first. Nor could he have known that Hitler would immediately oblige with a declaration of war against the United States. While American officials were aware by the beginning of December 1941 that Japanese forces might attack Southeast Asia and the Philippines at any moment, they had little conception that these forces would be able to reach all the way to Hawaii. The question of sheer incompetence on the part of relevant U.S. military and intelligence officials in failing to detect the Japanese attack was a separate and valid one, and a political hot potato throughout the war. In any case, the attack temporarily united Americans—Republicans as well as Democrats—in war against Japan and Germany, as Roosevelt never could have. As Arthur Vandenberg put it on December 8, 1941, "I still think we may have driven [Japan] needlessly into hostilities through our dogmatic diplomatic attitudes. . . . But . . . now we are in it. Nothing matters except victory."[21]

While congressional Republicans rallied energetically to the national war effort after Pearl Harbor, they continued to criticize and resist Roosevelt's domestic agenda with considerable intensity. Indeed, GOP members had been able since the late 1930s to form a "conservative coalition" in Congress together with sympathetic southern Democrats to resist any further New Deal reforms. The U.S. entry into World War II did not weaken this coalition. Taft played a leading role in articulating the wartime concerns of congressional conservatives and spoke for many of them when he said that the war might be used by liberal Democrats as a "cloak for New Deal measures." He and other conservatives nationwide resented the many new regulations, rationings, tax hikes, price controls, and proliferating bureaucracies that inevitably accompanied America's full-scale entry into war. They also resented the failure to make greater progress militarily against Japan in 1942. As it happened, these resentments were shared by much of the American public, and in the midterm elections of that year the voters registered their discontent by dealing incumbent Democrats a stinging defeat. A reputation for "isolationism" did little apparent damage to Republicans that fall. The election only strengthened the congressional conservative coalition, which proceeded to abolish several former New Deal agencies such as the Works Progress Administration. Significantly, however, the new Congress made no attempt to dismantle the basic framework of Roosevelt's domestic accomplishments from the 1930s, including programs such as Social Security, minimum wage laws, banking and securities regulation, and agricultural price supports. Meanwhile, government spending and federal authority expanded exponentially as the United States mobilized for total war.[22]

By 1943, the United States and its allies were experiencing military success, and a leading foreign policy question for Americans was what role their country would play in the world after the conclusion of the war. An overwhelming majority of U.S. citizens, between 70 and 85 percent, said they were prepared to see the United States take an "active part" in world affairs, as opposed to simply "minding its own business." Indeed, a common impression held by Americans during World War II was that they had failed in not following Woodrow Wilson's lead after World War I, and consequently his reputation made a dramatic comeback. The concept of a new League of Nations likewise became remarkably popular in the United States, since it matched traditional American liberal idealism with a readiness to assume broader responsibilities internationally. Public opinion polls consistently showed that U.S. membership in some sort of postwar world organization with "police power" was now very popular among Americans: between 60 and 70 percent in favor during 1942, with the numbers only climbing over time. There were no significant differences in the levels of support for such a world organization among Republicans as opposed to Democrats; popular majorities in each party were equally in favor. Internationalist, world federalist, and Wilsonian foreign policy lobbies such as the United Nations Association sprouted up and flourished in 1942–43. The leading figures and membership of such lobbies included Republicans as well as Democrats. But with the memory of Wilson's defeat under similar circumstances vividly in his mind, Roosevelt was initially reluctant to commit to specific plans for a new world peacekeeping organization, preferring to let internationalist lobbies and congressmen take the lead. The only foreign policy goals FDR laid out in public, beyond the military defeat of the Axis powers, were the very ambitious and idealistic yet inexact declarations of 1941, namely the Atlantic Charter together with the four freedoms identified in his State of the Union speech: freedom from fear, freedom from want, freedom of religion, and freedom of speech. Vice President Henry Wallace tried to fill the gap by laying out a postwar vision of his own—"the century of the common man"—which seemed to imply, among other things, massive postwar foreign aid programs to encourage international development worldwide. Consequently, as they waited for more precise proposals to emanate from the White House, Republicans were left to debate foreign policy among themselves, and they were far from united on this issue.[23]

At one end of the GOP spectrum were internationalists such as Henry Luce, Wendell Willkie, and Harold Stassen. Stassen, the young Republican governor of Minnesota up until 1943, staked out a position that was extreme even among internationalists by calling for world federalism. While the logical implications of this position were never accepted by anything like a majority of the American public, it held an unprecedented degree of support in 1943–45. A less improbable foreign policy vision came from the publisher Henry Luce. Even before Pearl Harbor, Luce had published an editorial in his widely read *Life* magazine entitled "The American Century." In it, he called unabashedly on Americans "to assume the leadership of the world," to act as "the powerhouse of the ideals of Freedom and Justice," and "to accept whole-heartedly our duty and our opportunity as the most powerful and vital nation in the world." Luce urged the United States to take the lead in establishing an open and liberal international economic order out of this global conflict, not only because of the commercial opportunities offered but, even more important, because otherwise free enterprise and democratic institutions would be unable to survive in the United States itself. He further suggested that "it was the manifest duty of this country to undertake to feed all the people of the world who as a result of this worldwide collapse of civilization are hungry and destitute," and that the United States ought to act as "the Good Samaritan of the entire world." Here was a kind of muscular idealism that appealed to a good many GOP internationalists.[24]

Of even greater immediate importance politically were the efforts of Wendell Willkie. Since losing the 1940 election, Willkie had continued to move in an increasingly internationalist and liberal direction on foreign policy as well as domestic. His 1943 book, *One World*, based on his global travels over the previous months, became one of the best-selling nonfiction books of all time. In it, he sketched a hopeful picture of "a new society of interdependent nations" emerging out of the war. "There are no distant points in the world any longer," he suggested, since "the world has become small not only on the map, but also in the minds of men." "There can be no peace for any part of the world," he stated, "unless the foundations of peace are made secure throughout all parts of the world." Willkie called for an end to European imperialism, for "freedom and self-rule" for colonial peoples. He praised the Soviet experiment as a dynamic meritocracy, "an effective society" that "works," and argued that it left Russians better off than they were before the Revolution of 1917. He had similarly flattering comments about China's Nationalists and Communists alike. He insisted that "the United Nations must become a common council, not only for the winning of the war but for the future welfare of mankind." "We must advance from the narrow idea of exclusive alliances and regional blocs," he said, "which in the end make for bigger and better wars, to effective organization of world unity." As did Luce and many others, Willkie predicted lasting cooperation with Moscow after the war. The book, like its author, had a "gee whiz" quality to it—sincere, well-intentioned, and in many ways naive. Yet the phenomenal popular and critical success of *One World* indicated that Willkie's liberal internationalist foreign policy ideas resonated with a very large segment of the American public, elite opinion, and numerous Republicans.[25]

Another, very different version of internationalism was put forward by Walter Lippmann, the influential veteran journalist with extensive ties to GOP interventionists. Lippmann was an apostate ex-Wilsonian and part of a discernible trend in the United States during World War II toward straightforward geopolitical reasoning on foreign policy matters. In his 1943 book, *U.S. Foreign Policy: Shield of the Republic*, Lippmann argued that since 1898, American diplomatic and strategic commitments had typically outrun the nation's willingness or ability to keep them. He therefore disparaged the making of universalistic postwar commitments that could not actually be kept. Instead, he called on Americans to recognize once and for all that they possessed a vital national interest in the freedom and security of what he called the Atlantic community, namely, Western Europe. The United States would have to maintain a strong naval presence on both sides of the Atlantic and Pacific after the war. Beyond that, Lippmann called for only limited U.S. engagements, under the umbrella of a standing postwar alliance joining the true great powers of the day—Great Britain, the Soviet Union, and the United States. This alliance would necessarily entail the neutralization of Eastern Europe, in order to meet Moscow's central security concern. Only by such measures could the core interests of each power be met without spiraling into violent conflict. Lippmann sought to educate his readers in the unsentimental realities of international balance of power politics as opposed to what he called idealistic "mirages" such as "world peace," "disarmament," "no entangling alliances," and "collective security." He asked Americans to recognize that any new League of Nations by itself would be unable to keep the peace in the absence of specific strategic commitments and alliances between individual nation-states. His thesis gained a wide, respectful reading and, unbeknownst to him, possessed certain uncanny similarities to Roosevelt's own nascent postwar plans, but this sort of explicit foreign policy realism still had a limited impact on the ways in which U.S. officials were prepared to discuss American diplomacy in public. More to the point, there is no indication that most Republican politicians or opinion leaders either wrote, spoke, or thought in strictly geopolitical terms when considering America's postwar world role. Indeed, even Lippmann did not, calling as he did for "no spheres of influence" but rather a "world-wide system of liberty under law."[26]

Senator Taft was skeptical of all such internationalist foreign policy visions; every one of them involved too many postwar entanglements and cessions of U.S. national sovereignty for his taste. While Taft supported the war effort after Pearl Harbor, he saw no reason to apologize for his prewar foreign policy. Roosevelt's four freedoms and Atlantic Charter, he felt, were simultaneously overambitious and too vague a basis on which to fight any war: how, for example, was the United States going to guarantee "freedom from want" worldwide? Taft resisted Roosevelt's apparent implication that U.S. wartime involvement constituted a "crusade" to "impose our idea of freedom" or intervene in the internal affairs of "every country." "The only effective way in which we can spread the four freedoms throughout the world," Taft argued, "is by the force of our own example." Henry Wallace's proposal for a "century of the common man" similarly struck Taft as, in practice, a call for the globalization of the New Deal—a kind of unwelcome "international WPA." Harold Stassen's concept of world federalism or a "super-state" he dismissed out of hand as "unsound and impractical." Henry Luce's advocacy of an "American century" to Taft "smacked of imperialism" and was not only "contrary to the ideals of the American people" but fundamentally unworkable: "It reminds me of the idealism of the bureaucrats in Washington who want to regulate the lives of every American along the lines that the bureaucrats think are best for them." As Taft put it, there "isn't the slightest evidence that we could make a success of our American raj," pointing as an example to Puerto Rico, "where we have been for forty-five years without relieving poverty or improving anyone's condition." Walter Lippmann's concept of a postwar great power alliance was likewise anathema to Taft. "Fundamentally," he said of Lippmann's proposal, "this is imperialism. Our fingers will be in every pie." "It derides the idea that we can defend the United States, or America," Taft commented, "without sea bases and air bases in Europe, Africa, and Asia." Taft saw no reason why Britain and the Soviet Union would not demand extensive spheres of influence of their own under such an arrangement, leading to endless great power rivalries. Moreover, it appeared to him to encourage the "existence of huge armaments," in themselves a "cause of war." And Willkie's vision of "One World" was particularly disturbing to Taft, since Willkie represented and influenced an important internationalist constituency in the Republican Party and beyond.

Taft's conception of America's proper postwar world role was to maintain strict limits on overseas engagements; preserve American national sovereignty; restore a strong foreign policy role for Congress; and keep a primary focus on domestic affairs. He did not want the United States to be a "meddlesome Mattie, interfering in every trouble throughout the world." He saw no urgent need, either in terms of Republican Party or U.S. national advantage, for an early or premature commitment to any specific proposals for postwar organization: "we can't out-intervention Roosevelt." Like his father, Taft placed great faith in the potential of "an international law and a Court to apply it," suggesting that the establishment of such law should precede rather than follow the creation of any supranational political organization. Unlike the more adamant anti-interventionists, he was willing to support U.S. membership in some sort of postwar international organization so long as it did not infringe unduly on the nation's sovereignty, but he argued that the primary burden for maintaining the peace should fall on regional powers rather than on the United States. As he put it, "I do not want to police Europe, or become involved in every little boundary dispute that there may be among the bitterly prejudiced and badly mixed races of Central Europe." Above all, he hoped to preserve a free hand for the United States going into the postwar era, and to minimize the influence within the Republican Party of Wendell Willkie, whom he viewed as "out to make as much trouble as possible."[27]

By 1943–44 an increasing number of congressional Republicans, especially from the Northeast—including senators such as George Aiken (R-VT), Warren Austin (R-VT), James Davis (R-PA), and Henry Cabot Lodge Jr. (R-MA)—had either been elected on or had shifted in the direction of foreign policy internationalism. GOP politicians could sense the changing winds of American popular opinion; a new league of nations was a winning political issue. Taft was unenthusiastic about this trend. With the senator from Ohio refusing to take the lead in working toward intra- or interparty cooperation on foreign policy matters, the way was open for Arthur Vandenberg to do so. Prior to Pearl Harbor, Vandenberg had been one of the leading anti-interventionists in the Republican Party. He later famously stated of December 7, 1941: "that day ended isolationism for any realist." Yet the phrase had a double meaning, even if unintentionally on his part, in that Vandenberg clearly realized that a reputation for isolationism had become a political liability for Republicans at the national level over the course of World War II, and hence no longer realistic in domestic political terms. As is evident from his private papers, Vandenberg did not convert to internationalism overnight. "If I have become an 'internationalist,'" he wrote in July 1943, "then black is white." What he did instead—with considerable political sensitivity—was to feel his way toward a stance that could unite both wings of the Republican Party, sideline Wendell Willkie, and neutralize any advantage the administration might have on foreign policy issues.

In September 1943, leading Republicans from Congress and around the country met at Mackinac Island, in Lake Huron, to develop a unified position on a new league of nations. Vandenberg played the critical mediating role, "hunting for the middle ground," as he put it, and cobbling together a statement which those attending could support. According to the Mackinac declaration, the Republican Party favored "responsible participation by the United States in a post-war cooperative organization among sovereign nations to prevent aggression," together with the preservation of congressional prerogatives in foreign affairs. This statement was criticized by ideologues on both sides as overly vague, but it served its purpose in providing the party with a reasonably unified position going into the 1944 election season. Internationalists applauded the Mackinac wording in favor of international organization, while many nationalists, including Taft, appreciated the affirmation of congressional authority and national sovereignty. This combination became the basic formula embraced by most members of the GOP in subsequent congressional debates and resolutions, and it in turn had a major influence on those debates. A Senate resolution of November 1943, for example, calling for American participation in a new "international authority with power to prevent aggression," included cautionary language very similar to the Mackinac statement, and carried by a vote of 85 to 5. Only the most ideological anti-interventionists, on the one hand, and the most ideological multilateralists, on the other, dissented from the new formula; even Taft was able to support it. The result was that a clear majority of Republican leaders signed on to a plausible position regarding any postwar league of nations: open to "bipartisan" cooperation and to certain forms of international organization, but still staunchly committed to the nation's sovereignty and its separation of powers. It was not a bad formula, politically speaking, and Vandenberg played the key role in its development.[28]

The next question was whether Republican Party members would re-affirm this middle-of-the-road policy position in the upcoming presidential primaries. The potential candidates spanned a broad spectrum on both foreign and domestic issues. Taft would have been a leading candidate for conservatives, but he had run a lackluster campaign four years earlier and had promised to stay out of the race in 1944 so that Ohio governor John Bricker could run. Bricker was a sentimental favorite with the midwestern wing of the party, a handsome and genial but otherwise unremarkable man. Another favorite candidate on the right was General Douglas MacArthur, the brilliant but egocentric commander of U.S. Army forces in the Southwestern Pacific. Wendell Willkie was the Roosevelt administration's favorite Republican: by this time staunchly liberal, internationalist, and highly dismissive of the conservative and anti-interventionist wings of the party. Harold Stassen also ran as a liberal internationalist Republican. Every one of these candidates fizzled as the primaries approached. Bricker never really impressed many party members as presidential material, however much they liked him; MacArthur sabotaged his own chances with a characteristically insubordinate and publicized letter to a congressional supporter; Willkie alienated regular Republicans with his open contempt for them and indifference to organizational matters; and Stassen's campaign failed to get off the ground, as the former governor was thousands of miles away on active service in the navy. Into the gap stepped Thomas Dewey. Dewey had been elected governor of New York in 1942 and immediately established a reputation as a formidably capable executive, able to win support from moderate and independent voters. He staked out a position as

a pragmatist on domestic economic issues, committed to a more effi-
cient, honest, and business-friendly government, but never suggested
that the New Deal framework be fundamentally altered or rolled back.
On foreign policy, his great weakness in 1940, he had since moved in a
more internationalist direction under the tutelage of Republican policy
expert John Foster Dulles. Dewey's instincts were practical rather than
fiercely ideological: he wanted above all to unite his party, win power,
and govern. He also loved to read public opinion polls, which seemed to
indicate that Republicans needed to adjust to the times or face continued political defeat at the national level. He therefore took a stand as a
moderate conservative internationalist, sensitive to the concerns of his
party's base but leaning toward the center on both foreign and domestic
issues. Dewey's priggish, calculating personality did not inspire affection,
and the Taft wing of the party mistrusted him, but he was clearly the
GOP's consensus candidate for president in 1944, and he sailed through
the primaries to win the nomination with ease.[29]

Dewey's campaign for president got off to a rousing start at the Republican Convention as he attacked "the dreary prospect" of four more
years of New Deal liberalism, with "interference piled on interference
and petty tyrannies rivaling the very regimentation with which we are
now at war." He communicated a sense of professionalism and was difficult to characterize as an extremist. Yet his campaign had trouble finding traction as the season wore on. Dewey tried attacking the White
House on foreign policy, implying that it was selling Poland out to Soviet
domination as part of an "immoral" exercise in great power politics,
"the rankest form of imperialism." He warned voters of radical influences within the Democratic Party—a potentially promising tack, especially since the Communist Party of the United States under Earl
Browder had temporarily disbanded itself while calling for FDR's reelection. Dewey further characterized the administration as "old and
tired," suggesting that Roosevelt's health was no longer up to the task of
governing. But with American forces advancing against both Axis powers, any depiction of the administration as incompetent lacked bite.
Moreover, the New Deal coalition remained immensely strong, and with
the war still on and going well, an insufficient number of voters saw
compelling reason to toss out an experienced incumbent president.

Roosevelt, for his part, ran a characteristically winning campaign, promised a cornucopia of postwar social benefits, deflected attacks, referred to his charming dog, and suggested that Dewey was in thrall to the right wing of the Republican Party. In the end, the electoral outcome closely resembled the one four years earlier: a respectable showing by Republicans in the Midwest and New England, but still a solid defeat for the GOP. From a foreign policy perspective, the most striking feature of the election was how similar the candidate's stands had been: both supported U.S. membership in a new united nations organization, empowered to act against aggression, but with no supranational police force of the kind favored by arch-internationalists. The only apparent difference between Dewey and FDR on this issue was whether Congress should retain the right to support or oppose the use of force once authorized by such a union of nations. Roosevelt, toward the end of the campaign, came out against such congressional prerogatives; Dewey hedged. In any case, the election saw the defeat of several leading congressional anti-interventionists from both parties, and was commonly interpreted as a mandate for internationalism—this despite the fact that domestic concerns were as usual uppermost for the average voter. The one issue that might have really damaged Roosevelt in 1944 was a public revelation that U.S. intelligence had already broken Japanese codes prior to Pearl Harbor; the surprise attack would then have been especially hard to explain in the simplified and overheated context of an election season. Dewey was informed of the code-breaking issue by Army Chief of Staff George Marshall but to his credit chose not to use it, knowing full well that such a public revelation would undoubtedly cost American lives in the Pacific.[30]

One foreign policy development that was barely discussed during the election campaign but would have immense long-term consequences was the rise of American cooperation with Great Britain in the development of a new international economic order. In July 1944, U.S. and British officials met at Bretton Woods, New Hampshire. They agreed on the creation of an international monetary fund, together with a world bank, to facilitate global trade, stabilize currency exchange, and promote reconstruction, investment, and development worldwide. The Bretton Woods Agreement represented a dramatic departure from both the autarchic policies of the 1930s and the international economic order of the nineteenth century, in that governments of leading Western nations would now take the lead in encouraging and managing an increasingly integrated global economy. Prominent Republicans, including Dewey, Dulles, Vandenberg, and several northeastern senators, had come to embrace over the course of the war both reciprocal free trade arrangements and the Bretton Woods framework, as did numerous export-oriented and financial interests associated with the party. Taft, on the other hand, was much more skeptical, as were midwestern Republicans in particular. These skeptics looked to maintain the traditional GOP policy of high tariffs and independent national economic development. Taft opposed the U.S. commitment to a regulated, worldwide multilateral economic system, preferring a bilateral and unilateral approach on monetary, financial, and commercial matters. He sought to "reserve our freedom of action" on foreign economic policy. He was furthermore unconvinced as a practical matter that currency stabilization could precede postwar reconstruction overseas. Yet he realized that recovering postwar national economies would need access to markets and raw materials from abroad. His solution was regional economic integration. He called for the establishment of local "customs unions" and "economic regions, each one to be as self-supporting as possible," as an alternative to global economic integration. In sum, Taft's willingness to go along with the establishment of a united nations organization did not translate into a willingness to go along with either free trade or the Bretton Woods Agreements; as of 1945, these foreign economic policy issues were still controversial in the GOP. The administration went ahead with the Bretton Woods framework regardless, and continued to reduce tariff barriers, with crucial support in both cases from a few internationalist Republicans. Taft and his supporters, on the other hand, remained adamantly committed to a mercantilist approach. As he put it to John Foster Dulles, who tried to explain to Taft the benefits of the Bretton Woods system: "I don't want to hear a thing about it . . . you might change my mind."[31]

With Allied armies closing in on Germany and Japan, the great remaining diplomatic question was the one of a postwar settlement. In January 1945, Roosevelt prepared to meet Stalin and Churchill at the

Black Sea resort of Yalta. Congressional Republicans were concerned that FDR was about to formally sanction Soviet and therefore Communist domination over Eastern Europe. On January 10, Vandenberg took the floor of the Senate to reiterate, in statesmanlike tones, his frequently expressed concern that "Russia's unilateral plan appears to contemplate the engulfment, directly or indirectly, of a surrounding circle of buffer states, contrary to what we thought we were fighting for in respect to the rights of small nations and a just peace." To his surprise, both the White House and the media picked up on a secondary theme of the speech, in which the senator agreed that no "nation hereafter can immunize itself by its own exclusive action," and interpreted it as a dramatic renunciation of his former "isolationism." Vandenberg was showered with attention by the international press as well as by the Roosevelt administration, which asked him to attend the upcoming United Nations conference at San Francisco as an American delegate. Conflicted but flattered, he agreed, and thus took the final step into his new role as the leading spokesman for GOP internationalists and a "bipartisan" foreign policy approach. Meanwhile, in February, the president met with Stalin at Yalta. Roosevelt had long since realized that Stalin was going to demand and be able to implement a Soviet sphere of influence in Eastern Europe, but the president hoped at least to secure Stalin's assurance that this sphere would be an "open" one, respectful of democratic electoral procedures and liberal trading arrangements. At Yalta, the Soviet dictator made clear his minimal security demands in Eastern Europe—namely, the creation of a set of buffer states—but ostensibly agreed to permit free and fair elections in Poland. Since it was the Red Army and not Anglo American forces that occupied Poland, there was little else Roosevelt could immediately do to protect democratic norms in that country. As details of the Yalta agreement leaked to the press, Republicans feared that their worst suspicions had been confirmed. Some conservatives denounced the agreement right away as a "new Munich," and Roosevelt's actions at Yalta turned into a leading foreign policy issue for the GOP in the coming years.[32]

A simultaneous and less controversial agreement involved the final creation of the United Nations. The contrast with the League of Nations debate of 1919–20 was striking. Roosevelt had proven to be far more flexible and politically sensitive than his mentor, Woodrow Wilson, in reaching out to and consulting with GOP internationalists. By 1945, an overwhelming majority of Republicans supported the UN's establishment. Part of the reason for this was that GOP concerns had been built in to the organization's framework; it did not fundamentally threaten U.S. national sovereignty. Moreover, American hopes for a peaceful postwar era were so genuinely high among Republicans and Democrats alike that the concept of a United Nations had taken on a kind of sacrosanct quality by the end of the war. Taft, like many other GOP nationalists and anti-interventionists, was still concerned about certain features of the proposed UN. He was disturbed by its emphasis on great power politics, through the institution of the Security Council veto system, and by its apparent reliance on force instead of international law. As he said, "we are not abolishing the causes of war. We are not abolishing militarism. We are enthroning it in a higher seat." Taft also continued to insist that Congress retain the right to support or oppose the use of force by the United States, regardless of UN actions. Yet in the end, he voted to ratify American membership in the United Nations Organization in July 1945, as did every other senator present except William Langer (R-ND) and Henrik Shipstead (R-MN). As one midwestern senator put it, "I'm the biggest isolationist that ever lived, but I'm sure as hell not going to vote against the [UN] Charter." Ratification was accompanied by senatorial paeans to the millennial peacekeeping potential of the new international organization. The American public, interestingly, was more skeptical: less than a third believed that the UN would be able to keep the peace for a period of fifty years.[33]

Superficially, the division of foreign policy opinion within the GOP by the end of World War II looked similar to that before Pearl Harbor. Old Guard conservatives, midwesterners, and rural representatives in Congress were still disproportionately protectionist, skeptical of multilateralism, and opposed to foreign entanglements and expenses. The interventionist or internationalist wing of the party continued to find its greatest strength among urban GOP moderates and northeasterners with ties to international trade, law, finance, foundations, Ivy League universities, and the executive branch of government. The balance within the party had shifted, however, as a result of the war itself. For one thing, German Americans, traditionally a key GOP constituency, no longer particularly opposed U.S. military engagement overseas. More important, the lesson drawn from the war by most Americans across the board was that the United States could never again retreat into the strategic nonentanglement of the interwar period. According to public opinion polls from 1945, more than three-quarters of the American people were now ready to take a more "active part" or "larger role" in world affairs; this included a solid majority of Republicans nationwide. The change in elite opinion was even more decisive. GOP opinion leaders, including upper-income and well-educated party members, were much more likely to support an activist or interventionist foreign policy immediately after World War II than before. Being tagged as an isolationist had clearly become an electoral liability at the national level. Consequently, a significant faction of internationalist Republicans had developed in Congress, even among conservatives and midwesterners, led by Arthur Vandenberg and prepared to cooperate with the incoming Truman administration on foreign policy issues. Anti-interventionists like Taft were rather quiescent on foreign affairs and primarily focused on domestic problems during Truman's first term. The stage was therefore set for the creation of a temporary and limited consensus between a majority of Republicans and a majority of Democrats on certain key international questions.[34]

During Truman's first term, Republicans mostly cooperated with the president's foreign policy agenda. The sheer pressure and pace of events abroad seemed to compel it. Over the winter of 1945–46, it became abundantly clear that Stalin was not about to allow genuinely free and fair elections in Poland. Moreover, the USSR was engaging in some clumsy and aggressive diplomatic probing outside its East European bailiwick, in Turkey and Iran. Congressional Republicans, led by Vandenberg, were alarmed and called for a firm line in relation to Moscow. Truman hardly needed such advice, since he was receiving exactly the same recommendation from leading State Department and cabinet officials, and was in any case a national security hawk and visceral anti-Communist at heart. In the opening weeks of 1946 the president made up his mind: as he put it, "I'm tired of babying the Soviets." The United States therefore began to shift toward a strategy of containment, under which it was assumed that continued negotiations with Moscow were essentially futile, given the implacably hostile nature of the Soviet regime. U.S. diplomatic, economic, and military support would henceforth be provided to a wide range of non-Communist countries, with the goal of denying the Soviet Union further gains. Initially, American officials hoped this could be done at minimal expense to the United States, but potential allies kept calling for increased and urgent financial support from Washington, raising fears of their imminent collapse. Consequently, over the next two years the Truman administration went to Congress to ask for foreign aid packages of tremendous size and scope: first, a $3.75 billion loan to Britain in 1946, then $400 million for Greece and Turkey the following year, then billions more in Marshall Plan aid to Western Europe beginning in 1948. As fiscal conservatives, Republicans balked at the price tag on these initiatives, and after their dramatic gains in the 1946 midterm elections they were back in control of Congress and well positioned to object. The critical factor that won over a majority of congressional GOP members to such expensive legislation was its anti-Communist intent. The administration was careful to court and consult with sympathetic Republicans such as Vandenberg, who as chairman of the Senate Foreign Relations Committee played a key role in shepherding the proposed foreign aid through the Senate. In fact, Vandenberg also helped ease the way for congressional assent and U.S. entry into NATO, even as the president's reelection campaign heated up. The result was that the "do-nothing" Republican Congress of 1947–48, as Truman called it, approved some of the most consequential initiatives in the history of American diplomacy.[35]

Taft, like many midwestern GOP conservatives, was deeply uneasy with the direction of U.S. foreign policy during this period. He viewed most of Truman's proposed foreign aid packages as wasteful, extravagant, taxpayer-financed giveaways—part of "the policy of scattering dollars freely around the world"—no more likely to solve international problems than were similar programs at home. In the cases of the Marshall Plan and U.S. aid to Greece and Turkey, as well as NATO, Taft further questioned whether such programs would not alarm, alienate, and provoke the Soviet Union in its own backyard. "If we assume a special position in Greece and Turkey," he said in 1947, "we can hardly . . . object to the Russians continuing their domination in Poland, Yugoslavia, Rumania, and Bulgaria." In fact, the senator's criticisms in some ways sounded remarkably like those of Henry Wallace, the left-wing secretary of commerce fired in September 1946 for questioning the administration's national security approach. Taft, like Wallace, denounced the entire drift of Truman's foreign policy as being in the direction of power politics and imperialism—supposedly corrupt Old World practices. Unlike Wallace, Taft also feared that Truman's foreign policies would encourage a continuation of Democratic New Deal methods at home, including higher taxes, inflation, budget deficits, and increased government "planning." Yet in the end, Taft voted for both the Marshall Plan and aid to Greece and Turkey. Apparently he realized that these programs were popular and that there was little to be gained politically by opposing them. Moreover, Taft was sincerely anti-Communist and therefore conflicted over several of the administration's requests. He really had no fundamental foreign policy alternative to offer at this point. His primary interest in 1947–48, as Senate majority leader, was in managing domestic legislation, and he allowed Vandenberg to take the lead among congressional Republicans on foreign affairs. Taft and his fellow conservatives did, however, have a major impact on elements of Truman's developing national security strategy. Defense spending was kept at a relatively low level throughout the late 1940s, in relation to America's new global commitments. This was in keeping with Republican demands. The specific and heavy reliance on airpower also reflected the preference of congressional conservatives. So did U.S. economic and military assistance to the beleaguered Chinese Nationalists under Chiang Kai-shek. Otherwise, foreign aid programs were often trimmed and cut around the edges to satisfy GOP critics. Finally, Truman's call for universal military training—a serious possibility at the time—was defeated in Congress, in large part as the result of the opposition of Republicans like Taft, who viewed it as overly coercive, militaristic, and even un-American. The United States instead settled on a program of selective service in 1948, one with generous deferments. As with many of America's early cold war policies, the overall outcome was a negotiated compromise incorporating domestic and specifically conservative GOP pressures in the direction of relatively low taxes, limited spending, and limited governmental coercion. Taft played an important role in shaping this compromise.[36]

Taft ran for the Republican presidential nomination again in 1948 as the favorite candidate of midwestern conservatives but was defeated by Governor Thomas Dewey as the more "electable" nominee. Truman was considered error-prone, and the Democratic New Deal coalition was hemorrhaging in multiple directions. While southern segregationist "Dixiecrats" launched an independent presidential campaign protesting Truman's liberal stance on civil rights, Henry Wallace launched his own presidential bid from the left wing of the party in opposition to Truman's hawkish, anti-Communist foreign policy. Dewey, expecting to win, ran a campaign that was dignified and moderate in tone but at the same time banal and uninspiring. Truman responded with a hard-hitting set of attacks in which he accused Dewey of being a "front man" for fascists as well as Old Guard conservatives who wanted to roll back FDR's New Deal. The accusation of fascism was obviously outrageous. The accusation that congressional conservatives like Taft sought to roll back much of the New Deal, on the other hand, had something to it, and it stuck. By striking this oppositional and combative tone, Truman rallied the core of the New Deal coalition in the North and West—including farmers, labor, Catholics, African Americans, and a majority of liberals—to eke out a victory in the November presidential election. While global affairs were not of primary concern to the electorate that year, Truman won credit from voters for pursuing a tough, anti-Communist foreign policy in a period of international crises without entangling his country in war. Dewey was viewed as credible and capable on foreign affairs, but since his positions differed little from Truman's, most voters saw no special reason to vote Republican on that issue. Henry Wallace, for his part, fizzled to less than 3 percent popular support in the November election and was easily dismissed, even by Socialist presidential candidate Norm Thomas, as "an apologist for the slave state of Russia." Dixiecrat Strom Thurmond won the electoral votes of four states, indicating profound Democratic vulnerabilities on civil rights, but when it came to foreign policy, southern segregationists had been vociferously anti-Communist all along. Consequently, and to the great frustration of conservative anti-interventionists like Taft, the election had the effect of further so-lidifying a bipartisan departure toward cold war internationalism, without benefiting the Republican Party in any way.[37]

The final creation of and U.S. entry into NATO in 1949 represented another major bipartisan foreign policy achievement for the Truman administration, one supported by most Republicans. It also represented one of Taft's last efforts to advocate a consistently noninterventionist foreign policy. Taft voted against the North Atlantic Treaty in the Senate, arguing that U.S. entry "necessarily divides the world into two armed camps" and would "promote war in the world rather than peace." The treaty of alliance, however, was popular with the American public and passed the Senate by a vote of 82 to 13. Taft again was in a small minority on a great foreign policy matter, but that was about to change. Over the course of 1949, GOP criticism of the administration's foreign policies increased dramatically. There were several reasons for this shift. First, Republicans resented their seeming inability to make political headway against the Democrats on domestic economic questions. Evidently the time had come to attack on foreign policy; certainly the strategy of bipartisan cooperation in that area had not won any presidential elections for the GOP in recent years. Second, congressional Old Guard Republicans possessed close ties with an increasingly influential and vocal "China lobby" committed to the unequivocal support of Chiang Kai-shek's Nationalists against Mao Zedong. The China issue became a focus for GOP discontent with the existing administration. Third, in the wake of Dewey's 1948 defeat, the conservative wing of the party took back the initiative from northeastern internationalists, and with Vandenberg sidelined by illness, Taft began to take a more active role in shaping the Republican approach on foreign policy matters. Fourth, a series of genuine national security setbacks and shocks over the course of 1949 provided a new set of issues with which to hammer the president. These shocks included the first successful Soviet atomic bomb test, in August 1949; the collapse of Nationalist forces in mainland China and the establishment of the People's Republic of China, only a few weeks later; and ongoing scandals and revelations regarding Soviet espionage in the United States.

Old Guard conservatives in particular were truly infuriated by this combination of events. Many of them, including Taft, had previously argued for increased aid to Chiang Kai-shek's Chinese Nationalists. They had regularly suggested that FDR and Truman were soft on communism. Now they believed they had been proven right. Moreover, they were inclined to suspect that such setbacks could not have occurred without the positive indulgence of the U.S. diplomatic corps and of Democratic administrations, whose New Deal policies they detested in any case. Taft, for example, was convinced that the State Department under both FDR and Truman had supported Soviet bloc advances at Yalta and again in China out of active sympathy for the Communist cause; he therefore called for a thorough purge of personnel at State. The Ohio senator had said as early as 1946 that the Democratic Party as a whole was "divided between Communism and Americanism." In the following years he continued to speak and write of Democrats as intimately connected to and infiltrated by Communists. Such sentiments were hardly uncommon on the Republican right. Democrats, for their part, had been accusing the Old Guard of fascist sympathies for much of the previous decade. It was within this already embittered political context, early in 1950, that many Republicans gravitated to the support of Joseph McCarthy, an otherwise unremarkable young senator from Wisconsin with a talent for publicity.[38]

In February 1950 McCarthy gave a speech in Wheeling, West Virginia, in which he falsely claimed to possess a list of 205 "members of the Communist Party and members of a spy ring . . . names that were known to the Secretary of State and who nevertheless are still working and shaping the policy of the State Department." Taft initially dismissed McCarthy's claims as "nonsense." They were both surprised when, over the course of the next few weeks, these charges drew tremendous popular attention. In fact, though the details were unknown to McCarthy, Communist espionage within the United States had created a genuine security nightmare for the Truman administration. During the late 1940s, U.S. officials had decoded the "Venona" cables, revealing an extensive Soviet-sponsored spy ring in the United States dating back to the 1930s. Soviet sources apparently included not only middle- to high-ranking government officials such as Alger Hiss, formerly FDR's assistant secretary of state for special political affairs, but engineers and scientists such as Julius Rosenberg, Klaus Fuchs, and Theodore Hall—in several cases, scientists whose information allowed the Soviets to build an atomic bomb a number of years earlier than they otherwise would have. Several hundred members of the American Communist Party likewise provided a broad support network for Soviet intelligence in the United States. Out of concern over leaks back to Moscow, the precise details of the Venona transcripts were kept secret from the American public, and even from the president. Truman nevertheless understood perfectly well the need for some sort of rational investigation of security risks inside the U.S. government, and introduced a comprehensive vetting process in 1947–48. While Truman was fiercely anti-Communist, he was reluctant to allow Republicans any advantage on this issue. His administration and its congressional allies were sometimes defensive and slow in admitting past security breaches, for example in dismissing the case of Alger Hiss as a politically motivated "red herring." Such accusations of purely partisan intent in turn infuriated Republicans, since further investigation into the existence of Soviet espionage in the United States seemed entirely appropriate under the circumstances.[39]

McCarthy's contribution, if it can be called that, to this combustible political situation was to take accusations of disloyalty to an entirely new level. First, he launched charges of Communist sympathy against his chosen targets in a manner that was uniquely reckless and unsubstantiated. Second, he made the absurd insinuation that the network of Communist-inspired disloyalty somehow included the president himself, along with Secretaries of State George Marshall and Dean Acheson—both outstanding public servants. Third, McCarthy insisted that the problem of treason extended not only to a limited number of agents but in effect to the country's entire liberal, northeastern, privileged and pedigreed governing class: as he put it at Wheeling, those "who have had all the benefits that the wealthiest nation on earth has had to offer—the finest homes, the finest college educations, and the finest jobs in Government we can give." This tone of outraged grassroots rebellion against perfidious elites was something of a departure for the GOP. A few Republicans and conservatives such as Whittaker Chambers recognized the danger of embracing McCarthy's wilder accusations. A more common response, however, among congressional Republicans was to maintain a certain distance from the Wisconsin senator while encouraging his freewheeling attacks. Taft, for example, told McCarthy to "keep it up," and that "if one case doesn't work out he should proceed with another." After all, McCarthy was simply expressing in more extreme form what many Old Guard Republicans like Taft already believed about the Democratic Party's direction since the 1930s. GOP leaders were therefore happy to use the burgeoning loyalty issue to bombard the Democrats, whose patriotism they suspected in any case. Anticommunism also provided the GOP with a popular issue that might allow them to break out of their northern rural base and appeal to traditionally Democratic constituencies such as Irish Catholics. The short-term political effect of McCarthy was indeed to benefit the Republicans, although not as much as is commonly suggested; a majority of Americans took McCarthy's antics with a grain of salt. The more significant long-term effect in the coming decades was unfortunately to identify McCarthy's tactics with anticommunism as a whole, and thereby to divert attention toward "McCarthyism" and away from Communist espionage and disloyalty as an actual problem.[40]

The Korean War proved to be the issue that more than any other would bring Republicans back to power. On June 25, 1950, North Korea launched a full-scale invasion of its southern neighbor. Surprised by this act of blatant aggression, the Truman administration quickly sent U.S. air, sea, and land forces to Korea, secured a UN resolution authorizing "police action" against the North, and deployed the U.S. Seventh Fleet in the Taiwan Strait. In September, U.S. commander Douglas MacArthur undertook a successful offensive against North Korean forces at Inchon, and was authorized to cross the 38th parallel in the hopes of reunifying the peninsula under a non-Communist government. All of these actions were applauded by even the most anti-administration Republicans, including Taft, in spite of his concern that the president had acted without congressional authorization. The Truman administration also began to increase defense spending dramatically, not only to support ongoing efforts in Korea but to improve conventional U.S. military capabilities across the board—notably in preparation for a major new ground deployment in Western Europe. In October, fearing Pyongyang's immediate collapse, Chinese forces started crossing the border into Korea. This again surprised American officials and ultimately led to severe U.S. military setbacks. By the time of the November midterm elections, as American casualties mounted, it was already clear that Korea might easily turn into a lengthy, costly stalemate for the United States. Popular dissatisfaction mounted in America over the prospect of such a stalemate, together with the economic restrictions and inflation associated with wartime, and this dissatisfaction expressed itself in losses for the Democratic Party that fall. Public support for President Truman's handling of the war dropped dramatically. Over the winter of 1950–51 U.S. troops were pushed back south, and bogged down in bloody combat with Chinese as well as North Korean forces. As frustrating as these developments were for the American public, they provided an unusual opportunity for critics on the right to argue for a change in strategy. Former president Herbert Hoover called for a return to "Fortress America," to avoid further entanglements on the European and Asian continents. Author James Burnham argued for a strategy of "liberation" whereby the United States would take the fight to Communist countries more aggressively. General MacArthur let it be known that he believed the United States should bomb Chinese bases in Manchuria while permitting Chinese Nationalist raids against the mainland. MacArthur's recommendations drew widespread support, not only from Republicans but from a majority of the U.S. public. A common feeling among many Americans at the time was that U.S. forces should either disengage from Korea or be allowed to attack China directly—one or the other. The mood, in short, was one of widespread frustration and dissatisfaction with the costs and limitations of containment.[41]

Taft seized the moment to put forward a conservative Republican alternative, encapsulated in his 1951 book, *A Foreign Policy for Americans*. The senator's central concern was that the strategy of containment was leading to endless expense and entanglement for the United States. In his view, these entanglements threatened nothing less than American traditions of limited government through a vast expansion of federal power and expenditure that would "wreck the country's economy and, in time, its morale." He therefore called for a less expensive policy of reliance on American technological and geographic strengths, one emphasizing U.S. atomic airpower and seapower, amplified by a ring of island bases around the Pacific and Atlantic Oceans, with only "occasional extensions of action into Europe, Asia, or Africa as promise success in selected areas." One implication of this strategy was to abstain from heavy ground commitments on the Eurasian mainland, notably in Western Europe, where allied governments were largely capable of defending themselves. In this way the United States could avoid the frustration, insolvency, and overextension of an unnecessarily global foreign policy role. At the same time, Taft called for an aggressive campaign of rollback against Communist countries, including energetic support for the Chinese Nationalists now based on Formosa. He favored stepped-up efforts at covert action, subversion, and psychological warfare against the entire Soviet bloc, and supported MacArthur's recommendation for escalated military action against the People's Republic of China. Only in this way would the United States seize the initiative back from the Soviet Union. Clearly, Taft had come a long way from his prior "isolationism." He was now a staunch cold warrior. He blamed America's foreign policy difficulties on the incompetence and disloyalty of leading officials in the Truman administration. He did not believe that the administration had taken the international and domestic danger from communism seriously enough. He described the USSR as "the greatest military threat from foreign sources we have faced since the days of the American Revolution," owing to its unique combination of industrial strength, missionary ardor, and nuclear weapons. He recognized, contrary to 1940–41, that the absorption of Western Europe under the influence of a hostile power would run against the vital interests of the United States. He called for the maintenance of congressional prerogatives in foreign policymaking. He also called, characteristically and tangentially, for the establishment of an international rule of law, to which end the UN had thus far proven inadequate.[42]

The administration responded to all such criticism by persisting in its chosen course in Korea and around the world. Truman and his leading advisers felt that disengagement from Korea would represent a severe blow to America's international credibility. Most of them also feared that striking against mainland China would risk bringing about a third world war. Consequently, they rejected MacArthur's increasingly public demands for military escalation. The defining moment came in April 1951, when Truman relieved General MacArthur for insubordination. This was a clear signal that rollback had been rejected, at least for now, and containment confirmed. Truman was reviled by Republicans for this

decision; nevertheless, the president had his way. Something similar occurred and at roughly the same moment over the question of deploying
several heavily armed U.S. divisions to Western Europe. Taft and his
supporters argued against this deployment, but the administration was
convinced that it was necessary to reassure West Europeans of American protection. Many congressional Republicans came to agree with the
president's position, and the Senate approved the sending of four American divisions to Europe with the proviso that any further deployments
would require congressional approval. In this case the final outcome was
rather anticlimactic, as Taft ultimately voted in favor of the new deployment, claiming to be satisfied with minor concessions from the White
House. Congressional conservatives led by Taft had more success in
shaping budgetary priorities: if defense spending had to go up, they insisted that at least taxes and domestic spending be limited. Still, Republicans were startled by the dramatic growth in federal expenditures during the Korean War. By 1951–52, even more moderate conservatives
were wondering if the combination of foreign wars and New Deal legacies was bankrupting the United States and distorting its system of
government.[43]

Alarmed by the apparently unstoppable trend toward a larger and
more intrusive role for the federal government in American life, Taft
decided to run for the presidency one last time. In 1952 he was better
organized, better financed, and more respected by party regulars than
ever before. Still, doubts lingered over whether he was perceived as too
right wing, too "isolationist," and too uncharismatic to be elected president. Northeastern GOP internationalists, led by figures such as Thomas
Dewey and Henry Cabot Lodge, arranged a movement to draft General
Dwight Eisenhower instead. Eisenhower was a fiscal conservative but
also a firm internationalist possessed of a winning style. Moreover,
Eisenhower was genuinely disturbed by the prospect of Taft as president, especially because of the senator's seemingly dismissive attitude
toward America's alliance commitments in Europe. In a remarkably
close-fought and bitter contest that came down to the floor of the 1952
Republican National Convention, the party ultimately decided for
Eisenhower on the basis of several contested southern delegations. Midwestern conservatives were furious at losing the nomination to the

party's northeastern faction for the fourth time in twelve years, but Taft was soon reassured that Eisenhower was a sincere anti-Communist and economic conservative who would work to keep taxes and spending under control. Whatever their differences, Republicans entered the general election that year energized, united, and justifiably optimistic about their chances. In reality, Taft and Eisenhower agreed on much more by this time than commonly recognized. They agreed, for example, on the need to keep a tight lid on foreign aid, defense spending, and expensive new commitments abroad, while pursuing a vigorously anti-Communist foreign policy. Both were attracted to the strategic uses of atomic airpower, in order to keep costs down; both were convinced economic conservatives. In other words, just as Eisenhower was no liberal, so Taft by the 1950s was no strict isolationist. Partly for this reason, the Ohio senator was able to play a surprisingly constructive role in working with the new administration, up until his sudden death from cancer in 1953. Yet as of the GOP Convention a year earlier, the Taft era in Republican Party politics ended, and the Eisenhower era began.[44]

Taft had represented the anti-interventionist wing of the Republican Party for more than a decade, and had usually done so with integrity. His greatest fear, consistently, was that an interventionist foreign policy would lead to the erosion of American traditions of limited government and to the growth of new bureaucratic controls, taxes, expenditures, and executive authority. In itself, this expectation was quite correct. Yet Taft never managed to hit on a successful alternative, either in political or policy terms, and it is impossible to escape the conclusion that on many of the great international questions of his day he was on the wrong side. To suggest in 1940–41 that the struggle against Nazi Germany was simply another of Europe's amoral balance of power wars and that the result could not greatly harm American interests was not credible. Neither was the suggestion that the United States could abstain from supporting Western Europe in the late 1940s without risking a major setback for the United States. Frustrated by his failure to win these arguments, and appalled by Communist advances overseas, Taft in effect leapfrogged over the Democrats after 1949 and began to argue for a foreign policy that was in several respects more interventionist than Truman's. Taft's intense anticommunism was no doubt sincere and well justified, but again, his specific criticisms of Truman's foreign policy in 1949–52 were largely unconvincing. Truman was right to doubt the staying power of Chiang Kai-shek's Nationalists on the Chinese mainland, right to fire General MacArthur, right not to escalate the Korean War into Manchuria, right to defend Dean Acheson and George Marshall against Joseph McCarthy, and right to deploy U.S. troops to Western Europe. Moreover, Truman and his leading advisers were in reality staunch anti-Communists, dedicated to not only containing but ultimately undermining the USSR; they understood the Soviet threat at least as well as Taft. It was simply incoherent to insist, as Taft did by the 1950s, that the United States must cut defense spending while simultaneously rolling back Soviet power worldwide. There was often a naive or unrealistic streak to Taft's foreign policy stands, especially with regard to his strange faith in the force of international law. He was always repulsed by great power politics. Perhaps the best one can say is that Taft represented with genuine conviction an older tradition of small-town, midwestern, conservative nonintervention whose passing was not altogether beneficial for the United States. Taft was a useful corrective. He never stopped warning of the dangers of overextension abroad, or the concomitant risks to limited government at home. As one historian has said of Taft and his supporters, "If some of them stubbornly believed in a pastoral Eden forever lost to reality, they could—at least until 1950—claim that they opposed extending this Eden by force."[45]

Chapter Three

Dwight Eisenhower

The Conservative as Balancer

Dwight Eisenhower was one of the most impressive and successful foreign policy presidents of the twentieth century. He ran for the Republican nomination in 1952 as a special favorite of GOP moderates and internationalists, but soon gathered broad national support as a figure of exceptional appeal. Eisenhower's overarching foreign policy goal was to contain communism and preserve America's world role without bankrupting the United States. In an era of repeated international crises, he provided strong, calm leadership and protected American interests while keeping the United States out of violent conflicts. He won over the bulk of Republicans, as probably no one else could have, to a posture of cold war internationalism. He struck balances with unusual aplomb between domestic and international priorities, American nationalism and diplomatic sensitivity, cold war activism and a deep desire for peace. Yet on domestic issues, and even on foreign policy, Eisenhower's brand of "modern Republicanism" had limited appeal to the GOP's conservative base, and fundamentally the party's organization and strength changed little during his time in office. His political successes were based on personal qualities that were virtually unique and did not translate into enduring partisan realignments or outlast his individual prestige.

While president, Eisenhower was viewed by contemporary critics as disturbingly passive and inarticulate—a likable grandfatherly figure, to be sure, but one who would rather play golf than run the government. In reality, as we today know from abundant archival evidence, Eisenhower was behind the scenes a commanding, highly intelligent, purposeful, and diligent chief executive, particularly in the realm of foreign policy. Raised in a pietistic, small-town environment in Kansas, Eisenhower was inculcated early on with self-discipline and hard work. As a young man he was athletic, gregarious, and popular, and out of an interest in national service he quickly decided on a military career. After attending West Point he served during the 1920s in an obscure post in Panama where he nevertheless used his time well to study Clausewitz and ponder the appropriate relationship between politics and armed force. Singled out for a series of distinguished staff assignments in the interwar years, he was noted by his superiors to be an unusually promising and capable officer. After the Japanese attack on Pearl Harbor, Army Chief of Staff George Marshall made Eisenhower head of the Army War Plans Division, and at that point his meteoric rise began. Eisenhower was soon made commander of U.S. forces in Europe, then in 1944 commander of Allied forces in Europe, giving him responsibility over the invasion and liberation of France. In this role he demonstrated great effectiveness and good will in reconciling and winning over both counterparts and subordinates from a wide array of countries, departments, and services. For the American public, the smiling, unpretentious "Ike" had the added quality of embodying managerial and military competence without in the least bit threatening democratic values. By the end of World War II he was a figure of genuinely worldwide popularity and renown. He returned to the United States to become chief of staff for the army, then president of Columbia University, and finally military commander of NATO. In 1951–52, Republican moderates and internationalists such as Governor Thomas Dewey of New York and Senator Henry Cabot Lodge of Massachusetts organized a movement to draft Eisenhower for president. Concerned by what he perceived as the Truman administration's drift toward fiscal irresponsibility, on the one hand, and the Republican drift toward neo-isolationism on the other, Eisenhower accepted the call, and after a hard-fought convention battle against conservative nationalist Robert Taft (R-OH), won the Republican nomination. Senator Richard Nixon (R-CA) was chosen as the GOP vice-presidential running mate because of his impeccable anti-Communist credentials, his

youth, his obvious political talents, his West Coast base, and his accept-
ability to every wing of the Republican Party.[1]

While Eisenhower's postconvention presidential campaign began in
a lackluster fashion, he soon shifted to a more aggressive approach in
reaching out to the GOP's Old Guard and adopting many of its longstanding criticisms of Truman. This had the intended effect of energiz-
ing Republicans and uniting the party. The strongest critique centered
on the Korean War. Eisenhower charged the Truman administration
with allowing that war to turn into a costly, lengthy stalemate. While he
was vague on specifics, the World War II hero promised in a dramatic
election campaign address to "go to Korea" to personally observe and
correct the situation. Eisenhower also suggested, more generally, that the
Democrats had failed to handle U.S. foreign policy with sufficient competence and resolve, whether in relation to China, Eastern Europe, or
the Soviet Union itself. The 1952 Republican Party platform condemned
Truman's policy of containment as "negative, futile, and immoral,"
promising instead to "revive the contagious, liberating influences which
are inherent in freedom." During the subsequent campaign, Eisenhower
spoke frequently of "liberating captive nations," though he was typically
careful to specify that such liberation could only come "by peaceful
means." On domestic issues, Eisenhower criticized the Democrats as the
party of excessive taxes, excessive spending, and "creeping socialism,"
thereby demonstrating his substantial agreement with conservative
Republicans on economic matters. He promised a "crusade" against
corruption in government. Finally, the issue of Communist disloyalty
within the United States encompassed both foreign and domestic issues,
and was likewise embraced by Eisenhower out of genuine concern, despite his intense distaste for Joseph McCarthy's methods. The general
left it to surrogates such as Nixon to make stinging personal attacks, for
example in calling Democratic presidential candidate Adlai Stevenson a
"PhD graduate of Dean Acheson's cowardly college of Communist containment." The outcome was a sweeping electoral victory for Eisenhower,
and for a new if narrow Republican majority in Congress. Ike improved
on Dewey's 1948 showing across the board, most strikingly in winning
the support of upper- and middle-income, urban and suburban white
southerners. The issue of communism also helped gain some votes for

Republicans among traditionally Democratic Irish and Polish Catholics. Yet the result was primarily a personal victory for Eisenhower rather than an indication of a new political era. Voters responded strongly to his special appeal and to the notion that he had the unique ability to solve the frustrating stalemate in Korea. The majority of Americans did not indicate, in polls, that they now identified as Republicans, or that they preferred the GOP to the Democrats on domestic economic issues— quite the opposite.[2]

Eisenhower assumed the presidency with a clear set of policy preferences, as well as a rather unusual administrative style. On domestic economic issues, in spite of popular impressions to the contrary, his instincts were quite conservative, against what he called "big government," the "welfare state," and the New Deal "gravy train." He shared the Republican Old Guard's concern that recent trends toward centralized federal planning, regulation, inflation, high taxes, and budget deficits would undermine both economic growth and individual freedom. Yet he also realized that a full return to the pre–New Deal era was not in the cards. For one thing, a majority of the American public clearly accepted and favored the basic New Deal framework. As he put it, "should any political party attempt to abolish social security and eliminate labor laws and farm programs, you would not hear of that party again in our political history." Furthermore, he believed that organizational changes in American society required the acceptance of some increased role for government in promoting social harmony and mediating between private group interests. Eisenhower therefore embraced, in practice, a moderately conservative stance on domestic economic issues, partly out of conviction and partly to make the Republican Party electable once again. He called this stance "the middle way" or "modern Republicanism," a moderate and consensus-building approach to which in any case he was well suited temperamentally. He applied the same centrist model to civil rights, the other great domestic issue of the day. Eisenhower was sympathetic to the goal of racial desegregation but preferred a cautious, gradual policy limited to areas under direct federal jurisdiction, such as the U.S. armed forces and the District of Columbia. Believing that broader social change would have to come voluntarily rather than through governmental coercion, he followed a middling course that frustrated diehard segregationists on the one side and African Americans and civil rights activists on the other.[3]

On foreign policy, Eisenhower's overriding priority was to reconcile America's new global role—which he fully embraced—with a greater sense of fiscal responsibility. He was convinced of the deadly threat from world communism, and that, as he put it in his inaugural address, "forces of good and evil are massed and armed as rarely before in history. . . . Freedom is pitted against slavery; lightness against the dark." Consequently, he believed that the United States had to maintain and strengthen its position at the head of anti-Communist coalitions worldwide, in support of what he called "collective security." This required not only military strength but also foreign aid, the expansion of international commerce, and consultation with members of friendly alliances. NATO was to him the single most important such alliance, but he did not rule out extensive U.S. involvement outside Western Europe. On the contrary, he considered much of the Third World to be of vital interest in America's competition with Moscow, both for economic reasons and out of concern for U.S. credibility and reputation. He therefore accepted much of the foreign policy legacy left to him by Truman and, if anything, argued for a more aggressive anti-Communist approach in regions such as East Asia. His main critique of Truman's foreign policy legacy was simply that it was too expensive. Eisenhower feared that indefinite defense expenditures on the scale of 1951–52 would overstrain America's finances, undermine its economic health, and in the end even alter its traditional way of life. As he put it, "we must not destroy what we are attempting to defend." Such an outcome would subvert the very purpose of the cold war. He therefore sought to keep a strict limit on the militarization of the American economy and to find a more sustainable balance between cold war internationalism and domestic fiscal concerns. This concern over costs led him toward the ready consideration of alternatives to expensive conventional militaries, such as covert action, psychological warfare, and nuclear threats. Eisenhower believed that the tone of U.S. alliance relations had to be respectful. As he said, "a platoon leader doesn't get his platoon to go that way by getting up and saying, 'I am smarter, I am bigger, I am stronger, I am the leader.' He gets men to go with him because they want to do it for him, because they believe in him." Yet Eisenhower viewed multilateralism as a practical rather than a doctrinal issue; he had no aversion to unilateral action in principle. He simply felt that international support, under certain circumstances, could enhance his ability to achieve U.S. foreign policy goals.[4] As put by a leading historian of Eisenhower's policy toward the UN:

> The administration . . . embraced the multilateral forum when it was perceived to best serve American interests, but ignored it with virtual impunity when it chose to act unilaterally. . . . Far from viewing the organization as an idealistic attempt at world government, the president considered it to be a useful instrument for protecting and advancing American foreign policy objectives, particularly in the traditional superpower conflict. . . . His rhetoric notwithstanding, [Eisenhower] had limited expectations for what could be accomplished through the UN.[5]

As president, Eisenhower pursued his foreign and domestic policy goals in a distinctive manner. In public, he frequently struck an uplifting yet banal tone, issuing statements that were vague and even garbled. Behind the scenes, however, he was active, precise, and hard-driving, a capable politician and a calculating strategist. His shrewd political sense was matched by an exceptional talent for net analysis. Through his military career, he had learned how to effectively organize and manage the decision-making process, particularly on matters of defense and foreign affairs. His method in these areas was to master the details of policy, utilize a strong staff system, insist on exhaustive, lively debate in regular meetings with advisers, explicitly weigh the costs and benefits of all conceivable alternatives, keep his options open, and maintain firm control of the entire process. While such a model on vital matters of state might seem obvious to an outsider, it is in fact distressingly uncommon. Eisenhower was therefore unusual in that he really did approach foreign policy decision making in a thoughtful, systematic, and careful manner. Moreover, he used the very same banal public style for which he was criticized to avoid controversy and deflect criticism, often in the direction of subordinates. Partly in this way, he maintained exceptionally high support from a public that saw him as above partisan politics altogether. His appointees were left to act as political lightning rods. Eisenhower's most important such appointment in the area of foreign policy was John Foster Dulles as secretary of state. Dulles was a leading and respected GOP internationalist with years of experience in diplomacy and ties to both wings of the Republican Party. He was a strong secretary, hectoring in style but very intelligent, knowledgeable, and skillful in negotiation. Eisenhower left Dulles considerable leeway in certain areas such as U.S. policy toward Europe, but on all matters the president retained final control. While Dulles's manner encouraged the perception that he was much more hard-line and more influential in foreign affairs than the president, neither of these things was true. The two men shared a basic worldview—conservative cold war internationalism—and Dulles never questioned Ike's ultimate authority. When it came to foreign policy, Eisenhower was in charge.[6]

Congress presented the most important domestic constraint upon the administration's ability to conduct American diplomacy. Ironically, it was Republicans rather than Democrats that gave Eisenhower the most trouble in this area, at least during his first term in office. The congressional Republican Party in 1953 was still badly divided on foreign policy issues between nationalists and internationalists. GOP nationalists were critical of foreign aid programs, advocates of atomic airpower, champions of Taiwan, opposed to diplomatic contact with Communist countries, skeptical of free trade, hostile toward the State Department, contemptuous of the UN, supportive of Joseph McCarthy, resistant to presidential authority, wary of America's Western European allies, enthusiastic about "rollback" in both Eastern Europe and China, jealous of U.S. national sovereignty, and suspicious of any foreign policy program—past or present—supported by liberal Democrats. GOP internationalists, on the other hand, supported presidential authority, foreign aid, free trade, NATO as well as the UN, and looked for bipartisan cooperation with Democrats on international matters. The nationalists tended to be very conservative on domestic economic issues, often midwesterners, from safely GOP rural and small-town districts. Examples included Senators John Bricker (R-OH), Styles Bridges (R-NH), Homer Capehart (R-IN), Everett Dirksen (R-IL), Bourke Hickenlooper (R-IA), William Jenner (R-IN), William Knowland (R-CA), William Langer (R-ND), Joseph McCarthy (R-WI), and Robert Taft (R-OH). They were frequently unhappy with Eisenhower, and he with them. The internationalists tended to be more moderate on domestic economics, often northeastern, from competitive, urban, suburban, or high-income regions. Examples included Senators George Aiken (R-VT), Prescott Bush (R-CT), James Duff (R-PA), and Henry Cabot Lodge, Jr. (R-MA). Obviously, Eisenhower was both a member and a leader of the internationalist wing—this had been a primary rationale for his presidency. In actual fact, the foreign policy course he followed was fundamentally a reflection of his own cold war internationalist beliefs; he never let the Old Guard determine basic decisions about war and peace. Yet he and Dulles were careful to cultivate and appease GOP nationalists in Congress. This meant that on certain diplomatic issues, especially symbolic ones, Eisenhower frequently tilted in the direction of Old Guard demands. In any case, the two wings of the GOP had more in common by this time than is usually recognized. Both wings were staunchly anti-Communist, hawkish, and economically conservative, committed to the cold war and to American military power; neither faction was truly isolationist, much less liberal in today's sense of the term. Moreover, many Republicans were inclined to support a new and popular Republican president more than they would have a Democrat, regardless of substantive policy concerns.[7]

Congressional Democrats presented no unified or coherent opposition to Eisenhower's first-term foreign policy initiatives. Indeed, on votes concerning diplomacy, foreign aid, and free trade, Eisenhower could usually count on the support of most northern Democrats. Southern Democrats, on the other hand, were moving in a distinctly nationalistic and oppositional direction during these years. Bitterly divided from the northern liberal wing of their own party over the emotional issue of civil rights, many white southerners grew increasingly skeptical of the liberal internationalist agenda altogether, including multilateral institutions and foreign aid programs to Third World countries. Southerners also began to abandon their traditional support of freer trade, partly because of economic changes as the region moved away from a cotton-based economy. This meant that Dixie Democrats were now frequently united with conservative midwestern Republicans in resisting Eisenhower's internationalist agenda on trade and foreign aid. Yet congressional southern Democrats remained staunch advocates of a strong national defense, if anything calling for higher levels of military spending than Eisenhower was willing to allow. The same was true of many Democrats from the North. Congressional leaders like Lyndon Johnson (D-TX) may have been skeptical of being dragged into new wartime entanglements, but they were also unwilling to be tagged as heading a party soft on national security. Democrats therefore largely supported the administration's foreign policy during the mid-1950s, in spite of grumbling on specific issues. In this, they matched the popular temper of the period, which was fundamentally deferential toward the president in pursuit of cold war anticommunism. Eisenhower and Dulles, for their part, were conscientious in consulting with opposing leaders in Congress, especially after the Democrats retook control of both chambers in the November 1954 midterm elections. Relations between the president and congressional leaders such as Johnson were generally remarkably good, and Old Guard Republicans could be forgiven for suspecting that Eisenhower preferred working with the Democrats to working with his own party on foreign affairs.[8]

The first and most pressing foreign policy matter on Eisenhower's agenda was to address the stalemate in Korea. Upon winning the 1952 presidential election, he visited the Korean peninsula, reviewed various military options, and came to the conclusion that the existing approach was bankrupt. Eisenhower therefore directed that the United States make contingency plans for tactical nuclear strikes against Chinese forces along the Yalu if armistice negotiations failed. The administration sent out subtle diplomatic signals to Beijing in May 1953 indicating that American nuclear use was a real possibility in the absence of successful talks. Chinese sources suggest that these particular signals were either dismissed or never received. Fortunately, China was by this time prepared to make significant diplomatic concessions on the critical issue of POW repatriation, not so much because of any specific nuclear threats but out of a more general fear of military escalation in the region. The death of Joseph Stalin in March 1953 also brought to power a new set of Soviet leaders interested in wrapping up the Korean conflict. The USSR consequently encouraged China and North Korea to make the needed concessions in order to reach a settlement. In July 1953, an armistice was finally signed, dividing the peninsula roughly halfway between North and South, and bringing the war to an uneasy close. Some conservative Republicans bemoaned the failure to reunite the Korean peninsula under non-Communist control, but for the great majority of the

American public, the war's end was a relief and a demonstration of Eisenhower's competence.[9]

Even as he brought the Korean War to a conclusion, Eisenhower faced a serious challenge in 1953–54 on foreign policy matters from within his own party. Having retaken power for the first time in twenty years, conservative GOP nationalists were determined to reassert congressional authority, stamp out any hint of Communist subversion, and repudiate the legacy of FDR and Truman. The 1952 fall election campaign represented only an uneasy truce between the major wings of the Republican Party. Once in office, Eisenhower's behavior was much more continuous with the Truman administration than Old Guard conservatives would have liked. Within its opening weeks, for example, the new administration nominated Charles Bohlen as ambassador to Moscow. Bohlen, a career diplomat, had assisted FDR at the Yalta conference, and was therefore anathema to GOP nationalists. Yet the administration managed to secure his nomination against the opposition of leading Old Guard senators. A similar uproar occurred at the very same time on the right over the question of an "Enslaved People's Resolution." Many GOP conservatives wanted a congressional resolution condemning previous Democratic administrations for entering into the Yalta agreements, but the new administration would not approve such a resolution. Eisenhower was willing to formally condemn the "enslavement" of Eastern Europe, but he would not condemn the Democrats or prior administrations for any supposed perfidy at Yalta. After heavy lobbying by the White House, debate was forestalled, and conservative nationalists never won the resolution they sought. A protracted intraparty dispute also occurred over the question of the Bricker amendment. For several years running, Senator John Bricker (R-OH) had called for a constitutional amendment preventing the federal government from using international agreements to enlarge its own jurisdiction over domestic issues. Specifically, Bricker proposed giving Congress the power to regulate "executive agreements" with other countries, agreements that had ballooned in number under FDR and Truman. The Bricker amendment embodied conservative GOP concerns over the erosion of congressional authority, national sovereignty, limited international commitments, and American constitutional traditions all at once. It gathered support from a wide variety of groups, including business interests, professional associations, and southern segregationist Democrats, the last of which were especially alarmed by the possibility of foreign or UN interference in southern racial practices. Eisenhower, characteristically, refused to fight the Bricker amendment in an open or direct fashion, and instead engaged in backstage bureaucratic maneuver to encourage its defeat. In the end, the amendment failed to pass through the Senate by a single vote—an outcome that represented something like Pickett's charge for the Old Guard of the Republican Party.[10]

Perhaps the most famous or infamous partisan dispute in 1953–54 was over the conduct of Joseph McCarthy. Eisenhower despised McCarthy's reckless tactics but genuinely shared the popular concern over Communist disloyalty, and out of the need for party unity he refused to take on McCarthy in 1953. The president initiated new internal security measures that were even stricter than those left behind by Truman. Congressional critics were allowed to drum a number of old China hands out of the State Department on suspicion of Communist sympathies, but still McCarthy was not satisfied. As the attention of the Wisconsin senator turned in 1954 to more powerful targets—notably, the U.S. Army—his popularity declined, and Eisenhower began to speak out against what he called "disregard of the standards of fair play." Working to undermine McCarthy behind the scenes, Eisenhower encouraged the senator's self-destruction during the Army-McCarthy hearings of 1954. In December of that year the Senate voted to censure McCarthy, dividing numerous Old Guard senators from many of their own Republican colleagues. Eisenhower was happy with the result and exasperated with continuing resistance from GOP arch-conservatives on one issue after another. As he put it, "I've had just about enough. If they want to leave the Republican Party . . . I'll go up and down the country, campaigning against them. I'll fight them right down the line." Yet Old Guard influence in the GOP on foreign policy matters was already ebbing significantly. Senator Robert Taft's untimely death from cancer in July 1953 robbed conservative nationalists of their most respected and influential leader. Numerous Old Guard members retired during the mid-1950s. In other cases, leading nationalists such as Everett Dirksen (R-IL) were gradually converted to the notion of an active presidency and a global role for the United States, in cooperation with the Democrats. Eisenhower repeatedly demonstrated that he would preserve executive authority and pursue a bipartisan internationalist foreign policy, whatever the Old Guard might say. Moreover, he did so without attacking or alienating most GOP conservatives. Indeed, he gave them much of what they wanted: an emphasis on atomic airpower, staunch support for Taiwan, strongly anti-Communist policies, and a commitment to the "liberation" of Eastern Europe. The result was a growing and truly broad consensus behind the basic foreign policy goals laid out by the administration. Rank-and-file Republicans, following Eisenhower's lead, were won over to a more internationalist stance. By 1955 the vast majority of Democrats and Republicans alike were ready to give the president the authority he requested to face crisis situations in East Asia, the Middle East, and elsewhere. In effect, the Old Guard had been not so much confronted by Ike on foreign policy matters as smothered and co-opted. In strictly political terms, it was a remarkable achievement.[11]

While the media's attention was focused on political pyrotechnics like those of McCarthy, Eisenhower began a substantial and thorough review of American national security policy. His central fear was that excessive defense spending not only risked turning the United States into an overly regimented "garrison state" but in the long run undermined the economic basis for U.S. military power. His goal, as he said, was therefore to achieve "security without paying the price of national bankruptcy." In an influential 1952 *Life* magazine article, John Foster Dulles had floated the concept of what became known as "massive retaliation," arguing that the United States should adopt a more aggressive strategy in relying on the open threat of immediate and overwhelming air strikes with nuclear weapons against the USSR in the case of any Soviet bloc aggression. While Eisenhower found Dulles's exact phrasing to be overly provocative, he was sympathetic to the notion of greater reliance on nuclear deterrence, in order to regain the cold war initiative from Moscow while keeping defense expenditures down. Eisenhower understood perfectly well that the consequences of any nuclear war would be "too horrible to contemplate." He did not believe that Soviet leaders really wanted a nuclear conflict any more than Americans did. As he put it, "these Communists are not early Christian martyrs"; they would not risk losing their own lives simply in order to spread their doctrine. This very fact meant that the United States could use the threat of such a terrible war to prevent and deter not only Soviet aggression but any limited Korea-like conflict as well. Eisenhower therefore settled on a national security strategy—the "New Look," as it was eventually called—that explicitly emphasized U.S. readiness to resort to nuclear retaliation against Soviet bloc advances. The new approach was formally approved in October 1953 after systematic debate with National Security Council directive 162/2, the basis for subsequent policies and revisions. This change in strategy allowed the administration to cut manpower levels as well as conventional military costs, reducing the total personnel of America's armed forces from 3.6 million to 2.8 million. Obviously, the conclusion of the Korean War helped in this regard, but the president also played a critical role in setting and maintaining a strict ceiling on defense spending. Total national security expenditures were reduced to under $50 billion for fiscal year 1954—significantly lower than Truman had envisioned—and were never to exceed that number for the rest of Eisenhower's time in office.[12]

Eisenhower also led a dramatic change in Republican Party positions on matters of foreign economic policy. The GOP had long been the party of protectionism; it had also been a party opposed to foreign assistance programs. Eisenhower, however, was openly committed to the expansion of world commerce, and to the multilateral trade regime established under FDR and Truman, not so much because of concern over particular corporate interests but rather as an essential component of America's global strategy in combating the spread of communism. For the same reason, Eisenhower had no interest in completely dismantling the set of foreign assistance programs established in the 1940s. Rather, he sought to prune existing foreign aid programs around the edges, in the hopes that private investment and "trade not aid" would act as primary engines for economic growth in the developing world. Ike's stance on commerce and foreign aid was controversial within the Republican Party. He faced stiff opposition on both issues from Old Guard and midwestern Republicans, who resisted freer trade and foreign assistance altogether. Yet the economic, ideological, and institutional bases for protectionism were not what they had once been, and congressional opposition was tactical rather than absolute. As on many other issues, Ike's preference was to avoid open schism within the GOP. He therefore compromised with congressional leaders on foreign economic policy. The resulting foreign aid levels and tariff reductions were less than Eisenhower would have liked, and controversy over foreign assistance continued, but the GOP in effect accepted executive leadership on the maintenance of an open international trading system. Presidential authority over reciprocal trade, as it was called, was extended for one year in 1953, then again for a year in 1954, after which time a new Democratic Congress was content to renew it in a more long-term fashion. A Republican president had successfully put his party's stamp of approval on America's postwar commitment to freer trade. This in itself was a major victory for the administration and a historic shift in GOP priorities.[13]

In relation to Western Europe, Eisenhower's first-term foreign policy emphasized the restoration and integration of America's allies in the hopes of allowing U.S. ground forces to come home. Eisenhower viewed Western Europe as central to the global balance of power, and was a firm supporter of NATO. He accepted the temporary stationing of American troops in Europe as a tripwire against any Soviet attack designed to trigger a U.S. nuclear response. He also believed that America's allies would soon have to provide the bulk of their own defense, especially in terms of manpower: "We cannot be a modern Rome guarding the far frontiers with our legions." Extensive overseas American military deployments, if unchecked, would according to Ike eventually lead to "national bankruptcy" for the United States. He therefore favored the integration of Europe as a "third great power complex in the world," one capable of standing up to Soviet pressure on its own. This could only mean German rearmament. In strictly military terms, the administration's initial proposal to that end was a transnational European defense community, to which Germany would contribute, but the French legislature balked at such a dramatic step and rejected it in August 1954. After Dulles threatened an "agonizing reappraisal" of America's European defense commitments, the British hit on an alternative: West Germany would be rearmed and admitted to NATO, with its sovereignty restored, but with a promise not to produce nuclear weapons and with allied troops stationed on German territory as an implicit control. This was sufficient to satisfy the French, and it proved to be a remarkably stable long-term solution. Yet Eisenhower never accepted the indefinite presence of a large American ground commitment in Europe. He continued to try to find ways of reducing that presence, even going so far as to initiate a process of "nuclear sharing" by which German and other allies were given effective tactical control over U.S. nuclear weapons in Europe. While Soviet leaders stewed over the alarming possibility of nuclear-armed German forces, Eisenhower simultaneously gave his blessing to the economic and political integration of Western Europe through the creation of a new European Economic Community.[14]

In Latin America, as in the rest of the developing world, Eisenhower's highest priority was anticommunism. In many cases this meant supporting autocratic regimes friendly to the United States against radical nationalist movements. Eisenhower believed, as he said, that "in the long run, the United States must back democracies." Nevertheless, he faced a dilemma that was also faced by every cold war president of either party: namely, whether to pressure allied yet autocratic regimes in the direction of democratic reform, when the very process of such pressure might simply undermine an American client and substitute a hostile autocracy in its place. Eisenhower's instinct in such cases was to bolster American allies. He also understood that numerous Third World nationalist and anticolonial movements were not directly controlled by either Communists or the Soviet Union. Yet he feared that the success of such movements might play into the hands of local Communist parties, and ultimately the USSR—even if unintentionally—by depriving the Western world of allies, bases, resources and credibility in its global contest with Moscow. Eisenhower was therefore sometimes very aggressive in opposing radical nationalists in the developing world, particularly when they appeared dependent on Communist support.[15]

Guatemala was a case in point. A nationalist government under Jacobo Arbenz had come to power in that country in 1951, introducing sweeping land reforms and expropriations against the interests of traditional elites as well as the United Fruit Company. For Eisenhower and Dulles, bananas were really not the issue. The administration's concern was that Arbenz was turning Guatemala toward communism. Nor was this fear completely unrealistic. By 1953–54, Arbenz did in fact consider himself a Communist, making most of his important decisions with a kitchen cabinet of local Communist Party leaders. As his wife later put it, Arbenz believed that "the triumph of communism in the world was inevitable and desirable." Anti-Arbenz forces in Guatemala—of which there were many within the army, the church, the landowners, and a discontented populace—turned to the United States for assistance. The discovery of Czech arms shipments to Arbenz's government in May 1954 provided an immediate justification for Eisenhower to act. He decided to authorize CIA support for a coup d'état the following month. The United States used air raids and radio broadcasts to convince Arbenz that an American invasion was imminent, at which point he fled the country, allowing an anti-Communist military government to take power. Both the Eisenhower administration and its critics drew mistaken conclusions from the outcome. The administration concluded that future covert actions against anti-American regimes would be easier than they really were. It also concluded that Moscow must have had a direct hand in local events. The administration's critics on this issue— of which there were many overseas, and a growing number in the United States over time—concluded that Arbenz had been a great democrat, that Communist influence on him had been nonexistent, that Washington had acted primarily in order to preserve the economic interests of the United Fruit Company, and that local events had been entirely dictated by the machinations of the United States. Neither set of conclusions testified to the fact that Guatemalans, through the struggle between local factions, had largely determined their own fate, which was to forcibly replace a thuggish and increasingly repressive left-wing government with a thuggish, repressive right-wing one. The American role in these events was significant but by itself insufficient; the Soviet role was virtually nonexistent. Nevertheless, the coup encouraged a false and growing legend of CIA omnipotence, and was widely resented in Latin America.[16]

In East Asia, the administration's policy was to bolster U.S. allies against China, the Soviet Union, and local Communist parties. This included, for example, military aid to American clients, as well as the 1954–55 creation of a Southeast Asian Treaty Organization (SEATO) with Australia, France, Great Britain, New Zealand, the Philippines,

Thailand, Pakistan, and the United States as members. Ike's greatest challenges in East Asia came over Taiwan and Indochina. In relation to Taiwan, Eisenhower entered office committed to the more aggressive support of Chiang Kai-shek's Nationalist government. One of the first actions Eisenhower took as president was to "unleash" Chiang by removing the U.S. Seventh Fleet from the Taiwan Strait. The implication was that Chiang's Nationalists were now free to roll back Communist control of mainland China. In reality, Eisenhower had no intention of being dragged into a Nationalist military effort to retake the mainland, but he was determined to defend Taiwan against any threat from Beijing. In 1954–55, Mao Zedong tested that commitment and initiated a series of crises by shelling Nationalist positions on the islands of Quemoy and Matsu. Eisenhower responded by (1) winning bipartisan support in Congress for an American military response, (2) threatening nuclear retaliation against a mainland invasion of Quemoy or Matsu, and (3) signing a formal defense pact with Taiwan. While the issue dragged on for years, no invasion ever came. Eisenhower and Dulles also took a consistently unyielding position against China's admittance to the United Nations, and against any formal U.S. diplomatic recognition of the Beijing government. The administration's uncompromising support for Taiwan on such issues was especially popular among Old Guard Republicans and the congressional China lobby. It was also part of a deliberate strategy to force a diplomatic wedge between Moscow and Beijing. Eisenhower and Dulles understood that Communist China was no Soviet puppet, and that the possibility existed of even greater Sino-Soviet discord. Yet they sought to encourage that discord by taking a very hard line against Beijing and thereby forcing it to make demands of Moscow—including full support against the United States over Taiwan—that Moscow could not accept without the unwanted risk of general war. This hard-line U.S. "wedge" strategy had its intended effect, as crises over Taiwan helped drive China and the Soviet Union farther apart, but it was a rather risky strategy, both in terms of alienating other U.S. allies and in terms of increasing the possibility of Sino-American war. Whether any other strategy would have promoted U.S. interests much more effectively is an open question; the evidence suggests that Mao was in fact profoundly hostile toward the United States during the

1950s and would probably have been hostile regardless of specific changes in American policy.[17]

In French Indochina, a Communist-led anticolonial movement, the Viet Minh, made dramatic military gains during Eisenhower's first year in office. By March 1954, a Viet Minh siege at the fortress of Dien Bien Phu left the French reeling. Eisenhower, his advisers, and congressional Republicans agreed that a Communist success in Indochina would constitute a terrible loss for the credibility of America's alliances in the region and throughout the world. Indeed, it was in relation to this crisis that the president came up with the so-called domino theory, saying, "you have a row of dominoes set up, you knock over the first one, and what will happen to the last one is the certainty that it will go over very quickly." Yet Eisenhower was equally strongly opposed to the introduction of U.S. troops into Indochina. He said he "simply could not imagine the United States putting ground forces anywhere in Southeast Asia" and described himself as "bitterly opposed . . . to such a course of action." Nor was the prospect of sending American troops to the relief of Dien Bien Phu popular with U.S. public opinion, even among Republicans. This still left the possibility of American air strikes against the Viet Minh, including the use of tactical nuclear weapons, something that Eisenhower and his advisers seriously considered in a series of no-holds-barred debates in the National Security Council. Consultation with Democratic and Republican leaders in Congress, however, revealed that they were deeply skeptical of any air strikes whatsoever, especially in the absence of British support or French colonial reforms. Their main objection was that air strikes were simply a halfway measure inevitably leading to ground intervention—a point with which Eisenhower was quite sympathetic. His belief on military matters, he said, was that "when you finally decide to resort to force you should plan no limits to its use." He therefore developed a set of necessary criteria for a U.S. military intervention in Indochina, precisely to avoid any sort of unsuccessful halfway approach. First, it would have to be done with the support of allies, notably Great Britain. Second, it would have to be done with the support of Congress. Third, the French themselves would have to make significant reforms in the direction of self-government for Indochina, as well as in their military efforts. Since the British refused to participate, that ruled out congressional support, which in turn ruled out U.S. intervention. Dien Bien Phu fell in May, the French position collapsed, and negotiations began in Geneva over the future of Indochina. Eisenhower seems to have known that the satisfaction of all three of his chosen criteria was highly unlikely, but by allowing Congress, the British, and the French to cancel one another out, he allowed responsibility for America's nonintervention to be dispersed. He also maintained the impression that the United States might intervene against the Viet Minh under different circumstances. This impression proved to be useful at the Geneva conference, in that the Viet Minh were pressured by Beijing to settle for half a loaf to avert U.S. countermeasures. In July 1954 Indochina was given its independence and divided into two halves, a Communist north and a non-Communist south. The Eisenhower administration refused to formally condone these results, partly out of domestic political concerns, but began to provide considerable U.S. military and economic aid to South Vietnam under the new government of Ngo Dinh Diem.[18]

In the Middle East, Eisenhower acted to oppose any trends that he thought might ultimately play into the hands of the Soviet Union. Sometimes this meant siding with local nationalist regimes, as he did with Egypt over the Suez in the fall of 1956; sometimes it meant acting against them. A leading example of the latter was the Iranian coup of August 1953. Iran's nationalist prime minister, Mohammed Mossadeq, had come to power two years earlier, calling for the expropriation of his country's oil resources from foreign companies. American oil majors hardly needed to buy Iranian oil, but the British felt threatened and urged covert action against Mossadeq. Moreover, Mossadeq's government seemed to U.S. officials to be headed toward a breakdown, with the Iranian Communist Party or Tudeh well positioned to pick up the pieces. It was the prospect of such a breakdown and the subsequent cutoff of oil supplies to U.S. allies in Western Europe that concerned Eisenhower and Dulles the most; they realized that direct U.S. oil interests were minimal, and that Iran's prime minster was no Communist. Soviet leaders were in fact deeply suspicious of Mossadeq. In a series of increasingly desperate and autocratic moves, the Iranian leader tried to play off Washington and Moscow, foreign and domestic opponents against one another, but the effort boomeranged as he alienated all of them simultaneously. Oppositional forces within Iran—including leading members of the military, landowning, and clerical classes—rallied around the country's monarch, the shah, and called for American intervention. While some mid-level U.S. officials on the spot were skeptical, Eisenhower agreed to support a coup d'état. CIA operatives distributed cash in Tehran to encourage popular demonstrations against Mossadeq's government. After considerable dithering from the shah, the subsequent coup placed him firmly in power, leaving Iran a close U.S. ally and recipient of American military and economic aid for many years. Soviet officials reluctantly concluded they had in effect suffered a cold war defeat and that they should have supported Mossadeq more directly. Ironically, the British still lost a considerable share of their previous oil interests in negotiations with the shah.[19]

In direct relations with the Soviet Union, Eisenhower pursued both a strategy of relentless military-diplomatic pressure and a strategy of working toward meaningful arms control. The strategy of pressure was publicly proclaimed in 1952–53 as one of "liberation"—a term that set Western European nerves on edge. The question was what liberation meant, in practice. One possibility was to militarily roll back the Soviet sphere in Eastern Europe, for example through "preventive" air strikes against the USSR before it developed a sizable nuclear arsenal of its own. Eisenhower "brought up this question more than once," as he put it, and "had never done so facetiously." In a thorough and wide-ranging 1953 review of U.S. strategic options conducted in the White House solarium, however, the president ruled out such a preventive war as senseless, unreliable, and impossibly dangerous, saying that "the only thing worse than losing a global war is winning one." That left covert action. In 1952 Dulles had proposed, for example, air drops behind the Iron Curtain to encourage anti-Communist resistance, but in reality the Truman administration had already experimented with such operations, and they generally ended in disaster: East European refugees were armed and lifted by the United States into the Soviet sphere, never to be heard from again. Dulles and his brother Allen, now director of the Central Intelligence Agency, soon realized that covert action was also unlikely to bring about the collapse of the Soviet bloc any time soon. Nor was Eisenhower really interested in risking general or nuclear war to liberate Eastern Europe. When East Germans rioted against their Communist government in June 1953, the United States sent food packages and its sympathy, but no military support. And when Hungarians rose up against their

Soviet overlords in the fall of 1956—partially under the encouragement of local operators working for Radio Free Europe—Eisenhower made it clear that the United States would not intervene, saying that Hungary was "as inaccessible to us as Tibet." The Red Army's subsequent destruction of the Hungarian rebellion made clear the limits of liberation. As Eisenhower ruefully concluded, "we have excited [the] Hungarians for all these years, and [are] now turning our backs on them when they are in a jam." John Foster Dulles raised the intriguing possibility that Washington could accept Moscow's diplomatic preeminence in the region, as in Finland, if national governments were permitted a genuinely free and democratic internal life. But the Eisenhower administration continued to insist that the existing Soviet occupation of Eastern Europe was illegitimate, if only as a long-term means of psychological warfare and an indication of concern.[20]

Eisenhower simultaneously tried to pursue realistic arms control agreements with the Soviet Union, an interest he indicated from his first year in office. Mutual arms reductions with Moscow would ease the cold war's financial burden on the United States, one of Eisenhower's highest priorities. It would also reduce the danger of unwanted escalation in a period of crisis—an especially urgent concern, given the immensely destructive nature of existing weapons. The death of Stalin in 1953 led Eisenhower to publicly outline that April what he called a "chance for peace." While skeptical of any fundamental change in Soviet intentions, he indicated a keen interest in cutting military expenditures, saying that "every gun that is made, every warship launched, every rocket fired signifies, in the final sense, a theft from those who hunger and are not fed." In December 1953, Eisenhower next outlined a plan entitled "atoms for peace." In it, he proposed that Washington and Moscow each direct a percentage of their nuclear materials toward an international agency, to be used for peaceful scientific and energy-related purposes. Finally, in 1955, the president put forward what he called "open skies," a proposal under which the United States and the USSR would each permit aerial inspection by the other of leading weapons sites as a confidence-building measure. In part, these diplomatic overtures were intended to demonstrate America's peaceful intentions to third parties in the cold war competition with Moscow, but Eisenhower referred to the need for mutual arms reductions so often in private that there is little reason to doubt his sincerity. Technological developments, in the form of the newly developed hydrogen bomb, had produced weapons far more destructive than those dropped on Hiroshima and Nagasaki. Eisenhower had seen internal government estimates of the appalling effects of any war fought with hydrogen bombs, and he concluded that if such a war came, "you might as well go out and shoot everyone you see and then shoot yourself." The testing alone of the new bomb was widely understood to produce dangerous radioactive fallout. Eisenhower was therefore committed to arms control as one way of reducing the likelihood of nuclear war. As it happened, the new Soviet leader, Nikita Khrushchev, had come to some similar conclusions, arguing that general warfare between communism and capitalism could no longer be considered inevitable in a thermonuclear age. Khrushchev was also interested, for his own domestic reasons, in pursuing deep mutual arms reductions with Washington. But as the leader of a closed society he would not accept intrusive verification procedures as proposed under "open skies." Nor did he pretend that the USSR would desist from spreading Soviet-style socialism abroad, most notably in the developing world. Eisenhower, for his part, did not pretend that he would stop trying to halt the spread of Soviet influence. Fundamental differences between the United States and the Soviet Union therefore continued, naturally enough, to prevent dramatic movement toward arms control. Still, a summit meeting with Soviet leaders at Geneva in 1955 produced informal agreement, if nothing else, that nuclear war had to be avoided, and Eisenhower's atoms for peace proposal saw fruition in 1957 with the creation of the International Atomic Energy Agency. Nor did the president give up on his hopes for careful reductions in superpower tensions. As he put it, "you don't promote the cause of peace by talking only to people with whom you agree."[21]

By 1956, Eisenhower had established an exceptionally strong basis on which to run for reelection. On domestic economic issues he had cut taxes, checked inflation, presided over a period of overall economic growth and prosperity, and halted the continued expansion of the federal government while demonstrating that a Republican president could be trusted not to dismantle the New Deal. On civil rights issues, the GOP under Ike was cautious but if anything less conservative and certainly less divided than the Democrats. "McCarthyism" had faded dramatically, put to rest by Eisenhower and the Republican establishment in a way that no Democratic administration could have. And on international affairs—the GOP's great issue advantage during the 1950s—the president had wrapped up the war in Korea, contained communism (for the most part), and kept the peace, winning high approval ratings for his conduct of U.S. foreign policy. Indeed, through no effort of his own, dual international crises over Hungary and the Suez mushroomed over the autumn of 1956, reminding many Americans that they preferred a steady hand on foreign affairs. Plus, voters continued to appreciate Ike's personal qualities of character. Facing an uphill electoral battle, the Democrats nominated for president the former Illinois governor Adlai Stevenson, just as they had in 1952. Stevenson criticized Eisenhower for allowing Communist gains to consolidate in Eastern Europe and Indochina. The Democratic candidate also called for a less militarized and less provocative foreign policy approach, including the unilateral suspension of U.S. nuclear testing along with an end to the draft. While the test ban proposal gave Stevenson's campaign a temporary lift, these criticisms, taken together, formed no coherent whole, and in this they were reflective of the Democratic Party's uncertainty at the time as to how to approach international and military affairs. Eisenhower was especially irritated by what he viewed as Stevenson's amateurish foray into issues of arms control, a foray he was eventually able to portray as irresponsible. In the end, Eisenhower won the electoral votes of virtually every region of the country outside the Deep South, recreating a similar outcome to 1952. He immediately called it a victory for "modern Republicanism." Again, however, it was very much a personal rather than a party victory, and the congressional GOP did not perform especially well in 1956. The votes that Stevenson won were largely due to persistent Democratic strengths in party identification and on domestic economic concerns—strengths that continued to play well for Democrats in Congress, as well as at the state and local level.[22]

U.S. foreign policy during Eisenhower's second term was dominated by the impression of crises and setbacks everywhere from the Middle East, Cuba, and Berlin to outer space. In the Middle East, Eisenhower and Dulles were alarmed as Egypt's nationalist leader, Gamal Abdul Nasser, took an increasingly anti-Western foreign policy line while accepting Soviet bloc arms sales and foreign aid. America's support for Egypt during the crucial phase of the 1956 Suez crisis had apparently won the United States little gratitude; the spread of Nasserism or radical Arab nationalism seemed only to benefit Moscow, and to undermine the influence of Washington's European allies in the region. In January 1957, Eisenhower therefore went to Congress and outlined the doctrine that would be named after him, proposing that the United States assume a new role in the Middle East by providing economic and military support "to secure and protect the territorial integrity and political independence of nations requesting such aid against overt armed aggression from any nation controlled by international communism." The new doctrine was tested most dramatically in Lebanon. When the president of that country, Camille Chamoun, called in July 1958 for U.S. aid against Nasserite and Communist subversion, Eisenhower sent in the Marines to support Chamoun's government. American officials on the spot quickly realized they were entangled in a sectarian power struggle that had little to do with communism. They consequently mediated a compromise agreement under which Chamoun stepped down from power, and by November the Marines were gone. U.S. intervention did maintain a pro-Western government in Lebanon, but Chamoun's behavior was part of a pattern in the Arab world by which governments manipulated U.S. concerns over communism to secure Washington's aid against local and domestic non-Communist rivals. Eisenhower was not unaware of this phenomenon but felt that even non-Communist nationalists or radicals in the Third World often functioned as de facto Soviet allies. In the end, U.S. opposition to Nasserism in the region only succeeded in boosting its credibility and fanning the flames of Arab resentment as popular hatred of British imperialism was now displaced onto the United States. The USSR, meanwhile, was able to pose as a friend of newly independent nations against Western colonialism. By the end of 1958 Eisenhower had concluded that it was pointless to set the United States against Nasser and his ilk. As Ike put it, "since we are about to get thrown out of the area, we might as well believe in Arab nationalism." This acceptance had remarkably few negative implications for the United States, since Nasser refused to be anyone's puppet and began falling out with his Soviet patrons almost immediately.[23]

An even more disturbing and proximate cold war development during the late 1950s was in Latin America. A 1958 visit by Vice President

Nixon to Venezuela was met with violent demonstrations, revealing deep reservoirs of anti-Americanism in that country. Revolutionary forces in Cuba simultaneously threatened to overthrow the regime of Fulgencio Batista, an American ally. Events in both Cuba and Venezuela seemed to indicate widespread resentment of U.S. policy in the region. Eisenhower responded by adjusting U.S. aid policy so as to increase developmental assistance to Latin America, a precursor to the later Alliance for Progress. He also began to pressure allies in the region to make democratic reforms, for example by abandoning U.S. support of the dictatorial Batista. When Fidel Castro's forces overthrew Batista at the beginning of 1959, Eisenhower indicated that he was willing to work with Castro, so long as Cuba's new leader refrained from taking an anti-American foreign policy line. Within months, however, Castro not only nationalized American assets on the island but began reaching out to Moscow as a potential trading partner and military supplier. The last was a step the United States would not tolerate, particularly so close to American shores, and so in 1960 Eisenhower approved Operation Pluto, a covert plan to topple Castro. These plans would soon be inherited and implemented by the Kennedy administration, though not in precisely the form that Eisenhower had envisioned. Ike's repeated comment to his advisers on the subject of Operation Pluto was prescient: "Boys, if you don't intend to go through with this, let's stop talking about it."[24]

Eisenhower was more successful in relation to Berlin. The formal status of that city, like the formal status of the two Germanys, had never been resolved to Moscow's satisfaction. In November 1958, Khrushchev issued an ultimatum, saying that Western access routes to Berlin would be cut off within six months in the absence of a treaty over the city's final status. Khrushchev's underlying purpose with this ultimatum was apparently to pressure the West's weak spot at Berlin to force broader negotiations over first, East Germany's official status, and second, West Germany's nuclearization. Eisenhower responded with characteristic calm. The need to reassure America's West German ally ruled out any formal U.S. recognition of East Germany or fundamental concessions over Berlin. Eisenhower was therefore unyielding on the West's basic access rights. Yet he was also determined not to overreact, especially since it might be hard to explain to the American public the necessity of a third world war over "the shape of the helmet of the official to whom we present credentials." The situation was further complicated, as Khrushchev realized, by NATO's untenable military stance in Berlin. Eisenhower's solution was to not even attempt a viable conventional defense of Berlin, since none existed, and since the very preparation for it might provoke Soviet counterreactions and local military "incidents," as well as excessive military spending by the United States. Instead, he ordered limited U.S. military replacements to Europe, built up allied support, and made plans to send a small armed convoy to West Berlin in case of any closure of access routes. He simultaneously made it clear that the United States was prepared to retaliate with an all-out nuclear response in case of any Warsaw Pact aggression against West Berlin. Khrushchev allowed the original six-month deadline to lapse, though he continued to threaten the same result. Eisenhower replied by inviting the Soviet leader to meet with him at Camp David, which he did in September 1959. At that summit, Eisenhower struck a diplomatic tone, stressing his desire to work toward a mutually satisfactory solution but maintaining the same substantive position as he urged Khrushchev to remove any suggestion of a time limit on Berlin as "inadvisable." The two leaders agreed to continue discussions over Berlin the following year. While the issue was never formally resolved during Eisenhower's time in office, the outcome in effect represented a victory for his administration, since Khrushchev backed down from prior threats and West Berlin remained free.[25]

The single biggest perceived foreign policy setback of Eisenhower's second term was the dramatic launching of the world's first artificial space satellite, *Sputnik*, by the Soviet Union in October 1957, only weeks after Moscow's successful test of an intercontinental ballistic missile (ICBM). *Sputnik* caused tremendous popular alarm in the United States. Coincidentally, a leading study of U.S. national security policy, the Gaither Committee Report, had already been presidentially commissioned and was submitted in November of that same year. The report recommended massive increases in defense expenditures, especially in the area of missile capabilities and homeland defense, to address supposed U.S. shortcomings in those areas. Predictions were made of a looming, dangerous "missile gap" between the two superpowers. The

U.S. armed services and congressional Democrats supported the Gaither report and chimed in with calls for greater spending on conventional military forces across the board. Many leading officials inside the administration and the GOP supported these recommendations. Still, Eisenhower resisted any radical increases in defense spending. First, he did not believe that *Sputnik* in itself carried much military significance. Second, while he recognized the importance of the new intercontinental ballistic missiles (ICBMs), the United States was well on its way to developing and deploying such missiles—farther ahead, in fact, than the Soviet Union. Third, the evidence from U-2 aerial reconnaissance flights over the USSR during the late 1950s did not suggest that any massive Soviet ICBM program actually existed. Fourth, in the absence of such conclusive evidence, Eisenhower was inclined to maintain a policy of fiscal conservatism in relation to defense spending, under the assumption that economic overextension and "garrison state" measures were as much a danger to the United States as Soviet missiles. Finally, and especially in relation to nuclear weapons, Eisenhower subscribed to a belief in strategic sufficiency. As he put it, there "comes a time . . . when a lead is not significant in the defensive arrangements of a country." If anything, the United States was building more nuclear weapons than it required for any conceivable usage: a stockpile of some 18,000 by 1960. Eisenhower therefore approved limited measures such as the planned deployment of intermediate-range ballistic missiles (IRBMs) to America's NATO allies, while heading off pressures for a more expensive response. The one thing he did not do was go to the Congress and the country, directly take on his critics, and explain why massive new defense expenditures were unnecessary. Yet his behavior in this regard was deliberate and public-spirited: he refused to lay out clear evidence in public of Moscow's limited missile capabilities despite the domestic political advantages that would have accrued because doing so would also have revealed the extent of America's reconnaissance programs, humiliated Khrushchev, and thereby destroyed any chances for an arms control agreement with the Soviet Union.[26]

Eisenhower hoped to reach a limited test ban agreement with the USSR before completing his second term. In fact, during the fall of 1958, the administration imposed a temporary moratorium on atmospheric nuclear tests reciprocally with Khrushchev. But the negotiation of a more formal treaty was bedeviled by genuine technical uncertainties over verification, as well as by Moscow's continuing resistance to anything more than extremely limited on-site inspections. Complicated test ban negotiations dragged on month after month. Then, in May 1960, just as Eisenhower was preparing for a summit meeting with Khrushchev in Paris, the Soviet Union shot down an American U-2 plane, capturing its pilot, Gary Powers. Khrushchev's demands for an American apology over this incident, and Eisenhower's refusal to give it, in effect torpedoed the Paris summit, along with any immediate hopes for a formal test ban. Eisenhower bitterly regretted both the U-2 incident and the failure to reach an arms control agreement with the Soviet Union, but the process begun by his administration would eventually culminate in the partial test ban and nuclear nonproliferation treaties of the 1960s.[27]

Democratic criticisms of Eisenhower's foreign policy mounted over the course of the late 1950s. In the Senate, Democratic liberals such as Hubert Humphrey (D-MN) and Mike Mansfield (D-MT) contended that the Eisenhower administration was insufficiently attuned to Third World socioeconomic problems and anticolonial feeling. They called for revamping and strengthening America's foreign aid program. At the same time, Democratic hawks such as Lyndon Johnson (D-TX) and Stuart Symington (D-MO) argued that the administration had neglected U.S. conventional military forces. They pointed to *Sputnik* as evidence of slippage in America's position relative to the Soviet Union and called for increased defense spending across the board. These critiques were skillfully combined in the 1960 presidential campaign of Senator John F. Kennedy (D-MA), who maintained that the Eisenhower years had been ones of passivity, permitting communism to make dramatic advances internationally. Kennedy and his advisers argued that the United States should make more of an effort to wean restive Third World publics from communism's appeal by emphasizing nation-building efforts in the developing world. This included everything from new foreign aid programs to energetic counterinsurgency efforts. Under a Kennedy administration, the United States would attempt to act as a kind of midwife to the Third World modernization process. The tone was one of militant optimism, programmatic activism, and confidence bordering on arrogance. As Kennedy's adviser Walt Rostow put it, "modern societies must be built, and we are prepared to help build them." The United States would have to build many new ICBMs, Kennedy argued, in order to close the missile gap. Conventional military forces would also have to be increased and used in a calibrated manner to give the United States a wider range of options in response to subtle forms of aggression. Fidel Castro would have to be confronted more directly. Even the perception of weakness, Kennedy believed, could be fatal to America's position in the world. He was therefore determined to maintain the indivisibility of America's worldwide cold war commitments even in places of little intrinsic strategic value. Where Eisenhower had supposedly allowed setbacks and drift, Kennedy was determined to go on the offensive and win back the initiative from Moscow.[28]

Kennedy's criticisms of U.S. foreign policy under Eisenhower were certainly bracing and politically useful, but in terms of their inherent policy merits they were mostly unconvincing. As should be clear from the previous pages, the notion that Eisenhower was passive in the face of Soviet or Communist challenges is absurd. Eisenhower was aggressive in containing Communist expansion, even in cases where the links to Moscow were highly tenuous and indirect. If anything, his administration could have been more relaxed in allowing genuinely non-Communist Third World nationalists like Nasser and Mossadeq to act as independent buffers between the Soviet bloc and the American one. But this was not the direction urged or taken by Kennedy. On the contrary, the Kennedy administration sought to engineer internal social changes in the developing world in a pro-American direction. Eisenhower was skeptical of such hugely ambitious, externally directed modernization efforts, and rightly so. Kennedy's call for increased cold war interventionism in the Third World was therefore exactly the wrong criticism to make. Nor was there any "missile gap" in relation to the USSR; Khrushchev had been bluffing. The only missile gap that existed under Eisenhower was one in favor of the United States, and orbital photographs that reached the White House in 1960–61 proved this definitively. Consequently, Eisenhower was right during the late 1950s—and he was virtually alone in this—when resisting massive new defense expenditures that would have constituted an irrelevant response to an imaginary threat. The more limited arguments of some of Eisenhower's critics for a broad and flexible range of defense capabilities were certainly plausible. "Massive retaliation" and the New Look limited America's military options and encouraged some blood-chilling U.S. nuclear threats over peripheral locations, but the limitation and the usage were both deliberate on Eisenhower's part. Not only did he seek to gain diplomatic leverage from these new weapons, he also relied on them precisely in order to avoid open conflict. So great was his determination to prevent a general nuclear war that he would permit no graduated or conventional escalation toward it. Moreover, the strategy seems to have worked. In cases such as Berlin and Quemoy-Matsu, direct military aggression was deterred, U.S. defense expenditures were limited, and major warfare was prevented.[29]

Eisenhower succeeded in conceiving, pursuing, and implementing a remarkably coherent foreign policy strategy during his time in office. His overarching goal was to hold down expenses and maintain America's form of limited government, while preserving U.S. international leadership and containing communism overseas. It is hardly surprising, in light of his background, that Eisenhower showed a mastery of military details relevant to foreign policy. What is not to be taken for granted is that he also showed keen insight into the appropriate relationship between military force and political considerations, both international and domestic. Allies were respected, supported, and consulted without entrapping the United States in unwanted conflicts. Defense capabilities were maintained without threatening the economic basis or political purpose of U.S. military power. Domestic support for foreign policy initiatives was built up and cultivated along both sides of the partisan aisle. Indeed, Eisenhower "internationalized" the GOP, including many Old Guard Republicans, as no one else could have, not only in relation to national security but also in free trade—a little-noted outcome that ought to be considered one of his major foreign policy achievements. Above all, through a series of dangerous turning points, from Dien Bien Phu to Hungary to Berlin, Eisenhower kept the United States out of war, showing impressive crisis management skills while protecting vital U.S. interests. He expected the Soviet Union to self-destruct in the long term, and therefore saw no need to attack it preventively. In fact, he sought to reduce both international tensions and U.S. military spending through the pursuit of careful arms control negotiations with Moscow. Yet he never deluded himself as to Soviet intentions. For the most part, his direction of U.S. foreign policy was calm, purposeful, and prudent. The last of these traits in particular is a critical and underrated virtue in national security affairs. Ike's foreign policy, like his entire presidency, was based on a series of balances. He balanced domestic political goals and imperatives with international ones. He balanced an unquestioned belief in America's form of government with a sense of realism as to its ease of export. He balanced hawkish anti-Communist convictions with a sincere desire for peace. He balanced cold war activism with a keen understanding that violent military entanglements were easier to get into than out of. He balanced a deep American nationalism with a willingness to engage in diplomacy. All of these balances made for a successful foreign policy record, leaving the United States in a strong international, economic, diplomatic, and military position in 1960–61 on which following administrations could build.

Eisenhower had less success in building or remaking the GOP in his own image. On foreign affairs, to be sure, he won over many regular Republicans to cold war internationalism—a lasting legacy. Yet leading GOP conservatives remained profoundly unhappy with certain features of Eisenhower's foreign policy, including repeated summit meetings with Soviet leaders, the failure to act on behalf of Hungarian rebels in 1956, extensive foreign economic aid programs, the loss of Cuba to communism, détente with the USSR, and the failure of "liberation" more generally. Moreover, on domestic political issues, Eisenhower left behind few lasting changes in either the makeup or strength of the Republican Party. Ike tried to cultivate a new generation of moderate Republicans, such as Prescott Bush of Connecticut and Jacob Javits of New York, but staunch conservatives, unreconciled to the New Deal, remained a powerful force in the congressional wing of the GOP and in the party's state and local organizations. Such conservatives supported Eisenhower out of expediency. "Modern Republicanism" seemed to them, and was, a slap in the face. Nor did the concept of modern Republicanism have much political, legislative, or conceptual success beyond the superficial. Intraparty factional differences remained profound. In truth, despite his private complaints over what he called the GOP's "dyed-in-the-wool reactionary fringe," Eisenhower had limited appetite for the nitty-gritty of party infighting. He did not attempt to undermine the party's conservative wing. In fact, he often agreed with conservatives on economic issues.[30]

Ike sought to appear above petty partisan politics, and in many ways he was. His tone was typically moderate, sensible, and accommodating; he blurred the differences between the two parties. He refused to either dismantle the New Deal or greatly expand upon it. He struck a balance between Republican and Democrat, left and right, that was broadly popular with the American public, but it could not outlast his unique prestige. In the words of political commentator Samuel Lubell, Eisenhower acted not as party-builder or a party-transformer but as "a substitute for a reshuffling of both parties." Ike had great personal electoral success, making the Republican Party electable again at the presidential level. This personal and presidential success did not, however, translate into comparable gains for the GOP in other electoral venues. The Democratic Party remained dominant in much of the country in terms of party identification, congressional representation, and state and local politics; the GOP was still the "minority party" nationwide. Republicans under Eisenhower built no effective party organizations in the South, where segregationist Democrats continued to predominate. Nor did the GOP make much political progress during the mid- to late 1950s in the Northeast, West, or Midwest. On the contrary, it was the Democratic Party that made congressional and state-level gains in those regions, particularly in the midterm elections of 1958. GOP conservatives complained that their party could hardly do worse if it took a straightforwardly right-wing stance. The stage was therefore set for a conservative resurgence within the Republican Party during the 1960s.[31]

Chapter Four

BARRY GOLDWATER

The Conservative as Hawk

SENATOR BARRY GOLDWATER never became president of the United States, but he had more of an impact on American political alignments over the long run than some presidents. This impact extended to foreign policy issues. During the 1960s, Goldwater called for an assertive foreign policy of worldwide anti-Communist rollback. He rejected arguments for containment, peaceful coexistence, arms control, or diplomatic engagement with the Soviet Union. Goldwater simultaneously called for a return to American traditions of limited government at home. His hardline foreign and domestic policy views found special favor with upwardly mobile, suburban conservatives in the nation's booming Sun Belt. The 1964 Goldwater presidential campaign brought Sun Belt suburbanites, libertarians, racial conservatives, and anti-Communist foreign policy hawks together into a new alliance. This insurgent coalition lost badly in the general election that autumn, but in the long term Goldwater's nomination indicated the direction the GOP would take on a wide variety of issues. Henceforth, support for defense spending and military intervention would be increasingly identified with domestic economic and social conservatism in the United States, and with the Republican rather than the Democratic Party.

The 1950s saw the emergence of a new and self-consciously conservative intellectual movement in the United States, one that would emerge into political influence during the following decade. This movement drew on three distinct strains of thought: classical liberal or libertarian theorists such as Friedrich Hayek and Milton Friedman, conservative traditionalist authors such as Russell Kirk and Richard Weaver, and militant anti-Communists such as Whittaker Chambers and James Burnham. The classical liberals championed free markets, private property, and individual enterprise, against existing trends toward centralized government planning. The traditionalists extolled ancient and medieval Western religiosity, ethics, and social order, against the apparent moral relativism and barbarism of the twentieth century. The anti-Communists—often former Marxists themselves—stressed the implacably aggressive, revolutionary, and messianic nature of communism and called for a strategy of "liberation" against any notions of peaceful coexistence or negotiation. Obviously, there were significant tensions in emphasis among these various strains of conservatism, for example in Russell Kirk's distaste for industrial capitalism as against Milton Friedman's celebration of it. Yet traditionalists and classical liberals agreed that the modern welfare state had erred in undermining an older American tradition of self-reliance, constitutionalism, and local self-government. They also agreed that communism represented the antithesis of everything they each valued. The question was then how to reconcile limited government at home with anticommunism abroad—a dilemma to which conservatives in the 1950s were painfully attuned. Initially, many classical liberal and traditionalist thinkers believed that the danger to limited government in the United States from an expanded national security state was at least as great as the danger from the USSR and its allies. For most such authors, however, the postwar spectacle of espionage scandal together with Communist expansion in Eastern Europe and Asia changed their minds. Analysts like James Burnham argued that in effect, a kind of Third World War had already been initiated by Moscow—a war that would be to the death, and a war that the West was in urgent danger of losing. Most right-wing intellectuals accepted this argument and agreed that an extensive U.S. defense establishment would have to be built up and if necessary used overseas to meet the Communist challenge. American conservatism thus shifted toward a more unreservedly hawkish and interventionist stance on foreign policy matters, with anticommunism as the critical ingredient. Those few strict libertarians or Old Right holdovers who did not accept this shift, such as Murray Rothbard, were marginalized into political irrelevance.

Conservative foreign policy commentators during the 1950s typically called for a rejection of containment in favor a more aggressive strategy against the Soviet Union. Authors like William F. Buckley Jr. combined this hawkish anti-Communist foreign policy stance with a staunch conservatism on domestic issues. Such ideological conservatives were utterly disgusted with the accommodating "modern Republicanism" of the Eisenhower era as having failed to roll back either communism or the New Deal. In 1954–55, Buckley therefore helped found and edit a new journal of opinion, *National Review*, to provide a forum for traditionalist, libertarian, and anti-Communist views. Buckley's presence gave the new conservatism an urbane, witty representation, along with a sense of intellectual coordination. Yet these journalistic endeavors would have mattered little had they not resonated with a significant segment of grassroots opinion on the right wing of the GOP. Many hardline conservatives in the Republican Party agreed with Buckley's *National Review* that international communism constituted "a blatant force of satanic utopianism. We consider 'coexistence' with communism neither desirable nor possible, nor honorable; we find ourselves irrevocably at war with communism and shall oppose any substitute for victory." GOP conservatives therefore wanted a more assertive policy against communism abroad, just as they wanted a more assertive policy against government spending, taxation, and regulation at home. By the end of the 1950s, such conservatives believed they had found in Senator Barry Goldwater their candidate for president.[1]

Goldwater was born in the Arizona Territory in 1909, the son of a Phoenix department store owner and the descendent of Jewish and Episcopalian ancestors. He grew up in an affluent home, attended a military academy in Virginia, and took over the family business in 1930. During World War II he flew with the Army Air Force, shuttling supplies to war zones in the Asia-Pacific theater. He remained in the Air Force Reserve after the war and continued to fly dozens of kinds of aircraft. Goldwater was elected to the Phoenix City Council in 1949 on an anticorruption platform, and to the U.S. Senate in 1952. Handsome, youthful, and transparently honest, the Arizona senator acquired a national reputation as a principled, uncompromising, and attractive new spokesman for the conservative wing of the Republican Party. A sought-after and inexhaustible stump speaker, Goldwater traveled the country as chairman of the National Republican Senatorial Committee, establishing useful connections with local party figures. While not the type to happily kiss babies, his manner of articulating the conservative position was unusually crisp, consistent, and cheerfully blunt, endearing him to supporters. In 1957 Goldwater took the lead in attacking President Eisenhower's proposed budget as a "bow to the siren song of socialism," profligate in expenditure. In fact, Eisenhower was fighting off demands for even greater spending from Democrats, but the Arizona senator felt the administration went too far. The 1957 budget fight, together with Goldwater's remarkably strong showing the following year in an otherwise disastrous midterm election for Republicans, established him as the party's preeminent conservative star. In the spring of 1960, his stock on the right rose further as he released a new book and surprise best-seller, *The Conscience of a Conservative*. Written with considerable assistance from *National Review* editor L. Brent Bozell, it galvanized the thinking of many young Republicans and remains the single best introduction to Goldwater's political views.[2]

Goldwater's central domestic concern was the relentless expansion in the size, scope, and authority of the federal government and its executive branch since the 1930s. He viewed this expansion as directly contrary to the intentions of the American founders, who had worried about the "corrupting influence of power" and therefore established a "system of restraints against the natural tendency of government to expand." This system of restraints, as he put it, had "fallen into disrepair." Instead, politicians from both parties had entered into a deleterious pattern of "buying votes with promises of 'free' hospitalization, 'free' retirement pay and so on." Yet these various government benefits were not actually free, since somebody had to pay for them, and since the very act of doing so required levels of taxation that were not only harmful to the nation's economy but confiscatory and wrong in principle. Goldwater's proposed alternative was to dramatically reduce the role of government in the nation's social and economic life, out of areas "in which it has no legitimate business." This would include, for example, cutting federal aid to education, ending farm subsidies, eliminating federal matching funds to states, and introducing a flat rather than a progressive or graduated income tax. It meant, in a nutshell, that "the government must withdraw from a whole series of programs that are outside its constitutional mandate—from social welfare programs, education, public power, agriculture, public housing, urban renewal and all the other activities that can be better performed by lower levels of government or by private institutions or by individuals." On the issue of civil rights, his position was effectively on the right wing of a party traditionally contemptuous of southern segregationists. Goldwater himself was no racial bigot or white supremacist. He had supported the Phoenix branch of the NAACP, helped desegregate the Arizona Air National Guard, voted for the Civil Rights Acts of 1957 and 1960, and recognized that the right to vote was clearly protected by existing federal laws. He insisted, however, that "the Constitution does not permit any interference whatsoever by the federal government in education," and that while he believed black and white children should attend the same schools, he was "not prepared . . . to impose that judgment of mine on the people of Mississippi or South Carolina." This left him skeptical of further federal legislation designed to enforce desegregation in the South. In other words, he tried to apply principles of voluntarism and local self-government to the controversy over civil rights as well as to national economic issues, whatever the outcome.[3]

On foreign policy, Goldwater was a staunch American nationalist and a hard-line anti-Communist hawk. He argued that "our national existence is once again threatened . . . confronted by a revolutionary world movement that possesses not only the will to dominate absolutely every square mile of the globe, but increasingly the capacity to do so." Yet he feared that many Americans, including the Republicans' own Eisenhower administration, indulged in unrealistic hopes of peaceful coexistence with the Soviet Union. The heart of the problem, in Goldwater's view, was that the Communists "are determined to win the conflict, and we are not." As he surveyed the international situation, he was highly critical of existing U.S. policies. America's cold war approach, he said, had been characterized by a "craven fear of death," overly focused on avoiding war as opposed to defeating world communism. Containment was a purely defensive strategy, and as such could not possibly succeed in the long run against an inherently aggressive, ruthless, and determined adversary. The U.S. foreign aid program was characterized by "waste and extravagance," he suggested, in some cases financing openly hostile regimes. Diplomatic negotiations, summits, and exchanges with the Soviet Union simply provided legitimacy to Communist advances. Moscow preached nuclear disarmament, he said, in order to neutralize American military strength in that area. The United Nations was a useless "international debating forum" and a financial burden on the U.S. taxpayer, providing "a unique forum for Communist propaganda" and potentially "leading to an unconstitutional surrender of American sovereignty." Such were the arguments Goldwater made as he called for a new strategy, "primarily offensive in character . . . to engage the enemy at times and places, and with weapons, of our own choosing." The United States needed to "achieve and maintain military superiority," the one major component of the federal budget where Goldwater was "not in favor of economizing." It needed, he said, to "develop tactical nuclear weapons for possible use in limited war," to offset Soviet conventional military advantages. It needed to reject any permanent nuclear test ban. It needed to protect "American honor—everywhere." It needed to cut foreign aid apart from limited loans to friendly states willing to share in the burden of their own defense. It needed to stop subordinating U.S. national interests to the UN. It needed to withdraw diplomatic recognition from the Soviet Union as an "outlaw" state, "neither legitimate nor permanent." It needed to support timely offensive action by Chinese Nationalists, South Korea, and South Vietnam against existing Communist regimes. Finally, it needed to provide all the paraphernalia of a full-fledged resistance movement behind the Iron Curtain, "encourage the captive peoples to revolt," and "be prepared to undertake military operations against vulnerable Communist regimes" while "discouraging premature uprisings" in order to avoid a repeat of the 1956 Hungarian disaster. In this way, Goldwater predicted that the United States would be able to "wage a war of attrition . . . to bring about the internal disintegration of the Communist empire."[4]

U.S. foreign policy under Eisenhower, as we saw earlier, was hardly guilty of the weakness, neglect, and naivety of which Goldwater accused it. Nevertheless, Goldwater's brand of militant anticommunism had a significant base of support in the Republican Party, as did his sharply conservative economic views. That base was not only intellectual or ideological but also regional and demographic: specifically, within the so-called Sun Belt. The 1950s and early 1960s saw rapid population growth and economic expansion in states such as California, Arizona, Texas, Florida, and Virginia. Transplanted small-town Yankees and midwesterners moved south and west in search of opportunity, bringing their Republican politics with them while adapting to local values. The suburban rings in which they lived around cities such as Los Angeles, San Diego, Phoenix, and Dallas were growing at a breakneck pace. Inhabitants of these new suburbs were often white-collar, increasingly affluent, religious, and intensely anti-Communist. They resented northeastern political and economic influence in local and national affairs. Many of them had close ties to the defense industry, to new business and financial interests in the South and West, or to extractive industries such as oil and gas. They further tended to be either indifferent or unsympathetic to the civil rights movement. Compared to the earlier generation of Old Guard Republicans, they were equally conservative but more hawkish on foreign policy, and more used to winning the political battles they fought. The Arizona senator was a very apt spokesman for these new Sun Belt conservatives, and while often overlooked or dismissed at the national level, they were growing in numbers and importance within both the GOP and the country as a whole. A Goldwater presidential candidacy had other crucial, potential sources of support: rural and small-town midwesterners, traditionally on the right wing of the Republican Party; new conservative student groups such as the Young Americans for Freedom; and authors and intellectuals affiliated with the *National Review*. Finally, on the fringe of the conservative movement from the late 1950s through the early 1960s were strange organizations such as the John Birch Society, led by Boston candy manufacturer Robert Welch, who once claimed that Dwight Eisenhower was a conscious agent of the international Communist conspiracy and that a majority of the United States was already under Communist control. The John Birch Society gave conservatives a bad name, but it had thousands of members, and figures like Barry Goldwater and William F. Buckley were reluctant to denounce it for fear of weakening and dividing the nascent political movement on the right. Numerous leading academics refused to distinguish between the libertarian politics of Barry Goldwater, the Catholic traditionalism of William F. Buckley, and the conspiracy theories of Robert Welch, instead lumping them together as members of a dispossessed, authoritarian "radical right" that threatened the very fabric of American democracy. In reality, the typical Goldwater supporters were neither radical nor dispossessed nor authoritarian but instead well-educated, successful, upper-income professionals and businessmen committed to political participation through democratic means, and of a strongly conservative bent.[5]

On the opposite end of the GOP, regionally and ideologically, was its liberal to moderate northeastern branch. Here the most celebrated figure was Nelson Rockefeller. As the scion of one of the world's wealthiest families, Rockefeller had the fame and riches that came with the name. He also happened to be something of a natural and self-confident politician, simultaneously ebullient and commanding. Having served during the mid-1950s in a series of foreign policy positions, he came to feel that the Eisenhower administration was insufficiently "dynamic." He supported increased spending on national defense, increased spending on domestic social programs, and a liberal position on civil rights. If the GOP's right wing felt the Eisenhower era had gone too far in modernizing the Republican Party, Rockefeller felt it had not gone far enough. He ran for governor of New York in 1958 and won handily, establishing himself immediately as a popular, formidable executive and a plausible presidential candidate on the moderate-liberal wing of the party. Rockefeller's success was representative of a general trend in that by 1960, Republicans in the Northeast were moving in a more liberal direction on domestic issues. In states with strong unions and big cities, GOP politicians were forced to adapt and reaffirm their support for traditional New Deal programs, simply to remain electorally competitive. Other prominent liberal northeastern Republicans in 1960 included Clifford Case (R-NJ), Kenneth Keating (R-NY), and Jacob Javits (R-NY) in the Senate and John Lindsay (R-NY) in the House of Representatives. Northeastern party moderates—actually a more numerous and influential group than the liberals—included senators such as Prescott Bush (R-CT) and Hugh Scott (R-PA), as well as UN ambassador Henry Cabot Lodge. GOP moderates typically supported civil rights for African Americans, in some cases enthusiastically so. By northeastern standards, such Republicans were centrist rather than left wing on economic issues. Indeed, this was part of their appeal to the general public, in that they promised not to dismantle but to administer the welfare state with greater fiscal responsibility and honesty than their Democratic counterparts. A number of their leading figures were, like Rockefeller, of patrician background. As of 1960, moderate and liberal northeastern Republicans still dominated an impressive network of leading banks, corporations, law firms, private foundations, and newspapers centered in New York. Convinced internationalists, they supported foreign aid, the Atlantic alliance, and the United Nations. They were used to being able to pick the Republican presidential nominee. In a sense, they were used to running the country. Yet the conservative base of the GOP remained strong within the party throughout much of the nation at both the congressional and the local level, unreconciled to "modern Republicanism," and East Coast establishment figures like Rockefeller were increasingly out of step with that conservative base. As northeastern Republicans stepped to the left on domestic issues, the ideological polarization in the GOP grew. Nor was the Northeast the only regional basis for moderate Republicanism, which had significant outposts of support in the upper Midwest and along the northern Pacific coast, especially in the Senate and among state governors.[6]

Caught in the middle of this looming intraparty struggle was the GOP's congressional leadership. Republicans entered the 1960s with only a small minority in Congress, a minority further divided among conservative, moderate, and liberal factions. This made positive action in Congress difficult for the GOP. The Old Guard midwestern heart of the party had been decimated by age and defeat. Nor were congressional figures like Senate minority leader Everett Dirksen (R-IL) inclined to reorient the Republican Party in any direction, right or left. Dirksen may be taken as representative of the GOP's congressional wing at this time. A onetime member of the party's Old Guard, he had become convinced during the Eisenhower years of the need for a global foreign policy and a strong presidency. While he was a solid midwestern conservative, he did not seek to disturb whatever postwar bipartisan consensus existed in favor of American internationalism abroad and a mixed economy at home. His style was conciliatory rather than ideological. In practice, he mainly tried to hold the GOP caucus together, sometimes cooperating with Democratic factions on specific matters, sometimes blocking or amending liberal legislation. The one issue on which Dirksen, Goldwater, and Rockefeller could all agree was the need for a strong national defense and a hawkish, anti-Communist foreign policy.[7]

The race for the 1960 Republican presidential nomination indicated ominous fault lines in the Republican Party. Goldwater was the sentimental favorite of southern and western GOP conservatives. Rockefeller was the sentimental favorite of northeastern GOP liberals. Vice President Richard Nixon was respected, articulate, experienced, and the obvious choice for party regulars. When both Goldwater and Rockefeller declined to run, Nixon gathered up delegates and proceeded toward the nominating convention. He attempted through studied vagueness to straddle the differences between liberals and conservatives within his own party, a balancing act that in this case pleased neither faction. Then in May 1960, U.S.-Soviet relations suddenly took a turn for the worse when an American U-2 reconnaissance aircraft was shot down over the USSR. Rockefeller took the opportunity the following month to make a dramatic public announcement decrying the GOP's supposed lack of direction, and called on the party to assume a more activist agenda on domestic as well as foreign affairs. The implication was that the New York governor was back in the race; he seems to have hoped, unrealistically, that he could somehow unsettle the upcoming Republican National Convention and be drafted in the space of a few weeks. Nixon in fact had the nomination sewn up, but on the eve of the convention he met with Rockefeller in Manhattan in an attempt to appease him, issuing what became known as the "Treaty of Fifth Avenue." In it, Nixon pledged himself to increased defense spending, an activist domestic economic policy, and a liberal stance on civil rights. GOP conservatives were outraged by this backroom attempt at liberalization; Goldwater called it the "Munich of the Republican Party." An intense debate resulted at the convention over the civil rights issue in particular. Nevertheless, Nixon's and Rockefeller's underlying preferences were reflected in the final GOP platform, which was hawkish on defense, moderate on economics, and cautiously liberal on civil rights. Nixon easily won his party's nomination, selecting Henry Cabot Lodge as his running mate.

The convention led to several important long-term consequences. Rockefeller alienated not only conservatives but mainstream party regulars and professionals with his idiosyncratic attempt to bypass normal nominating procedures. Goldwater, meanwhile, established himself as a loyal party man. When invited by conservative supporters at the convention to let his name stand for the nomination, he refused, asking them to "grow up" and support Richard Nixon, in order to eventually "take this party back." The effect of these words was to galvanize conservative discontent and make Goldwater the right's undoubted favorite for 1964.[8]

The 1960 presidential election, a famously close-run thing, did not turn primarily on foreign policy issues. Both Nixon and his Democratic opponent, Senator John F. Kennedy (D-MA), campaigned as ardent internationalists and anti-Communist hawks. Nixon called for unflinching military support of Taiwan against China over the islands of Quemoy and Matsu. Kennedy tried to outflank his opponent by demanding a more vigorous prosecution of cold war policies overall. This led to a bizarre, ironic exchange in their fourth televised presidential debate, during which Kennedy urged U.S. action against Castro and Nixon demurred, even though both of them knew that covert operations were already in the works. Kennedy also harped on America's supposed missile gap in relation to the Soviet Union. In the end, however, voters gave Nixon the edge on foreign policy experience, just as they gave Republicans the edge as the party most likely to keep the United States at peace. When voters were asked to compare the two candidates personally, they gave Nixon a slight overall advantage as more seasoned, although admittedly less charming than Kennedy. The senator's great asset in 1960 was simply that self-identified Democrats greatly outnumbered self-identified Republicans, and that the Democratic Party was viewed by more voters as preferable to the GOP on the pocketbook concerns of ordinary Americans. In the absence of unusually favorable conditions and towering national heroes like General Eisenhower, the Republicans were likely to lose from the start. In choosing Senator Lyndon Johnson (D-TX) Kennedy also made a stronger vice-presidential pick than Nixon did, and ran a less error-prone, less reactive and more compelling campaign. Nixon, for example, somehow managed to lose both the African American vote and diehard segregationists to Kennedy at the same time, even though the nominees' positions on civil rights were substantially similar. The Democratic candidate's Catholicism was a major implicit issue in the election, but it seems to have hurt him as much as it helped, driving away Protestant voters while pulling in Catholics. Overall, it was one of the least ideological presidential campaigns in modern American history, as both candidates called for a strong federal government, new domestic spending, methodical progress on civil rights, and energetic internationalism. Nixon managed to win electoral votes in much of the West, Midwest, Rim South, and parts of New England, but Kennedy's strength in major northern industrial centers and the Deep South, together with his narrow and controversial margin in key states such as Illinois and Texas, gave the Massachusetts senator the White House.[9]

Kennedy's victory left the Republicans in weak condition. The party's stalwart congressional leaders, Everett Dirksen (R-IL) in the Senate and Charles Halleck (R-IN) in the House, worked with conservative southern Democrats to block elements of the administration's domestic program, but on the whole they came across as stodgy and obstructionist compared to the popular, active young president. The GOP found it difficult to provide effective, convincing, and coherent opposition to Kennedy. To give himself cover on what had become a regular weak spot for Democrats, the president appointed to his foreign policy team several prominent Republicans, including Robert McNamara at Defense, John McCone at the CIA, and Douglas Dillon at Treasury. During his first eighteen months in office, Kennedy pursued a policy of global containment of communism that was alternatively careful, aggressive, and erratic. He presided over major increases in U.S. defense spending; supported negotiations with Communists to establish a coalition government in Laos, hoping to neutralize that country as a cold war battlefield; lent uncertain support to an ill-fated effort at overthrowing Cuba's government in the Bay of Pigs; pursued on-again, off-again nuclear test ban negotiations with Moscow; escalated the U.S. military presence in Vietnam; presented a rather shaky presence against Khrushchev at the Vienna summit of 1961; approved new covert action plans against Fidel Castro; and held firm over renewed Soviet threats in relation to Berlin, while allowing the Communist bloc to build a wall separating eastern and western zones in that city. The response of GOP congressional leaders in each of these cases was typically to call for and reaffirm hard-line cold war stands overseas while supporting and deferring to the president in moments of crisis. Goldwater, like many other conservative anti-Communists, felt that this did not go nearly far enough. While he and Kennedy liked one another personally, Goldwater quickly became convinced that the president's foreign policies were "weak-kneed" and ineffectual. The Arizona senator believed, for example, that Kennedy had "clearly lost his nerve" and shown a "rather gutless character" in failing to provide anti-Castro forces with sufficient air cover at the Bay of Pigs. He attacked the administration for permitting the Soviets and their East German allies to build the Berlin Wall unmolested. He denounced any and all negotiations with Communists, whether over Laos or a nuclear test ban, as futile and self-defeating concessions. He argued for a strategy not of containment but of "victory" in relation to the Communist world. Most pointedly, he called for the overthrow of Fidel Castro's regime, whether through blockade, covert action, or direct invasion—an issue that he felt could help Republicans going into 1962 midterm elections, on the premise that "Communist governments will not be tolerated in the Western hemisphere."[10]

Even as Goldwater made these demands, over the summer of 1962 the Soviet Union was deploying medium-range ballistic missiles and nuclear warheads to Cuba. While Kennedy was aware of a Soviet military buildup on the Caribbean island, he was not aware of its precise nature or extent. Toward the end of August, Senator Kenneth Keating (R-NY) began to publicly insist that Moscow was shipping missiles to Cuba. The source and validity of his information were unclear. Republicans called for U.S. action against Castro; it promised to be an issue in the upcoming midterm elections. Not realizing that Keating was on to something, Kennedy responded in September by assuring the American public that no "offensive" Soviet weapons deployment had been observed and that any such weapons in the region would be unacceptable. On October 16, 1962, the president was informed that U.S. reconnaissance had in fact discovered the existence of Soviet missiles in Cuba. He formed an Executive Committee of the National Security Council to deliberate secretly for several days over the appropriate American response, consulting with Republican leaders in and out of Congress and receiving their support. It is sometimes suggested that Kennedy's subsequent public demand for the missiles' removal was caused primarily by domestic political concerns, but in reality there is little evidence for that claim. Domestic political factors obviously shaped the precise framing of the president's decisions but were often discussed in private as a constraint on rather than a reason for action. The driving consideration was the administration's perception of U.S. national interests. As virtually any other president would have, Kennedy viewed the placement of Soviet nuclear weapons in the Caribbean as an intolerable threat to the security and cold war standing of the United States. The fact that Republicans in Congress, the press, and the NSC's Executive Committee demanded a hard line on the missiles only reinforced his determination to have them removed. The majority of the American public was not clamoring for war but was instead deeply alarmed by the possibility of a U.S.-Soviet nuclear exchange, while supportive and deferential toward the president. At the same time, there was popular, congressional, and bureaucratic pressure to do something in the face of the Soviet offense. Kennedy's decision to impose a naval blockade on Cuba and wait before further military action was therefore well received by most Americans, and constituted an effective response on its own merits. The real domestic political complications came with the final settlement. Kennedy and Khrushchev agreed that the Soviet missiles would be removed, in exchange for the later removal of similar U.S. missiles from Turkey along with an open American promise not to invade Cuba. The full agreement was kept highly secret to prevent domestic political criticism of it in the United States, but even its public results were bitterly resented by Republican hawks. Goldwater viewed the promise not to invade Cuba as a victory for Castro and a humiliating defeat for the United States. Foot-dragging by Khrushchev over the missiles' removal from the Caribbean also threw Soviet compliance into question. Nevertheless, the American people were mostly relieved to have avoided World War III, crediting Kennedy with a capable handling of the crisis. The rather mixed outcome does not seem to have helped either party very much in the midterm elections a few days later. Instead, it neutralized Cuba as a potentially damaging issue for the Democrats while allowing them to play to their contemporary strengths: party identity, domestic economic issues, and a charismatic president viewed as increasingly successful. The November electoral results were largely a wash, with dramatic gains for neither party, but since presidents normally lose seats in midterm elections, this was interpreted as a mandate for the administration, especially since the internal balance of the Democratic congressional caucus shifted in favor of its liberal northern wing.[11]

In the wake of the 1962 midterm elections, there was a leadership vacuum in the GOP. Richard Nixon ran for governor of California that same year and lost, effectively removing him as a presidential candidate. Nelson Rockefeller seemed the prohibitive favorite for the upcoming nomination but was still viewed as unreliable by party regulars and conservatives, a problem further aggravated by his 1963 divorce and remarriage. Goldwater was the clear favorite of the Republican right, but he had little interest in running for president and preferred to fight his battles through the Senate. A small group of conservative GOP strategists, politicians, and businessmen responded in 1961–63 by forming a tenacious campaign to draft Goldwater. They were poorly financed at first, but as compensation they were remarkably well organized, dedicated, and politically shrewd. Their central insights were that demographic changes and population growth had given western and southern states new prominence electorally, that considerable grassroots support existed for the conservative, anti-Communist Goldwater in such states, that Republican Party organizations in those same states were often weak and ripe for the picking, and that southern white Democrats could also be won over through a conservative stance on civil rights. Under the relatively closed primary system of the early 1960s, the advantage went to the candidate with the ability to mobilize committed followers at the precinct and county level. Goldwater had such followers, despite his ambivalence about running. By the fall of 1963, he was ready to try for the White House. The subsequent assassination of John F. Kennedy shocked and saddened Goldwater, who had hoped to conduct a principled battle of ideas with his friend. Goldwater also realized that the American public would not repudiate Lyndon Johnson, the successor to the fallen president, less than a year after Kennedy's untimely death. Nevertheless the Arizona senator went forward in an uncharacteristically grim fashion and announced his candidacy in January 1964. The

Draft Goldwater campaign encouraged enthusiastic conservatives to attend local party meetings and stand for local positions, in order to then select conservative delegates to the national convention. GOP moderates were outmaneuvered and flabbergasted; Goldwater's edge in the number of supporting delegates was gained long before the convention was held. He faced several opponents from the liberal-moderate wing of the party, including Henry Cabot Lodge and Nelson Rockefeller, but they were disorganized and failed to coalesce around a single figure. Goldwater took the lead and gathered up delegates throughout the West and South during the opening months of 1964. In the crucial June primary in California, he narrowly beat Rockefeller and effectively won the nomination.[12]

Simultaneous with the presidential primaries, the nation moved toward a climactic debate on civil rights, with Goldwater playing an important part. Early in 1964 President Lyndon Johnson pressed forward with sweeping legislation to formally outlaw racial segregation in public places. As with Eisenhower and Kennedy before him, one of Johnson's leading concerns was that the failure to address civil rights for African Americans could damage the United States' reputation in its cold war competition with Moscow. Goldwater opposed the new bill as an unwarranted extension of federal power. A few Republican senators joined him in that stance. Many more, like Everett Dirksen—midwestern GOP conservatives as well as northeastern liberals and moderates—were convinced that the time had come for such legislation. The major bloc of opposition in the Senate, broken only after a filibuster, came as so many times before from traditionally segregationist southern Democrats, not Republicans. Yet the Goldwater presidential campaign scrambled and confused traditional political loyalties by taking a clear stand against the 1964 civil rights bill even as a Democratic president and most congressional Republicans supported it.[13]

Goldwater's position on civil rights reinforced the impression that he was an unusually right-wing presidential candidate. Well before his nomination, widespread attention and alarm had mounted over the new conservative political activism associated with the senator. As early as 1961, then president Kennedy had drawn the public's attention to what he called the "extreme right," suggesting links between conservative Republicans and fringe groups like the John Birch Society and encouraging a journalistic furor over the supposed authoritarian threat from within. He even went so far as to have the Internal Revenue Service investigate conservative groups like the Young Americans for Freedom. In 1963, a frustrated Nelson Rockefeller had denounced Goldwater's activist supporters as "the radical right," "extremist groups, carefully organized, well-financed and operating through the tactics of ruthless, rough-shod intimidation." These charges were hard to shake off completely, coming from the senator's own party. Goldwater in turn made a number of off-the-cuff and damaging remarks on his way to the nomination, for example in publicly musing that the United States might use tactical nuclear weapons to defoliate the jungles of Vietnam. By the summer of 1964, establishment GOP leaders had good reason to fear that Goldwater would be viewed as too extreme by the general public. The Republican Convention that July, an unintended showcase of party disunity, did little to dispel this image. Civil rights activists, journalists, leading Democrats, and even noted Republicans such as Rockefeller openly compared Goldwater and his supporters at the convention to Hitler and the Nazi party. Naturally outraged, and having won back the party's presidential nomination to a clear conservative stance for the first time since the 1930s, Goldwater and his delegates were in no mood to compromise. An open fight broke out over the party platform on civil rights, as well as on the issue of "extremism." Moderates were rebuffed in both cases. The resulting 1964 Republican platform stated that civil rights concerns were "a matter of heart" rather than a cause for further legislation, and called for significant reductions in domestic spending. On foreign policy, the platform recommended that the United States "move decisively to assure victory in South Vietnam," demanded a strategy of "victory," denounced negotiations with the Soviet Union, supported Cuban "freedom fighters," and called for the "eventual liberation" of Communist regimes. Goldwater's acceptance speech was similarly uncompromising. He lambasted the Democrats for supposedly allowing Communist advances in Cuba, Berlin, Laos, and Vietnam; called for Americans to return to traditional pre–New Deal ideals rather than "stagnate in a swampland of collectivism"; and argued that "extremism in the defense of liberty is no vice." The speech showed little effort at

keep Saigon afloat and attention focused on his cherished domestic agenda while securing himself from hawkish critics like Goldwater. In political terms, this worked beautifully at first. The majority of the American public was not eager to engage in full-scale warfare in Southeast Asia; popular opinion was in fact fluid, uncertain, and divided on the issue. This made an incremental, stopgap approach politically appealing, as the supposedly moderate option. Militarily, however, such an approach was bound to be rather ineffectual against a determined adversary like the Vietnamese Communists, as many of the president's military and civilian advisers realized. It was precisely for this reason that Goldwater had called during the presidential campaign for a full-scale national effort in Vietnam, but Johnson was unwilling to concede the point. When in August 1964 a confusing naval incident occurred in the Gulf of Tonkin, Johnson took the opportunity to request authorization from Congress to take any necessary action against Vietnamese Communist forces. The subsequent Gulf of Tonkin Resolution protected Johnson's right flank against Goldwater going into the November elections and reinforced the president's sought-after image as a steady, careful, and responsible steward of the nation's strategic interests. Indeed, in the middle of an election season, Goldwater called Johnson's response to the Gulf of Tonkin "the only thing he [the president] can do under the circumstances." Congressional Republicans supported Johnson over the Gulf of Tonkin—and over Vietnam generally—even more strongly than did the Democrats, as the president himself admitted. The administration began a limited bombing campaign against targets throughout Vietnam early in 1965, followed by the gradual introduction of major U.S. ground forces that same year. The American public initially rallied to the U.S. war effort, as did the overwhelming majority of leading Republicans. A few GOP liberals, such as Senator George Aiken (R-VT), questioned the need for military escalation and called for a negotiated settlement. A much more common Republican response, typified by Senate minority leader Everett Dirksen, was to support the war and propose, if anything, stronger measures. GOP conservatives such as Barry Goldwater, now out of office, and Senator John Tower (R-TX) were particularly drawn to this last alternative, calling on Johnson to eschew negotiations, formally declare war, and unleash U.S. airpower against

North Vietnam. Everett Dirksen, Richard Nixon, and former president Eisenhower offered similar recommendations. For the most part, however, Republicans in and out of Congress simply played the role of loyal opposition, deferring to the president as commander-in-chief.[16]

At home, the GOP's lopsided defeat in 1964 left the party divided and uncertain as to how to recover. Party liberals like Jacob Javits argued that Republicans needed to repudiate the right, focus on the problems of major northern cities, and make a determined bid for the votes of African Americans, urbanites, and reform-minded suburban professionals throughout the nation. Republicans on the right believed that Goldwater's ideas had been seriously misrepresented and that the future of the GOP still lay in a southern, western, and conservative direction. Moderate party regulars and professionals said the time had come to get back to the nation's ideological center. The various factions competed for control over the GOP in 1965–66. Yet the lesson drawn by most Republicans of every faction was that they needed to work together much more effectively to avoid common defeat. The dominant theme on all sides was one of tonal moderation. The eccentric John Birch Society, for example, was finally and convincingly denounced by William F. Buckley, a sign of the right's new political realism. Conservative GOP politicians stopped talking about repealing the New Deal. Pragmatic and effective new party leaders began to emerge, such as Representative Gerald Ford of Michigan, selected as House minority leader in 1965. Above all, a sudden change in the national temper brought unexpected opportunities for Republicans on issues of race, crime, and social disruption. On civil rights, the Johnson administration's focus shifted from incontrovertible freedoms such as voting toward more complex and intractable issues such as African American housing, jobs, and poverty in northern cities. Immense expectations were raised for a new era of economic and racial equality. Simultaneously, race riots broke out in major American cities, causing widespread destruction. Prominent liberals publicly empathized with the rioting rather than condemn it. The civil rights movement splintered, giving rise to an increasingly militant black nationalism. Numerous Great Society welfare programs proved to be expensive, unpopular, and counterproductive. Violent crime climbed dramatically. The Supreme Court under Chief Justice Earl Warren continued

a decadelong trend of controversial, liberal rulings that protected criminal defendants, relaxed obscenity laws, and banned prayer in public
schools. An emerging counterculture upset traditional social mores and
questioned the nation's virtue. Student radicals led antiwar demonstrations on university campuses. All of these developments shocked and
appalled many socially traditional working-class and lower-middle-
class white Democrats, alienating them from their party's liberal elite,
which now appeared insular, patronizing, and indulgent of lawlessness
rather than sympathetic toward their concerns.[17]

The issue of the Vietnam War was related to voters' preferences on
domestic social developments, but not in a simple or straightforward
way. It was not the case, for example, that disaffected white Democrats
were all unreservedly hawkish on Vietnam. Rather, they associated unruly antiwar demonstrators with the same trends they disliked so intensely at home: riots, crime, extreme permissiveness, and social breakdown. As of autumn 1966, a majority of Americans within both parties
continued to support the White House over Vietnam, but discontent
climbed as U.S. casualties rose and the military stalemate continued.
This discontented public opinion splintered in two directions: the first,
to negotiate a settlement and disengage, and the second, to escalate the
U.S. military effort even further. The second option was consistently the
more popular of the two. GOP liberals nudged toward a position calling
for U.S. withdrawal and a diplomatic solution to the war. Most leading
Republicans, including the party's congressional leadership, and certainly its conservative wing, favored the opposite approach, supporting
the war and calling on the president to take the fight to North Vietnam
more aggressively. A frequent theme from both sides, however, was that
the Johnson administration had got the United States bogged down in a
bloody, mismanaged quagmire and had been dishonest about the war's
true nature and extent. Vietnam was hardly the preeminent issue in the
1966 midterm elections, but it played into Democratic losses that year.
Capitalizing on fresh discontent over President Johnson, the war, inflation, race riots, new welfare programs, crime, unpopular judicial rulings, and broader social change, the Republicans were able to make
gains nationwide, picking up forty-seven seats in the House of Representatives, three in the Senate, and several new state governorships.
Each faction in the party could point to promising, sympathetic young

leaders who had been elected or reelected in 1966. Northern liberals and moderates could point to newly elected senators Charles Percy (R-IL), Mark Hatfield (R-OR), and Edward Brooke (R-MA), along with Nelson Rockefeller, reelected as governor of New York. Percy and Hatfield campaigned and won on relatively dovish foreign policy platforms. Conservatives, on the other hand, could point to Senator Howard Baker, newly elected from Tennessee; Senator John Tower, reelected in Texas; and Paul Laxalt and Ronald Reagan, newly elected as governors of Nevada and California, respectively—all of them from Sun Belt states. It was not yet evident which party faction would win the 1968 presidential nomination, nor was it obvious what the GOP's precise foreign policy stance would be, but it was clear that Republicans were confident of and oriented toward electoral success as the next election approached.[18]

One final trend of considerable long-term significance to the Republican Party and U.S. foreign policy was the emergence during the mid-1960s of a number of disillusioned leftist intellectuals, eventually described by their critics as "neoconservatives." The original group consisted of figures such as Irving Kristol, Daniel Bell, and Irving Howe—academics and cultural critics from Jewish working-class or lower-middle-class background who had attended City College of New York and flirted with Trotskyism during the 1930s and 1940s. Out of their disgust with Stalin's tyranny, these intellectuals came to appreciate major elements of American democracy and to rally in its defense against the Soviet Union. By the mid-1960s, these same authors perceived a related home-grown danger in the revolutionary rhetoric of the New Left, which they viewed as a noxious mixture of sentimental anarchism combined with apologies for left-wing dictators overseas. Kristol and Bell also came to believe that many of the Johnson administration's Great Society programs had been overly ambitious, and they were joined in that belief by gentile neoconservative authors and policy experts such as James Wilson and Daniel Patrick Moynihan. The typical neoconservative argument usually took for granted the good intentions and worthy goals of liberal welfare measures but pointed to their perverse, unintended consequences. For example, if inner-city riots grew out of a deep-rooted culture of poverty, as Moynihan suggested, then more government welfare spending might not be the best response when it rewarded the rioters without changing their culture. These and similar concerns were voiced in a new journal, *The Public Interest*, founded by Kristol and Bell in 1965. Its tone was empirical, topical, and social-scientific, offering concrete and well-grounded recommendations on current policy issues. Such methods provided new respectability to traditional conservative arguments, but what really gave them an audience was the fact that so many other Americans by the late 1960s shared the belief that Great Society liberalism had overextended itself.

Early neoconservative writings focused on domestic problems, but Kristol also wrote on foreign policy, convinced as he was that the country's liberal intelligentsia was undermining the morale, pragmatism, and self-confidence of America's leadership class in its critical struggle with world communism. In a characteristic 1967 piece in *Foreign Affairs*, Kristol hoped to see the triumph of "a new set of more specific principles that will relate the ideals which sustain the American democracy to the harsh and nasty imperatives of imperial power." He argued that the consistent and unblemished promotion of liberal ideals overseas could hardly be the sole criterion for a great power's international behavior; geopolitical considerations necessarily intruded. As he put it, "Whereas a national community is governed by principles by which one takes one's intellectual and moral bearings, the nations of the world do not constitute such a community and propose few principles by which their conduct may be evaluated. What this adds up to is that ideology can obtain exasperatingly little purchase over the realities of foreign policy. . . . Our State Department may find it necessary, if disagreeable, to support military dictatorships in certain countries, at certain times." Yet America's intellectual class, according to Kristol, was increasingly unwilling to accept international realities and responsibilities, preferring flights of moralism instead. He and his associates were also appalled by the New Left's sympathy for the Palestinian struggle against Israel, sympathy revealed during the Six Days' War of 1967. Neoconservatives in the 1960s still had little use or feeling for Republicanism, whether of the midwestern, Sun Belt, or WASP variety; they were essentially cold war liberal Democrats and retrospective admirers of FDR. They had no interest in dismantling the New Deal, returning to an anti-interventionist foreign policy, or blocking the great civil rights acts of 1964–65. Several of them never abandoned their liberal or social democratic convictions on domestic issues. For Irving Kristol, on the other hand, cold war liberalism proved to be only a way station on the path from Marxist thought across the ideological spectrum to conservatism. Yet it would be a form of intellectual conservatism with a difference: lively, polemical, metropolitan, fully reconciled to the nation's postwar political order, and with a taste for sectarian combat.[19]

As for Barry Goldwater, he returned to the Senate after the 1968 elections and served capably in that office for another eighteen years. The Arizona senator became a kind of folk hero for the GOP and a consistent spokesman for its libertarian strain into the 1990s. His 1964 presidential campaign had done nothing less than reshape American politics, bringing to the fore an insurgent Republican coalition based in the nation's South and West: conservative on economics, conservative on race, ideologically hard-edged, and aggressively hawkish on foreign policy. This new coalition was repudiated at the polls in 1964; the majority of the American public was simply not ready, under existing conditions, to embrace such a departure from existing centrist orthodoxy. Nor was it entirely obvious at the time that the Goldwater campaign was anything more than an aberration. Liberal, moderate, internationalist, and even dovish Republicans were still very influential. In the long run, however, Goldwater had indicated the direction the GOP would take in coming decades. His campaign sparked the creation of a genuinely grassroots conservative movement and political network. After 1964, members of this network adapted, reorganized, and remained a powerful force within the Republican Party. The ultimate implications for the relationship of U.S. foreign policy to party politics were considerable. Support for military spending and intervention overseas would increasingly be identified in American politics with staunch conservatism on both economic and racial issues, and with the GOP rather than the Democrats. Such had not been the case during the early cold war period. For this to redound politically in favor of the Republican Party, however, liberal Democrats would also have to question the cold war consensus and move to the left on foreign and domestic policy. As it happened, they were already beginning to do so.

Chapter Five

RICHARD NIXON AND HENRY KISSINGER

Realists as Conservatives

THE NIXON-KISSINGER FOREIGN POLICY team of 1969 to 1974 epitomizes Republican foreign policy realism. Richard Nixon was a thoroughgoing political pragmatist with an instinctive dislike of liberal elites, a readiness to embrace government activism on economic matters, and a penchant for bold, innovative departures in international affairs. Henry Kissinger was a brilliant and in many ways a deeply conservative foreign policy strategist who believed that revolutionary states such as the Soviet Union could be constrained peacefully through the careful coordination of military power and diplomacy. Together, these two presided over a skillful reorientation of American diplomacy that put great power relations and geopolitics first. They slowly extricated the United States from Vietnam, opened up ties to China, consolidated America's strategic position worldwide, and pursued sophisticated versions of containment in relation to the Soviet Union. The one inherent problem with this approach was not that it was unusually immoral, ephemeral, or unsuccessful—it was none of these things—but that it downplayed the continuing and very real power of ideological factors in Soviet foreign policy.

In party political terms, Nixon was arguably the first modern Republican president to reach out specifically to cultural and national security conservatives, across party lines. He had considerable personal electoral success with his center-right combination of populist cultural conservatism, economic activism, and foreign policy realism, but this success did

not translate into new Republican majorities. In particular, Nixon's behavior over the Watergate scandal eventually weakened or discredited
much of his policy approach, even where there was no necessary connection. GOP conservatives and anti-Communist foreign policy hawks
were thus ultimately empowered, in a strange twist of fate, to attack
1970s policies of arms control and détente, about which they had never
been enthusiastic.

An assessment of Richard Nixon's foreign policy, like everything else
about him, is vulnerable to what might be called a bad-faith model: as if
nothing that he did could possibly be admirable, or done for the right
reasons. Remembered primarily for Watergate or for his personality,
Nixon is hard to like. There was never any question about his intelligence, political skill, or capacity for hard work: he had all of these qualities in abundance. The questions that always lingered had to do with his
character and his personal appeal. Nixon was capable of bold, creative,
even visionary departures in policy. Yet he could also be disappointingly
petty, jealous, and vindictive—indeed, remarkably so, in someone so
accomplished. He compounded these genuine faults with a more superficial weakness that nevertheless hurt him politically, namely, an intense
social and physical awkwardness. While he pretended to be otherwise,
Nixon was in fact an extremely shy, reflective, and private man, uncomfortable around other people. In a sense it was a testament to his remarkable tenacity, ability, and intellect that he climbed to the summit of
the American political system, despite being fundamentally ill-suited to
electoral politics. Foreign affairs were his special strength, and his particular interest. During the early 1970s, his international policies were
considered a remarkable practical success, even by many Americans
who otherwise disliked him and considered him unethical. Today, however, the conventional wisdom in academic circles is overwhelmingly
critical, with the Nixon-Kissinger foreign policy legacy commonly characterized not only as immoral but as frequently inept and largely ephemeral. Indeed, the criticism sometimes slips into a mode as petty as Nixon
could be, obsessed with gossip and small-scale maneuver. The following
analysis reveals something very different.[1]

Richard Nixon was born in Yorba Linda, California, to parents of limited means. His mother was a serene, pious Quaker, his father, a combative, struggling small businessman. In his memoirs, Nixon said that he lay in bed as a child and dreamed of traveling to "far-off places." He was a serious, determined student, attending Duke University Law School before returning to Southern California. Nixon identified early on with the centrist, internationalist wing of the Republican Party, supporting Wendell Willkie for president in 1940. He worked in the Office of Price Administration in 1942—an experience that soured him on government bureaucracy—followed by service in the Pacific theater with the U.S. Navy, where he acquired a talent for playing poker. He was approached by local Republicans to run for California's twelfth congressional district in 1946, a race in which he demonstrated many of the traits for which he would become famous: keen debating skills, thorough preparation, and sharply partisan attacks. In Congress, he acquired a national reputation as a leading anti-Communist by taking up the case of Whittaker Chambers against Alger Hiss, a case in which Hiss was eventually found guilty of perjury. Nixon ran successfully for the U.S. Senate in 1950, and was chosen by Dwight Eisenhower as his running mate only two years later. After another hard-hitting campaign, he served capably as vice president, gaining particular attention for his expanding knowledge, experience and toughness in foreign policy matters. Nixon's 1960 presidential campaign was dignified but uninspired; his 1962 run for governor of California was also unsuccessful. His political career apparently over, he retired to legal practice in New York. The mid-1960s were fruitful for Nixon as he broadened his cultural and intellectual horizons, reading and traveling widely. He faithfully supported Barry Goldwater in 1964 and Republicans nationwide in 1966, earning credit as a staunch party loyalist. By 1967 he was once again a leading, active candidate for the White House.[2]

The most plausible alternatives to Nixon for the 1968 Republican presidential nomination were all governors: Ronald Reagan of California, Nelson Rockefeller of New York, and George Romney of Michigan. Ideologically, Reagan was located on the right wing of the party, Rockefeller on the left, and Romney on the center-left, with Nixon in the middle. Initially, Romney seemed to be the favorite, but he self-destructed in 1967 when he claimed that his previously hawkish stance on Vietnam had been the result of "brainwashing" by the U.S. military. Rockefeller had considerable support from northeastern GOP liberals but not much beyond that, and his presidential campaign was characteristically erratic. The regularly underestimated Reagan was in fact Nixon's most serious rival, especially since the party's center of gravity had shifted to the right since 1960. Reagan, while new to elected office, was already immensely popular with the party's conservative grass roots, especially in the South and West. Well aware of these dynamics, Nixon made great effort to reach out to the GOP right wing, including those he called the "Buckleyites" at the *National Review*, and to cultivate their support. The effort paid off. Partly out of appreciation for his constant party loyalty, leading conservative politicians such as Barry Goldwater and John Tower endorsed Nixon early on. Just as GOP moderates saw Nixon as insurance against the right, so GOP conservatives saw him as insurance against the left. He was the consensus candidate, acceptable to every faction, and the particular favorite of seasoned party professionals. He also performed well in the primaries against all opponents. The one lingering possibility working against him was that southern Republicans might bolt toward the more charismatic and straightforwardly conservative Reagan at the party's August convention. Nixon responded by reassuring southern delegates, led by Senator Strom Thurmond of South Carolina, on several key points. Specifically, Nixon suggested that he would support a strong national defense, including anti-ballistic missile systems; safeguard southern textile industries with protective tariffs; do no more to enforce desegregation than was already required by law; appoint southern judges; and pick a running mate acceptable to conservatives. On the last of these points, Nixon ultimately selected Maryland governor Spiro Agnew, a Rockefeller Republican who nevertheless endeared himself to the party's right wing by taking a hard line against race riots in Baltimore. This was all sufficient to win the support of Thurmond and other southern Republicans, who played a central role in giving Nixon the nomination. In his acceptance speech at the party convention, Nixon highlighted the failure of the Johnson administration to end either the war in Vietnam or escalating crime, racial violence, and social unrest at home. He called for "order" and "respect for law," which he characterized as the reasonable concern of the "great majority" of "forgotten Americans, the non-shouters, the non-demonstrators . . . decent people; they work and they save and they pay their taxes and they care." He suggested that power be restored from the federal government to the cities and states. Finally, he called for a "complete reappraisal" of American foreign policy commitments and a new "era of negotiations," beginning with an "honorable end to the war" in Vietnam. With this, Nixon left the convention in a strong position to win the presidency.[3]

A leading reason for the Republicans' assumed edge going into the 1968 general election was the absolute disarray among Democrats. The year began with a massive Communist assault in Vietnam, the Tet Offensive, that, while militarily unsuccessful, shook the confidence of the American public, press, and political establishment. In the New Hampshire primaries, Senator Eugene McCarthy challenged incumbent Lyndon Johnson for the Democratic presidential nomination on an antiwar platform and performed remarkably well. Senator Robert Kennedy (D-NY) next jumped into the race on a similar platform. Johnson responded by announcing his withdrawal from any reelection campaign, and proposed new efforts at peace negotiations with Hanoi. Americans were subsequently horrified that spring and summer by the senseless killings of Martin Luther King and Robert Kennedy. With the escalation of assassinations, campus unrest, violent demonstrations, antiwar feeling, crime, race riots, and talk of revolution, the nation appeared to be suffering a kind of collective nervous breakdown. The political effects of all this were much worse for Democrats than Republicans. College-educated liberals and African Americans tended to favor rapid disengagement from Vietnam and new social programs to address the "root causes" of riots and crime. White working-class, Catholic, and southern Democrats, on the other hand, whatever their feelings on the war, tended to resent rising social disorder, along with its upper-middle-class apologists. Democrats were thus badly fractured. The party establishment rallied to a traditional and ebullient cold war liberal, Vice President Hubert Humphrey, as its preferred presidential candidate, which in turn triggered a disastrous confrontation between antiwar activists and Chicago police at the Democratic Convention in August. The nation watched, live, as the party of Franklin Roosevelt tore itself apart on national television; more viewers sympathized with the police than with the activists. Meanwhile, former Alabama governor George Wallace launched a rip-roaring independent populist campaign targeted against the social, economic, and policy elites of both major parties. His base of support was among culturally conservative Democrats, particularly in the South, approving of New Deal economic programs but disgusted with recent liberal positions on civil rights, race riots, crime, and Vietnam. Wallace in fact ran considerably to the right of Nixon on social issues, leaving the Republican candidate in the middle on such issues between Humphrey on one side and Wallace on the other.

With the Democrats so bitterly divided, the election seemed Nixon's to lose, which he subsequently almost did owing to a very cautious campaign that, although meticulous, steady, and professional, was also uncharismatic and vague on specifics. Humphrey fought to win back both antiwar doves and New Deal voters with proposals for a new halt to U.S. bombing in Vietnam, together with traditional party appeals on pocketbook concerns. In the end, this succeeded in piecing together much of the old Democratic coalition in the Northeast and Midwest, including Catholics, unions, and working-class voters. Throughout most of the South, however, support for the Democrats at the presidential level virtually collapsed, and even among northern Catholic and working-class voters both Nixon and Wallace made significant inroads on the basis of social concerns. In the end, Nixon barely edged out Humphrey in the popular vote, winning several key states by narrow margins. The Republican campaign played particularly well in the West. Nixon also picked up the electoral votes of numerous midwestern and northeastern states, along with parts of the outer South, such as Virginia and Florida. With his explicit appeal to racial moderates rather than would-be segregationists, Nixon won northern white Protestants, middle-class suburbanites, and white-collar professionals nationwide. Wallace received all of his electoral votes from the Deep South.

The effect of Vietnam on the overall election result was subtle and indirect. For one thing, the positions of Humphrey and Nixon on the war were not all that different: both took middle-of-the-road stands, both favored an honorable conclusion to the war, both opposed immediate U.S. withdrawal, and both supported Johnson's efforts at a negotiated solution. This meant that there was little to choose from between the two. Indeed, the most openly hawkish candidate in 1968 was George Wallace, even though he generally appeared more infuriated by antiwar demonstrators than by the Viet Cong. Moderate hawks and moderate doves could and did plausibly vote for either Humphrey or Nixon; extremists were likely to be satisfied by neither. Democrats and Republicans both tried to manipulate the prospect of autumn peace negotiations over Vietnam to help their respective candidates in the U.S. presidential election. Johnson attempted to engineer an agreed-upon bombing halt with North and South Vietnam to help Humphrey in the election's final days. The Nixon campaign privately discouraged the Saigon government from agreeing to any such halt. In all likelihood such intrigue had little effect in Vietnam, where the South's president Nguyen Van Thieu was determined to oppose a U.S. bombing halt in any case. Nor could Johnson reveal the Republican campaign's private contact with Saigon, since evidence of it came from a legally dubious wiretap that he himself had ordered. Yet the Vietnam issue still influenced the election in other and more legitimate ways, and on balance it damaged Humphrey. The vice president simply could not escape the fact that this frustrating stalemate had occurred under a Democratic administration of which he was a part. Voters were therefore ready for a fresh alternative. The issue of Vietnam was bound up in the minds of many Americans with rising social disorder at home, which also redounded against the Democrats, since this disorder had occurred on their watch and was widely resented even by millions of their core constituents. Nixon was further able to convincingly present himself as the more capable hand on foreign policy matters, which presumably would aid in the resolution of America's Vietnam entanglement one way or another. Humphrey and Nixon did not disagree fundamentally over the issue of Vietnam, but in the absence of that issue Humphrey would have had a better chance in a very narrow race.[4]

Nixon's liberal critics frequently depicted him as extremely right-wing and also utterly devoid of core convictions—two positions logically incompatible with one another. Actually, neither depiction was entirely true. Nixon was privately and sincerely convinced, for example, of the political and moral bankruptcy of what he called the country's

"Eastern establishment" or "leader class" by the late 1960s, a class that for him included prominent liberals, the elite press, most academics, and the federal bureaucracy. This was a core conviction. He genuinely identified with the social and pocketbook concerns of working-class and lower-middle-class Americans. He was further convinced of the verity of certain traditional values, including family, country, religiosity, hard work, and the ethic of the self-made man. All of this made him a natural spokesman for cultural conservatives of modest income, as indeed for Middle America more generally. The question was then how to translate these broad values or instincts into specific policies, and here he was extremely flexible. For one thing, he sought to build a new majority coalition in American politics, and believed that he could not do so by taking an orthodox GOP position on domestic economic issues; popular and congressional pressure in the opposite direction was simply too strong in the early 1970s. Moreover, unlike previous Republican leaders, such as Goldwater, Eisenhower, and Taft, Nixon really had no principled objection to government activism in relation to the economy. He had never been especially conservative on fiscal matters, and he viewed his party's traditional reputation on them as an electoral liability. He further possessed an inherent liking for dramatic, creative public initiatives, and was willing to listen to recommendations from an ideologically diverse range of assistants. Nixon was therefore remarkably open to new domestic policy departures in almost any direction, and in fact, federal regulation, spending, and bureaucracy all increased dramatically on his watch. The Nixon administration expanded affirmative action for racial minorities, supported the proposed equal rights amendment, quietly oversaw a decisive period of school desegregation in the South, proposed a guaranteed annual income for the poor, expanded Social Security and health care benefits, established the Environmental Protection Agency, increased government spending on the arts, and introduced sweeping new regulations regarding consumer safety. This was hardly a stereotypically right-wing record. The overall direction was rationalized by that unconventional Democrat Daniel Patrick Moynihan, one of Nixon's favorite advisers, as "Tory men and Whig measures," best exemplified in Britain's nineteenth-century conservative leader Benjamin Disraeli. Nixon hoped, like Disraeli, to build a new, popular basis for a party of the center right. In this regard, the president's highly visible stands against selected targets such as the forced busing of schoolchildren or unruly antiwar demonstrators made perfect sense for him politically, since these were issues on which the conservative position and the popular position were one and the same. When the conservative position and the popular one diverged on domestic policy, he usually took the more popular course.[5]

Nixon was far more interested in the substance of foreign policy, and here he was frequently willing to take unpopular positions. As a freshman in Congress, for example, his southern California constituents had overwhelmingly opposed the Marshall Plan; he responded by supporting it anyway, convinced as he was of its necessity. To be sure, Nixon as president was obsessed with the precise domestic political presentation, timing, and reception of foreign policy decisions, but he also possessed an underlying and well-considered agenda for American diplomacy by 1969 apart from such considerations. International politics fascinated him and tended to bring out his more impressive qualities. He had a shrewd sense of global power relations and of competing national interests in world affairs. He was able to conceptualize innovative, long-term strategies and then act on them in a bold and tactically skillful manner. He had no illusions that the USSR and mainland China were anything other than capable, determined adversaries of the United States, but his hawkish anticommunism was leavened by two distinctly personal factors. First, he was supremely pragmatic, and came to see that U.S. national interests were ill-served by the absence of useful communication with major rivals. Second, he aspired to be what he called a "peacemaker," no doubt influenced by his mother's Quakerism, and he spoke of this aspiration so often in private over the years that there is little reason to doubt its sincerity. By 1968 he had a developing vision of the need for multiple new departures in American foreign relations. As he explained in a *Foreign Affairs* article from the previous year, mainland China had to be brought into the international system on a healthier basis. Negotiations needed to be encouraged with the Soviet Union. America's international commitments had to be reestablished on steadier and more solid ground, with increased contributions from U.S. allies. In relation to Vietnam, Nixon told various aides and associates that he "would stop that war. Fast." A conventional military victory, he recognized, was "no longer possible." Yet the United States could not simply withdraw in humiliation: some creative solution had to be found, combining diplomacy, counterinsurgency, the decisive use of force, and "progressive de-Americanization," to preserve South Vietnam and by extension U.S. credibility. Above all, policy in Southeast Asia needed to be reconceived in its proper place as only one element in America's larger global strategy. To implement all of these changes, Nixon was determined to be in effect his own secretary of state, and to direct foreign policy out of the White House. He would be considerably aided in that task by his national security adviser, Henry Kissinger.[6]

Kissinger was a German Jewish refugee from Hitler's Nazi regime and a direct observer as a child of Germany's descent from democracy into tyranny, lawlessness, and racial persecution. The experience left him skeptical that moralistic proclamations could uphold civilized order in the absence of supporting physical force. It also left him convinced of America's value as a power for good in the world. Kissinger immigrated to the United States and served in the U.S. Army during World War II, followed by a brilliant academic career as a student and then professor at Harvard. His writings from the 1950s and 1960s reveal a well-considered, coherent, and deeply conservative philosophy of international politics. In Kissinger's view, the modern era was characterized by the spread of ideologically charged "prophetic" leaders and revolutionary states that challenged traditional diplomatic norms along with the foundations of international order. Yet it was possible to constrain such states, and at the same time prevent war, through the firm and careful coordination of military power and diplomacy. Here he took his inspiration from the example of great nineteenth-century European statesmen such as Austria's Metternich, Britain's Castlereagh, and Germany's Bismarck. Each of these figures, while flawed, nevertheless showed great skill and ingenuity in promoting his country's interest while ultimately serving the cause of peace. Kissinger believed that statesmanship was still possible in the modern era. He believed that the realm of international politics was perpetually one of deadly competition over basic values and interests between self-regarding nation-states. Yet he also believed that this competition could and ought to be limited by policies of balance, reciprocity, and restraint, even among ideologically disparate states. The United States, in his view, had been fortunate and secluded enough historically to be able to indulge in cycles of moralistic crusading abroad followed by periods of frustrated disengagement. This erratic pattern was no longer tenable in the nuclear era. Kissinger urged a steadier and more realistic approach to America's foreign affairs, one grounded in the realization that international conflict was not about to disappear following some final victory over hostile forces. The implications for U.S. foreign policy by 1968 were several. Kissinger sought to preserve the essence of containment. He was unconvinced that an immediate withdrawal from Vietnam would bolster America's reputation. At the same time, he argued that Washington had to negotiate a responsible end to that conflict, while opening up ties with mainland China. Both initiatives would improve America's diplomatic options in an increasingly multipolar international system. The United States, Kissinger suggested, needed to tone down the assumption that peace and security depended on the forcible promotion of democracy, or that "American remedies can work everywhere." The time had come for recognition of limits, precisely in order to sustain a leading U.S. role in the world.[7]

Nixon apparently decided to appoint Kissinger his national security adviser upon meeting him. The president-elect appreciated Kissinger's foreign policy views and sensed that he would be a useful addition to the administration. Kissinger did not disappoint; in fact, he showed a striking talent for bureaucratic maneuver. He did not expect the State Department's compartmentalized bureaucracy to help him in formulating a creative strategy of globally interrelated parts. He therefore immediately set about organizing a variety of interagency procedures to ensure that his office would form the primary locus for the coordination, planning, and review of U.S. foreign policy. He also appointed an exceptional group of staff members to aid him in that respect. Kissinger became the predominant figure among Nixon's foreign policy advisers, eclipsing Secretary of State William Rogers. Yet this predominance depended entirely on the president's support. In the end, as Kissinger recognized, it was Nixon who set the basic priorities and made the major decisions, certainly well into 1973. In any case, the two men were so like-minded on foreign policy that they formed a genuine intellectual partnership.[8]

The domestic political circumstances inherited by Nixon in 1969 were ill-suited to the conduct of a coherent foreign policy. Stalemate in Vietnam had encouraged a breakdown in America's cold war consensus and fresh skepticism regarding military intervention abroad. Of particular and lasting significance was the rise of a new, articulate, dovish school of foreign policy thought in the United States during the late 1960s and early 1970s, a school sometimes called "post–cold war internationalism." The new doves criticized U.S. cold war containment policies and questioned the necessity for American military intervention against communism. They opposed U.S. military aid to authoritarian regimes on the right, and called for better relations with China and the Soviet Union. Doves demanded cuts in defense spending and a shift in budgetary priorities toward domestic social expenditures. They recommended a scaling back of U.S. military commitments overseas. They urged attention to nonmilitary issues such as global poverty and economic development, and sympathized with "national liberation" movements in the developing world. Finally, they opposed the war in Vietnam as senseless and immoral, and called for U.S. disengagement. Dovish opinion tended to be especially strong among elite opinion-makers in the press, the academy, and religious institutions. Ranged against the doves were anti-Communist hawks who continued to accept the premises of America's military commitments overseas. Liberals in both parties generally became more dovish during the Nixon years, while conservatives remained cold war hawks, but the hawk-dove division as yet bore almost no relationship to party identification among the general public. The relative strength of hawks and doves depended on the specific issue, venue, and moment; there were many varieties and shades of opinion in between the two positions. On the question of Vietnam, for example, a majority of Americans viewed the war as a mistake by 1969. Yet most also opposed any sudden or humiliating U.S. retreat from Vietnam and resented campus demonstrations by antiwar protestors. The American people, including Republican voters as a whole, were thus left somewhat conflicted by the clash between hawks and doves, a condition to which Nixon was acutely sensitive.[9]

The breakdown in the cold war consensus translated into profound ideological divisions in Congress over foreign policy, with cleavages cutting across party lines. Democrats in particular, while still in control of a large congressional majority, were deeply split over national security issues. Liberal northern Democrats such as Senators Frank Church (D-ID), Michael Mansfield (D-MT), and Edmund Muskie (D-ME) tended to be increasingly dovish on Vietnam, rejecting traditional cold war policies during the early 1970s. A notable exception to this tendency was Senator Henry "Scoop" Jackson (D-WA), a liberal Democrat who was also a prominent national security hawk. The substitution of Nixon for Johnson no doubt freed up many northern Democrats from supporting a war of which they had become privately skeptical by 1968. Conservative southern Democrats, on the other hand, such as Senators Richard Russell (D-GA) and John Stennis (D-MS), tended to support Nixon over Vietnam and to favor hawkish cold war policies more generally, in keeping with the preferences of their own constituents. The congressional Republican Party was less starkly divided, but a significant number of GOP liberals, including Senators Edward Brooke (R-MA), John Sherman Cooper (R-KY), Charles Goodell (R-NY), Mark Hatfield (R-OR), Jacob Javits (R-NY), and Charles Percy (R-IL), were dovish on Vietnam and attracted to a new post–cold war internationalism. Conservative Republicans and moderate GOP regulars, together with hawkish southern Democrats, formed Nixon's base of support on international and military matters. This usually left a majority in Congress supportive of the president's wartime policies during his first term, depending on the precise issue at hand. Yet even many Republicans were frustrated by the passivity that Congress had shown over major foreign policy decisions in recent years, and the congressional mood would become less and less deferential toward the president from 1969 on. Congressional doves began as a minority, but the political momentum was clearly in their favor.[10]

In establishing a sense of diplomatic priorities, Nixon and Kissinger sought to place great power relations at the top. The two men looked to reestablish that distinction between vital interests and peripheral ones that is essential to any solvent and sustainable foreign policy. For too long, as in Vietnam, the United States had pursued policies with great intensity in peripheral regions without putting them properly in their broader global context. Great power relations were by definition of vital interest; peripheral commitments had to be analyzed in terms of their effect on such relations. Nixon and Kissinger also looked to replace ideological with geopolitical considerations as the primary basis for the identification of national security threats. As Kissinger put it in 1969, "we will judge other countries, including Communist countries . . . on the basis of their actions and not on the basis of their domestic ideology." The USSR was indeed a serious rival to the United States, but primarily because of its military power and foreign policy behavior, not because of its internal form of government. Power, not ideology, was the best starting point for thinking about international affairs. This led to some interesting conclusions. Nixon and Kissinger both believed that power had become increasingly diffuse and multidimensional in the international system since 1945. Militarily, there were still two superpowers, in a separate category from other nations. Economically, however, there were now at least five major centers of power, with Western Europe, Japan, and China added to the United States and the USSR. Moreover, from a geopolitical as opposed to an ideological perspective, the USSR and China were each other's enemies rather than socialist brethren. This meant new opportunities for American diplomacy. A power political perspective, furthermore, unlike an ideological one, allowed for the pursuit of hard-nosed negotiation with hostile powers in limited areas of mutual advantage even alongside continued competition with such powers. It also encouraged a desire to limit America's material commitments in locations of peripheral interest. Altogether, paradoxically, a foreign policy based on straightforward power politics might avoid further Vietnam-type entanglements while allowing for more constructive relations with America's cold war adversaries. If China and the USSR were thought of primarily as great powers rather than simply ideological enemies of the United States, then there was considerable room for diplomacy with Moscow and Beijing.[11]

Upon entering the White House, Nixon instructed Kissinger to begin investigating "possibilities of rapprochement with the Chinese." Such rapprochement would presumably bring the United States diplomatic leverage in relation to the USSR while stealing a potential political issue from the Democrats. Sino-Soviet border clashes in 1969 provided an unexpected starting point. When Moscow inquired into the likely American response to a preventive Soviet strike against Chinese nuclear facilities, Nixon and Kissinger made it clear that they would oppose any such action. As the president explained, "We're not doing this because we love the Chinese. We just have to see to it that we play both sides." Nixon further eased trade and travel restrictions with the mainland, removed the Seventh Fleet from permanent patrol of the Taiwan Strait, and asked diplomatic intermediaries in France, Romania, and Pakistan to pass on his interest in better relations to Beijing. Mao was intrigued, but considerable political obstacles remained in China. The same was true in the United States, where Nixon feared a severe backlash from conservatives and anti-Communists should he reach out to China or abandon Taiwan. Initial diplomatic overtures were therefore careful, limited, secretive, and vague on both sides.[12]

Nixon and Kissinger were also interested in serious negotiations with Moscow on a wide range of issues, including Vietnam, Berlin, and arms control. After several years of energetic military buildup, the USSR by 1969 had for the first time attained rough parity with the United States in intercontinental ballistic missiles (ICBMs); American military forces were meanwhile level and on their way to being reduced. Nixon realized that strategic parity was an accomplished fact and sought through arms control negotiations to prevent the USSR from moving even further ahead, especially since the United States was bogged down in Vietnam and unlikely to outspend the USSR militarily under current domestic political conditions. Soviet leaders had their own reasons for welcoming diplomacy with Washington: they were concerned about China, in need of Western trade and technology, and desirous that the United States recognize Moscow's political-military equality along with its sphere in Eastern Europe. Both Soviet and American leaders also sought to prevent inevitable cold war crises in the Third World from entangling the two superpowers in deadly confrontation. Kissinger quickly established a backchannel with Soviet ambassador Anatoly Dobrynin to begin negotiations in a variety of areas. Nixon informed Dobrynin that diplomatic progress would be "linked": if Moscow wanted movement on arms control, for example, it had to help the United States diplomatically in Vietnam. In the fall of 1969, negotiations began on the Strategic Arms Limitation Talks (SALT). The Soviet leadership resisted the concept of "linkage," which meant that diplomatic progress was in fact delayed, but when it eventually came it would be comprehensive. Nixon also sought to gain a bargaining chip with Moscow in arms control talks by moving ahead with the testing and development of anti-ballistic missile (ABM) systems, an area in which the United States had a technological advantage. The 1969–70 Senate debate over whether to support the ABM program turned out to be extremely close and contentious, in one case passing by a single vote, revealing deep ideological divisions between conservative hawks and liberal doves that cut across party lines and lasted throughout the Nixon years.[13]

With regard to the protection of American allies in the developing world, and in the context of intense military, fiscal, and domestic pressures due to Vietnam, Nixon and Kissinger sought devolution of primary responsibility away from the United States and toward the allies' own self-defense. As Kissinger put it, "America cannot—and will not—conceive all the plans, design all the programs, execute all the decisions and undertake all the defense of the free nations of the world." This pattern of devolution became known as the Guam Doctrine or the Nixon Doctrine, after remarks the president made on the island of Guam in the summer of 1969. Nixon indicated that the United States would begin withdrawing its troops from Vietnam, while increasing arms sales and economic and military aid to Saigon—a policy eventually known as "Vietnamization," and recommended by Secretary of Defense Melvin Laird. With this policy, Nixon hoped, South Vietnam could be given the means to defend itself at less cost to the United States in terms of both dollars and manpower. A similar model was applied to other U.S. allies such as Iran, Israel, Saudi Arabia, and South Africa: increased arms sales and foreign aid, in the hopes that these nations could act as regional "policemen" in their respective neighborhoods without the need for direct American intervention. Part and parcel of this approach was to downplay U.S. interference in the internal affairs of regional powers. Nixon and Kissinger were skeptical that Washington had either the knowledge or the ability to engineer domestic socioeconomic or political change in developing countries, so they refrained from making such changes a top priority in U.S. policy with friendly regimes. Clients would not be hectored on issues of democracy and human rights. Instead, the United States would bolster local allies, including autocratic ones, in the expectation that there could hardly be anything worse for American interests or democracy in the long run than the replacement of such allies by regimes both autocratic and unfriendly.[14]

Of course, the immediate foreign policy priority for Nixon in 1969 was to end the Vietnam War on terms satisfactory to the United States. This proved more difficult than he had hoped, to say the least. Hanoi continued to insist, as part of any peace agreement, on the unilateral withdrawal of American troops from Vietnam and the replacement of Saigon's President Thieu with a mixed coalition government. Nixon refused both of these terms as tantamount to surrender, and looked for other ways to pressure the North. While the president hoped for diplomatic assistance from the USSR as the price of better relations with Washington, Moscow proved either unwilling or unable to lever its ally in Hanoi into major concessions at the conference table. This left U.S. military pressure. To that end, Nixon and Kissinger initiated the bombing of North Vietnamese bases and supply lines in Cambodia during the spring of 1969, an operation kept secret from even the highest American political and military authorities. That summer, the president further ordered the Joint Chiefs of Staff to prepare plans for a devastating bombing campaign, dubbed "Duck Hook," that was aimed at destroying North Vietnam's extensive dike system along with its political resistance. Nixon simultaneously warned Ho Chi Minh that the United States would launch "measures of great consequence and force" in the absence of major diplomatic concessions by November 1, a warning Ho dismissed. In October the president went so far as to place American nuclear forces on alert, to indicate the seriousness of the threat to Hanoi. Yet the U.S. Joint Chiefs were skeptical that Duck Hook would have its intended effect, and massive antiwar protests were building in the United States by the fall of 1969—nationwide demonstrations of an increasingly respectable, peaceful, middle-class nature, known as the "Moratorium." Nixon responded to the protests in a characteristic manner: stylistically defiant but substantively accommodating. On November 3 he gave a major public address in which he called on the great "silent majority" of Americans to support the U.S. war effort in Vietnam, rather than allow policy to be made by street demonstrations. The address was a great success in domestic political terms, undercutting the antiwar movement and rallying popular support for Nixon. Still, the content of the speech was an indication of U.S. military de-escalation. Hanoi had called Nixon's bluff, and Duck Hook was never launched; the fear of domestic political backlash constrained the president in that regard. Instead, Nixon tried to buy time and ease antiwar pressures by slowly withdrawing American troops from the theater of combat under the policy of Vietnamization begun earlier that year. The troop withdrawals were popular in the United States but alarming to Saigon and opposed by Kissinger, since they obviously undermined U.S. diplomatic leverage with Hanoi. Meanwhile, Senate doves tried unsuccessfully to limit or defund American military operations in Vietnam, finally securing a congressional amendment in December 1969 to forbid the introduction of U.S. ground troops into Laos—a symbolic victory, and a harbinger of things to come.[15]

In 1970, Nixon tried to use a similar combination of troop withdrawals, public appeals, diplomatic overtures, and sudden threats of force to maintain fading domestic support for the war while preserving a non-Communist government in Saigon. Frustrated by the cancellation of Duck Hook the previous autumn, in search of a "bold stroke," and understanding that Hanoi's military sanctuaries in Cambodia played a central role in the Communists' strategy, Nixon decided to launch an incursion of U.S. ground troops into that country in coordination with its government, U.S. airpower, and the South Vietnamese. On April 30, 1970, Nixon announced the Cambodian incursion to the American public, drawing a parallel between his foreign and domestic adversaries by condemning "mindless attacks on the great institutions which have been created by free civilizations in the last 500 years." While a plurality of U.S. public opinion supported the invasion, the outcry from the critics, including numerous executive branch opponents, was even more severe than Nixon had anticipated. Passionate antiwar protests flared up on university campuses, leading to the killing of four young people at Kent State University on May 4. Nixon was shocked by these killings and contemptuous of the reemerging protests. Senate doves answered by repealing the Gulf of Tonkin Resolution and passing legislation forbidding new funds to any U.S. ground forces remaining in Cambodia as of July 1. Nixon now faced the threat of defection over the war from several moderate to conservative Republicans in Congress. As he put it later that summer, "when the Right starts wanting to get out, for whatever reason, that's our problem." Nixon responded on June 30 by informing the nation that U.S. troops would withdraw from Cambodia, having accomplished their mission. In fact, the invasion had been tightly circumscribed from the very beginning, with public announcements of its precise extent and duration undermining its potential impact on the North Vietnamese. The Cambodian incursion nevertheless disrupted Hanoi's military efforts and set back preparations for a conventional invasion of the South by the North. It also revealed that the United States was as bitterly polarized as ever over the war in Vietnam, a polarization that Nixon almost seemed to welcome.[16]

The president approached the 1970 midterm elections hoping to make significant gains for the GOP in Congress through an emphasis on social issues. The success of his "silent majority" speech the previous year led him to believe that a majority of voters could be rallied around conservative themes so long as these were defined in cultural and patriotic terms rather than in Goldwater-type opposition to traditional New Deal programs. Several members of Nixon's administration, including Vice President Spiro Agnew, White House Chief of Staff Bob Haldeman, and speechwriter Pat Buchanan, agreed that Republicans could become a majority party in the country through what Agnew called "positive polarization" along social and cultural lines. As Haldeman noted, "there are twice as many conservatives as Republicans" in the United States; the challenge was to redefine the lines of party division. Foreign policy, and specifically the war in Vietnam, played into this redefinition. A majority of Americans, whatever their feelings about Vietnam, clearly resented the more unruly antiwar demonstrations and associated them with unwelcome social disorder; in this sense, Vietnam was also a "social issue." Nixon therefore decided to "emphasize anticrime, anti-demonstrations, anti-drug, anti-obscenity" and to attack protestors and politicians who "counsel defeat and humiliation for America." Agnew played an even more aggressive role in the 1970 campaign, attacking the press and the "radical liberalism" of leading Democrats as "a whimpering isolationism in foreign policy . . . and a pusillanimous pussyfooting on the critical issue of law and order." The results, however, were disappointing for Nixon and the Republicans, who made few electoral gains and in fact lost seats in the House of Representatives on a platform that struck many voters as overly shrill. Most congressional Democrats were well-entrenched politically, able to play successfully on local and pocketbook concerns in a year of stalled economic growth, and with such an ideologically diverse group many Democratic members were difficult to characterize as culturally "radical." Nixon's one striking win, ironically, was in backing the victorious third-party conservative James Buckley against New York's liberal Republican senator Charles Goodell—technically a loss for the GOP, but a gain for conservatives and for the White House, since Goodell had often bucked Nixon on Vietnam, but Buckley would not.[17]

By early 1971, Nixon was convinced that his reelection was in serious jeopardy. His approval ratings were not especially high; the previous year's midterm elections had been a disappointment; he had no major foreign policy accomplishments he could point to; the war in Vietnam dragged on, more unpopular than ever; economic conditions at home seemed to be worsening; and he was running in a dead heat in early polls against some potential Democratic presidential candidates such as Senator Ed Muskie. It was in this context that the president began to engineer what one author called "the great Nixon turnaround." The turnaround started with, of all things, a dramatic change in international monetary policy, an issue area that Nixon in truth found baffling and obscure. Since 1944, under the Bretton Woods system, the U.S. had played a stabilizing role in world money matters by agreeing to exchange dollars for gold at a fixed price. Other currencies were in turn pegged to the dollar at fixed rates, alterable only by international agreement. Even before Nixon entered the White House, however, with America's relative financial and economic position deteriorating, the Bretton Woods regime was breaking down, and by August 1971 there was real fear of a run on the dollar. The president met with his economic advisers that month to determine his response. One alternative was a period of domestic economic austerity, to stabilize the dollar, but with his reelection looming Nixon was uninterested in that option. Moreover, both he and many of his leading advisers believed that America's economic health, autonomy, and freedom of action had to come before the maintenance of financial obligations that the United States could no longer afford. Nixon therefore settled on an abrupt decision of historic importance:

the United States would indefinitely suspend the dollar's convertibility into gold. U.S. allies were not consulted. The president was especially influenced in this by his domineering secretary of the treasury, Texas Democrat John Connally, who, like Nixon, favored sudden, sweeping policy initiatives regardless of their content and who once summed up his foreign economic philosophy by saying, "My basic approach is that the foreigners are out to screw us. Our job is to screw them first." In effect, the original Bretton Woods system was dead. This decision to close the gold window was combined with the dramatic announcement of new wage and price controls to counter inflation, along with a temporary surcharge on imports, all under the unfortunate Leninist heading of a "New Economic Policy." These policy changes, taken together, were internationally disruptive, unilateral, nationalistic, and in the case of wage and price controls not only politically unprincipled but economically counterproductive. They were also extremely popular in the United States, with Democrats arguing that if anything, the new economic controls did not go far enough. Of course, some of these measures would do more harm than good to the American economy in the long run, as even Nixon himself later admitted, but they had their intended short-term effect, which was to help encourage a miniature economic boom that bolstered his chances of reelection.[18]

Nixon achieved a series of equally dramatic and better-considered foreign policy successes in 1971–72 with regard to China, the USSR, and Vietnam. Each of them was the result of years of preparation. In the case of China, by 1971 Mao was looking for international relief from his own Cultural Revolution and was ready for high-level U.S. diplomatic visitations, convinced as he was that the threat from the USSR was now greater than any danger from a United States apparently disengaging from the region. Kissinger was invited to travel to China in July of that year, a trip conducted in great secrecy and subsequently announced by Nixon together with plans for a presidential visit to Beijing. With the notable exception of conservative intellectuals, the great majority of America's attentive public and political elites were shocked and delighted by this announcement; U.S. Asian allies and the Soviet Union alike were simply shocked, as it left them diplomatically adrift. That autumn, the United States supported mainland China's full admission into the UN.

The hard part came as the Nixon administration unwillingly watched Taiwan expelled from the UN General Assembly, an act that particularly enraged the Republican right. Meanwhile, Kissinger visited China again and hit on what would become a lasting formula to smooth over Sino-American differences on Taiwan: both major powers would agree that there was only "one China" and that Taiwan was part of it, without needing to agree on the legitimacy of Taiwan's government. In February 1972, Nixon visited the People's Republic of China, the first president to do so, under intensive media coverage worldwide. Mao charmed Nixon, telling him "I voted for you during your election. . . . I like rightists." Nixon stated his conviction that "what is important is not a nation's internal political philosophy." The two leaders issued the Shanghai Communiqué, formally outlining the "one China" policy and indicating common opposition to Soviet "hegemony." The United States agreed to eventually withdraw militarily from Taiwan while verbally reaffirming its immediate defense commitments to that island. Overall, the visit was a great success in diplomatic, substantive, and public relations terms. Sino-American trade and cultural exchanges soon expanded. But the bedrock of this new rapprochement was a tacit and growing alliance against Moscow that was based on overlapping security interests. In Mao's words from 1973, "we can work together to commonly deal with a bastard."[19]

As with China, so U.S. negotiations with the Soviet Union bore fruit by 1971–72. The initial breakthrough was over Berlin. Under the Quadripartite Agreement of September 1971—prodded by the example of West Germany's "Ostpolitik"—Moscow agreed to a legal basis for civilian access from the Federal Republic of Germany into West Berlin in exchange for American acceptance of the Soviet bloc's de facto control over East Berlin. In effect, the two sides agreed to formally recognize the partition of Berlin, thus stabilizing the city's situation and removing it as a perennial flash point in superpower relations. Nixon stated that he hoped this agreement would encourage "normalization on East-West relations generally." The president was invited to come to Moscow in May 1972 and meet with Secretary-General Leonid Brezhnev in order to sign a sweeping set of military, diplomatic, and economic agreements. The centerpiece was SALT I, the first major arms control treaty to limit the production and deployment (as opposed to the testing) of nuclear weapons. Under SALT I, the two superpowers agreed to freeze much of their existing nuclear arsenals at existing levels: roughly 1,600 ICBMs for the USSR and 1,054 for the United States. Submarine-launched ballistic missiles were similarly frozen at 950 for the USSR and 710 for the United States. These numerical advantages for the USSR were offset by America's technological edge at the time in Multiple Independently Targetable Reentry Vehicles, or MIRVs, allowing several nuclear warheads with differing targets to be placed on a single missile. The United States was able to maintain its advantage in long-range bombers, and the U.S.-allied nuclear arsenals of France and Great Britain were not counted toward American totals. Associated U.S.-Soviet agreements included an Anti-Ballistic Missile Treaty, limiting each side to two ABM emplacements; a trade agreement giving the USSR most-favored nation status; and a Statement of Basic Principles according to which the superpowers agreed to "avoid military confrontation" while renouncing "efforts to obtain unilateral advantage." While this latter renunciation was entirely unrealistic, most of these treaties and arrangements were achievements of real substance, and the atmosphere surrounding the Moscow summit was genuinely constructive. Congressional hawks were leery of the various new superpower agreements; congressional doves felt they did not go far enough. Nevertheless, both the Moscow summit and its resulting treaties were popular with the American public, and SALT I passed the Senate in September 1972 by an overwhelming majority after Senator Henry Jackson (D-WA) and his allies clarified that they would not accept U.S. numerical inferiority in classes of weaponry with future arms control negotiations.[20]

Improved U.S.-Soviet relations in the early 1970s were frequently described in the press as "détente," yet the complexity of the strategy was not always made clear. For Nixon and Kissinger, détente was a version of anti-Soviet containment, or more properly a supplement to it. They took it for granted that the USSR would continue to be a geopolitical competitor of the United States, but they sought to restrain and discipline that competition in order to reduce the risk of nuclear war. Arms control and trade agreements would be among the "carrots" to give Moscow a new incentive for achieving international stability. The military-diplomatic "sticks" of containment would remain in place. Rewards as well as penalties would thus be used together to constrain Soviet expansion. Nixon's opening to China played a vital role in this strategy, in that a tacit Sino-American alliance shifted the global balance of power against Moscow. It also gave the United States increased diplomatic leverage in terms of better relations with the Soviet Union. This triangular great power arrangement, with the United States in a pivotal position, in turn allowed the United States to scale back somewhat on its international military and economic commitments without seriously endangering American interests. As time went on, Kissinger began to speak of his hope that détente might lead to internal changes within the USSR, and thereby to the end of the cold war, but the Nixon-Kissinger approach did not require domestic Soviet change as a precondition for negotiations. Rather, its primary goal was to balance Soviet power at reduced cost to the United States.[21]

One of the original short-term purposes of détente had been to improve the prospects for a diplomatic settlement over Vietnam. By 1971–72, that effort had finally begun to pay off as well, although only in coordination with the exercise of American military power. Popular and congressional pressures for U.S. disengagement from Vietnam built in 1971, even as American troops continued to come home. As Republican Senate leader Hugh Scott observed, "The hawks are all ex-hawks. . . . We just can't hold the line any longer on numbers." In May 1971, recognizing that the current position was unsustainable, Nixon made a major diplomatic concession to Hanoi, agreeing to the principle of unilateral American rather than mutual troop withdrawals from South Vietnam. Yet the North, confident of ultimate U.S. withdrawal in any case, continued to insist on the deposition of Saigon's government under President Thieu. In March 1972, North Vietnam launched a massive conventional assault against the South, the "Easter Offensive." South Vietnamese forces reeled under attack. The very survival of the Saigon regime was in doubt, under the shadow of the upcoming Moscow superpower summit. Nixon's response, decided on over the objections of several of his leading advisers, was much like the one he had rejected in 1969: stepped-up U.S. air strikes against the North Vietnamese, this time entitled Operation Linebacker, combined with the mining of the North's harbors. Public opinion polls showed a majority of Americans supporting these actions, even if congressional doves did not. Operation Linebacker was more successful than previous such bombings, relying as it did on precise attacks against conventional military formations together with their supply lines, and it brought the Easter offensive to a halt. The Moscow summit went ahead regardless; Soviet leaders had too much at stake to cancel it over U.S. actions in Vietnam. Hanoi was now under pressure from China and the USSR to compromise with Washington over the Paris peace talks. Realizing that Nixon was likely to win reelection, shaken by the effects of Operation Linebacker, and encouraged by the hope that South Vietnam could eventually be conquered regardless, Hanoi finally conceded on the main sticking point by October 1972 and agreed that Thieu could remain in power under a cease-fire agreement. As Kissinger told Nixon, commenting on consecutive diplomatic coups in Beijing, Moscow, and Paris, "you've got three for three." The administration had the essentials of a peace accord; the only question was whether Saigon's President Thieu would accept. Thieu, understandably, recoiled at the notion that North Vietnamese forces would remain in the South while U.S. forces did not—the American concession of the previous year. He initially rejected the agreement out of hand. Nixon was reluctant to force it on Thieu, or to be criticized for doing so and for pulling an "October surprise" in the days before the U.S. presidential election. Yet Washington and Hanoi were close to a cease-fire agreement, and Nixon hoped to gain some credit for it; hence Kissinger's public statement on October 26, however ill-advised, that "peace is at hand."[22]

The image of diplomatic successes with Beijing, Moscow, and Hanoi served Nixon well in his 1972 reelection campaign, as he knew they would. Indeed, by the autumn of 1972 the last U.S. combat battalion was withdrawn from Vietnam, and military conscription was being phased out in the United States—developments that removed much of the impetus from the antiwar movement. The majority of the American public gave Nixon credit for trying to extricate the United States from that war with some shred of dignity. Détente with the USSR and diplomatic openings to mainland China were also broadly supported by public opinion, even though bitterly resented by leading conservative activists and intellectuals. Altogether, by mid-1972 Nixon was widely viewed by the general public as a highly successful and capable foreign policy president, an impression that helped him politically. He could also point to short-term growth in the American economy, spurred by the measures of the New Economic Policy. As he prepared for the fall campaign, Nixon campaigned against the busing of children to racially integrated schools; took hard-line conservative positions on crime, drugs, campus demonstrations, and judicial appointments; and stood against amnesty for Vietnam draft deserters. At the same time, he took credit for increased government spending and regulation of health care, education, consumer safety, and the environment, while lauding the wage and price controls of the previous year. This ideologically androgynous combination of stands on both foreign and domestic policy did not win the full enthusiasm of either the left wing or the right wing of the Republican Party, but it was broadly popular and well attuned to the preferences of the average American voter. After staving off minor primary challenges from Congressmen John Ashbrook (R-OH) and Pete McCloskey (R-CA)—reflecting discontent among GOP conservatives and GOP liberals, respectively—Nixon secured the endorsement of Republican politicians across the board and set out to dismantle his main opponent in the fall. [23]

The president's task was made much easier by the Democrats, who were a deeply divided party by 1972. Plausible Democratic presidential nominees included everyone from segregationist Governor George Wallace of Alabama on the right, through liberal hawkish Senator Scoop Jackson (D-WA) in the middle, through Hubert Humphrey and Senator Ed Muskie (D-ME) on the center-left, to Senators Ted Kennedy (D-MA) and George McGovern (D-SD) on the left. Kennedy was charismatic but tainted by scandal, and did not run; Muskie imploded on the campaign trail; Jackson had his particular constituency but never caught fire; and Wallace campaigned well but was shot and maimed during the primary season. That left Humphrey as the conventional choice, but McGovern was able to build a popular base on the left wing of the party among liberal activists and secure the nomination under new rules laid down after 1968. McGovern's nomination at the 1972 convention represented the definitive repudiation of old party bosses like Mayor Daley of Chicago, who revered the Democrats' New Deal legacy but tended to be culturally conservative and hawkish on foreign policy. It represented the triumph of dovish, post–cold war internationalism in the Democratic Party, triggering a minor exodus from that party of hawkish anti-Communist voters and intellectuals to Nixon and the GOP. It further represented the triumph of a new wave of "purist," issue-oriented, insurgent activists committed to a more consistently liberal set of positions on social, economic, and foreign policies. In this it bore a striking resemblance to the 1964 Goldwater campaign, even though it was its mirror image ideologically, and as with the Goldwater campaign, so McGovern's presidential bid turned into an electoral fiasco. The Democratic Convention itself was a public relations disaster, highlighting the party's organizational disarray together with its capture by a smorgasbord of single-issue activists. McGovern took policy stands that were well to the left of the average American voter on a wide variety of issues, including crime, abortion, drugs, amnesty, taxation, welfare, and civil rights. He called for immediate and complete U.S. disengagement from Vietnam, and later offered to get down on his hands and knees in order to secure peace with Hanoi. These were the sort of statements that alienated many traditional party supporters. Indeed, Nixon turned out to be closer than McGovern to the issue preferences not only of most Americans but of large numbers of self-identified Democrats as well. The McGovern campaign further made a critical series of tactical gaffes and damaging campaign decisions, notably in the selection of unvetted Senator Thomas Eagleton (D-MO) as its vice-presidential candidate. The November outcome was a landslide: Nixon captured the votes not only of regular Republicans but also of millions of conservative to moderate Democrats nationwide. He won a majority of Catholic voters and union households—both previously Democratic stalwarts. He won an overwhelming majority of white voters throughout the South. In political terms, these were historic achievements for a Republican presidential candidate. Yet this was also very much a personal rather than a partisan success. Nixon chose to distance himself in 1972 from the GOP label, and he did little to assist or even associate with other Republicans. His landslide victory had no coat-tails: the GOP gained only a few seats in the House, and lost two in the Senate. Many southern white voters, for example, continued to vote for moderate or conservative Democrats at the congressional level, and Nixon did not discourage them from doing so. Nor did the number of voters who self-identified as Republicans increase appreciably under Nixon. The president had won personal vindication for his attempts to create a "new majority," but it was not a party-building success.[24]

Turning back to Vietnam after the 1972 election, Nixon made a final effort to create a tolerable diplomatic solution before an increasingly dovish Congress forced one on him. In October, Saigon's President Thieu had balked at the agreement reached between Hanoi and Washington; by December, Thieu's intransigence had caused North Vietnam to backtrack on its own concessions, and peace talks broke down completely. Nixon decided to launch one last set of air strikes against the North, Operation Linebacker II, also known as the "Christmas bombings," although air strikes were halted on Christmas Day. These new bombings were highly controversial in the United States, and the international outcry against American air strikes in Vietnam was greater than ever. Swedish premier Olaf Palme compared the Christmas bombings to the genocidal methods of Nazi Germany. In reality, the air strikes were conducted with new targeting technologies allowing unprecedented regard for precision and civilian immunity and bore no comparison to the Allied city-busting bombings of World War II, much less to Nazi methods. The purpose of Operation Linebacker II was to demonstrate America's continued willingness to support Thieu's regime with U.S. airpower, undermine North Vietnam's capacity for a conventional military invasion of the South, and thereby encourage both Saigon and Hanoi to come back to the bargaining table. It worked in each of these regards. By the end of December, under diplomatic pressure from Moscow and Beijing, North Vietnam was again ready to compromise, and the U.S. air strikes were ended. Meanwhile, Nixon wrote Thieu repeatedly, assuring him in a series of private letters that the United States would "respond with full force" to any Northern violation of the cease-fire agreement, promising continued U.S. military and economic aid to Saigon and suggesting that Thieu's failure to sign that agreement might result in his complete abandonment by the United States. With the greatest reluctance, Thieu finally accepted, paving the way for the Paris Peace Accords of January 1973. The outlines were fundamentally those reached by Kissinger and Le Duc Tho the previous October: U.S. troops would withdraw from Vietnam, while North Vietnamese forces already in the South would remain; Thieu's government would stay in power; and American prisoners of war would be returned home. The Paris peace agreement was universally popular in the United States, boosting Nixon's popularity and credibility on foreign policy issues one more time. The question of substance was whether it would actually be enforced.[25]

Criticism of Nixon's and Kissinger's Vietnam policy has long maintained, first, that they had no intention of achieving a workable peace or preserving South Vietnam in the long run but unnecessarily dragged out the war while deviously looking for nothing more than a "decent interval" to protect Nixon's political fortunes, and second, that they had no intention of keeping the peace but deviously looked to maintain warlike U.S. engagement against North Vietnam even after 1973. As is common with criticism of Nixon, the two critiques, both passionately held, are mutually contradictory and incompatible. The second critique is at least closer to the truth, even though stated hyperbolically. There is simply no evidence that Nixon and Kissinger were indifferent to the fate of South Vietnam after U.S. withdrawal and a mountain of evidence against it. Certainly, they recognized that the government in Saigon was painfully incapable of standing against Hanoi on its own, and feared that it could not, but they continued to hope that with American aid and air strikes if necessary, South Vietnam could be preserved even in the absence of U.S. ground forces. Nor was this an entirely unrealistic hope, for exactly this outcome was achieved against North Vietnam in 1972. Indeed, by that year U.S. counterinsurgency efforts had won considerable success against Viet Cong guerrillas and Saigon had recovered control over most of its own countryside, leaving Hanoi no option but a risky, massive conventional invasion along the lines of the Easter offensive. The secrecy of Nixon and Kissinger's approach was sometimes gratuitous, as with the Cambodian bombings of 1969 and the presidential promises to Thieu of 1972–73. Whatever the advantages of secrecy, American democracy and diplomacy would have been better served by a more forthright method in these cases. Nixon's private assurances to Saigon, however, were little different from his public commitments at the time, guaranteeing U.S. enforcement of the Paris Accords, and on the question of Cambodia there really were compelling arguments against allowing that country to operate—against the will of its own government—as a North Vietnamese supply zone free from U.S. interference.[26]

What many of the critics believe, in essence, is that the central goal of working to preserve South Vietnam was wrong, and that any efforts in that direction were therefore wrong. Phrased as a coherent policy alternative, this means the United States should have withdrawn from Vietnam in 1969 under any diplomatic conditions Hanoi would accept. Yet this is clearly not what most U.S. citizens believed in 1969, when Nixon entered the White House. On the contrary, a majority of Americans at that time, while frustrated with the war, still hoped to salvage the U.S. effort while somehow disengaging from it. It was exactly this popular sentiment that Nixon's policies reflected. Nor were Hanoi or Saigon ready to compromise in 1969, any more than the United States was. The United States and North Vietnam fought for several more years precisely to determine their relative strength on the ground, the only serious basis for any peace settlement. Strangely, antiwar critics at home and abroad rarely blamed Hanoi for its intransigence on key points of negotiation—only the United States. Nor did these critics focus on the totalitarian nature of the North Vietnamese government. Rather, many of them unconscionably romanticized that government while reviling the United States for defending a less authoritarian regime in Saigon. Nixon and Kissinger sincerely believed that a sudden American capitulation in Vietnam would damage U.S. credibility in the world. This belief has stood the test of time; the eventual 1975 outcome in Vietnam was obviously a loss for the United States and a victory for its enemies. Perhaps it would have been better to have never intervened in Vietnam in the first place, if the United States was unwilling or unable to pursue that war in a successful manner. But again, Nixon and Kissinger did not create America's military involvement in Indochina; they inherited it, by which point the range of viable options had narrowed considerably. They did in fact extricate the United States from Vietnam. Surely one of the great ironies of the period is that some of their most vociferous critics, urging even more rapid withdrawal, were the very people who had supported President Johnson's decision for U.S. military escalation in the first place.

With respect to Nixon and Kissinger's foreign policies in other parts of the world, it has often been suggested that these men subordinated regional issues to major power relations and cold war concerns. Stated in that manner, this is really more of a statement of fact than an inherent cause for criticism. The more serious and implicit question in that statement is whether the Nixon administration viewed selected regional crises as playing into Moscow's hands when really they did not. An early answer to this question can be offered by comparing the administration's responses to two very different crises: the first in Chile, the second in the Middle East. In 1970, a close three-way election in Chile resulted in the victory of Salvador Allende and his Popular Unity coalition. Allende was a Marxist and a friend of Fidel Castro's, in close contact with the KGB. The Nixon administration witnessed the electoral success of numerous leftist governments in Latin America, and so long as they did not threaten to become Soviet allies, Nixon and Kissinger were indifferent to their domestic economic planning. In the case of Allende, however, they feared on the existing evidence that he would turn Chile into "another Cuba, a satellite of the Soviet Union." Nixon therefore ordered the CIA to begin efforts to prevent Allende's installation as president of Chile and, when that failed, to work toward his overthrow. This included financial support for Allende's opponents, economic sanctions against his government, and attempts to encourage a military coup against him. Nixon need hardly have bothered. As was often the case with Marxist governments, Allende's domestic economic measures were dogmatic and incompetent, driving the Chilean economy into the ground and triggering massive resentment and upheaval all on their own. Allende's allies on the left wing of his Popular Unity movement urged him to apply a suitably Leninist approach and impose a dictatorship—a process of paramilitary violence that they began on their own initiative, largely unchecked by him. Allende, much to their disappointment and the disgust of his Soviet patrons, seemed torn between militant revolutionary romanticism and a nagging unwillingness to completely abandon constitutional forms. Chile continued to spiral downward into a worsening

condition of strikes, food shortages, street violence, and lawless confrontation on the left and right. Repeated coup attempts finally reached
a culminating point in September 1973 when the Chilean army rallied
around its chief, General Pinochet, to topple Allende from power. In all
likelihood the Chilean president killed himself as the army assaulted his
palace; there was no popular uprising to defend him. The Nixon administration had no direct involvement in or knowledge of Pinochet's coup
but was obviously happy at the result, and helped contribute to it indirectly through the covert activities of the previous three years. Pinochet
quickly cracked down on the Chilean left and imposed a regime that was
simultaneously repressive, pro-American, economically successful, and
reliably anti-Communist. Nixon's and Kissinger's embrace of covert action in this case was similar to the policies of previous cold war presidents such as Eisenhower and Kennedy, except for the crucial fact that
Allende—unlike Castro, for example—had been elected democratically.
The United States could probably have watched the Chilean president
self-destruct without any heavy-handed interference or consequent
blemish. Instead, Allende turned out to be far more useful dead than
alive to the Soviet Union and its allies since he became the focus of a
longstanding and heavily distorted legend of martyrdom for the anti-
American left worldwide. Even a 1975 U.S. Senate investigation accepted
the fiction that Allende had been "independent" of Soviet influence—if
independent is taken to mean not on the payroll of the KGB.[27]

Nixon and Kissinger paid little attention at first to the Middle East.
They worked, as Lyndon Johnson had before them, to support Israel,
contain the USSR, and maintain U.S.-allied regimes such as those of
Jordan, Iran, and Saudi Arabia. On October 6, 1973, the Jewish holiday
of Yom Kippur, American officials were shocked when the armed forces
of Egypt, Syria, and Iraq—all nominally Soviet allies—launched a massive, coordinated attack on Israel. Nixon was preoccupied with the Watergate scandal at the time. The main consequence of his preoccupation
was that Kissinger, by now secretary of state, played an even more prominent role in shaping America's diplomatic responses; both Nixon and
Kissinger worried that such responses could be incapacitated by domestic scandal. Otherwise, the substance of U.S. policy in this crisis was

much what it would have been without Watergate. Kissinger quickly determined that American interests and long-term regional peace prospects were best served in the Yom Kippur War by the prevention of an overwhelming victory or defeat on either side. He and Nixon arranged for a U.S. airlift of weapons and supplies worth over $2 billion to Israel to prevent its collapse. In protest, oil-exporting Arab nations announced a petroleum embargo against the United States—a foreign policy tool that Nixon and Kissinger had not anticipated, and a very effective one, as the United States and its allies had become quite dependent on oil imports from these nations. As the tide of battle turned against the Arabs, Israel threatened to encircle and destroy an entire Egyptian army. A UN resolution called for a cease-fire and an end to hostilities. Soviet leaders, alarmed by the possibility of Egypt's catastrophic defeat, warned that they were prepared to intervene unilaterally to save the Egyptians if the United States did not cooperate in implementing the UN cease-fire resolution. While Kissinger shared Moscow's interest in saving the Egyptian army, he had no intention of allowing the USSR to introduce its armed forces into the region in this way. On the evening of October 24, in the absence of an incapacitated president but with his approval, Kissinger and top U.S. military officials decided to put America's armed forces on heightened worldwide nuclear alert. Soviet leaders were taken aback but responded as hoped by withdrawing their earlier threat. Moscow and Washington then cooperated in arranging for a regional cease-fire, as well as an end to their own brief but alarming confrontation. Both Israel and the Egyptian army were thus saved. Moreover, Kissinger realized during this crisis that Egypt's President Sadat was neither simply bent on Israel's destruction nor a tool of the Soviet Union; rather, Sadat was trying to demonstrate his determination to win back Egypt's lost territories from the Arab-Israeli war of 1967 as a basis for subsequent peace. Kissinger therefore set out to improve relations with Sadat, which he did, and to encourage the piecemeal disengagement of Arab and Israeli forces as a first step toward regional stabilization. Nixon was particularly eager to see an end to the Arab oil embargo, which affected the average American more directly than virtually any other foreign policy development of the period apart from Vietnam; this also argued for active U.S. diplomacy in a mediating role. During the winter of 1973–74, shuttling back and forth between regional capitals in the Middle East, Kissinger nudged and cajoled the hostile parties toward an initial, limited peace. Moscow was shut out of this process. By the spring of 1974 the American secretary of state had secured disengagement agreements between Israel and Egypt, as well as Israel and Syria. The oil embargo was lifted, and U.S. regional preeminence demonstrated; only Washington seemed able to satisfy Arab demands with regard to Israel. Egypt consequently moved from being a Soviet ally to an American one. This was all groundwork for President Carter's later Camp David Accords, on the principle of "land for peace." All in all, it was a remarkable demonstration of Kissinger's diplomatic skill, adaptability, and sensitivity to regional context. He understood that Sadat was independent of Soviet influence, and acted accordingly.[28]

While the blossoming of the Watergate scandal in 1973 did not increase congressional influence over U.S. foreign policy in crisis situations such as the Yom Kippur War, it had a noticeable impact on other parts of Nixon's and Kissinger's grand design, for example in Vietnam. An increasingly dovish Congress had moved toward shutting down U.S. commitments in Vietnam even before Watergate, a movement that now accelerated. Even many otherwise hard-line anti-Communist southern Democrats and Republicans joined in these efforts. In May 1973, Congress cut off funding for U.S. bombing in Cambodia. The next month, Congress banned U.S. combat engagement in Vietnam altogether. Economic and military aid to Saigon was also cut back from presidential requests. Finally, in October of that same year, Congress passed the War Powers Act, which among other things required the president to terminate any U.S. military involvement overseas within sixty to ninety days in the absence of explicit congressional approval. While this act proved to be largely symbolic, it clearly represented a congressional attempt to reassert war-making authority, and specifically to repudiate any further U.S. military engagement in Vietnam. Obviously, such legislative actions made it extremely difficult for Nixon and Kissinger to enforce the Paris Peace Accords, as they had hoped to do, through the threat of continued American support for Saigon together with selective U.S. air strikes. The government of North Vietnam reasonably concluded that it would soon be able to attempt a major offensive against the South free from decisive U.S. opposition.[29]

Domestic political criticism from different directions also complicated Nixon's and Kissinger's continued efforts at détente with the Soviet Union. Senator Henry "Scoop" Jackson (D-WA) and his staff assistant, Richard Perle, proved to be particularly effective critics. In autumn 1972, Jackson introduced an amendment to the Nixon administration's new trade agreement with Moscow and implicitly demanded that the Soviet Union allow the increased emigration of Jews to Israel in exchange for most-favored-nation (MFN) trade status with the United States. Representative Charles Vanik (D-OH) introduced a companion amendment in the House of Representatives the following year. Conditions on emigration had not been part of the administration's original agreement with Moscow. Nevertheless, the Jackson-Vanik amendment became something of a cause célèbre, gathering support from across the American political spectrum and positioning Jackson for a future presidential bid. Liberals appreciated the focus on human rights. Conservatives appreciated the hard line against Moscow. Jewish Americans appreciated the call for increased emigration. U.S. labor organizations appreciated the opposition to trade with the Soviet Union. The result was that Jackson-Vanik gathered overwhelming support in Congress, passing the House and Senate in 1973–74 despite protests from the White House. Kissinger reacted by trying to accommodate Jackson's concerns and win Soviet concessions on emigration, but when such concessions were secured, Jackson responded by escalating his demands. Disgusted with the process, in January 1975 Moscow finally repudiated the entire MFN agreement with the United States and imposed fresh restrictions on Jewish emigrants. By that time, of course, Nixon had been forced out of office, and the United States had a new president.[30]

Gerald Ford entered the White House in August 1974 determined to maintain the basic outlines of the Nixon-Kissinger foreign policy. Ford had been minority leader in the House of Representatives since 1965, replacing Spiro Agnew as vice president in 1973. Ford's unpretentious manner and skepticism regarding governmental activism encouraged mistaken popular caricatures of him as something of a directionless bumbler. In fact, he possessed keen analytic abilities and was particularly knowledgeable about economic issues. On both domestic and international policy, Ford knew what he wanted. He was a traditional Republican conservative on economic issues, more orthodox in such matters than Nixon, and a hawkish but pragmatic cold war internationalist on foreign policy and defense. His conciliatory style, initial commitment to détente, and moderation on social issues encouraged the perception among GOP conservatives that Ford was more "liberal" than he really was. Ford had an excellent working relationship with Kissinger, agreed with his approach, and kept him on as both secretary of state and national security adviser. Kissinger remained the preeminent figure in American diplomacy under the new president, though hardly an uncontested one. The Ford transition therefore witnessed a striking continuity in foreign policy from the Nixon years. Nevertheless, the strategy of détente faced growing resistance from various quarters even before Nixon's resignation. Jackson-Vanik was only one example of such resistance. Of particular long-term significance was the attack on arms control from conservatives and national security hawks in both parties. Most politically influential hawks had been willing to support détente with Moscow in 1972, whatever their misgivings, in order to focus on Vietnam. By 1974, however, an informal and bipartisan coalition of hawks and conservatives was developing, led by key figures such as Secretary of Defense James Schlesinger, the Joint Chiefs of Staff, Scoop Jackson, and noted defense experts, deeply suspicious of Soviet intentions and skeptical of further arms control agreements. Everyone from Senator Jackson to Leonid Brezhnev claimed to be open to a second SALT treaty based on the concept of strategic equality between the superpowers; the question was how to handle precise limitations on specific weapons systems. American hawks such as Schlesinger and Jackson preferred that any new limitations weigh much more heavily on the Soviets than on the United States, an entirely understandable preference in itself but one that made agreement from Moscow unlikely. Under these domestic political pressures, Ford met Brezhnev at Vladivostok in November 1974, without any conclusive deal on SALT II. Instead, the two leaders signed a number of secondary and symbolic accords while reaffirming their mutual desire for the preservation of détente. That same month, the Republican Party suffered one of its worst losses ever in the congressional midterm elections. The primary issues were Watergate and the nation's economy. While foreign policy had little to do with these losses, they had an impact on foreign policy all the same. Liberal, dovish, reform-minded northern Democrats were now in a very strong position, empowered to block anti-Communist U.S. interventions overseas. In this way, the Ford administration was whipsawed domestically, from the right on arms control, from the left on intervention, and from both sides on the issue of human rights in the Soviet Union.[31]

Ford and Kissinger continued to hope for a SALT II agreement with Moscow. Partly for that reason, they acceded to Soviet sensitivities in two important cases during 1975, despite resistance from several of Ford's other advisers. First, when the exiled Soviet dissident writer Alexander Solzhenitsyn visited the United States that summer, Ford followed Kissinger's advice not to meet with Solzhenitsyn at the White House. This decision was seized on by conservatives and anti-Communists as a vivid illustration of the moral bankruptcy of détente. Second, Ford and Kissinger agreed to offer formal recognition of the existing territorial settlement in Europe—a longstanding goal of the USSR, finally reached at the Helsinki Conference of July–August 1975. Soviet leaders believed that such recognition would help bolster the internal and external security and legitimacy of their East European client states. Moscow's chief concession in exchange, insisted on by America's Western allies, was a written commitment to respect human rights and political dissent in its East European sphere—the so-called "third basket" of the Helsinki Accords, and one that Soviet leaders had no intention of honoring. Moscow also agreed to provide advance notice of military maneuvers along NATO's eastern borders and to permit the change of territorial boundaries in Europe through peaceful negotiation. Both sides assented to the principle of noninterference in the internal, sovereign affairs of other countries—a stipulation that appeared to contradict basket three but that supposedly gave East European countries some insurance against outright Soviet invasion along the lines of Czechoslovakia in 1968. Kissinger helped negotiate the accord in order to create further linkages under détente and to cultivate some geopolitical diversity in the USSR's European sphere, but he found Helsinki's earnest legalities to be almost comical in their assumption of great practical effect. As he said of the written details, "they can write in Swahili for all I care." The Helsinki agreement was not popular in the United States, where it was criticized by both liberals and conservatives as a selling out the peoples of Eastern Europe. Yet to the surprise of Kissinger, Brezhnev, and American critics of Helsinki alike, the agreement ultimately encouraged a bubbling up of political dissent in the Soviet bloc republics. This dissent was repressed at the time but is now recognized as having been one of the key factors in the weakening of Communist rule in Europe.[32]

The year 1975 also saw the complete and unhappy resolution of America's war in Indochina. Over the winter of 1974–75, Hanoi began a major conventional military offensive against the forces of South Vietnam. Ford and Kissinger responded by requesting congressional approval for fresh U.S. aid for Saigon. More skeptical than ever of the utility of such aid, Congress replied by cutting back requested payments or refusing them altogether. If America's ally in South Vietnam had ever possessed a chance to survive, it was doomed by the drying up of U.S. support, a pattern that had already begun under Nixon. Saigon's government and armed forces were increasingly plagued by shortages of supplies, desertion, and low morale, along with critical military miscalculations by President Thieu. The final advance by North Vietnamese forces in the spring of 1975 came with stunning speed. Thieu continued to assume to the very end that American help would rescue his regime, for example with U.S. air strikes, since Nixon and Kissinger had promised as much in 1972–73, but Ford had not been privy to those assurances and never seriously considered using airpower against the North Vietnamese in 1975. Kissinger was tormented by his inability to secure greater help for Saigon, but Congress and the American public, including most conservatives and Republicans, clearly had no appetite for any further military involvement, and Ford's decisions reflected that political reality. On April 23, Ford was cheered by Tulane University students when he declared that the war in Vietnam was "finished as far as America is concerned." A last-minute and hastily planned U.S. evacuation of Saigon a few days later concluded with indelible images of America's greatest foreign policy failure. Remarkably, Ford escaped domestic political criticism for these events. His standing as a Republican cold war hawk no doubt made it easier for him to survive the potential charge that he had "lost" Indochina. More to the point, by 1975 very few Americans wanted to fight in Vietnam or even think about that country, now under the rule of a fiercely authoritarian, militarized, and hostile regime allied with the Soviet Union.[33]

The fall of Saigon, however, did happen to coincide with a naval incident that demonstrated the limits of Americans' willingness to suffer continued international humiliations. On May 12, 1975, Cambodia's Khmer Rouge government seized the U.S. merchant ship *Mayaguez* in the Gulf of Siam, taking its crew prisoner. When Ford met with the National Security Council to formulate his response, as one observer put it, "there wasn't a dove in the place." The president and his advisers, particularly Kissinger, agreed the situation was intolerable and that the United States needed to respond aggressively. Publicly describing the Cambodian action as a case of international "piracy," Ford calmly ordered an American aircraft carrier to the site, assembled an amphibious task force, and demanded the unconditional return of the crew of the *Mayaguez*. Indeed, he eventually decided not only to forcibly rescue the American crew but to punish Cambodia with air strikes for daring to challenge the United States in this way. When consulted by the president, leading congressional Democrats were skeptical, questioning the wisdom and legality of a military response, but Ford disagreed, saying "it is better to do too much than too little." With hazy intelligence reports, the president directed U.S. Marines to land on the island of Koh Tang, where they did heavy fighting, expecting to locate the *Mayaguez*, only to find that the merchant ship's crew had been moved. The crew was then discovered on a fishing vessel at sea and rescued, having been released by the Cambodians simultaneously with American military operations. Ford's approval ratings shot up temporarily in the wake of this crisis, as Congress and the American public applauded his firm handling of the case. Ford could hardly have been unaware, only two weeks after the fall of Saigon, and with his administration struggling on numerous domestic issues, that a forceful resolution of the situation would redound to his benefit politically. Yet the administration's response was driven by a powerful conviction, precisely because of the counterexample of Vietnam, that the United States had to "draw the line," in Kissinger's words, and demonstrate internationally that it could not be coerced indefinitely.[34]

The demonstration did not last long. Within months the United States again revealed its limited appetite for even the most indirect military entanglements abroad, this time in sub-Saharan Africa, where the final stages of European decolonization triggered competing cold war interventions by Havana, Moscow, and Washington. In 1974, Portugal's new government decided to terminate control over its colonial possessions, including, notably, Angola. Three tribally based factions now struggled for power in that soon-to-be independent country: the Marxist-oriented Popular Front for the Liberation of Angola (MPLA), supported by Cuba and the Soviet Union, the National Front for the Liberation of Angola (FNLA), supported by China and Zaire, and the National Union for the Total Independence of Angola (UNITA), led by the charismatic yet opportunistic Jonas Savimbi. The United States had ties to both the FNLA and UNITA but provided little material aid to either. Of all the outside powers, Castro's Cuba was the most eager to intervene, as a way to demonstrate its revolutionary credentials and help a Marxist government take power in Africa. Initially skeptical, Soviet authorities were pulled in by Castro's enthusiasm, authorizing air and sea lift support for a major Cuban troop presence in Angola. Meanwhile, at Kissinger's recommendation, President Ford in July 1975 authorized U.S. covert aid to the FNLA and UNITA, amounting to over $30 million by year's end. South Africa also intervened directly on behalf of the FNLA, but with Cuban help the MPLA entered Angola's capital that November and proclaimed itself the new nation's government. Leading congressional Democrats in the United States discovered the existence of American covert operations in Angola and decided to shut them down, arguing that the Ford administration had provoked Soviet intervention, that Cuba was not a Soviet proxy, that South Africa was an unacceptable ally, and that covert operations were wrong in principle. In December 1975, the U.S. Senate voted by a veto-proof margin of 54 to 22 to terminate American involvement. Many of the national security hawks who had criticized Kissinger over détente, Helsinki, and arms control were nowhere to be found during this debate. With memories of Vietnam still very fresh, and in the middle of withering congressional and journalistic criticism of the CIA,

there was little popular support in the United States at the time for covert involvement in another country's civil war. The end of American
assistance sealed the fate of the FNLA, which was thoroughly defeated
by the start of 1976. Jonas Savimbi's UNITA retreated to the country's
southern bushes to wage protracted war against the MPLA, now recognized by other African countries as Angola's official government, and a
formal ally of the Soviet Union as of October 1976. The American failure in Angola helped convince Ford and Kissinger to adopt a new policy
toward Africa that year, a policy designed to undercut support for communism on that continent by lending U.S. support to majority rule in
Rhodesia, Namibia, and South Africa. Soviet leaders, for their part, were
surprised by their own success in helping to establish a genuinely Marxist regime in Africa, a success that encouraged new confidence in similar revolutionary possibilities throughout the developing world.[35]

By 1975–76, Ford's policy of détente was under sharp attack from
both liberals and conservatives, as was Kissinger, its human epitome.
Liberals increasingly dismissed Kissinger's version of détente as nothing
more than a cover for the propping up of right-wing dictators overseas
while criticizing the secretary of state as a secretive, Machiavellian figure, indifferent to human rights internationally. Leading conservatives
meanwhile characterized détente as nothing more than a disguised form
of appeasement and surrender, pointing to the fall of Saigon, Helsinki,
Solzhenitsyn's visit, Angola, and the entire SALT process as supposed
examples of endless concessions and retreat before communism. In fact,
the GOP's right wing had never been entirely happy with Ford, and after
his 1974 selection of Nelson Rockefeller as vice president, numerous
conservatives decided to oppose him. They found their candidate in
California's governor Ronald Reagan, who mounted a remarkably strong
challenge for the upcoming Republican presidential nomination. Reagan championed a politics to the right of Ford: stylistically aggressive,
staunchly conservative on social issues, and unabashedly hawkish and
nationalistic on foreign policy. Indeed, Reagan's foreign policy criticisms
led Ford to abandon use of the word "détente" by the spring of 1976. The
California governor did very well in that year's Republican primaries,
coming close to defeating the incumbent president, but in the end, Ford

narrowly secured the nomination by winning moderate, northeastern, and midwestern Republicans. Reagan and his supporters did, however, force some important concessions at the summer GOP Convention, notably through the insertion of a "morality in foreign policy" platform critical of détente, Helsinki, and "secret agreements." For a party to condemn its own foreign policy was certainly an unconventional way to win an election. Still, the platform was a true indication of political trends within the GOP.

Ford's Democratic opponent in 1976 was Georgia's governor Jimmy Carter, a shrewd politician who matched the contemporary national mood by offering himself as a fresh, capable, and honest figure from outside the Washington establishment. On foreign policy, the ideologically dexterous Carter criticized the White House from the left and right simultaneously. From the left, he recommended modest cuts in defense spending, opposed arms sales to foreign dictatorships, accused Ford of trying to "start a new Vietnam in Angola," and called for a new focus on human rights overseas. From the right, he accused Ford and Kissinger of being "out-traded" by Moscow in a variety of settings, including the Helsinki Conference. From both left and right, he attacked Kissinger's foreign policy approach as "amoral." The most well-known contribution of any foreign policy issue during the election came in the form of Ford's infamous gaffe at the second televised debate with Carter that fall, at which the president was asked a question implicitly about the so-called "Sonnenfeldt Doctrine." Helmut Sonnenfeldt was a State Department counselor who had suggested to a group of American ambassadors in private that the United States would like to see Eastern Europe's relationship with the USSR develop in a more "organic" direction, free from Soviet coercive power. This suggestion was innocuous enough, and entirely in keeping with official American hopes since FDR, but as it leaked to the press in the context of the Helsinki Accords it raised criticisms that Ford had approved a Soviet sphere of influence in Eastern Europe. Ford was eager to deny any such approval, but when asked about it during the TV debate he mangled his answer, declaring simply that "there is no Soviet domination of Eastern Europe." Given the opportunity over a period of several days to clarify his response, he refused to do so, making the situation even worse. The problem was not so much the policy specifics as the already popular caricature of Ford as dim-witted—as if he was unaware that Soviet tanks occupied large parts of Eastern Europe. In any case, even after this absurd imbroglio, Ford continued to outpoll Carter on foreign policy. When asked which candidate and party could better handle U.S. foreign relations, Americans consistently gave a significant edge to Ford over Carter and Republicans over Democrats. Kissinger's realism, competence, and success always played better with the general public than with ideological activists in either party, and the secretary of state remained a respected asset to Ford going into the fall election. Indeed, by 1976 foreign policy was about the only issue advantage the GOP had, and a diminished one, since the public's attention was overwhelmingly focused on domestic concerns. Popular unease over the state of the economy, together with the still-powerful shadow of Watergate, hurt Ford's reelection chances badly, and as a born-again Christian from the Deep South, Carter was difficult to dismiss as a McGovern-style liberal. Democrats further retained a massive two-to-one edge in voter identification. In spite of these advantages, the Georgia governor only barely won the presidency that fall. Insofar as foreign policy influenced the election, it appears to have helped Ford.[36]

If we conceive of Nixon, Kissinger, and Ford as pursuing a broadly continuous foreign policy approach, the simplest way to evaluate its overall success or failure is to compare America's international position by 1976 to the one inherited in 1969. In 1969, the United States was bogged down in and preoccupied by a costly stalemate in Vietnam, one that had already shattered America's cold war consensus, encouraging violent social conflict in the United States. In the following years, Nixon and Kissinger extricated the United States from Vietnam, thus reducing a source of severe domestic controversy, while improving American relations with China and the USSR. This in turn allowed them to balance Soviet power, retrench strategically, and maintain an internationalist foreign policy without undue expense, a policy maintained under Ford. By 1976, consequently, the United States was in a considerably improved position relative to 1969, both at home and abroad. It was only this improved foundation that allowed Jimmy Carter to argue that the United States should pay more attention to issues such as human rights overseas—issues that would have seemed distinctly secondary in the absence of domestic or international peace and stability.

As time went on, congressional criticism rained down on détente from both left and right. Yet these very same congressional critics denied the Nixon and Ford administrations the tools to make détente work. Congressional hawks denied the White House the ability to provide Moscow incentives for cooperation through arms control or trade agreements. Congressional doves denied it the ability to bolster U.S. defense spending, preserve American intelligence capacities, or even attempt to block Marxist advances in Vietnam and Angola. Obviously, without carrots or sticks, the United States could not expect to either contain or to tame Soviet power. Nevertheless, many of the foreign policy innovations from the Nixon-Kissinger era had lasting effects. The diplomatic opening to China is only the most obvious one. Kissinger initiated a peace process in the Middle East that paved the way for subsequent administrations. Détente with Moscow also had enduring impact. Superpower relations were made more predictable and transparent; the risk of nuclear war was reduced. And while détente may have actually bolstered the security and legitimacy of the Soviet bloc in the short term, in the long term it helped undermine it by encouraging a freer flow of people and ideas both across and behind the Iron Curtain. Such achievements are hardly ephemeral. Nor is the example that Nixon and Kissinger left behind of a strategy for handling hostile states. Their approach was bold, practical, and tough-minded. They tried to create a new version of containment using every form of power available to them, whether in the form of positive or negative incentives, carrots or sticks, to check and balance a dangerous adversary without resorting to either war or surrender. Whatever its flaws, this was a strategy of enduring relevance, and one that current policymakers would be well advised to consider when facing similar dangers.

The charge of exceptional immorality leveled so often against the Nixon-Kissinger foreign policy approach is also seriously overdone. In international politics, morality must surely include taking responsibility for real-world outcomes, and not simply issuing self-gratifying proclamations of principle or intent. The proposed Jackson-Vanik amendment was a case in point. Nixon and Kissinger actually secured greater levels of emigration for Soviet Jews than did Jackson-Vanik, which managed to undermine Jewish emigration and Soviet-American relations at the same time. Yet according to the conventional lexicon of American politics, the Nixon-Kissinger foreign policy approach was immoral, while Jackson-Vanik was an example of moral concern. This is the sort of morality we can do without. Nixon and Kissinger upheld traditional cold war policies and methods of containment just as the majority of America's cultural and intellectual elite turned against such policies and methods. For doing so, these two men were considered uniquely unethical. In reality, however, they used the very same tools that other cold war presidents used, including military intervention, covert operations, secret diplomacy, ties to illiberal regimes, and unilateral action, to combat the spread of Soviet influence internationally. If anything, their approach was refreshingly candid, in that they did not further claim to possess the key to social progress worldwide. Their focus was on containing the expanding influence of an authoritarian superpower while at the same time avoiding a nuclear holocaust—both of which were entirely moral as well as prudentially necessary goals. In pursuit of those goals, they were highly and sometimes excessively secretive, but in the complete absence of that secrecy, it is questionable whether they could have brought about the opening to China, détente with Moscow, arms control, the Middle East peace talks, or any of the accomplishments otherwise hailed by so many opponents of "secret diplomacy."

The single greatest obstacle to truly cooperative superpower relations in the 1970s was neither Nixon nor Kissinger nor any of their domestic critics but the Soviet Union. The Nixon-Kissinger approach assumed that the importance of domestic ideology could be downplayed in major power relations. In the case of the USSR, however, ideology mattered. Even as they appreciated a reduction in the risk of nuclear war, Soviet leaders continued to aim at the expansion of the socialist bloc into the developing world. When opportunities for expansion arose, as in Vietnam and Angola, they seized them, supporting their local allies. Kissinger hoped, in a sense, to recreate Europe's historic concert of powers at a global level, but no such concert was possible with nations whose foreign policies were powerfully shaped by Marxist-Leninist ideas. The Soviet Union continued to promote socialist revolution internationally;

the United States opposed it. As these ideological differences were once again revealed as basic during the mid-1970s, popular support for détente faded inside the United States, creating a feedback effect between political complications at home and abroad.

Domestically, Nixon attempted to create a new center-right majority in American politics, one based on active management of the nation's economy together with a culturally conservative populist appeal on issues such as law and order. The foreign policy complement to this coalition was hawkish defiance over Vietnam combined with modest strategic devolution and careful improvements in U.S. relations with China and the Soviet Union. Nixon had much success in winning support for his center-right approach at the presidential level, but even before Watergate he was unable to translate that success into a specifically Republican majority, and often seemed uninterested in doing so. His pirouettes across the political spectrum on both domestic and foreign policy issues baffled liberals and conservatives alike and left his administration without an ideological base. The Watergate scandal was crucial in undermining Nixon's foreign policy legacy, but not simply for the reasons commonly cited. Certainly, Watergate weakened the authority of the presidency, ruling out firm U.S. responses in Vietnam and Angola in 1974–75, but the liberal congressional challenge to cold war policies began before Watergate and would probably have occurred regardless. The more subtle and important long-term consequence of Watergate for U.S. diplomacy was that it tended to discredit the version of foreign policy realism associated with Nixon, not only among American opinion elites generally but among conservative Republicans in particular. To put it bluntly, Nixon's dishonorable behavior over Watergate stained everything it touched, even in cases where the relationship was tendentious and the stain undeserved. Numerous other presidents had managed and would manage to pursue successful, realistic foreign policies, framed in traditionally American terms, without embarrassing the country through revelations of shabby personal misconduct. After Watergate, however, the policy of détente, like Nixon's foreign policy realism more generally, was easier to caricature as somehow inherently immoral, since it was apparently part of a package that included mendacity and scandal. GOP conservatives had always been skeptical of détente in any case. In a quirk of history, Watergate empowered them to challenge the Nixon-Kissinger foreign policy approach altogether, and gave them good reason to do so, in order to claim back the mantle of morality from the likes of Jimmy Carter. Both parties thus hoped to bury Richard Nixon. Yet Nixon's political legacy was enduring. He was the first modern Republican to win the White House by reaching out specifically to cultural and national security conservatives across party lines—a task made easier by contemporary internal changes among Democrats. The realignment of America's political parties over social and foreign policy issues had only begun, and Nixon helped point the way.

Chapter Six

RONALD REAGAN

The Idealist as Hawk

RONALD REAGAN is the central conservative Republican leader of the past seventy years. He redefined the image of the American right and catalyzed conservative predominance in the GOP, leaving that party stronger and more coherent than at any time since the 1920s. In relation to party politics, he took the Goldwater coalition of Sun Belt conservatives and expanded on it dramatically, fusing business-oriented Republicans into a broad alliance with previously Democratic southerners, evangelicals, culturally traditionalist Catholics, and national security hawks. In relation to foreign policy, he pursued a fundamentally daring, ideologically charged strategy of aggressive anti-Communist containment and indirect rollback, leavened by considerable tactical pragmatism and flexibility. Reagan looked to use every available foreign policy instrument to pressure the Soviet Union, with the long-term goal of weakening the USSR and reducing cold war tensions on American terms. He succeeded not only by being relentless in this effort but by a willingness to negotiate from strength, and by avoiding protracted military interventions that might endanger the larger cause. In the end, Reagan changed the terms of debate in American politics, and by refusing to overreach either domestically or internationally, he ensured that Republican conservatism would continue to be a dominant political force years after he left office.

By the mid-1970s, in the aftermath of Watergate, the Republican Party was at a low point in its long history. For most Americans, the party's

main associations were either with scandal, hard times, or wealthy business interests—none of which was particularly appealing politically.
Less than a quarter of U.S. voters identified as Republican. There was
serious talk as to whether the GOP would survive another generation.
Compounding this frustration for Republican conservatives was the
feeling that the two major parties differed little on foreign policy, social,
or even economic issues. Self-described conservatives outnumbered
self-described liberals nationwide by almost two to one, yet conservatives seemed to control neither party; each party had important internal
factions preventing any clear ideological choice. For the Republicans,
northeastern moderates and liberals, epitomized by Gerald Ford's vice
president, Nelson Rockefeller, provided a counterweight to conservative
influence. For the Democrats, southern moderates and conservatives
provided a similar counterweight to liberal influence. Indeed, there were
more self-identified conservative Democrats than conservative Republicans in America in 1976. On social issues such as abortion, both parties
were internally divided, in Congress and among the electorate. On foreign policy and defense there was similar confusion, as the Democrats
still had a significant hawkish faction, while Republican administrations
pursued détente with major Communist powers. The presidential election of 1976, featuring two relatively moderate candidates, confirmed
that policy differences between the two parties were not great and that
elections like those of 1964 or 1972 might have been exceptional. Leading activists on the right such as William Rusher argued for the creation
of a new third party, based on a clear conservative platform, but they
had little success. Nor were they able to capture the GOP in 1976. Yet
there were numerous subtle and long-term factors working in their
favor, and within five years the situation would be radically different,
with energized conservatives dominating the Republican Party, the Senate, the White House, the political agenda, and the nation's foreign policy. At the head of that transformation was the apparently improbable
figure of Ronald Reagan.[1]

Reagan was born in small-town Illinois in 1911. His mother was a
serene, religious woman, his father a garrulous shoe salesman with a
drinking problem. Reagan was shy as a child, developing into a genial,
popular, handsome young man while retaining a certain emotional de-

tachment from those around him. Industrious and ambitious, he worked as a radio sports announcer in Iowa during the Great Depression before moving to California to seek his fortune in the movie industry. Signing on with Warner Brothers in 1937, he became a dependable and well-liked actor who helped make training films for the Army Air Corps during World War II. Politically, throughout the 1930s and 1940s he was a New Deal Democrat and a fan of Franklin Roosevelt. Reagan was made president of the Screen Actors Guild (SAG) in 1947, an experience that taught him several things. As a union leader, he became an effective negotiator who typically started from a demanding position but then bargained and compromised as necessary, preferring half a loaf to none. He was surprised to learn the lengths to which American Communists would go in their attempts to influence labor unions within the entertainment industry, for example in physically threatening him, an experience that helped turn him into a visceral anti-Communist. His time in Hollywood also gave him skill in communication and a worldly success and self-confidence predating any political career, all of which would prove very useful. In 1954 he began working as a spokesman for General Electric on television as well as in person, meeting with workers and management all around the country. His contact with the business sector and his autodidactic reading during this portion of his life confirmed in him a growing conservatism on economic matters. Reagan became convinced that government regulation, taxes, and spending were crowding out free enterprise, a crowding that he felt personally as he moved into the highest income percentile, where taxes were indeed very high at the time. He cultivated a set address that he delivered in his visits to GE plants nationwide, warning of the dangers of government planning and extolling the benefits of the private sector. By the early 1960s Reagan's speeches had grown so explicitly political that he and GE parted ways. He became, as it were, a leading conservative activist in the state of California, finally switching his party affiliation to the GOP in 1962. During the U.S. presidential campaign two years later, Reagan was asked to deliver a nationally televised address on behalf of Republican candidate Barry Goldwater. In that speech, which he had in effect been practicing for a decade, Reagan warned of the twin danger to American traditions of individual freedom from big government at home and communism

From the mid-1960s onward, Reagan was regularly mentioned as a possible GOP presidential candidate. He made a brief run in 1968, and turned out to be Nixon's most formidable opponent, but by his own admission Reagan was not yet fully ready, and the party's now crucial bloc of southern conservatives backed Nixon instead. By the time Reagan stepped down as governor of California at the beginning of 1975, circumstances were very different. Watergate had led to the accession of Gerald Ford, a president whom Reagan (wrongly) dismissed as a lightweight, a caretaker, and a creature of the despised Richard Nixon. Sensing Ford's vulnerability, Reagan decided to challenge him for the GOP presidential nomination. To do so against a sitting president was remarkably bold, but Ford had certain real political weaknesses, since many Americans shared Reagan's impressions of him. The former California governor, moreover, had the significant advantage that he was already the leading national spokesman for a clear message of uncompromising conservatism on social, economic, and foreign policy issues within a party that was largely and increasingly conservative at its base. Reagan therefore initially led Ford in Republican primary polls, but got off to a poor start by stumbling in his presentation on economic details. Ford's narrow but surprising win in the 1976 New Hampshire primary rescued his candidacy and gave him subsequent momentum, especially as he could count on the benefits of incumbency. Reagan fought back in North Carolina and Texas by hitting on themes of American nationalism in relation to foreign policy. Specifically, he attacked Ford's proposal to hand control of the Panama Canal over to Panama, saying that "we bought it, we paid for it, we built it, it's ours and we intend to keep it." More generally, he attacked the Ford-Kissinger policy of détente as an unprincipled sellout of Eastern Europe's "captive nations," characterized arms control with Moscow as futile, and argued for significant increases in defense spending to match the Soviet military's own long-term buildup. These foreign policy and national security criticisms very much resonated among GOP conservatives, leading Reagan to a dramatic comeback and a series of southern primary victories. He continued to win the support of grassroots party conservatives, particularly in the South and West; Ford, on the other hand, won party leaders, moderates, and northeasterners, as well as the critical swing votes of many fellow midwestern conservatives. The two candidates battled their way to the Republican Convention in a close, hard-fought contest that Reagan barely lost. He and his supporters were bitterly disappointed, but in fact it was one of the most successful and propitious losses in modern American politics. Reagan's delegates managed to pull the 1976 Republican Convention, and indeed the Ford administration, significantly to the right on a variety of issues, including foreign policy, and the GOP establishment was once again put on notice that Sun Belt conservatives were a powerful and growing force in the Republican Party. Reagan himself had made an impressive showing, ending with an emotional appeal to GOP delegates at the summer convention and emerging as the obvious favorite for 1980. Indeed, had he actually won the nomination in 1976, he might very well have failed politically, either against Carter that fall or in the sense that even as president, Reagan would have been forced to govern the country in the extremely difficult circumstances of the late 1970s. As it was, that bad hand of cards was dealt to Georgia's Democratic governor Jimmy Carter, a hand he in turn played badly.[4]

To some extent, Carter had difficulty in establishing a coherent foreign policy of any kind. His advisers were deeply divided in their fundamental assumptions, and he frequently seemed internally ambivalent as well. Yet insofar as Carter had a clear international agenda, he was arguably the only U.S. president to try to break from cold war assumptions while the cold war still continued. Particularly during his first year in office, he called for a new approach emphasizing human rights, international organizations, global poverty, energy, and interdependence. Carter made modest cuts in defense spending and canceled the production of both the B-1 bomber and the so-called neutron bomb in 1977–78. He negotiated a second Strategic Arms Limitation Treaty (SALT II) with the Soviet Union, following on the earlier 1972 accord. He hoped for the continuation of détente, while criticizing Moscow on human rights. In relation to America's allies in the developing world, he attempted to isolate the regional sources of conflict and address them free from what he called "the inordinate fear of Communism." This approach bore fruit in some cases, notably in the Middle East, where Carter mediated the historic Camp David peace agreement between Israel and Egypt. The same approach also led him to the conclusive negotiation of a set of treaties over the Panama Canal. In other cases, however, Carter's desire to promote democratic human rights and downplay anti-American radicalism actually backfired, as in Nicaragua and Iran, where admittedly rotten but existing U.S. allies were half-heartedly pressured and inadvertently destabilized rather than simply supported in the face of violent domestic challenges. Soviet leaders, for their part, did not know quite what to make of Carter. They very much resented his emphasis on human rights and his early, amateurish proposals on arms control but continued to believe that détente could be maintained alongside the careful advancement of the socialist bloc within the developing world. As it became clearer to Carter that Soviet leaders had not renounced the latter goal, for example in relation to the Horn of Africa, he grew increasingly uncertain over his initial foreign policy approach and more open to arguments from his relatively hawkish national security adviser Zbigniew Brzezinski. International complications to Carter's early agenda were matched in the United States by fierce and growing criticism from the right.[5]

Conservative critiques of Carter's foreign policy came from several directions. First was the "New Right," a distinct set of lobby groups and individuals that developed in the mid- to late 1970s committed to a different form of conservative politics that focused on social populism, anti-establishment resentments, and American nationalism rather than on traditional fiscal austerity or strict party loyalty. Leading New Right figures and organizations included Richard Viguerie, Howard Phillips, Terry Dolan, Paul Weyrich, the Conservative Caucus, the Committee for the Survival of a Free Congress, and the National Conservative Political Action Committee. These groups used innovative direct mail techniques to raise money and build grassroots pressure on contemporary hot-button issues on the theory, as stated by Terry Dolan, that "the shriller you are, the easier it is to raise funds." One such set of issues was in the area of U.S. foreign and national security policy, where the New Right embraced a nationalistic stance opposing any erosion of America's international or military position. New Right lobbies played a central role in 1977–78 fighting against the ratification of Carter's Panama Canal treaties. Opinion polls revealed that a majority of the American public was not enamored of the idea of handing back control of the Canal Zone to Panama. To many in the United States, that canal seemed to symbolize America's twentieth-century achievements, just as its loss could symbolize American retreat and decline. New Right advocates and organizations seized the issue and led a concerted campaign against the canal treaties. These treaties were particularly unpopular among conservatives in the South and West. Carter fought back on the Panama Canal issue with focus and determination. In doing so, he had the approval of the nation's foreign policy establishment and of political moderates in both parties, including, crucially, Senate minority leader Howard Baker (R-TN). The canal treaties even gained the support of certain leading foreign policy hawks such as William F. Buckley, convinced as he was of the need to meet the aspirations of the Panamanian people for self-determination. Treaty reservations leaving the United States the right to defend the Canal Zone were enough to win the Senate's approval in 1978 by a single vote above the necessary two-thirds. The outcome was a genuine achievement for Carter, but in political terms it was something of a pyrrhic victory, since it empowered the New Right organizationally, ate up the president's political capital on foreign policy matters, and bolstered his image as an international accommodationist rather than a tough-minded steward of American interests. The New Right targeted numerous congressional liberals in both parties in the midterm elections of 1978, pointing, among other things, to the liberals' support for the canal "giveaway." While Panama was only one issue among many in those midterms, it helped lead to the defeat of several liberals and the election of more conservative candidates, a trend that augured badly for Carter.[6]

A second and more powerful critique of Carter's foreign policy was leveled against his overall approach on arms control, cold war competition, and U.S.-Soviet relations. Numerous national security hawks in both parties were deeply disturbed by existing policies of détente even before 1976. Only days after Carter's election in November of that year, a leading group of such hawks formed the Committee on the Present Danger (CPD) to organize and make their case. The CPD has often been described as a neoconservative lobby. It would be more precise to say that the committee's most important members, such as Paul Nitze and

Eugene Rostow, were establishment cold war Democrats with years of experience and credibility in U.S. national security policy, and that they were disturbed by unfavorable international trends in the 1970s as well as by the dovish foreign policy drift of their own party since 1968. Other notable CPD members included hawkish anti-Communist academics and intellectuals such as Jeane Kirkpatrick, Richard Pipes, and Norman Podhoretz, most of whom were still Democrats during the late 1970s. They were joined by traditional Republican cold warriors. In this sense, the CPD acted as a meeting point for a wide range of foreign policy hawks from both parties, new and old. Their one common trait was that they sought a return to the vigorous policies of anti-Communist containment pursued by Democratic and Republican presidents prior to the fiasco in Vietnam. CPD members worried that the United States had lost the nerve to compete with the USSR internationally. They argued that the Soviet Union had been building up its military power and worldwide reach since the mid-1960s, while the United States mistakenly scaled back and retrenched. The USSR possessed, for example, both a blue-water navy and multiple new Third World alliances that had not existed only a few years before. The CPD called for increases in U.S. defense spending to match the Soviet Union's. Beyond that, it argued for an entirely different mindset, one that recognized the continuing and deadly threat from the USSR as a one-party dictatorship and military superpower bent on global domination and possessed of a revolutionary ideology. CPD members focused special attention on SALT II. Specifically, they argued that SALT II would entrench existing strategic imbalances in favor of the Soviet Union and allow for the possibility of a nuclear first strike by Moscow against the United States. The CPD pointed out that Soviet leaders thought of nuclear warfare differently from Americans: while the loss of millions of compatriot civilians might be unthinkable in Washington, it was not unthinkable in Moscow, where massive civilian defense and anti-ballistic-missile projects went ahead regardless of treaty restrictions. The nightmare scenario was therefore one in which the United States or its allies would be vulnerable to nuclear blackmail by a militarily superior Soviet Union.

Contrary to CPD claims, the prospect of retaliation by invulnerable U.S. submarine-launched missiles made a nuclear first strike profoundly unappealing to Moscow, but in many other ways the CPD was essentially right about Soviet intentions and capabilities. Committee members made their case against SALT II in a wide range of venues, including journals, newspapers, magazines, and television, and their arguments had an impact, especially as the general public grew more alarmed over the apparent decline in America's relative international and military position. By the time the Senate opened hearings on SALT II in the summer of 1979, the treaty was headed for trouble, as leading GOP moderates such as Howard Baker leaned against it. Carter's whole foreign policy approach simultaneously came under sharp criticism from neoconservative intellectuals, who acted as the elite shock troops of American anticommunism by the late 1970s, still hoping for the arrival of a hawkish Democrat as president. One such intellectual, Jeane Kirkpatrick, made a particularly influential case against Carter's foreign policy, saying in a widely read 1979 *Commentary* article that the administration had inadvertently strengthened undemocratic anti-American radicals in countries such as Nicaragua and Iran by pressuring allied regimes on issues of democracy and human rights. What Carter failed to realize, she suggested, in conducting the cold war struggle against Moscow, was that authoritarian regimes on the right could and did sometimes evolve into liberal democracies without threatening vital U.S. interests. Marxist-Leninist dictatorships, on the other hand, like the totalitarian Nazi regime, not only were implacably hostile toward the United States but incapable of internal reform, possessing as they did a true monopoly of power over both state and civil society. The danger for liberal Americans was therefore in mistaking and encouraging any social change in friendly but authoritarian states as necessarily for the better. As Kirkpatrick put it, referring to Carter's policies of democracy promotion, "hurried efforts to force complex and unfamiliar political practices on societies lacking the requisite political culture . . . not only fail to produce the desired outcomes; if they are undertaken at a time when the traditional regime is under attack, they actually facilitate the job of the insurgents."[7]

Ronald Reagan was in full agreement with the various criticisms made of Carter, SALT II, and détente by members of the CPD; in fact, he served on the CPD's executive board. In a series of radio addresses during the mid- to late 1970s, as he prepared for another run at the presidency, Reagan presented the conservative foreign policy case to the listening public in his usual folksy manner, describing détente as "what a farmer has with his turkey—until Thanksgiving Day." Like other fervent national security hawks at the time, he warned of the dangers of appeasement, nuclear blackmail, U.S. defense cuts, parchment guarantees, Soviet expansionism, and a potential first strike against the United States. He called for the restoration of U.S. "strategic superiority" and a much more aggressive set of foreign and defense policies against the Soviet Union, including unequivocal support for anti-Communist allies overseas. Yet Reagan also revealed in these radio addresses, and in other speeches, letters, and private conversations, a perspective that was distinctly his own. For one thing, Reagan simply hated nuclear weapons and wanted to see them eventually abolished. He feared that the cold war might lead to a nuclear holocaust and was appalled by the notion that America's national security rested on the doctrine of mutually assured destruction, a doctrine he called "the craziest thing I ever heard of." Just as important, Reagan was convinced that Soviet communism could not last as a viable socioeconomic system, that it was fundamentally brittle and doomed, "a form of insanity," as he put it, "a temporary aberration which will one day disappear from the earth" since it failed to meet a variety of natural human needs. Indeed, Reagan had great confidence in the ability of his country's free market system to outperform the USSR economically, so long as America's market power was leveraged militarily: "the Soviet Union cannot possibly match us in an arms race," he declared. Reagan therefore recommended well before 1980 that the United States build up its armed forces energetically, precisely in order to pressure the Soviet Union into deep, mutual arms reductions on terms favorable to the United States, thus reducing the danger of nuclear war. As he told his friend Richard Allen in 1977, Reagan's ultimate goal was neither indefinite coexistence nor indefinite struggle with the USSR, but rather "we win and they lose." In arguing this particular combination of themes during the 1970s, Reagan was virtually alone. Still, he was obviously in deep sympathy with more conventional GOP foreign policy hawks, who recognized that he was by far their most like-minded and charismatic national spokesmen.[8]

Reagan's path to the presidency also benefited from the rise of various conservative movements, ideas and organizations during the mid- to late 1970s, organizations motivated primarily by concern over domestic issues. Social conservatives, disaffected with liberal national trends on issues such as abortion, prayer in schools, and women in the workplace, organized into new groups with genuine grassroots appeal. The special role of New Right lobbies in this regard has already been mentioned. Another example of mobilized social conservatism was Phyllis Schlafly's Eagle Forum, an organization that had remarkable impact in stalling and eventually defeating the proposed equal rights amendment. The most consequential such development in the long run was the political mobilization of evangelical Protestants behind conservative social positions. Carter did very well electorally with evangelical voters in 1976, but many were quickly alienated from his administration on a range of issues, notably by the threatened removal of tax exemptions from certain private Christian schools in 1978. The following year, consequently, with the help of New Right activists, Jerry Falwell founded the Moral Majority, an organization committed to registering and turning out evangelical voters on behalf of socially conservative candidates. Economic issues also provided grist for the new conservatism of the late 1970s. Alarmed by long-term trends in favor of ever-expanding government spending, taxes, and regulation, American business interests mobilized politically through the Chamber of Commerce and the National Association of Manufacturers on behalf of tax cuts, deregulation, and limited expenditures. Nor were such concerns confined to large corporate interests. With taxes high and inflation in the double digits, ordinary small property owners, taxpayers, and homeowners were deeply dissatisfied with national economic developments and open to conservative solutions. Such solutions were offered through an assortment of conservative economic ideas, newly plausible under the circumstances: monetarism, public choice theory, and supply-side economics, all championed by credible, articulate public spokesmen such as Milton Friedman. The 1978 California tax revolt manifested in Proposition 13 was a harbinger of things to come, in that a majority of the state's voters supported strict limitations on taxes. Congress began to move in a similar direction, toward tax cuts, at about the same time. All these conservative issues, ideas, and organizations, moreover, received intellectual and institutional support and coordination from the creation and expansion of think tanks on the right, such as the Heritage Foundation. These research institutions were in turn financed by individual and corporate sponsors, by wealthy conservatives such as Joseph Coors, and by nonprofits such as the Richardson Foundation, the John M. Olin Foundation, and the Scaife Foundation. Irving Kristol played a particularly important role in brokering targeted fundraising efforts on behalf of conservative ideas and institutions, eventually taking a post himself at the American Enterprise Institute. Hence, there was already a deep, wide-ranging network of new social, economic, and intellectual organizations on the right, helping to promote conservative causes in the country, Congress, and the Republican Party, even before Ronald Reagan entered the White House.[9]

Reagan was well aware of the newly mobilized strength and political potential of social as well as economic conservatives, and he looked self-consciously to assemble them into a winning coalition. An address that he gave to the Conservative Political Action Conference in February 1977 was indicative of his goals. In that address, he spoke of a "new, lasting majority" that would reach out to culturally conservative "blue-collar, ethnic and religious groups . . . traditionally associated with the Democratic Party" and "combine the two major segments contemporary American conservatism into one politically effective whole." Republicans would have to shed their "country club-big business image" and make "room for the man and the woman in the factories, for the farmer, for the cop on the beat," embrace clear conservative principles, and "communicate those principles to the American people in language they understand." Interestingly, Reagan took it for granted in this speech that social and economic conservatives would agree on foreign policy goals, including a fierce anti-Communism and "maintaining a superior national defense, second to none."[10]

One final factor that worked in Reagan's favor during the mid- to late 1970s was the rightward trend in the congressional Republican Party. Entering GOP senators and congressmen tended to be more conservative than retiring ones, on social and foreign policy as well as economic issues. Indeed, New Right activists made a point by 1978 of targeting liberal Republicans for defeat in party primaries, sometimes with striking success. Incoming GOP representatives also frequently hailed from southern and western states; their numerical weight in the Republican caucus continued to grow, and they tended to be more sharply conservative than their northeastern colleagues. The ongoing rise of the Sun Belt in the country and in the GOP pulled the party farther right and made it the primary electoral vessel for some of the nation's fastest expanding economic and political interests. The overall result was that conservatives had already achieved practical dominance of the Republican Party before Reagan announced his 1980 run for the White House. The only serious interparty debate was between relatively moderate, typically northeastern or midwestern conservatives like Gerald Ford and more hard-line Sun Belt conservatives like Reagan. Genuinely left-of-center liberals were disappearing as a major force in the GOP, despite their high prolife and storied traditions.[11]

The Carter administration entered its final period of crisis in the closing weeks of 1979 as U.S. hostages were taken in Iran. Initially, the American public rallied to Carter's side over the hostage crisis, helping him to fend off a serious primary challenge for the Democratic presidential nomination from liberal champion Senator Edward Kennedy (D-MA.) As the crisis wore on, however, month after month, it reinforced the impression of Carter as a weak foreign policy leader, particularly after a disastrous hostage rescue attempt in April 1980. The president's problems were further compounded by the Soviet invasion of Afghanistan at the end of 1979. Carter himself described this invasion as the most serious threat to world peace since World War II, and declared that it opened his eyes to the continuing threat from the USSR. He proceeded to ratchet up a new anti-Soviet foreign policy line that included increased defense spending, the pulling of SALT II from consideration by the Senate, the early provision of covert aid to anti-Communist forces in Afghanistan and Nicaragua, and the enunciation of the Carter Doctrine, under which the United States pledged to defend Persian Gulf states from any threat of Soviet aggression. Yet Carter's late-term conversion to cold war verities was somewhat unconvincing, and in political terms it lent fresh credibility to the arguments that anti-Communist hawks like Reagan had been making all along.

Reagan announced his candidacy for the presidency in 1979 and was the presumed Republican front-runner as the leader of the party's now dominant conservative faction. His most plausible potential challengers for the GOP nomination—former president Gerald Ford, Tennessee senator Howard Baker, former Texas governor and treasury secretary John Connally, Illinois representative John Anderson, and former Texas representative and CIA director George H. W. Bush—were all based to a greater or lesser extent in the more moderate wing of the party, and they all faced the same dilemma of how to rally opposition to Reagan while still winning conservative support. Connally's well-financed but idiosyncratic campaign flamed out quickly, as did the respected Baker's, and Ford never chose to enter the race. Instead, it was Bush who became the leading alternative to Reagan among GOP moderates, after a surprise victory in the Iowa caucus. Bush went on to win several northeastern and midwestern states but could not overcome Reagan's underlying strength among conservative southern and western Republicans. John Anderson made an even more lasting run than Bush, winning the support of GOP liberals and deciding in the end to run for president as an independent against both Reagan and Carter. The Republican National Convention that summer was more a coronation than a fight. Conservative ideas had clearly won out inside the party, on issues ranging from national defense to taxes to abortion. Reagan's acceptance speech to GOP delegates offered broad, uplifting themes of national economic, social, and military renewal without abandoning conservative positions on specific issues. The nominee struck a conciliatory tone toward party moderates and made considerable effort to reach out to them, notably by naming Bush as his vice-presidential running mate. Republicans left the 1980 convention unified and confident of victory in November.[12]

In a sense, one might have expected Reagan to lose in 1980, since he was correctly perceived as considerably to the right of center by a majority of voters in a country where most place themselves roughly in the middle ideologically. Certainly Carter expected to be able to defeat Reagan as an aging former actor and "extreme" right-winger prone to verbal gaffes, but several important factors interfered with the incumbent president's expectations. First, Carter himself was perceived by the fall of 1980 as equally or even more distant, to the left, from the average voter's

own positions on numerous issues, including defense spending, inflation, busing, affirmative action, the death penalty, government regulation, taxes, and prayer in schools. On some of these issues, such as defense spending, the American public had moved noticeably rightward
since the mid-1970s; on others, such as busing and prayer in schools,
the conservative position had long been popular with a majority of
voters. The Democratic Party's continued leftward movement on social
issues, in particular, as evidenced by the party's 1980 convention platform, helped to reinforce the ideological distance between the Democrats' liberal leadership and elements of its own white working-class
base. Second, Carter was simply viewed by most Americans as a failed
president in 1980, above all because of poor economic conditions and
regardless of ideology. With the nation's economy mired in an unhappy
state of high unemployment, high interest rates, and high inflation simultaneously, the Democrats lost their usual trump card as the party
best able to protect the jobs and pocketbooks of working Americans. Third, Reagan was an attractive candidate on the stump, offering a
clear, hopeful message of strong leadership, definite policy change, and
soaring optimism, as against Carter's increasingly dour presentation. A
televised presidential debate between the two major candidates that
October helped lay to rest certain lingering doubts about Reagan, as he
presented himself in a calm, reasonable, self-assured manner, asking
voters the fundamental question as to whether they were better off under
Carter as president. Foreign policy entered into the election in a number
of contradictory ways, and not always to Reagan's benefit. Many Americans were genuinely concerned that as president he would increase the
risk of war, a concern that Carter stressed to great advantage. At the
same time, however, a majority of voters believed that Reagan would do
better than Carter at strengthening U.S. armed forces and bolstering respect for the United States overseas, a theme that carried particular res-
onance in the wake of the sometimes humiliating foreign policy crises of
1979–80. An initially promising and trumpeted but ultimately fruitless
burst of presidential activity surrounding the Iran hostage negotiations
during the final days of the campaign only served to remind voters of
their exasperation with that demeaning episode, and helped turn the
final election results against Carter. In the end, Reagan won every state

in the union except Georgia, Minnesota, Hawaii, West Virginia, Maryland, and Rhode Island. He held on to moderate Republicans, inspired the GOP's right wing, and won over independents while securing the support of a remarkable 41 percent of self-described conservative Democrats nationwide. With his distinct mantra of a restored national defense, unabashed patriotism, economic recovery, and conservative social values, Reagan ran particularly strong among white southern Democrats and was also very competitive with culturally traditionalist northern Catholics in working-class and lower-middle-class neighborhoods. John Anderson, for his part, received over 6 percent of the vote, doing especially well among young bicoastal, liberal, and independent college-educated professionals. At the congressional level, Republicans took control of the Senate for the first time in decades and made major gains in the House of Representatives. The New Right and its evangelical allies played an important role at the margins in several GOP congressional victories, as well as in mobilizing socially conservative voters for Reagan on key issues such as abortion. While the overall election results did not necessarily represent any sudden, comprehensive national realignment in favor of the Republican Party, they could certainly be interpreted as a mandate to revive the nation's economic and military strength on the part of a new president, who after all had campaigned on a remarkably ideological platform.[13]

Foreign policy was only one of several major concerns to the new president. As chief executive, Reagan presided over a very broad political coalition. Even his conservative base of support was itself composed of a diverse array of constituencies. The coalition led by Reagan included traditional Republicans, small-town midwesterners, evangelical Protestants, pro-life Catholics, small businessmen, farmers, populists, libertarians, nationalists, New Right activists, white southerners, neoconservative intellectuals, former segregationists, major corporate interests, Wall Street types, suburbanite professionals, right-wing students, and independents, along with numerous hawkish or culturally conservative Democrats. Needless to say, such a coalition contained multiple internal tensions. For example, working-class Catholics might appreciate Reagan's moral traditionalism but shy away from his proposed budget cuts. Northeastern fiscal conservatives might appreciate Reagan's proposed budget cuts but worry about his unyielding policies on arms control. In essence, the Reagan coalition really addressed three separate policy dimensions: economic, social, and international. Some key constituencies and congressional representatives were conservative on one or two dimensions, but not all three. In fact, few Americans in 1981 were staunchly conservative on all social, economic, and foreign policy issues, consistently. Yet Reagan had considerable success in holding his center-right coalition together, both in Congress and in the country. He did it in several ways. He offered valued symbolic or policy rewards to core factions. He began from an audacious, right-wing starting point on the issues, while showing considerable practicality and adaptability in implementation. He won credit for being a leader of conviction, while also being sufficiently pragmatic to win over political moderates. And he presided over his coalition with a keen sense of timing, dexterity, and personal charisma. A leading illustration of Reagan at his most effective was the budget debate of 1981. The president proposed deep tax cuts that year, both as part of a conservative economic agenda and to help stimulate the economy out of recession. Ideally, he would have also preferred to balance the budget, but he found radical cuts in domestic social spending to be politically impossible, and was furthermore committed to a significant increase in military expenditure. He therefore bargained and consulted with Congress, secured the tax cuts and the defense increase, while accepting existing political constraints on domestic spending cuts—a combination that obviously led to increased deficits. At the same time, he avoided controversial social legislation or direct military action abroad that might endanger his domestic economic program. Economic conservatives liked the tax cuts. Foreign policy conservatives liked the defense increase. Polls showed that most Americans supported both measures. Reagan secured an impressive, momentum-building political victory with his base, Congress, and the broader public simultaneously. Social conservatives received little substantively in 1981 but continued to favor Reagan, out of an understanding that he shared their goals and led a broad coalition effort. Ideological purists of various types found the continued high levels of social spending and resulting budget deficits, the careful avoidance of military entanglements, and the limited legislative action on social issues to be unacceptable, but the purists missed the point: Reagan had revealed his true priorities and accomplished most of what he wanted in 1981, both politically and in terms of policy substance, without breaking his coalition apart.[14]

Like every president, Reagan had his own unique style for directing foreign policy. A common caricature at the time was that he was little more than the creature of his handlers, likable enough but unintelligent and not really in command: an "amiable dunce," in the words of Clark Clifford. Another contemporary caricature was that he was a dangerously purist right-wing ideologue—difficult to envision, admittedly, if he was simply the unthinking creature of other, stronger-willed men. In any case, neither of these cartoon images was really true. The evidence of Reagan's copious letters written before and during his presidency to critics and supporters alike reveal a thoughtful, earnest, diligent author who knows his own mind and is possessed of considerable common sense. Certainly, Reagan's manner as president was to set broad policy goals, while usually leaving the detailed implementation to his subordinates. Sometimes his described goals were so broad that his advisers were unclear as to his precise wishes. This in turn encouraged heated, even public arguments over foreign policy between leading officials, notably after 1982 between Secretary of Defense Caspar Weinberger and Secretary of State George Shultz on issues such as arms control and military intervention. Reagan disliked bureaucratic intrigue among his advisers but had little taste for policing their squabbles or confronting them personally. He frequently failed to manage his subordinates or monitor policy implementation in a sufficiently vigorous fashion. Yet this failing was more than made up for by Reagan's good qualities as a leader. He offered an unusually compelling, unclouded, overall policy vision that rallied and inspired his supporters and advisers. Whatever their other differences, Reagan's subordinates shared his overarching conservative cold war internationalism. He was the administration's best public spokesman, a winning and persuasive voice on behalf of its basic priorities. He was capable and tenacious in negotiation. He was politically shrewd, with an excellent feeling for U.S. public opinion, and furthermore willing and able to work his congressional counterparts with persuasion, charm, arm-twisting or bargaining, as necessary. In crises he was careful, self-possessed, and ready to persevere after making a decision. In fact, Reagan was often inclined, for better or worse, to defy the collective wisdom of existing bureaucratic, congressional, popular, or allied recommendations to pursue a controversial or unconventional path that he believed right. A short list of such convictions would include his positions on missile defense, aid to the Contras, the underlying weakness of the Soviet Union, and deep reductions in nuclear arms. On the major foreign policy decisions of his administration, he was clearly the one in charge. Those who thought to play that role themselves—such as his first secretary of state, Alexander Haig—were soon removed from influence. And while Reagan started from a set of genuine, passionately held core beliefs regarding the proper course of American diplomacy, he was noticeably unwilling to risk massive policy or political failure for the sake of strict ideological purity. In other words, he was generally businesslike and flexible in a tactical sense, in pursuit of a fundamentally daring, ideologically charged foreign policy strategy combining elements of indirect rollback with aggressive anti-Communist containment. That strategy took time to fully develop, but from the very first year of the new administration, several components were visible.[15]

First, Reagan launched an accelerated U.S. military buildup. This entailed increased expenditures on weapons systems such as the MX intercontinental ballistic missile, Trident submarines, and the B-1 bomber; research and development on new systems such as the Trident II submarine–launched missile and the B-2 bomber; greater spending on pay, readiness, mobility, airlift, and amphibious capabilities; qualitative improvements in military training and doctrine; and quantitative improvements in the sheer number of ships, tanks, aircraft, and personnel available. The purpose of this buildup, in Reagan's mind, was not only to reassure allies and deter the Soviet Union but to restore U.S. diplomatic leverage with Moscow down the road. Reagan had little difficulty in securing major increases in military spending from Congress during his first year in office, popular as such increases were at the time, both with the general public and congressional Republicans, and with a crucial faction of hawkish, mostly southern Democrats. Such expenditures were obviously in tension with the administration's other declared fiscal priorities, such as a balanced budget, but Reagan was unwilling to cut back in this area, saying that "defense is not a budget issue. You spend what you need."[16]

Second, Reagan offered indirect U.S. military aid, weapons, training, and logistics to anti-Communist insurgents in Nicaragua and Afghanistan. CIA director William Casey was an especially energetic advocate of such aid, arguing that it could impose heavy costs on the Soviet bloc at relatively little expense to the United States. Support for Afghanistan's mujahideen against an occupying Soviet army was relatively uncontroversial in the United States, and tended to increase each year. Nicaragua was much trickier, politically. Reagan and his subordinates worried that the Sandinistas were for all practical purposes a new Soviet ally in America's backyard, providing support to local Marxist revolutionaries such as El Salvador's Farabundo Marti National Liberation Front (FMLN). Indeed, Secretary of State Al Haig argued in 1981 for a U.S. naval blockade of Havana to "go to the source" and intercept Cuban supplies flowing to the Sandinistas, saying "give me the word and I'll make that island a fucking parking lot." Reagan was profoundly leery of any such direct action against Cuba or Nicaragua, as were his military and political advisers, but he was determined to frustrate anti-American forces in the region, and to that end began supplying covert U.S. aid to counterrevolutionary "Contras" inside Nicaragua. As details regarding U.S. Contra aid leaked to the press, it created serious controversy. Liberals in Congress, the media, and the academy argued, predictably and with great fervor, that the Sandinistas were not really Soviet allies but instead independent social progressives, that the real source of trouble in Central America was not communism but poverty, political oppression, and mistaken U.S. policies, that the Contras were nothing but a disgraceful bunch of thugs, and that the administration's military entanglements in the region could easily turn into another Vietnam. The majority of the American public was uncertain about most of these points but knew that it opposed "another Vietnam," and consequently tended to be deeply skeptical toward any U.S. military intervention whatsoever in Central America, even in the form of indirect or covert aid. This popular skepticism lent political weight to liberal criticisms, and so began a lengthy, seesaw battle between leading Democrats and the administration over U.S. Contra policy, with congressional moderates in both parties playing a pivotal role from case to case. By the end of 1984, under the Boland amendments, Congress specifically forbade the Pentagon or any U.S. intelligence agencies from providing support to paramilitary activities inside Nicaragua. The Reagan administration had more immediate success in helping to prevent the FMLN and its allies from winning El Salvador's civil war.[17]

Third, Reagan downplayed the necessity of any immediate superpower arms control agreement, arguing that the United States and its allies needed to bolster their defenses first. Administration officials were particularly concerned that recently deployed Soviet SS-20 theater-range missiles undermined the credibility of America's nuclear deterrent in Europe. Allied NATO governments shared this concern, and for that very reason had already agreed in 1979 to host the deployment of U.S. Pershing II intermediate-range missiles and Tomahawk cruise missiles. Reagan was determined to go ahead with the planned deployment of the so-called Euromissiles and to avoid any unfavorable arms control commitments in the meantime, a determination that alarmed large segments of European and American public opinion as needlessly belligerent. From 1981 to 1983, a nuclear freeze movement developed in the United States advocating a freeze on the production, testing, and deployment of nuclear weapons, with support from leading experts, lobbies, celebrities, House Democrats, and, if contemporary public opinion polls were to be believed, an overwhelming majority of Americans. Reagan faced strong popular, congressional, and European pressures to make some sort of positive arms control proposal to Moscow. He responded by offering that the United States and the Soviet Union both dismantle any planned or existing deployments of intermediate-range nuclear missiles in Europe, the so-called zero option. This proposal was understood all around to be distinctly favorable to the United States, since it entailed far greater cuts on the Soviet side than the American side. There was no real prospect in the early 1980s that Moscow would accept such an offer. Indeed, some of Reagan's more hard-line appointees may have liked the zero option precisely for that reason, but Reagan himself was rather unusual in that he appears from the very beginning to have wanted deep, mutual cuts in nuclear weapons after and only after the restoration of U.S. diplomatic and military leverage. In any case, he was not swayed. Desultory arms control talks over intermediate-range nuclear forces (INFs) were conducted in Geneva, with negotiating positions far apart. Soviet leaders hoped that Western peace movements would undermine support for Reagan's position. Massive rallies were held in the United States and Europe against the missile deployments and in favor of a nuclear freeze. In Europe, the popular pressure was so great as to almost break allied governments, but with the election or reelection of staunch cold war allies such as Helmut Kohl, Margaret Thatcher, and François Mitterand the alliance held, and the deployments went ahead. The Soviet Union responded by walking out of the Geneva INF talks at the end of 1983, leaving superpower relations at their lowest point in more than twenty years.[18]

Fourth, Reagan disputed Communist rule in Eastern Europe, particularly Poland, and sought to loosen Moscow's hold on the region. At the time Reagan entered office, Poland's Warsaw Pact government was facing severe challenge from the union movement Solidarity. Fearing a potential Soviet invasion, Poland's leaders imposed martial law in December 1981. Reagan was appalled by these developments but saw them as a golden opportunity to contest, delegitimize, and undermine communism in its central bailiwick, saying, "We may never get another chance like this in our lifetime." He recognized that the United States was in no position to challenge the USSR militarily in Poland, and did not want to raise false hopes to that effect. Instead, he imposed U.S. economic sanctions against Poland, warned Moscow not to invade that country, denounced Communist domination over the region, and began to provide covert aid to Solidarity with the help of American labor unions. This covert aid was provided in close coordination with the Vatican and Pope John Paul II, who as a charismatic, Polish-born pontiff offered crucial moral support to anti-Communist dissent in Eastern Europe.[19]

Fifth, and with the Polish crackdown as the immediate justification, Reagan attempted to wage economic warfare against the Soviet Union itself. Reagan was disturbed by the notion that the West had in any way subsidized the Soviet economy during the 1970s. He was particularly concerned that private firms were helping in the construction of a Soviet pipeline carrying natural gas from Siberia to various West European countries—potentially leaving those countries dangerously dependent on Soviet energy supplies, while earning much-needed hard currency for the USSR. At the same time, he believed that the Soviet Union was highly vulnerable to economic pressure because of its own internal weaknesses and malfunctions. He looked to deny Western money, trade, or technology to the Eastern bloc and, as he said at the time, to "lean on the Soviets until they go broke." To the consternation of numerous U.S. corporations and NATO allies alike, Reagan therefore shut down American participation in Soviet pipeline construction, and tried to pressure the Europeans to do the same. The pipeline issue became a protracted source of transatlantic tension. Reagan never succeeded in winning allied cooperation on this issue, and in 1983 existing pipeline sanctions were scaled back. His efforts at economic warfare, however, succeeded in several other ways. The construction of the Siberian pipeline was frustrated, hampered, and delayed through U.S. efforts. In one remarkable instance the United States even managed to supply unknowing Soviet agents with faulty technology for use in pipeline construction, leading to a massive line explosion in Siberia in 1982. Saudi Arabia was pressed to increase its daily output of oil and thereby drive down world prices, in the knowledge that this would dry up Soviet revenues from oil and gas exports—a process that actually did occur after 1985, to Moscow's great consternation. The Reagan administration also imposed during its first term other restrictions on trade, credit, and technology transfer to the USSR, with the cooperation of NATO allies in many cases, and with cumulatively painful effects on the Soviet economy.[20]

Sixth, Reagan offered a sharp rhetorical, ideological challenge to Soviet communism as a socioeconomic and political system. In a series of striking first term speeches he went far outside diplomatic niceties to question not only the morality and legitimacy but the very tenability of both the USSR and its ruling philosophy. In 1981, Reagan spoke at Notre Dame University, saying that "the West won't contain Communism, it will transcend Communism. We will not bother to renounce it, we'll dismiss it as a bizarre chapter in human history whose last pages are even now being written." In 1982, he addressed the British Parliament, neatly turning Marxist theory on its head by describing a "great revolutionary crisis" within Soviet society, "a society where productive forces are hampered by political ones," and consequently predicting a "march of freedom and democracy which will leave Marxism-Leninism on the ash heap of history." In 1983, in a speech to the National Association of Evangelicals, Reagan memorably described the USSR as an "evil empire." These speeches made plain Reagan's conviction that the Soviet regime was fundamentally immoral, dysfunctional, and doomed. Such language was also intended to throw Moscow on the defensive psychologically, to fight back in the cold war propaganda war, to rally domestic and allied support for anti-Soviet policies, to inspire political dissidents in the Eastern bloc, and to provide a positive, persuasive alternative to communism through the example of liberal democracy and open markets. The Reagan administration simultaneously increased funding on tools of public diplomacy such as Radio Free Europe and Voice of America, in order to carry the U.S. message behind the Iron Curtain. Crusading language was thus a distinct and deliberate component of the Reagan foreign policy strategy, a component the administration believed came at minimal cost.[21]

Seventh, Reagan embarked on a major effort to build a national missile defense system. The Republican Party platform had endorsed such a system in 1980. The issue remained largely dormant until March 1983, when Reagan surprised even his top advisers and took to the airwaves to announce the Strategic Defense Initiative (SDI). Immediately dubbed "Star Wars" by the media, SDI represented a startling reversal of existing U.S. policies on nuclear weapons, mutual deterrence, and arms control dating back to the 1960s. Several of his closest allies and advisers warned Reagan against such a reversal, but he was adamant in favor of missile defense, reflecting his longstanding horror at doctrines of mutual assured destruction. Reagan saw no reason to prevent the United States from at least making the effort to protect its citizens against the threat of nuclear attack, and he believed that the United States was well positioned to compete in the arena of high technology with the Soviet Union. Such competition might in turn help pressure Moscow into serious arms control negotiations. SDI also provided a way in which to undercut the political momentum of the nuclear freeze movement, since Reagan's declared goal with missile defense was to "free the world from the threat of nuclear war." Critics at home and abroad argued that missile defense was destabilizing and provocative, that it was too expensive, that it was technologically impossible, and that it violated existing treaties. This last point was a bit rich coming from the Soviet Union, which had long since been working on its own national missile defense system without fastidious concern for either the spirit or the letter of the 1972 ABM treaty. Several of the other criticisms were plausible enough individually, though less so collectively, since SDI could hardly be dangerously effectual and thoroughly ineffectual at the very same time. As Reagan said, "If it's no good how come the Russians are so upset?"[22]

All seven of these components, from increased defense spending to SDI, were part of an overall hard-line strategy by which Reagan sought to pressure, challenge, and weaken the Soviet bloc through military, political, technological, ideological, and economic competition worldwide. That strategy did not come together all at once. Its precise implementation was the subject of fierce bureaucratic struggles within the administration. Yet the documentary evidence clearly indicates that Reagan had a distinctive, coherent, self-conscious approach for waging cold war against the USSR more relentlessly than at any time since the 1950s. Of the many declassified National Security Decisions Directives pointing to such an approach during the Reagan era, two may be singled out as indicative: NSDD-32 ,"U.S. National Security Strategy," from May 1982, and NSDD-75, "U.S. Relations with the USSR," from January 1983. NSDD-32 declared that the administration's goal was "to contain and reverse the expansion of Soviet control and military presence throughout the world," to "weaken the Soviet alliance system by forcing the USSR to bear the brunt of its economic shortcomings, and to encourage long-term liberalizing and nationalist tendencies within the Soviet Union and allied countries." NSDD-75 repeated and expanded on these themes, aiming at "evolutionary change within the Soviet Union itself" and pointing to "a number of important weaknesses and vulnerabilities within the Soviet empire which the United States should exploit," for example in relation to Poland, Afghanistan, Soviet currency reserves, and the issue of human rights. In a sense these directives were a return to early cold war American strategy. They aimed at not only the containment but the rollback, where possible, of Soviet power. They imposed costs on the USSR and its allies at multiple weak points using a wide array of negative sanctions and policy instruments. They sought to ensure that "East-West economic relations do not facilitate the Soviet military buildup." They made the internal as well as external behavior of the USSR a central point of criticism and concern. They looked to use the power of nationalism "to encourage Soviet allies to distance themselves from Moscow." They asserted the "superiority of U.S. and Western values . . . over the repressive features of Soviet Communism," and they viewed the cold war as a central, defining struggle between two ways of life, inevitable given the nature of the Soviet regime. The goal here was American preponderance, reassertion, and cold war success, not military, political, or moral parity with the USSR. Moreover, Reagan played a central, active role in the formation of this approach. One need not suggest that he foresaw the exact manner of the USSR's collapse or deny that internal debates were rampant within his administration to admit that Reagan did indeed have a deliberate, overarching, and aggressive strategy for fighting the cold war, based on personal assumptions going back decades and laid out in documentation at the time.[23]

If Reagan was a genuinely intransigent anti-Communist hawk, it is worth pointing out that from the beginning, his foreign policy strategy also included important self-imposed limitations. In practice, and despite his crusading rhetoric, he was generally cautious and careful regarding direct U.S. military intervention overseas. The direct interventions that Reagan did authorize were usually brief, small-scale, likely to succeed, and popular at home; when they were not, he quietly extricated himself and the United States from unfavorable conditions. Grenada and Lebanon are the leading and contrasting examples. The small island nation of Grenada was under the leadership of pro-Cuban Prime Minister Maurice Bishop and his Marxist "New Jewel" movement when Reagan entered the White House. Bishop's government received financial assistance from Moscow and military and technical assistance from Cuba. On October 13, 1983, a violent coup from within the ruling party led to Bishop's execution along with the institution of an equally radical new government. Reagan and his leading advisers did not really know which particular leftist faction was now in charge of Grenada. They were concerned that it was in the process of becoming "a Soviet-Cuban colony," as the president put it, astride Caribbean sea-lanes to and from the Panama Canal. They looked to demonstrate American power and seize the opportunity to overthrow a local Marxist government at low cost to the United States. They also saw the possibility of a dangerous hostage situation involving the several hundred U.S. medical students living in Grenada. Reagan therefore decided on an American invasion to topple Grenada's new junta and secure the safety of U.S. citizens. The latter point was particularly stressed in the president's public address explaining the invasion, which took place suddenly on October 25 amid considerable secrecy, and eventually involved some six to seven thousand U.S. troops. Much of the American public was initially rather puzzled and wary of U.S. intervention, but after its rapid success—and with the relief of American students vividly demonstrated on national television—rallied to Reagan's decision. Congressional Democratic leaders such as Speaker of the House Tip O'Neill raised critical questions and grumbled that they had not been seriously consulted, which was true, but in the wake of obvious popular support for the invasion most of them dropped the issue. Overseas, the invasion was extremely unpopular, as even the closest U.S. allies, such as Britain's Margaret Thatcher, condemned it, but the support of the Organization of Eastern Caribbean States gave Reagan some limited international legitimacy. Operationally, the invasion was a "sloppy success," in the words of General Colin Powell, revealing as it did real problems with intelligence and coordination among U.S. armed services. In any case, the administration and its supporters were happy to have pulled off the direct rollback of a Marxist regime, however small, and the majority of the American public seemed to appreciate the short, sharp, and effective use of U.S. military power.[24]

Lebanon was plagued throughout the 1980s by a many-sided civil war that involved government forces, the Palestinian Liberation Organization (PLO), and Christian, Shiite, and Sunni militias. By July 1982, Syria and Israel had each intervened directly and militarily to support their respective Lebanese allies. Reagan saw Syrian involvement as an indirect extension of Soviet influence in the region and was inclined toward U.S. intervention in Lebanon to counteract such influence. The prospect of placing the American military directly in Lebanon was vigorously criticized by the Joint Chiefs of Staff, Secretary of Defense Caspar Weinberger, and numerous State Department regional experts, but Secretary of State George Shultz argued that U.S. intervention would help pacify Lebanon, support its central government, and enhance regional prospects for Arab-Israeli peace. Reagan was persuaded that Shultz was right, and therefore authorized American military deployment to Lebanon in August 1982 as part of a multinational peacekeeping force, while keeping that deployment small and tightly restricted as a concession to critics inside the administration. At first the mission went well. American troops helped evacuate PLO forces from Beirut, as intended, and left after only a matter of weeks. In September 1982, however, as the local violence continued, the Marines were sent back into Beirut under vague and contradictory instructions to somehow keep the peace without becoming too deeply involved in Lebanon's wider civil war. The factional warfare did not abate, and inevitably, the Marines were drawn into conflict with local militias. Opinion polls showed that the Lebanon deployment was increasingly unpopular inside the United States. On October 23, 1983, a suicide bomber drove an explosives-laden truck into U.S. Marine barracks in Beirut, killing more than two hundred U.S. servicemen. Reagan, his advisers, and the American public were stunned by the attack. After a short-term rally and retaliation on the part of the United States, it became increasingly clear to most of Reagan's military and political advisers—as to a majority of the general public—that there was no constructive way for the Marines to remain in Beirut without risking further such attacks. Nor were congressional Republicans eager to see American forces entangled in Lebanon's civil war as the 1984 U.S. elections loomed. Reagan was initially very reluctant to withdraw U.S. troops or "cut and run" under pressure, but finally agreed to do so in February 1984, describing the withdrawal as a "redeployment" of Marines to American ships offshore in the Mediterranean. Islamist terrorists in the region drew the obvious lesson that the United States could be successfully coerced through the infliction of American casualties, a lesson that never could have been drawn if U.S. troops had not been deployed under such unpromising conditions in the first place. In the United States, however, the decision to withdraw the Marines from Lebanon was popular and widely supported, removing it as a potentially damaging issue going into the 1984 election season. The successful 1983 intervention in Grenada helped erase the stain of failure in Lebanon, providing political cover at home and abroad as Reagan withdrew from Beirut's bloody complications. This covering effect could not have been entirely premeditated or foreseen, since plans to invade Grenada were largely complete before news of the Marine barracks truck bombing reached Washington on October 23, 1983.[25]

Reagan's aggressive anti-Soviet foreign policies carried certain risks. The combination of America's military buildup, anti-Communist interventions, denunciatory rhetoric, SDI, and unyielding stance on arms control left Moscow shaken, alarmed, and defensive. Renewed cold war tensions came to a head in the fall of 1983. In September of that year, a South Korean civilian airliner, KAL 007, wandered into Soviet airspace. Local Soviet military authorities mistook the airliner for a U.S. military aircraft and shot it down, killing sixty-one U.S. citizens on board. Reagan publicly denounced this action as a "crime against humanity" while privately warning that "we've got to protect against overreaction." When he learned of Moscow's mistaken identification of the aircraft, he was hardly reassured, since it meant that Soviet officials were either appallingly incompetent or willing to gamble on a violent military incident with U.S. armed forces. That November, an even more dangerous moment occurred when NATO held military exercises entitled Able Archer. Such exercises were standard practice, but in the context of a heightened cold war atmosphere, leading Soviet officials, including Secretary General Yuri Andropov, became convinced that the United States might use Able Archer as a ruse to launch a nuclear first strike against the USSR. Under such circumstances, Soviet war plans called for a preemptive first strike in response. Obviously, the attack never came, but when Reagan was told how seriously Moscow had taken this possibility, he was deeply disturbed. Since he had no intention of doing any such thing, it simply had not occurred to him that Soviet leaders might genuinely fear a U.S. nuclear attack. Reagan therefore decided to give private reassurances to Moscow as well as a major public speech in January 1984 to lower superpower tensions and reduce the risk of accidental or preemptive nuclear war. In a highly personal address, he said that "people want to raise their children in a world without fear," and called on the superpowers to establish a "better working relationship" in order to address "priority number one" of "reducing the risk of war." As he put it, "the fact that neither of us likes the other system is no reason to refuse to talk." The speech did not entail a fundamental change or reversal of Reagan's other hard-line policies on SDI, Nicaragua, Afghanistan, or military spending; the basic outlines of his anti-Communist strategy remained the same, as did the substance of his position on arms control. Indeed, by the beginning of 1984 Reagan could and did argue that it was his reassertion of U.S. military power that put Washington in an improved position to negotiate from strength. But the January speech was a notable development in that its tone was primarily pacific and conciliatory—a development duly noted in Moscow. Reagan made a similar address to the UN General Assembly that September. Among their other effects, such speeches helped reassure U.S. public opinion that Reagan sought meaningful arms control, and that he shared the fervent and popular American desire to avoid war with the Soviet Union. This reassurance would be vital going into the 1984 reelection campaign, as several of Reagan's leading advisers, including his wife Nancy, well understood.[26]

The Democratic Party nominated a decent but conventional liberal insider, former vice president Walter Mondale, as its candidate for president in 1984. His nomination illustrated that the Democrats were in no mood yet to seriously question existing party orthodoxies; indeed, Mondale was more of a traditional liberal than Jimmy Carter had ever been. Still, Democrats hoped to make political headway against Reagan on a wide range of issues, including economic inequality, social spending, the growing budget deficit, unemployment, women's rights, and the environment. With regard to foreign policy and defense, Mondale called for a much less hawkish approach, emphasizing international peace, arms control, constrained military spending, opposition to covert action in Central America, and the risks of nuclear war under a Reagan administration. Democrats had reason to think that this platform might work politically, as public opinion polls initially showed the average voter marginally closer to Mondale's position than to Reagan's on a number of leading issues. In the area of foreign policy, as an illustration, U.S. aid to the Contras was very unpopular. The public was also deeply concerned about the danger of nuclear war, and ready to emphasize arms control over the development of new weapons systems. Yet Mondale's hoped-for issue advantages never really materialized. On the contrary, as voters began to focus on the question of which candidate they better trusted to manage these difficult issues, Reagan regularly came out ahead, on numerous domestic as well as foreign policy matters. Voters could see, for example, that Reagan was in practice quite circumspect in avoiding open conflict with the Soviet Union. In the end, they gave him credit for restoring U.S. military strength and self-confidence while keeping the peace. His quick success in Grenada, like his disengagement from Lebanon, reinforced the perception that he was determined to avoid failed, protracted entanglements overseas. The war-and-peace issue was thus neutralized so as not to benefit Mondale. Moreover, a majority of voters simply liked Reagan: they appreciated his cheerful, winning manner and thought of him as a strong, honest, and capable leader who had restored a sense of national pride. But the single biggest factor working in his favor was the domestic economic recovery. By 1983–84, with considerable help from the Federal Reserve, inflation had been broken, taxes were reduced, unemployment and interest rates were both down, and the economy was growing at a healthy rate. Mondale consequently had a hard time making the case that Republican rule had been materially bad for middle-income Americans.

The final electoral result was a landslide in which Reagan won the popular vote by a margin of over eighteen points, including a majority in every state but Minnesota. White southerners and evangelicals voted for Reagan to an even greater extent than in 1980, as did younger voters. The president also won solid majorities of white working-class and white Catholic voters. Mondale was reduced to a base constituency of African Americans, liberals, labor unions, Jewish voters, Hispanics, and only the lowest-income white supporters. While 1984 was a highly polarized presidential election in ideological terms, it was also very much a referendum on practical performance. Under generally prosperous, peacetime conditions, U.S. voters did what they usually do, and rewarded the incumbent—hardly surprising in itself. The interesting point is that Reagan was able to portray his reelection as vindication of an unusually sharp conservative agenda. While that agenda had always been popular

with core supporters, major elements of it were otherwise quite controversial, including the president's aggressive anticommunism efforts
overseas. The average American voter in 1984 was ideologically moderate, positioned somewhere between Reagan and Mondale on foreign
policy as well as domestic. As Reagan fully realized, it was only broad,
practical success and tactical flexibility in governing that gave his sharp
conservative agenda continued political viability.[27]

The most consequential development in world politics during the
months following Reagan's reelection was the coming to power of
Mikhail Gorbachev as leader of the USSR. Gorbachev was a convinced
Communist, dedicated to the strengthening of the Soviet Union, but
unlike his immediate predecessors he was also refreshingly human, dynamic, reform-minded, and ready to experiment with new policy ideas
at home and abroad. On foreign and defense policy, he realized that the
expansionary Soviet approach of the Brezhnev era had backfired, leaving Moscow overextended in an expensive, counterproductive arms
race with the United States. Reagan, for his part, had been trying for
years to engage some Soviet leader in diplomatic dialogue, however limited, but as he said, "they keep dying on me." He recognized in Gorbachev the possibility of a more promising interlocutor. They met for
the first time at the Geneva summit of November 1985. Gorbachev argued for arms control and against SDI, while Reagan pressed the Soviet
leader on human rights and regional issues such as Afghanistan. They
reached no formal agreement but managed to release a joint statement
agreeing on a common agenda, and further declaring that a "nuclear
war cannot be won and must never be fought." This in itself was a long
way from the diplomatic deep freeze of autumn 1983. Moreover, the two
leaders hit it off as human beings, establishing a personal trust and rap-
port. They were ready to negotiate; it was clear there would be further
summits. In October 1986, Reagan and Gorbachev met again, in Reykjavik, Iceland. This time the two men entered into detailed, extensive
bargaining over their mutual nuclear arsenals. Gorbachev offered not
only to eliminate all intermediate-range missiles in Europe but to cut all
strategic weapons by 50 percent. The United States countered with an
even more sweeping offer to abolish all ballistic missiles within ten years.
Gorbachev raised the stakes again by recommending the elimination of

nuclear weapons altogether, an astonishing proposal to which Reagan happily agreed. The one sticking point was the SDI, which alarmed Soviet leaders. Gorbachev insisted that the United States confine future SDI research to the laboratory; Reagan refused, committed as he was to that program. The meeting thus broke up in frustration, with the two superpowers having been on the verge of nuclear abolition. Both Reagan and Gorbachev soon realized that Reykjavik represented progress, not failure, in how far they had come. Cold war tensions had thawed considerably. A new arms control agreement was only a matter of time. In reality, the prospect of nuclear abolition was profoundly unsettling to America's leading allies, numerous administration officials and many defense experts alike, since it dismantled the primary U.S. deterrent in relation to Western Europe and elsewhere. Negotiations over a more limited and achievable arms control accord continued.[28]

Even as Reagan and Gorbachev pursued diplomacy, superpower cold war competition persisted. Neither leader saw any contradiction in this, since military or geopolitical pressure might bring success at the bargaining table. Gorbachev continued to build up Soviet armed forces, while trying to win the war in Afghanistan. Reagan, for his part, increased spending on SDI, and provided fresh support for rebellious forces within the Soviet bloc. Indeed it was not until 1985 that journalist Charles Krauthammer popularized the term "Reagan Doctrine" to describe the administration's policy of supporting anti-Communist insurgents in the Third World. It was never entirely clear if the goal of the Reagan Doctrine was to pressure local Marxist governments such as Nicaragua's into diplomatic settlement or instead to simply overthrow them; administration officials did not agree among themselves on this point, and Reagan gave various speeches indicating either direction. Nor was the Reagan Doctrine ever really applied comprehensively against all Marxist regimes in the developing world, for example in Cuba, Ethiopia, Cambodia, or Mozambique, where U.S. covert efforts were either minimal or nonexistent. Still, in the case of Afghanistan, the Reagan administration significantly increased U.S. aid to anti-Communist insurgents in 1985–86, with the declared purpose under NSDD-166 of not only frustrating but defeating and ejecting Soviet forces from that country. American weaponry, advisers, and logistical support began to arrive through Pakistan on a massive scale. The delivery of U.S. Stinger anti-aircraft missiles in particular dealt a severe blow to Soviet helicopter gunships and helped turn the tide militarily in Afghanistan. The administration was also able to win new support from Congress for Jonas Savimbi's UNITA rebel forces in Angola, against the local pro-Soviet regime and its Cuban backers.[29]

As always, Nicaragua was more difficult. With military aid from U.S. defense or intelligence agencies forbidden to the Contras under the Boland amendment, the administration was severely constricted in what it could do. Nevertheless, Reagan told his National Security Council (NSC) staffer Oliver North to keep the Contras together "body and soul." Taking this as a clear mandate from a president often elliptical on details, the free-wheeling North and his superiors at the NSC proceeded to solicit third-party funding for Nicaragua's anti-Communist insurgents from international and private American donors. Reagan simultaneously sought to free U.S. hostages in Lebanon by providing for the sale and shipment of American weapons through Israel to "moderate" factions in Iran with supposed influence over the fate of those hostages—all this despite the fact that U.S. law and the administration itself publicly forbade arms sales to Iran. Oliver North came up with the "neat idea," as he called it, of taking the money earned from the Iranian arms sale and diverting it to the Nicaraguan Contras—another way of circumventing congressional limitations on U.S. covert aid. In effect, the NSC staff conducted their own private foreign policy, free from presidential supervision. When news of these half-baked arrangements began leaking to the press in November 1986, Reagan faced the greatest scandal of his administration; his presidential approval ratings dropped more than twenty points. Shaken and initially in denial, Reagan eventually did what Nixon never had. He authorized a full investigation, cleaned house, and took responsibility for the scandal. By the summer of 1987 the president's approval ratings were back up over 60 percent, but the Iran–Contra arms affair revealed to the general public what White House insiders had long known, namely, that Reagan was not a particularly strong manager. In a curious sense, this may have saved his administration, since Reagan was able to plausibly argue that he had not known of all the machinations going on beneath him by various NSC staff. Yet it was clearly the president himself who had pushed forward the arms-for-hostages deal at crucial moments, over the combined objections of leading advisers such as Shultz and Weinberger. No evidence was ever found that Reagan specifically authorized the diversion of funds to the Contras, and independent counsel Lawrence Walsh determined that the president had committed no criminal wrongdoing capable of successful prosecution. The Iran–Contra arms scandal provided evidence, among other things, of the fierce determination of many inside the Reagan administration to support anti-Communist insurgents overseas, even to the point of provoking a domestic political and legal crisis. One of the many ironies of this crisis was that some centrist congressional Democrats had already moved to reinstate limited U.S. aid to the Contras in 1985–86, before the scandal broke. The revelations of the Iran–Contra arms affair meant that even such limited aid would be wound up by Congress in 1987–88. Meanwhile, Reagan's well-intentioned efforts to purchase freedom for U.S. hostages in Lebanon ensured that the hostage-takers viewed the United States as an easy mark; more American hostages were taken than freed as a result of this ill-conceived initiative.[30]

The Iran–Contra arms scandal temporarily distracted the White House from foreign policy while ultimately creating added political incentive to produce some sort of diplomatic achievement before Reagan left office. A strong majority of U.S. public and congressional opinion stood in favor of an arms control agreement with Moscow by 1987. The loss of Republican control over the Senate in the 1986 midterm elections only added to these pressures. Reagan was sensitive to the changing domestic political climate and wanted something to show for his years of hawkish foreign and defense policies. Fortunately, few U.S. concessions on arms control were necessary, given Moscow's increasingly conciliating stance. Over the course of 1987, Gorbachev agreed to the mutual and verifiable elimination of medium and intermediate-range land-based nuclear arms, decoupled from concerns over SDI or long-range strategic arsenals. In effect, he conceded to Reagan's 1981 "zero option." Reagan was happy to accept this concession, having long aimed himself at mutual, favorable reductions in nuclear weapons. Consequently, at the Washington summit of December 1987, the two superpower leaders signed the Intermediate Nuclear Forces Treaty, eliminating an entire

just than undemocratic ones; he spoke and wrote regularly and sponta-
neously on this subject for years before entering the White House. His
administration created the National Endowment for Democracy (NED)
in 1983 to provide training, technical aid, and financial support for
democratic practices, including free elections, overseas. In contrast to
some previous cold war administrations, there was no case under Reagan of CIA intervention against a democratically elected leader or government. Yet the former California governor shared Jeane Kirkpatrick's
conviction that there could hardly be anything worse for the cause of
democracy—not to mention American interests—than the triumph of
communism overseas. When Reagan first became president, therefore,
his primary and immediate concern in relation to anti-Communist allies abroad was to bolster them, not to sanction or hector them on
human rights. There was considerable room for U.S. officials to implement country-specific policies, case by case. In relation to South Africa,
for example, Assistant Secretary of State for African Affairs Chester
Crocker pursued a policy of "constructive engagement," reassuring the
apartheid regime of U.S. support against communism while trying to
gradually nudge Pretoria in a positive direction on democracy and
human rights as well as regional security issues. Similar American policies were pursued in relation to El Salvador. Reagan spoke of anti-
Communist insurgents such as the Nicaraguan Contras as "the moral
equivalent of our founding fathers," but in practice these insurgents were
supported by Reagan whether or not they lived up to Jeffersonian standards. Reagan was therefore quite circumscribed in his efforts at democracy promotion abroad, regardless of ringing speeches and no doubt
sincere democratic convictions. He seems to have thought mainly in
terms of the United States as an example or model to other countries of
a flourishing democracy rather than as having an obligation to forcibly
promote democracy overseas. An important turning point on this issue
came in 1986, when U.S. ally Ferdinand Marcos of the Philippines faced
possible overthrow by domestic opponents. Reagan's instinct was to
back Marcos, but in this particular case the main opposition was neither
Communist nor anti-American. The entire U.S. foreign policy establishment emerged in favor of helping to ease the corrupt, autocratic Marcos
out of power, of which Reagan was finally convinced. Other U.S. allies in

Chile and South Korea were also pressed more aggressively on human rights and democratic practices at about the same time, at the behest of U.S. officials such as Assistant Secretary of State for Inter-American Affairs Elliot Abrams. The administration thus turned from gradualism and quiet diplomacy toward a rather more assertive approach in favor of democratic reforms among anti-Communist authoritarians. When Reagan left office, there were considerably more democracies in Latin American and East Asia than there had been when he entered. While the primary sources of democratization in such countries were both complicated and internal, the combination of U.S. reassurance, practical assistance, and occasional pointed pressure during the 1980s probably helped push several American allies in a more democratic direction.[32]

Reagan's embrace of the language of worldwide democracy promotion encouraged observers to ask whether his administration represented the triumph of "neoconservatism." Undoubtedly, Reagan's foreign policy struck themes consistent with contemporary neoconservative ideas: American exceptionalism, fierce anticommunism, a certain muscular idealism, and an unapologetic defense of U.S. values and interests abroad. He himself possessed elements of a neoconservative background, as a former New Deal Democrat with personal experience of Communist tactics. Numerous figures commonly described as neoconservative, such as Jeane Kirkpatrick, Richard Pipes, Elliot Abrams, and Richard Perle, held prominent positions in the Reagan administration. It was reasonable to suggest after 1980 that the neoconservatives had finally arrived at real influence. Certainly they felt Reagan was one of their own, to a greater extent than any prior Republican president. Still, Reagan presided over a broad coalition of which neoconservatives were only a small part. In practice, he pursued a foreign policy that many of them often found to be insufficiently bold or assertive. The distinctions between neoconservatives and the traditional GOP right wing had also somewhat faded by the 1980s, as they merged into one another intellectually, politically, and organizationally. Nor did neoconservatives necessarily agree among themselves over issues such as whether to press Latin American allies on democracy promotion, or whether Reagan had faltered in the struggle against communism. Kirkpatrick, for example, was satisfied with Reagan's overall record in conducting the cold war against Moscow, while arguing for a gradualist approach on the issue of allied democratization. Elliot Abrams, on the other hand, came to see strong reformist pressure in cases like Pinochet's Chile as essential. Norman Podhoretz, for his part, wrote a series of increasingly embittered articles against Reagan's foreign policy, dismissing it as "appeasement" for failing to roll back the Soviet bloc more aggressively. Fortunately, Reagan paid little attention to the latter criticism, and continued to pursue his own course.[33]

When Reagan left office in January 1989, the cold war was not over, but it had thawed to an unprecedented degree. U.S.-Soviet negotiations were well under way on the mutual, deep reduction of long-range nuclear weapons. Gorbachev had announced further, unilateral disarmament measures. Indeed, Moscow was scaling back on military commitments worldwide, and accommodating the United States on one issue after another. Soviet troops were on their way out of Afghanistan; Cuban troops would soon be out of Angola. Regional peace agreements had been reached in both of these war-torn countries and on terms agreeable to Washington. A similar agreement would eventually be reached in Nicaragua, leading to the Sandinistas' defeat in democratic elections. Poland and other East European countries would break free of Communist control within only a few months. While Reagan did not cause these developments single-handedly, he certainly contributed to them. He perceived early on that the USSR and its clients were vulnerable at important points. He deliberately sought to force Soviet leaders to make difficult choices between guns and butter, between international strategic position and domestic base, by pressuring Moscow militarily, economically, technologically, diplomatically, and ideologically. This was a high-risk strategy. The USSR could have responded in a variety of ways. Fortunately, it happened to find a leader in Mikhail Gorbachev, who reacted to American pressure not by lashing out or cracking down but by accommodating the United States and its allies in order to focus on domestic reform. Reagan's critics today argue that the Soviet Union was bound to collapse regardless, but this is not what they argued at the time. The contemporary argument against Reagan was that he risked World War III by refusing to initially recognize and conciliate the Soviet Union as an enduring, respected superpower equal to the United States. In reality, virtually no one, Reagan included, foresaw the precise manner or moment in which the USSR would collapse, yet surely he deserves credit for seeing—unlike many of his own supporters—that communism was fundamentally weak rather than strong. Reagan had great and justified faith in the ability of the United States to outlast its authoritarian adversaries. He looked to negotiate from strength. First, he pursued a diplomatic and military hard line against the Soviet Union, building up American power and setting Moscow on the defensive. This appalled many on the left. Then he opened up to that same Soviet adversary, improved relations, and concluded a far-reaching arms control agreement. This appalled many on the right. In fact, Reagan had better judgment than his critics on the left or the right. He used every policy instrument at his disposal to pursue a bold, deliberate strategy of pressuring the USSR, with the long-term intent of reducing cold war tensions on American terms. And he succeeded. It was a remarkable performance. If anything, his foreign policy performance was so successful in the end that it carried the danger of mistaken imitation by lesser leaders under very different circumstances. Reagan did not succeed simply by being intransigent. He did not succeed simply by being willing to negotiate. He succeeded by combining and alternating between these qualities, at the right time and in the right way. Reagan's stirring foreign policy rhetoric was and is also easily misinterpreted, through the impression that he was a gung-ho military interventionist. In fact, he was usually careful and cautious with regard to the use of the military, preferring indirect, covert, or brief, small-scale U.S. interventions to large ones. There was no equivalent of Korea, Vietnam, or Iraq on Reagan's watch. Nor did Reagan attempt to roll back the Soviet empire through the direct use of U.S. armed forces. On the contrary, he frequently tried to reassure Soviet leaders that he would not attack them. Part of the secret of his success was no doubt the ability to convince supporters of his core convictions while simultaneously pursuing policies that were actually more circumspect and less interventionist than would have been obvious from his rhetoric. This practical restraint in turn reassured the general American public of Reagan's good sense and helped maintain sufficient domestic support for his overall strategy.[34]

Reagan's domestic political accomplishments were scarcely less impressive than his foreign policy. To be sure, there were clear limitations on these accomplishments. Contrary to the hopes of many conservatives and the fears of many liberals, there was no radical reduction in government spending under Reagan. Nor was there a Republican majority in the country as yet, apart from the presidential level: the GOP took the Senate, only to lose it, and never made much headway in the House of Representatives. Meanwhile the Democratic Party and its allies still had great residual if disorganized strength in Congress, the federal bureaucracy, and the country, particularly on traditional New Deal pocketbook issues. Yet despite all these limitations—and precisely because he did not overreach beyond them—Reagan had a greater impact on American politics than any president since Franklin Roosevelt. He curbed the growth in domestic government expenditures, cut discretionary social spending in real terms, helped break inflation, and instituted dramatically deep tax cuts. Unintentionally or not, the effect of these tax cuts was to rule out ambitious new domestic spending programs for years to come. Partly because of his policies, the nation's economy entered into a period of protracted growth and innovation. He changed the face of the courts by appointing conservative judges. He used the presidential bully pulpit to speak out with effect on behalf of moral traditionalism, free enterprise, and America's global role. He helped restore a sense of national morale, after the tedious self-flagellations of the late 1960s and 1970s. He changed the terms of debate. Subsequent White House hopefuls in both major parties would be forced to move in Reagan's direction, to the right, both rhetorically and substantively, to remain viable at the national level. The Republican Party was also in better shape when Reagan stepped down than it had been prior to 1980. It had a clear identity and a sense of ideological confidence and cohesion. It was organizationally stronger and more competitive at many levels, in part owing to Reagan's deliberate efforts at party building. Indeed, Reagan was the first president in decades to complete two terms as a popular chief executive and then hand over the White House to his chosen successor. He redefined conservatism in the United States as well as the GOP, adapting conservative ideas to American realities and appealing beyond the traditional Republican base. In fact, he appropriated important themes—apparently in all sincerity—from liberal icons such as Thomas Paine, FDR, and John F. Kennedy, including images of spirited idealism, forward progress, populism, and an American mission. Reagan offered a vivid, enduring example of a self-described conservative as president who was optimistic, principled, and successful, neither bitter, stiff-necked, nor gloomy. He shattered a weakened but previously dominant national Democratic coalition and replaced it with a conservative Republican one as the most dynamic political power in the country. He brought foreign policy hawks, economic conservatives, and social traditionalists, including many onetime Democrats, into a single alliance, then led this alliance to a winning position both within the GOP and within the United States. That alliance, moreover, outlasted him, held together as it was by a set of ideas. He accomplished what would have once seemed inconceivable in America: he made not only the Republican Party but a self-consciously conservative party appear to be the force of the future. In all, he was a much greater figure than the cognoscenti realized at the time, more consequential, skillful, and pragmatic, but also more determined and relentless. Most presidents seem to shrink in significance as their tenure recedes in time. Reagan only looms larger: sunny, single-minded, and remote.[35]

Chapter Seven

GEORGE H. W. BUSH

The Conservative as Realist

As PRESIDENT, George H. W. Bush was temperamentally rather than ideologically conservative. He emphasized caution, stability, and prudence in international as well as domestic public matters. On foreign policy, Bush was often criticized for supposed timidity. In reality, however, he guided American diplomacy with considerable strength, skill, and success through a period of dramatic global upheaval, locking in changes of lasting benefit to the United States in relation to Germany, Eastern Europe, the collapsing Soviet Union, Latin America, arms control, democracy promotion, and international trade. The general American public, including most Republicans, appreciated Bush's capable and effective foreign policy approach but grew dissatisfied with him on domestic issues.

The end of the cold war and the election of President Clinton left Republicans somewhat uncertain as to their foreign policy priorities. GOP nationalists, anti-interventionists, hawks, and realists each made the case for alternative U.S. approaches overseas. Most congressional Republican nationalists focused on domestic matters and were skeptical of Clinton administration arguments for humanitarian intervention, arms control, foreign aid, and international organization. Conservative anti-interventionists like Pat Buchanan went much further and argued for dismantling many of America's postwar international commitments. At the other end of the foreign policy spectrum, a new generation of GOP hawks called for preventive military action, benign U.S. hegemony, and rogue state rollback overseas. Republican realists continued to rec-

selected Senator Dan Quayle (R-IN) as his running mate and promised "no new taxes" if elected president. The Democratic nominee that year was an uninspiring technocrat, Governor Michael Dukakis of Massachusetts. Early in the race, the Democrat led in the polls, but Bush put together a hard-hitting campaign that stressed Dukakis's liberal positions on issues such as crime, taxes, defense spending, the death penalty, and civil liberties. The governor's ineffectual response to these characterizations allowed Bush to define the election as an ideological contest between liberal and conservative cultural values—a definition that favored the GOP. Nor were most voters really all that dissatisfied with the Republican record of the previous four to eight years. On the contrary, the mid-1980s had been a period generally of economic growth and foreign policy success for Americans, and Reagan was a popular president during his final year in office. Bush was therefore well positioned to win election, as Reagan's vice president and the obvious custodian of the era's peace and prosperity. Dukakis ran strongly with core Democratic constituencies, including liberals, African Americans, organized labor, Hispanics, and working-class Catholics. He won states in the Pacific Northwest, New York, New England, and the upper Midwest. Bush ran well virtually everywhere else, winning not only traditional Republican northern middle-class Protestant voters but also white southerners, middle-class Catholics, born-again Christians, and working-class whites nationwide. Foreign policy and defense played an important part in the vice president's victory, despite decreased popular concern over the Soviet threat. Among those who said in exit polls that defense was a top priority—some 23 percent of voters, altogether—an astonishing 84 percent voted for Bush over Dukakis. Clearly, Bush was able to successfully portray himself as the more experienced, steady hand on international affairs, better able to manage America's foreign relations while keeping the nation militarily strong. This portrayal, moreover, was part of an overall Republican appeal—maddeningly vague in the opinion of liberals but nevertheless potent—in which patriotism was bundled together with cultural conservatism to define Dukakis as somehow outside the mainstream of traditional American values. The vice president consequently succeeded Reagan in the White House with a convincing electoral win, although without coat-tails or friendly majorities in Congress.[2]

Both before and during his presidency, Bush's critics on the left and the right often accused him of having no discernible fixed principles. In fact, Bush had a very clear set of core convictions, but they had more to do with character than with precise issue positions. Bush put great emphasis on the values of family, personal decency, humility, courtesy, civic duty, and love of country, and to a greater extent than most, he practiced what he preached. On economic issues, he was skeptical of governmental solutions to socioeconomic problems. He frequently mentioned the Hippocratic Oath—"first, do no harm"—as a useful guideline for those in power. In this sense, he was a conservative. Yet his conservatism was more dispositional than ideological in nature. He did not, for example, seek a dramatic rollback of the federal government's role in the nation's economy, and while interested in policy details he had no sweeping agenda for domestic legislation in a conservative direction. On social issues, Bush began his electoral career in the 1960s as a pro-choice Republican, and he tended toward moderation rather than right-wing positions. As his career advanced and the party moved to the right, Bush adopted the conservative stance on controversies such as abortion. Foreign policy was really Bush's primary interest. He held the belief, common to his background and generation, that the United States had to play a leading role in the world, maintain robust armed forces, contain the Soviet Union, combat aggression, work with U.S. allies, and promote free trade internationally. For Bush, the lessons of the 1930s were very personal, and they pointed in the direction of American military strength and resistance to dictators. He was convinced that by the late 1980s democratic changes were sweeping the globe. Yet in foreign policy as elsewhere, Bush stressed prudence and pragmatism. He placed immense value on international stability, and he recognized that such stability required great caution and care with regard to specific policy initiatives. This recognition was reflected in the overall tenor of his foreign policy team, where James Baker as secretary of state, Brent Scowcroft as national security adviser, and Dick Cheney as secretary of defense worked together in an unusually cohesive, collegial, and effective manner. Bush set the tone for this team by taking a hands-on approach that valued professionalism, competence, and personal relationships rather than ideological abstractions. His instinct was not to offer grand designs for

neutral or ambiguous in its foreign policy orientation. Bush and Secretary of State Baker soon took the lead in paving the way for the reunification of Germany, in close coordination with Kohl, through intense, step-by-step personal diplomacy. The greatest obstacle they faced in this endeavor was the very strong feeling in Moscow against any independent resurgence of German power. Bush and Baker responded by promoting the so-called "Two plus Four" framework for reunification talks, beginning with the two Germanys and including the four World War II allied powers: Britain, France, the United States, and the Soviet Union. In this way, Moscow and other European countries could be reassured that unification would only originate within the context of a multilateral, gradual, consultative approach, and with full regard for allied security concerns. Early in 1990, Gorbachev accepted the premise of German self-determination through unification—a dramatic concession in itself. This still left the question of whether a united Germany would be a member of NATO, and here Gorbachev remained firmly opposed. Bush, Baker, and Kohl offered a number of inducements to win Gorbachev's acceptance on this point. They promised that Germany's borders with Poland would be inviolate, that German armed forces would be strictly limited, that Germany would abstain from developing nuclear weapons, that NATO would reform its military posture into a more purely defensive direction; that pan-European security structures would be strengthened and upgraded, that NATO forces would stay out of eastern Germany for several years, and that the West would provide financial aid to Moscow to ease the process of reunification. The turning point came at the Washington summit of May 1990, when Bush asked Gorbachev whether nations had the right to choose their own foreign alliances, under the principle of self-determination. To the astonishment of those gathered, Gorbachev said yes. His precarious domestic position by this time no doubt played a crucial role in this change of heart, as did the numerous inducements and reassurances laid out by Germany and the United States. Gorbachev was also apparently persuaded, in the end, that it might be more dangerous to have a united Germany outside than inside NATO. Nevertheless it was an astonishing surrender of the Soviet position in Central Europe. By the end of July 1990 Moscow had agreed to German reunification within NATO. The Two plus Four talks were concluded, and Allied occupation rights were relinquished. On October 3, 1990, the two Germanys formally reunited—an outcome that would have been unthinkable to most observers less than a year before.[5]

While the fall of communism went ahead peacefully in much of Europe, the outcome was very different in China. Like many other Marxist regimes at the time, the People's Republic of China was under internal, popular pressure for democratic reform. In June 1989, the Chinese government responded with a brutally violent crackdown in Beijing's Tiananmen Square, killing thousands of unarmed protestors. American opinion was shocked at these events. Bush declared publicly that he "deplored" the massacre, but insisted on placing it within the context of overall U.S. foreign policy interests. For Bush, the strategic relationship with China, one of the world's greatest powers, was vital to the United States. So were Sino-American economic ties. Bush was loath to in any way encourage massive social or political upheaval within China. He believed that continued U.S. economic and political engagement with China would best serve the cause of reform in that country. Moreover, he felt that from his own personal experience he understood the Chinese. Consequently he initially refused to impose anything more than limited measures of protest against Beijing, for example cutting off military exchanges and exports to China. The president's very measured course was clearly out of step with popular and elite opinion in the United States, which was outraged across party lines by the Tiananmen Square massacre. Conservative Republicans in Congress and the press joined with liberal Democrats in protesting the weakness of Bush's response. By a margin of 418 to 0, the U.S. House of Representatives imposed tougher sanctions on China. Beijing's reply to all of this was uncommunicative and intransigent. Bush went out of his way to reassure the Chinese government privately that he had no desire to see a weakening of Sino-American relations. As news of such reassurances leaked out, they seemed further evidence of an excessively conciliatory response to a shamelessly repressive dictatorship. The president and Congress then settled into a kind of prolonged, legislative trench warfare over U.S. policy toward China. Protectionist sentiment merged with human rights concerns to create a powerful congressional lobby against Sino-American trade. Nevertheless, Bush was able to use his veto, together

with a minimally supportive bloc in the U.S. Senate, to stave off protectionist pressures and preserve working relations with Beijing. He was
also able to use the annual renewal of China's most-favored-nation trade
status to win freedom for a number of Chinese political dissidents.
Eventually Sino-American relations crept back toward normality, but
China's image in the United States had changed dramatically and for the
worse.[6]

Bush also faced a significant foreign policy challenge during his first
year in office over the Central American republic of Panama. That country's dictator, Manuel Noriega, had been a cold war ally of the United
States, but was an embarrassment to Washington by the late 1980s in
part because of his continuing and extensive involvement with the region's drug trade. In May 1989, Noriega nullified election results in
which Panama's democratic opposition had won. President Bush called
on Noriega to step down, but the Panamanian strongman defied the
United States as his personal police force beat up political opponents.
That October, a bungled coup attempt against Noriega was easily defeated. Washington had remained aloof from the coup; Bush resolved to
plan more seriously for Noriega's overthrow. On December 16, 1989, an
incident occurred in which members of the Panamanian Defense Force
harassed and attacked several U.S. soldiers together with their depen-
dents. Bush seized on the incident to launch a sudden, full-scale invasion only a few days later. With the president hoping to avoid any half-
hearted or inconclusive effort, more than twenty thousand U.S. troops
took part. Democratic and Republican congressional leaders were informed of the coming military action hours before it took place. Taken
by surprise, Noriega's forces were quickly overwhelmed and defeated.
Noriega himself was apprehended two weeks later. Bush neither asked
for nor received foreign support for the invasion. International criticism
was widespread but superficial; Noriega was a difficult figure around
which to rally world opinion, and Gorbachev in particular was muted in
his criticism. In the United States, the invasion's decisive results, together
with its location in a country of longstanding interest to the United
States, led most Americans to rally to the president, bolstering his reputation as a strong foreign policy leader. Noriega's democratic opponents

were seated as the legitimate rulers of Panama. Most Panamanians were happy to be rid of Noriega, and while succeeding governments were hardly model democracies, they were a considerable improvement on his rule, and certainly friendlier to the United States. The safety of the Canal Zone and of American citizens in Panama was ensured, if there had ever been any doubt.[7]

The largest U.S. military action undertaken during the Bush years was against Saddam Hussein's Iraq. The Bush administration inherited Ronald Reagan's policy toward Saddam, which was to treat Iraq as a geopolitical counterweight to Iranian Islamist influence in the region. In 1989, Bush approved the continuation of U.S. agricultural commodity credits to Baghdad and tried to maintain working relations with Iraq, but Saddam needed massive economic help as a result of his costly war against Iran, and he fixed on Kuwait as an easy, oil-rich target. On August 2, 1990, Iraqi forces invaded and occupied Kuwait. The invasion was a surprise to the Bush administration as well as to the rest of the world, and was stunning in its brazenly aggressive quality. Saddam now controlled or threatened the heart of the world's largest oil supply. Bush quickly decided on a firm U.S. response, declaring, "This will not stand." The immediate concern in Washington was over the security of Saudi Arabia and its immense oil fields. Tens of thousands of American troops were deployed by Bush to protect the Saudi kingdom, an action that met with no major congressional opposition. Prodded by Washington, the United Nations Security Council approved sweeping economic sanctions against Iraq. In a striking reversal of traditional cold war patterns, the Soviet Union under Gorbachev supported these sanctions and worked with the Bush administration closely throughout the crisis. The president used his penchant for personal diplomacy to help construct a broad international coalition against Saddam, a coalition that included not only Western allies such as Britain and France but also Arab powers such as Egypt and Syria. Bush appears to have decided within weeks, if not days, of Saddam's invasion that the United States would have to go to war to force Iraq out of Kuwait. Still, he delayed any further announcement regarding American troop deployments until after the 1990 midterm elections. He built domestic support for his actions in the Gulf by referring to a long-term U.S. foreign policy goal, a "new world order" characterized by international peace, democracy, free trade, and collective security, "a world where the rule of law supplants the rule of the jungle." While striking in their universality, such themes were hardly new in American diplomatic history, but very much reflective of long-standing U.S. liberal internationalist traditions.[8]

Iraq's invasion of Kuwait happened to occur during protracted budget negotiations between Congress and the White House. These negotiations were a very uncomfortable experience for Bush, who felt intense pressure to raise taxes in order to bring the federal budget deficit under control, and who preferred to focus on foreign policy in any case. It would be surprising if Bush had not virtually welcomed the opportunity to turn his attention to international affairs. Not only was he on stronger ground politically when it came to national security issues as opposed to domestic economics, the Persian Gulf crisis was also an opportunity to disprove common charges of indecisive leadership. Nor was any of this incompatible with a sincere conviction that Saddam's occupation of Kuwait had to be reversed for reasons of U.S. national interest. Bush's strong initial response to the Iraqi invasion sent his approval ratings rocketing upward in August 1990. Indeed, he hoped to convert this new popular support into political leverage with Congress over the budget, but had little success in doing so. In a badly managed, poorly explained, and humiliating series of maneuvers, Bush finally agreed in October 1990 to a budget for fiscal year 1991 that included increased taxation. In the process he managed to seriously alienate both Republican conservatives and the general public by going back on his 1988 promise not to raise taxes. Nor did he receive credit for trying to reduce the deficit. On the contrary, by the fall of 1990 a clear majority of the public disapproved of the president's handling of the national economy. As popular, journalistic, and congressional attention switched back from Iraq to domestic economic matters that September and October, Bush's approval ratings dropped by more than twenty percentage points. Republican candidates in the November congressional midterm elections were encouraged in numerous cases to avoid association with the president. The election results confirmed that Bush had been unable to help his party very much by using the issue of Iraq: Republicans suffered losses, if modest ones, leaving the midterm elections as more or less a draw in partisan terms. But the budget fiasco of 1990 was a severe, lasting blow to Bush's standing with multiple constituencies.[9]

A few days after the 1990 congressional midterms, Bush announced the doubling of U.S. forces in the Persian Gulf region from a quarter of a million to half a million troops. The only purpose of such an extensive deployment was to prepare for offensive action against Iraqi forces in Kuwait. This announcement triggered serious domestic political opposition in the United States. The vast majority of congressional Republicans rallied to the president's deployment, but most Democrats in and out of Congress objected, arguing that war was unnecessary and that economic sanctions be given time to work. Bush did not believe that sanctions by themselves would force Iraq from Kuwait, nor was he particularly interested in postponing the point of decision. In his mind, delays would only lead to the fraying of the existing coalition against Saddam, robbing the United States of its ability to compel Iraq. In November 1990 Bush secured a UN resolution authorizing the use of force to liberate Kuwait in the absence of an Iraqi withdrawal by January 15, 1991. This UN resolution in turn gave the administration considerable political cover at home. On January 9, 1991, Bush had Baker meet one last time with his Iraqi counterpart for talks in Geneva, but in truth, the moment for diplomatic compromise was over: Saddam would not agree to a completely unconditional withdrawal and the United States would not agree to anything less. Days later, both houses of Congress voted in favor of the use of force against Iraq, with a pivotal bloc of hawkish and mostly southern Democrats joining the Republicans in support of Bush. Devastating American air strikes against Iraq and its armed forces began on January 16. After more than a month of such strikes, U.S. and allied ground troops began the liberation of Kuwait on February 24. The land war lasted barely four days, during which the Iraqi army was overwhelmed. Allied casualties were amazingly low in a showcase of America's reformed, post-Vietnam military prowess. Viewing further slaughter as unnecessary, Bush authorized a cease-fire, and the war came to an end. The president appears to have believed that Saddam would soon be overthrown in some sort of internal military coup. Indeed, Bush made the mistake of publicly suggesting that ordinary

Iraqis might rise up and topple Saddam, creating the erroneous impression of prospective material U.S. aid for such action. When Kurdish and Shiite Iraqis did in fact rebel against Saddam's regime, in the following days, the Bush administration did nothing concrete to support them, and had never intended to. Saddam's forces put down the Kurdish and Shiite uprisings with brutal effectiveness. Stung by the image of consequent massacres, Bush offered humanitarian relief and implemented U.S.-enforced no-fly zones over southern and northern Iraq in which Saddam's aircraft would be forbidden from operating. The United States settled in to a lengthy period of containing Iraq through sanctions, military deterrence, selected air strikes, and UN inspections. Critics later argued that Bush should have ordered American forces "on to Baghdad" to overthrow Saddam, but the president had no mandate for this either domestically or internationally, and, as subsequent events revealed, any such mission would have been fraught with immense difficulties. Bush and his leading advisers were particularly concerned that a fragmented Iraq might act as a power vacuum, letting in Iranian influence. They saw no American interest in a U.S. occupation of Iraq, and wisely decided to avoid any deeper military entanglement in that country.

The fate of both Gorbachev and the USSR itself continued to be highly uncertain throughout 1991. In January of that year, the Soviet leader took advantage of America's preoccupation in the Persian Gulf to crack down on national separatists in the Baltic states. While this crackdown triggered widespread condemnation in the United States, Bush's response was muted. Washington was gaining a great deal by working with Gorbachev in the case of Iraq, as well as over arms control and in numerous other locations such as Nicaragua and Angola. As usual, Bush preferred to see isolated aspects of foreign policy behavior in the overall context of great power relations, and in his view the United States could not afford to abandon all other gains in relation to Soviet-American relations because of concern over one particular event. He therefore refused to take very punitive actions such as economic sanctions versus Moscow on the issue of Baltic separatism, or to vigorously support the Baltic states against Gorbachev in their search for independence. The issue soon died down as Soviet hard-liners were again set back politically. In July 1991, Bush and Gorbachev met in Moscow to sign the Strategic Arms Reduction Treaty (START I), cutting the number of nuclear warheads on both sides to a maximum of six thousand. The United States further offered the Soviet Union certain commercial benefits such as most-favored-nation status in trade relations. During the same visit, Bush traveled to Ukraine and warned its people against the dangers of what he called "suicidal nationalism." The address was soon dubbed Bush's "Chicken Kiev" speech by columnist William Safire for its refusal to more energetically support national self-determination among the republics of the USSR. Less than three weeks later, in response to this very prospect of nationalist separatism, Soviet hard-liners launched a coup against Gorbachev. The misbegotten effort quickly collapsed, and once Gorbachev returned to power he terminated the Communist Party's political monopoly and permitted the Baltic states to separate from Moscow. By the end of the year the USSR had formally disbanded into its component nations, with Boris Yeltsin taking control of a now non-Communist Russia.[10]

Looking back at the 1989–91 period in U.S.-Soviet relations as a whole, the Bush administration was often criticized in the United States, notably by conservatives such as Safire, for failing to more fully support movements toward national self-determination in the Soviet Union and Eastern Europe. In reality, however, Bush's low-key use of U.S. economic and diplomatic leverage over Moscow severely constrained Gorbachev's ability to smother nationalist movements, for example in the Baltic states. Such easy criticism on the part of American pundits also failed to account for the possible costs of abandoning a remarkably conciliatory partner in Mikhail Gorbachev. A more belligerent U.S. policy toward Moscow in 1989–91 may very well have strengthened rather than weakened Soviet hard-liners, allowing them to challenge Gorbachev with greater speed and effect than they eventually did in August 1991. The outcome then might not have been freedom for Soviet and East European peoples but Communist repression, as in China. Moreover, the precipitous or violent collapse of the Soviet Union was not something to consider casually; the prospect of thousands of nuclear weapons scattered throughout a suddenly failed state was one that no responsible American government could picture without grave misgivings. The notion that Bush and his foreign policy team were somehow "soft" on Gorbachev is nonsense. Bush pressed for and won dramatic Soviet foreign policy accommodations across the board, over Eastern Europe, arms control, Germany, the Persian Gulf, and Third World conflicts. On one issue after another, Gorbachev conceded and cooperated, while Bush pocketed the gains. The fact that he did so without simultaneously assuming a truculent or chest-beating tone was to Bush's credit, since it helped ease the process of Soviet concession. The exact wording of his 1991 speech in Ukraine may have been misjudged, but the overall approach of Bush's Soviet policies was not. The actual consequence of that approach, insofar as the United States possessed the ability to influence events in the Soviet bloc, was the complete collapse of communism in Eastern Europe and the breakup of the USSR under surprisingly peaceful conditions. Such events would have been regarded as science fiction only a few years before; it is difficult to see how the outcome could have been much more favorable to the United States.

The year 1992 brought a new set of difficult foreign policy challenges that threatened to make a mockery of Bush's depiction of a benign new world order. With the cold war over, the pressure was building—in the middle of a presidential election campaign—for the United States to intervene in cases of largely humanitarian as opposed to economic or geopolitical interest. Bosnia and Somalia were the leading examples. The violent breakup of Yugoslavia in 1991–92 had led to the creation of various independent republics, including Bosnia, itself dissolving into Croat, Serb, and Moslem factions, each relying on external support. Serbia in particular under Slobodan Milosevic supported Bosnian Serb paramilitaries in their vicious attacks on Moslem civilians in the hopes of carving out a greater Serbia within the region. In the case of Somalia, the disintegration of the central government had led to conditions of widespread starvation, aggravated by the depredations of local warlords. Both cases could plausibly be viewed as examples of intolerable violence by local aggressors against innocent civilians, requiring U.S. intervention. The same cases could also be viewed as undoubtedly tragic but intractable examples of civil disorder powered by historic ethnic animosities and not amenable to American military solutions. The U.S. Joint Chiefs of Staff, as well as President Bush and his leading advisers, very much inclined toward the latter view, especially early on. Leading liberals from Congress, the press, the State Department, and various human rights groups offered the opposing interpretation and called for humanitarian intervention in both Bosnia and Somalia, with increasing effect over the summer and fall of 1992. Of crucial political importance was the fact that certain leading conservative hawks such as Jeane Kirkpatrick and Richard Perle joined in the call for U.S. military action against the Serbs. The pressure for intervention was magnified as the Democratic nominee for president that year, Bill Clinton, attacked Bush for failing to do more in Bosnia. Bush was under contradictory political pressures. On the one hand, calls were building to "do something" in Bosnia and Somalia for humanitarian reasons. On the other hand, as Bush well understood, these calls did not reflect any real popular appetite for costly U.S. military interventions, and if such an intervention turned sour the president believed domestic political support for the mission would quickly dry up. Any major military initiatives were forestalled until after the November election. Fearing that a new Clinton administration might entangle the American military in unpromising Balkan conditions, and perhaps hoping to relieve some of the pressure to intervene in such cases, the Joint Chiefs of Staff finally agreed to a U.S. mission in the Horn of Africa during the waning days of the Bush White House. More than twenty thousand American troops would be deployed to Somalia not to disarm the warlords or build a new national government but simply to ensure the safe supply of food to civilians. Under this limited mission, Bush was confident that U.S. forces would be able to return home within a few months, hand over further responsibilities to the UN, meet an obvious humanitarian need, bolster the reputation of the United States, and burnish his own legacy as president. As it turned out, while thousands of lives were indeed saved through humanitarian relief, the question inevitably arose of what to do next about the warlords who had helped cause the starvation in the first place. In 1993, the United States would dramatically expand its mission in Somalia, with fateful consequences, but all this took place under a new American president. In the case of the former Yugoslavia, the Bush administration authorized the creation of certain no-fly zones over Bosnian skies and usefully warned Milosevic not to expand his aggressive actions into Kosovo, yet apart from these actions Bush continued to the end to resist any major U.S. military intervention. As he said on August 4, 1992, in reference to Bosnia as well as Iraq: "Before I'd commit

the president for the Republican nomination. Buchanan ran as a protectionist and a nationalist on foreign policy, opposed not only to the Gulf War but to most existing U.S. commitments abroad; a thoroughgoing conservative on social issues; and a populist who understood the general frustration over lost jobs and economic hardship. In the 1992 New Hampshire primary he approached 40 percent of the vote—a remarkable showing against an incumbent president of the same party. Exit polls indicated that the primary source of Buchanan's support was not foreign policy concerns but rather discontent over the economy, regardless of ideology. While he did not go on to win any individual state, Buchanan secured almost three million votes in the GOP primaries that year and ran a feisty campaign that hobbled the president. In response, Bush tried to shore up his support from the right at the summer's Republican Convention by taking unmistakably clear conservative stands on social issues such as abortion. This had the intended effect but in turn alienated more moderate voters, both in and out of the GOP. Another hobbling effect on Bush was administered by the eccentric Texas billionaire Ross Perot, who ran as an independent candidate for president on the premise that the entire American political system was broken and that he alone could fix it. Perot had no particular foreign policy ideas apart from ill-considered opposition to NAFTA, but he did focus attention on the continuing budget deficit at home and acted as a vessel of discontent for independents frustrated with both major parties.

Meanwhile, the Democrats nominated Arkansas governor Bill Clinton, a charming, intelligent, and politically gifted liberal-moderate surrounded by lingering questions about his character. Clinton ran an effective, aggressive fall campaign against the incumbent president, emphasizing pocketbook issues. He did not run as an antiwar liberal but rather as a relatively hawkish and idealistic internationalist with a primary focus on the nation's economy. He avoided controversial cultural issues and reinforced his image as a new breed of centrist Democrat by choosing Tennessee senator Al Gore as his running mate. Bush fought back with an energetic but unfocused appeal that stressed foreign policy leadership, moral traditionalism, and Clinton's personal weaknesses, but offered no clearly defined domestic agenda for the next four years. In the end, Clinton defeated both Bush and Perot that November with a plurality of the vote nationwide and a solid majority in the Electoral College. Bush continued to dominate overwhelmingly among voters most concerned about international issues, but by 1992, with the collapse of Soviet Union, this was such a small group that it did him little good. Indeed, a majority of voters by that year were prepared to say that no lasting benefit had come out of Kuwait's liberation, and even the cold war seemed a distant memory; anxiety over America's international economic competitiveness was now widespread, and the general mood was one of unease rather than triumph over previous foreign policy successes. The election results showed that Bush held on to conservative Republicans, evangelicals, and upper-income voters but lost crucial ground to Clinton among middle-class, white-collar, and Catholic voters throughout the country. Perot did special damage to Bush among independents and moderate Republicans dissatisfied over national economic conditions, and Perot's 19 percent of the popular vote was one of the best ever for a third-party candidate. Overall it was one of the worst showings for a Republican presidential nominee in the twentieth century, as Bush won less than 38 percent of the popular vote, but the party was not as weak as it seemed, and the GOP actually made modest gains that autumn in the House of Representatives.[13]

Bush was often accused during his four years in the White House of lacking a visionary approach to both politics and foreign policy. Certainly, his inability to clearly communicate an identifiable domestic agenda, whether conservative or not, was a serious political weakness. His style was typically characterized by caution and self-restraint. Yet a sense of self-restraint does not, in itself, indicate the lack of a coherent governing approach, much less a lack of thoughtfulness. On the contrary, self-restraint in policy often flows from thoughtfulness, just as self-described visionaries are frequently the farthest thing from being truly thoughtful. Bush was conservative, in the literal sense of the word. A central feature of his approach was to try to prevent avoidable mistakes. This is a goal that is easily dismissed only by those without close knowledge of international or domestic policy conundrums. As it happens, modern American politics is not particularly well-suited to an openly modest governing philosophy. Instead, the common demand is for what Bush knowingly called "the vision thing." In foreign policy, this means at the very least linking day-to-day decisions to an overarching sense of how they serve consensual American values such as democracy and self-government. It also means giving the impression of boldness. Bush had the peculiar quality of actually pursuing bold foreign policies that did promote American values abroad, without being able to articulate as much publicly in a very convincing way. Consequently he was criticized for being timid and indifferent to moral concerns in international affairs. He should have done much more, critics said: he should have unequivocally supported freedom for nations living under Soviet domination, early on; he should have punished China for Tiananmen Square; he should have gone on to Baghdad and overthrown the dictator Saddam Hussein; he should have moved energetically against ethnic cleansing in Bosnia. What all such criticisms had in common was that the critics making them, unlike Bush, did not have to take responsibility for the hidden costs or negative consequences of such actions. Bush was hardly indifferent to the moral content of his policies, but he was not inclined either by background or by temperament to conduct international affairs by bumper sticker. He insisted on weighing the merits of individual foreign policy decisions in terms of their inevitable trade-offs in other venues. The final decisions he took in each case may not have provided the most immediate emotional satisfaction for the political pundit, but they were generally the right ones to take. By pursuing a firm but careful course, Bush helped lock in international changes of dramatic and lasting benefit to the United States in relation to Germany, Eastern Europe, the former Soviet Union, Latin America, democracy promotion, arms control, and trade. He marshaled domestic and global support behind a thoroughly necessary and successful effort to reverse Saddam Hussein's potential stranglehold over world oil supplies. The fact that Bush did not go further in selected instances and provoke Moscow beyond all limits, ruin relations with China, or entangle the United States in low-intensity conflict in Iraq, is very much to his credit. During a crucial period of international transition and in a wide variety of areas, Bush's foreign policy was conducted for the most part with admirable skill and success. Nor did the American people fail to recognize his effectiveness in world affairs. Rather, they credited him with considerable ability in that arena, while rejecting his 1992 reelection bid on other grounds. Something similar might be said of GOP conservatives. Fundamentally, most conservatives did not become unhappy with Bush because of his foreign policy but because of his domestic governing approach. From their point of view he proved an inadequate custodian of the Reagan legacy, regardless of his international achievements. Bush was therefore left without much of a political base by 1992—a lesson that his son, George W., would not forget.

Republicans and U.S. Foreign Policy during the Clinton Era

Bill Clinton entered the White House in 1993 with a primary focus on domestic rather than international issues, but he and his team brought with them certain foreign policy assumptions that differed from those of George H. W. Bush. First, Clinton and his advisers believed that economic matters of trade, investment, and globalization had supplanted interstate conflict and national security at the very top of the international policy agenda. Second, they believed that the nature of national security had itself been transformed by the rise of supposedly new challenges such as ethnic conflict, civil war, weapons proliferation, the environment, and non-state actors. Third, they believed that these nontraditional security challenges could best be handled through American participation in peacekeeping and nation-building missions beneath the rubric of multilateral institutions such as the UN. Finally, they believed that the United States should be more consistent than it had been during the cold war in promoting democracy and human rights overseas. As a consequence, the Clinton administration was noticeably willing to declare that the United States had a vital interest in geopolitically peripheral cases of civil disorder for essentially humanitarian reasons. Indeed, Clinton had criticized Bush in 1992 for refusing to promote democracy and human rights aggressively enough in places such as China, Bosnia, Haiti, and Somalia. These criticisms were also a way to showcase Clinton's credentials as a centrist "New Democrat," willing to stand up for American values and interests overseas. At the same time, once in power, Clinton revealed little appetite in such cases for sustaining truly high costs or heavy risk, whether in terms of U.S. military casualties, financial expenditures, or political capital, to promote the stated foreign policy goals. The contradiction between pronounced ends and unprovided means played itself out in multiple instances in 1993–94. In relation to China, the Clinton administration began by threatening to link good trade relations to Beijing's human rights conduct, only to back off that stance and embrace "engagement." In Bosnia, the administration declared itself against the ethnic cleansing of Moslem civilians by Serb paramilitaries but did nothing significant to stop it. In Haiti, the administration endured a series of humiliations before indicating a readiness to topple that country's military junta. In Somalia, the administration revised the existing U.S. and UN mission from the delivery of food supplies to the reconstruction of an entire failed state. Yet as the United States and its partners had neither the desire nor the ability to really impose order in Somalia, that mission degenerated into a series of confused manhunts against recalcitrant warlords. The deaths of eighteen American soldiers in one such manhunt on the streets of Mogadishu in October 1993 brought the entire nation-building project into question. Moreover, even as Clinton called for increased action in cases of humanitarian concern, he proposed modest cuts in expenditures on the very armed forces required to carry out such missions.[14]

Republicans were often uncertain over how exactly to respond to Clinton's foreign policy agenda. The GOP's conservative base as well as its congressional wing shifted toward an increasingly oppositional stance during the 1990s regarding foreign aid, international institutions, and U.S. military intervention overseas. There were several reasons for this shift and for new intraparty divisions over foreign affairs. Reagan and to a lesser extent Bush had provided rallying points for party regulars. Now, in the absence of executive responsibility, GOP members were free to pursue their own inclinations. As the Republican Party continued to become more southern and more conservative, it was drawn to a new unilateralism in foreign affairs. There was a temptation to oppose whatever President Clinton supported, not only for partisan and ideological reasons but also since many Republicans simply disliked the man. Yet GOP confusion and opposition were rooted in a more serious intellectual problem. With the end of the cold war and the collapse of communism, all Americans were searching for guidelines as to the conduct of U.S. foreign policy. Possessing more relative international power but facing no single clear external threat, the United States was freer to pursue a wide range of foreign policy goals, and at the same time less compelled to do so. Anticommunism had provided especially strong glue for the Republican Party and the conservative movement over several decades. Consequently it was not at all obvious to GOP conservatives, any more than to Americans as a whole, what precise role in the world the United States should now play, or what doctrine should guide it in doing so. Republicans during the Clinton years were in general agreement that the president's handling of American foreign policy was disturbingly weak and ineffectual, but they did not agree on an overarching alternative. Instead, they split into four main schools of thought: realists, nationalists, interventionists, and anti-interventionists.[15]

GOP realists sought to preserve existing U.S. alliance commitments in Europe and Asia and to support regional balances of power on those continents. They did not expect international competition to disappear with the end of the cold war or with the spread of market democracies. They were generally skeptical of humanitarian intervention in locations peripheral to American national security. They argued for the selective use of force to support vital U.S. interests but were otherwise wary of strategic overextension. They had no objection to the use of multilateral institutions, foreign aid, and diplomatic exchange to promote U.S. goals—in fact, they supported foreign affairs expenditures—but they saw such policy tools as instrumental rather than as ends in themselves. They did not make the internal political fate or complexion of other countries their main cause of concern but focused on concrete U.S. interests abroad, whether economic or geopolitical. Once American credibility was committed to a given policy, whether or not GOP realists agreed with the initial decision, they tended to favor the robust use of power to ensure success. Republican realism during the Clinton era was best represented in the views and statements of former U.S. foreign policy leaders such as James Baker, Brent Scowcroft, and Henry Kissinger—veterans, not coincidentally, of the Nixon and Bush administrations. It was also the basic perspective of leading GOP senators expert in foreign affairs, notably Richard Lugar (R-IN) and Chuck Hagel (R-NE). Republican realism was the implicit outlook of many career U.S. diplomats and soldiers such as Colin Powell, chairman of the Joint Chiefs of Staff from 1989 to 1993. It furthermore gained support from numerous first-generation neoconservative intellectuals such as Irving Kristol, who suggested that with the end of the cold war, "the function of the United States is not to spread democracy around the world."[16]

Republican nationalists in the 1990s sought to preserve a free hand for the United States in world affairs. They were profoundly skeptical of international organizations or treaties that might infringe on U.S. national sovereignty. They viewed the UN in particular as a corrupt, bloated, ineffective bureaucracy dominated by anti-American shibboleths. They were very resistant to sending or maintaining U.S. troops on peacekeeping and nation-building missions abroad, especially under UN auspices. They called for deep cuts or even the elimination of foreign aid programs and foreign affairs expenditures as wasteful and unnecessary. They expressed deep suspicion of the State Department and its norms and conventions as unproductive of U.S. security. At the same time, GOP nationalists had no objection to the vigorous assertion of American power overseas. Indeed they castigated the Clinton administration for failing to maintain U.S. primacy with sufficient energy. They called for increased expenditures on America's armed forces. They supported the construction of a national missile defense system. They demanded a hard line against anti-American autocrats in Cuba, North Korea, Iraq, and Iran. They called for vigilance against the potential spread of Russian or Chinese power in Europe and Asia. They were staunch supporters of U.S. allies such as Israel, Taiwan, and the newly liberated nations of Eastern Europe. And they were capable of outrage over human rights abuses in cases such as China and Bosnia. Republican nationalism was arguably the predominant foreign policy perspective among the GOP's conservative base in the Clinton era. It was also a view common inside the party's congressional wing, particularly in the House of Representatives. The single most visible and influential spokesman for Republican foreign policy nationalism during this period was the polarizing figure of Senator Jesse Helms (R-NC), ranking member of the Senate Foreign Relations Committee. An arch-conservative on social issues, given to caustic statements, Helms was simultaneously a skillful parliamentarian possessed of clear foreign policy ideas. Helms used his leading position in the Senate to call for UN reform, State Department reorganization, and cuts in foreign aid. He led congressional battles against arms control agreements and international treaties that were in his view unverifiable or constraining upon America's ability to defend itself, and had a major impact on U.S. foreign policy in the Clinton years.[17]

GOP hawks or interventionists called for the aggressive promotion of democracy and American military predominance worldwide, through preventive military action if necessary. They worried that international order would unravel without regular American activism and viewed existing multilateral institutions as no substitute for such activism. They argued for bold strategies of counterproliferation and regime change with regard to "rogue states" such as Iraq, Iran, and North Korea. They recommended the firm containment of potential great power challengers in China and Russia. They urged dramatic increases in defense spending. They also supported robust U.S. military intervention even in semiperipheral regions such as the Balkans, not only for idealistic reasons—that is, to stop mass killings—but because they felt that America's credibility as a global power was on the line in such cases. This last point in particular—the readiness to argue for the use of force in locations of essentially peripheral strategic interest—distinguished GOP interventionists from many of their fellow conservatives during the 1990s, often putting them in a minority position in their own party. Indeed, a few neoconservatives such as Joshua Muravchik went so far as to endorse Bill Clinton for president in 1992 precisely because of the Democratic governor's hard-line campaign stance on Bosnia. In practice, idealistic hawks like Muravchik were very disappointed with Clinton, as they were with congressional Republicans much of the time. GOP foreign policy interventionists relied on crucial support from key sympathetic congressional leaders such as Newt Gingrich (R-GA) and Bob Dole (R-KS) to secure what victories they could during the Clinton years. At think tanks such as the American Enterprise Institute and in publications like *Commentary* and the *Weekly Standard*, conservative hawks, including Muravchik, Elliot Abrams, Zalmay Khalilzad, Robert Kagan, William Kristol, Richard Perle, and Paul Wolfowitz, put forward their case for an alternative and distinctly assertive GOP foreign policy position. Kagan and Kristol especially, through a series of influential articles beginning in the mid-1990s, argued for the United States to exercise a "benevolent global hegemony" based on "military supremacy" and the "remoralization of American foreign policy." Their presentation of a clear alternative vision of muscular idealism was meant not only to rectify what these authors saw as disturbing trends in American foreign policy but also to give their party an inspiring and winning issue in electoral terms. GOP hawks found common ground with GOP nationalists on a variety of issues such as military spending and missile defense. Still, most rank-and file Republicans revealed little enthusiasm at the time for signing on whole-heartedly to a truly interventionist foreign policy vision. Hawks like Kristol and Kagan were able to witness and encourage some Republican support for armed intervention in cases such as Kosovo, but their sweeping calls for a U.S.-enforced world order held only limited appeal to most conservatives in the Clinton era. The relative weakness of the GOP's interventionist faction in the 1990s was part of a striking disunity over foreign policy issues not only inside the Republican Party but even among neoconservative intellectuals. With the collapse of communism in Eastern Europe, Jeane Kirkpatrick, for example, suggested that the United States could return to being a "normal country in a normal time," and that it was "not within the United States' power to democratize the world." Irving Kristol made similar statements. Nevertheless, the alternative of a distinctly assertive and idealistic Republican foreign policy vision continued to exist, pushed forward for the most part by a new generation of advocates.[18]

At the other end of the foreign policy spectrum, conservative anti-interventionists rejected the entire premise, shared by leading Republicans and Democrats alike, of a continued worldwide military and diplomatic role for the United States. Anti-interventionists argued that with the collapse of the Soviet Union, the United States could dismantle most of its bases and alliances in Europe and Asia. They called on the United States to stop intervening militarily in the affairs of other countries. They urged the termination of American membership in international organizations and insisted on the preservation of U.S. national sovereignty. Conservative anti-interventionism was itself composed of two distinct subgroupings. The first was the libertarians, notably those associated with the Cato Institute, committed to a strictly limited role for the federal government in foreign as well as domestic affairs. The second was the "paleoconservatives." Paleoconservatives were staunch traditional-ists in cultural, economic, and international matters, unreconciled to modern liberalism in any form. They combined these traits with a pro-found opposition to immigration, free trade, and globalization. Exam-ples of paleoconservative intellectuals included Samuel Francis and Paul Gottfried. The only nationally known politician in the 1990s who really put forward a clear paleoconservative agenda was Pat Buchanan. Buchanan did surprisingly well in the New Hampshire primaries of 1992 and 1996 with his runs for the Republican presidential nomina-tion, but there is little evidence that he did so as a result of his starkly anti-interventionist foreign policy stands. In fact, Buchanan's anti-interventionism was more of a liability than an asset in the GOP, eventu-ally forcing him into third-party politics. His fate was emblematic of the role of conservative anti-interventionists in the Republican Party. While many GOP conservatives shared their skepticism for liberal globalism, few were willing to go as far in rejecting the common assumptions of U.S. foreign policy since 1945. The anti-interventionists thus provided intellectually intriguing critiques but remained politically marginal throughout the 1990s, with little practical effect on Republican Party politics.[19]

Tensions between realists, nationalists, interventionists, and anti-interventionists helped shape GOP foreign policy stands during the Clinton era, beginning with the Congress of 1993–94. The issue of Bos-nia was a prime example. Some prominent Republican politicians, in-cluding Senate minority leader Bob Dole (R-KS), pressed the Clinton administration to lift the international arms embargo against that coun-try, arm the Bosnian Moslems, and bomb Serbian forces—an option known as "lift and strike." Others, such as Senator John McCain (R-AZ), worried that such escalation would only lead to an open-ended U.S. military quagmire in the Balkans. Congressional Republicans found no consensus on this issue. In the cases of Somalia and Haiti, there was greater intraparty GOP unity against intervention. When the Somali mission slid into disaster over the fall of 1993, Republicans joined con-gressional Democrats in calling for American troops to be removed from that country. The GOP was also generally united on the undesir-ability of any armed U.S. intervention in the case of Haiti. When Clinton went to Congress for final approval of NAFTA, it was congressional Republicans that gave him the majority of his support. But even on the issue of free trade there was significant skepticism and resistance in some quarters of the Republican Party, particularly with regard to U.S. trade with China.[20]

By the fall of 1994, Clinton had fumbled a number of major domestic as well as foreign policy initiatives, belying his image as a capable, centrist New Democrat. House Republicans led by Newt Gingrich (R-GA) tapped into popular dissatisfaction with Clinton and successfully nationalized the midterm elections that November on the basis of a ten-point "Contract with America." The GOP subsequently gained fifty-two seats in the House and eight in the Senate, creating the first solid Republican congressional majority in decades. For the most part, the Contract with America and its advocates focused on domestic issues such as welfare, taxes, a balanced budget, congressional term limits, and crime. Foreign policy was not the primary interest of most Contract-era Republicans, nor was it an issue on which they always agreed. Still, GOP members were able to rally around several points regarding international and military affairs in 1994. They excoriated Clinton's handling of national security matters and called for increased military spending, national missile defense, cuts in foreign aid, UN reform, NATO expansion, and a prohibition against placing American troops under foreign command. The Contract was therefore not so much interventionist or anti-interventionist on foreign policy issues as strikingly nationalist in tone. While world events were neither the leading reason for Democratic losses in 1994 nor of highest priority to most of Clinton's Republican critics, U.S. foreign policy would be affected by the GOP takeover of Congress, particularly since entering Republican freshmen in the House of Representatives tended to be relatively uninterested in foreign affairs and lacking in the internationalist pieties of an earlier generation.[21]

The new GOP congressional majority pressed Clinton on several major foreign policy matters in 1995–96. In the Senate, Jesse Helms, now chairman of the Senate Foreign Relations Committee, led the push for deep cuts in foreign aid, along with sweeping reforms at the State Department. He also initiated stringent new economic sanctions against Fidel Castro's Cuba in the form of the Helms-Burton law, stipulating that the United States would sanction not only Castro's regime but any foreign firms that traded with it. Meanwhile, Bob Dole built bipartisan support for the option of "lift and strike," securing a veto-proof Senate majority of 69 to 29 in July 1995 in favor of ending the international arms embargo against Bosnia. This congressional pressure, combined with deteriorating events on the ground in the Balkans, finally forced Clinton to seize the initiative. Fearing a looming disaster that might endanger America's international credibility along with his own presidency, Clinton authorized air strikes against Serb forces in Bosnia and approved U.S. military support for Bosnian Moslems and Croatians. Hard-nosed negotiations held in Dayton, Ohio, produced a set of accords in November that ended Bosnia's civil war and created a loose multi-ethnic federation stitched together by international support. To help enforce the Dayton Accords, Clinton turned to Congress and requested that U.S. peacekeepers be deployed to the Balkans. Congressional Republicans were unenthusiastic. In fact, there was heated opposition to any such deployment among House conservatives. Only with the cooperation of Dole and Gingrich did Clinton succeed in winning just enough congressional support by the end of the year to send American troops to Bosnia. Conservative Republicans were also frustrated over the direction of U.S. foreign policy in other ways. Several leading military or international policy items in the Contract with America, like much of the rest of it, eventually died in the House, the Senate, or at the hands of a presidential veto. A striking example of this was the fate of national missile defense legislation, struck down by a combination of Democrats and twenty-four GOP fiscal conservatives in the House of Representatives. Yet the Republican Party in 1995–96 clearly pulled Clinton to the right on foreign and military issues as well as on domestic policy.[22]

Republicans entered the 1996 presidential election season hopeful that foreign policy and national security issues would help defeat Bill Clinton. Once General Colin Powell decided not to run, the leading GOP candidates for the White House were Bob Dole, Pat Buchanan, billionaire Steve Forbes, Senator Phil Gramm (R-TX), and former Tennessee governor Lamar Alexander. Forbes and Gramm appealed most directly to economic conservatives. Buchanan offered a distinct mixture of protectionist nationalism and social conservatism, attacking Wall Street and alarming the party establishment. Alexander and Dole each offered a mainstream, center-right candidacy. Buchanan and Forbes managed to split the solidly conservative vote in several early primaries, leaving a wide opening for the more moderate and established front-runner Dole. Neither Gramm nor Alexander ever achieved any momentum. Dole's candidacy generated little excitement but was acceptable to most party factions, leaving the respected Kansas senator to sweep through the remaining primaries after South Carolina. The Dole campaign tried to hit President Clinton on military and international issues while creating a foreign policy platform that would reconcile GOP hawks, realists, and nationalists. At their convention that summer, Republicans urged the restoration of "American world leadership" in "a difficult and dangerous world" via "peace through strength." They reiterated earlier calls for national missile defense, increased military spending, and NATO expansion. The party platform denounced Clinton's handling of U.S. foreign affairs as rudderless, weak, and incompetent, particularly with regard to cases of military intervention. Voters most concerned about international policy and defense still gave Republicans the advantage on those issues, but by 1996 Clinton had inoculated himself against criticism to some extent with a series of relatively successful peacemaking efforts in Bosnia and the Middle East. Charges of foreign policy incompetence simply did not carry much weight that year, and in any case were of little concern to most Americans in an apparently peaceful and prosperous time. Moreover, Clinton's partial co-opting of conservative policy recommendations left Dole with less to say against him. Ideologically moderate voters still had lingering doubts about Clinton's personal character but appreciated his handling of the nation's economy and his tack to the political center in 1995–96. The Dole campaign thus achieved little traction against Clinton, who was easily reelected in November, although by slightly less than half of the electorate, since Ross Perot won more than 8 percent of the popular vote.[23]

The GOP and the White House continued to spar over foreign policy during Clinton's second term in office. On a number of issues, congressional Republicans again nudged American policy in their desired direction. Such was the case, for example, with national missile defense.

The combination of North Korean missile tests and recommendations from a commission led by former secretary of defense Donald Rumsfeld allowed Republicans to push Clinton toward increased funding for the development of missile defense systems. Multiple arms control initiatives were also subject to the skeptical eye of GOP majorities in Congress. In cases where congressional Republicans were seriously divided, as over the Chemical Weapons Convention, the administration was able to secure passage of a major arms control treaty. In cases where Republicans were more or less united, as against the Comprehensive Test Ban Treaty on nuclear testing, Clinton's arms control proposals went down to defeat. Congressional conservatives were able to delay or prevent American entry into other multilateral agreements such as the Kyoto Protocol and the International Criminal Court. Meanwhile, Jesse Helms fought long-running battles over funding for the UN and the State Department. In the end, Helms secured important concessions regarding both institutions. Several U.S. diplomatic agencies were cut in funding, reorganized, and folded directly into the State Department. And with regard to the UN, American back dues were paid in exchange for internal UN reforms and a permanent reduction in the percentage of the organization's budget owed by the United States. The Clinton foreign policy era concluded with the incongruous sight of Jesse Helms addressing the UN directly, warning of possible American withdrawal from that organization in the absence of further reforms. Yet Helms completed his chairmanship of the Senate Foreign Relations Committee by championing not only UN reform but Third World debt forgiveness and aid to Africa, in the latter case directly to needy recipients rather than through corrupt regional governments.[24]

Republican pressure on Clinton did not necessarily indicate GOP unity. As is often the case with parties out of power, Republicans in the late 1990s were unable to find a wholly united voice on international issues. No event in Clinton's second term highlighted the ongoing foreign policy divisions within the GOP as much as the war over Kosovo. A small province in Serb-dominated Yugoslavia, Kosovo was inhabited by ethnic Albanians determined to assert their independence. As international talks over Kosovo's political status faltered in 1998–99, Serbian leader Slobodan Milosevic moved to crack down on the breakaway

province. Determined to prevent the same kind of atrocities and humiliations that had occurred years earlier over Bosnia, the Clinton administration launched military action against Yugoslavia in March 1999.
Yet Clinton initially made clear that he had no intention of deploying
U.S. ground troops, only airpower against Serbian targets. Republicans
found these events deeply frustrating. Many of them, particularly conservative nationalists such as Senator Kay Bailey Hutchison (R-TX), believed the United States had no compelling strategic or moral interest in
Kosovo's independence in the first place. Others, such as Senators John
McCain and Richard Lugar, felt that if the United States was to go to war,
it ought to be with full force, rather than under stifling limitations or
with airpower alone. The congressional GOP response to the war in
Kosovo was therefore incoherent, as indicated by a strange series of
votes that spring. On March 23, 1999, sixteen Republican senators
joined with most Democrats in supporting U.S. air strikes in Yugoslavia.
On April 28, the House of Representatives refused in a tie vote to support those same air strikes, and prohibited the use of American ground
troops unless authorized. Then in May, the Senate tabled a resolution
supporting "all necessary means" to win the war. At the same time, both
the Senate and the House continued to fund military operations. Congressional Republicans as a unit thereby refused to either support, oppose, or defund what many of them viewed as "Clinton's war." It was not
one of the GOP's proudest moments.[25]

Numerous Republican national security hawks and interventionists
worried that the United States had entered a prolonged period in which
it shirked its responsibilities abroad. They were frustrated by their inability to make much headway politically against either Bill Clinton or a
post–cold war lack of attention to foreign affairs in their own party. The
conservative movement as a whole seemed divided, confused, and uninterested in foreign policy, and drawn toward a rather narrow nationalism insofar as it was interested. The only GOP presidential candidate
who really inspired passion among his supporters over international issues was Pat Buchanan, and he advocated less rather than more American engagement overseas. *Weekly Standard* editors William Kristol and
Robert Kagan responded in 1996–97 by encouraging the creation of the
Project for the New American Century (PNAC), with links to leading

conservative journals, think tanks, interest groups, and foundations. PNAC's stated purpose was to "make the case and rally support" for "a Reaganite policy of military strength and moral clarity" committed to "preserving and extending an international order friendly to our security, our prosperity, and our principles." While hardly the immense influence later claimed by conspiracy theorists, and possessed of virtually no infrastructure, PNAC was a useful way of gathering together Republican foreign policy hawks of similar points of view and publicizing their recommendations in the form of brief memos to Congress and other interested parties. PNAC, for example, called on President Clinton in January 1998 to undertake "military action" aimed at "removing Saddam Hussein and his regime from power"—a position not too far removed from the American political mainstream by that time, as Congress simultaneously passed the Iraq Liberation Act with a similar declared purpose by an overwhelming margin. PNAC signatories included not only obvious confreres such as Elliot Abrams, Richard Perle, Norman Podhoretz, and Paul Wolfowitz, but also conservative Republican politicians and former office holders such as Gary Bauer, Jeb Bush, Dick Cheney, Steve Forbes, Dan Quayle, and Donald Rumsfeld. Many of its signatories would go on to participate in the administration of George W. Bush. The formation of this network did not mean that GOP hawks had yet won the political struggle over foreign policy; in fact, they did not even hold preponderant influence inside their own party. Still, they did offer a distinct, visible, and potentially winning set of ideas regarding American diplomacy and national security—a set of ideas that could be taken off the shelf, as it were, by sympathetic leaders in a time of crisis. These ideas would be commonly described as "neoconservative," but the original neoconservatives, such as Irving Kristol and Jeane Kirkpatrick, had been deeply skeptical of projects for U.S. democracy promotion and regime change overseas. Groups like PNAC were therefore in the process of redefining not only what it meant to be a Republican on foreign policy, but what it meant to be a neoconservative.[26]

Chapter Eight

George W. Bush

The Nationalist as Interventionist

PRESIDENT GEORGE W. BUSH followed a path of "big government conservatism" both at home and abroad. He presided over major increases in domestic social spending, as well as a sweepingly ambitious attempt to democratize the Middle East. Neither of these legacies would necessarily have been predictable from his 2000 presidential campaign, which emphasized conservatism at home and extra caution regarding nation-building missions overseas. Still, the kernels of Bush's distinctive governing approach were there from the start. In domestic policy, Bush was a self-described "compassionate conservative," confident that governmental power could be used to morally worthy ends. In foreign policy he was an instinctive American nationalist, believing in his country's global mission and favoring an uncompromising approach toward U.S. adversaries. Prior to the terrorist attacks of September 2001, Bush was skeptical toward arguments for military intervention overseas. After the impact of those attacks, he embraced a declared national security strategy of regime change, democratization, and preventive warfare in relation to potential threats. Iraq was turned into the main proving ground for this high-risk and in many ways idealistic strategy. Under Bush's ultimate guidance, the invasion and early occupation of Iraq were conducted with boundless optimism, inattention to local circumstance, and a serious lack of preparation for postwar reconstruction, counterinsurgency, and stability operations. This lack of preparation in turn encouraged the rise of widespread sectarian violence in that country. Bush eventually corrected his mistakes by embracing a strengthening and reordering of U.S. efforts inside Iraq. The surge, as it was called, rescued

Iraqis from continued descent into civil war and disaster, but it did not entirely rescue the Republican Party from association with an initially mismanaged war. Bush's political and ideological legacy to conservatives was consequently more mixed, disorienting, and uncertain than he would have liked, despite numerous underappreciated successes in foreign policy and counterterrorism efforts.

George W. Bush was more a product of Texas than his father had ever been. Although born in Connecticut in 1946, George W. was raised in Midland, attending public elementary school and imbibing the social mores of a conservative, religious, Sun Belt oil town. The young Bush's experience at elite eastern private institutions—first Andover, then Yale—was not entirely happy. He was a lackluster student, resentful of perceived East Coast snobbery and contemptuous of 1960s campus activism. Yet early on he showed qualities of irrepressible gregariousness that made him a natural politician. Bush enlisted in the Texas Air National Guard, then completed an MBA at Harvard. He went into the oil business but never made much money from it. Nor was he successful in his 1978 run for Congress. For several years his life appeared rather rambunctious and directionless, especially in contrast to his accomplished father's. Then he moved toward greater stability. First he married Laura Walker and became a devoted family man. Then he began to reflect on his own Christian convictions and practices with much greater seriousness. In 1986, he swore off alcohol entirely. Bush found that the rigor imparted through familial and religious commitment could be both calming and empowering. He channeled his newfound self-discipline into supporting his father's political ambitions, acting as a conduit to religious conservatives during the 1988 presidential campaign. He gained an unequaled apprenticeship in the gritty realities of modern electoral politics by observing and participating in his father's career. Along the way, he drew several important lessons and developed inclinations that would help guide him politically: the need to define one's own agenda, an aptitude for personal politics, a determination to focus on essentials, and a refusal to be outflanked from the right. Bush finally found business success by becoming managing general partner of the

Texas Rangers, a job to which he was well-suited. The position offered cash, publicity, and credibility, acting as a springboard for an independent political career. In 1994 he ran for governor of Texas against an incumbent Democrat, the feisty Ann Richards. Bush refused to trade personal insults with Richards. Instead he ran a highly disciplined, successful challenge against her by presenting a sincere, engaging demeanor and focusing on a few well-chosen issues, such as welfare, crime, and education. As governor, Bush worked with Texas Democrats to pass legislation and was soon viewed as an effective, popular executive—one of a cohort of pragmatic, conservative Republican governors that might take their party back into the White House. He won reelection in 1998 by a landslide, immediately making him a leading candidate for the 2000 GOP presidential nomination.[1]

Bush's potential appeal in 2000 was that of what Stephen Skowronek calls the "orthodox innovator." An orthodox innovator is a president who promises to complete the agenda of an existing dominant political coalition through unswerving devotion while offering tactical changes to keep that coalition winning and relevant. This is exactly what Bush promised to do. If we take Reagan-style conservatism as the single most dynamic and powerful political force in the country during the 1980s and 1990s, then Bush's promise was to be a faithful servant of the Reagan legacy. Yet the tactical innovations he offered were considerable indeed. The centerpiece of Bush's message as he ran for the presidency in 1999–2000 was what he labeled "compassionate conservatism." In a narrow sense, this meant that Bush advocated federal support for religious charities to help combat problems such as poverty, hunger, and drug abuse. In a broader sense, it meant that Bush was willing to use governmental power to conservative ends. While Bush advocated lower levels of federal taxation, spending, and regulation than did the Democrats, he did not run as a libertarian or limited government conservative. On the contrary, he promised ambitious new government programs in health care and education while distancing himself from those in his own party who he claimed were inclined to "balance the budget on the backs of the poor." In part, this was based on a political calculation that Republicans would not take back the White House if they seemed hard-hearted on social and economic issues. Compassionate conservatism was therefore a winning slogan because of its potential appeal to evangelical Protestants, women, Catholic swing voters, and moderate suburbanites all at once. Still, there is no doubt that it also reflected Bush's own genuine assumptions regarding the appropriate role of government. Bush had a longstanding personal interest in the potential of church-associated organizations to address inner-city dysfunctions. More generally, his religious convictions and belief in a strong federal power were central to his developing version of conservatism. He had no particular objection to activist government. In fact, he was confident that government could help engineer constructive changes in American social life in a conservative direction. This was an important shift in emphasis from Ronald Reagan and one that contained the seed of unanticipated outcomes in both domestic and foreign policy.[2]

As Bush launched his bid for the presidency, international affairs were neither his area of expertise nor the central focus of his campaign. Still, Republicans hoped to benefit from traditional party advantages on the issue of national security, and Bush made it part of his overall appeal. For tutorials in military and world affairs, he relied on the "Vulcans," a team of former defense and foreign policy officials led by Condoleezza Rice and Paul Wolfowitz. With their help, Bush crafted a message that resonated with his own instincts. He called for increased defense spending, military modernization, and national missile defense. He criticized the Clinton administration for overextending America's armed forces on humanitarian and nation-building missions of questionable interest to the United States. He promised to be more careful and selective with regard to the use of force overseas. He also urged a tougher stance toward real or potential U.S. adversaries such as China, North Korea, and Iraq. Bush lauded the expansion of democracy and free trade as being very much in America's interest. At the same time, he was deeply skeptical of the benefits of U.S. membership in numerous multilateral agreements such as the Kyoto Protocol, the International Criminal Court, and the ABM Treaty. The overarching tone was that of a candidate who looked to maintain a forward global presence for the United States—albeit on American terms—while safeguarding U.S. military capabilities and focusing on concrete national interests. This particular platform had the advantage of rallying Republicans, differentiating Bush, and hitting at perennial Democratic weaknesses on issues of national defense. It was also a platform that held something for every foreign policy faction in the GOP, including realists, hawks, nationalists, and even anti-interventionists. Indeed, Bush's efforts to bridge intraparty differences on foreign policy led him to some awkward hedging during the 1999 war over Kosovo: it was Senator John McCain (R-AZ), not Bush, who came out of the Kosovo episode as the most clear-minded and impressive of the GOP presidential candidates on foreign policy. The Texas governor would have to locate his initial appeal to Republican primary voters on other issues.[3]

The GOP candidates for president in 2000 included Gary Bauer, Steve Forbes, Alan Keyes, and John McCain. Forbes ran to Bush's right, and both Bauer and Keyes ran as socially conservative purists, while McCain ran to Bush's left on certain domestic issues such as taxes. Bush's well-organized campaign team, his impressive fundraising, his family name, and his mainstream conservatism all made him the natural frontrunner, but McCain launched a serious challenge with a reform-oriented message and a solid win in the New Hampshire primary. The Arizona senator had special appeal to Republican moderates, independents, and foreign policy hawks, reinforced by his heroic Vietnam war record and his straight-shooting persona. The South Carolina primary became the crucial testing ground, which Bush won convincingly by emphasizing his conservative and Christian beliefs and credentials. The lack of viable challengers to Bush's right, and his frequent public references to his own religious faith, were critical in making him the most plausible candidate for social conservatives. McCain battled back to win in Michigan before speaking out in frustrated indignation against leaders of the Religious Right. This in turn allowed Bush to solidify support at the base of the Republican Party, and he hardly lost a primary afterward outside of New England.[4]

Bush's fall campaign kicked off with a GOP Convention that emphasized diversity, inclusiveness, and compassion, ad nauseam. His Democratic opponent, Vice President Al Gore, was respected for his broad policy knowledge and experience but somehow appeared both ideologically shifting and personally wooden. The fall debates between the two candidates only reinforced popular concerns about Gore's tendency toward pomposity and exaggeration, despite his admitted seriousness on the issues. He never seemed to fix on a settled theme or persona. Bush, on the other hand, came across as personally grounded, despite doubts regarding his intellectual heft. The Bush campaign was furthermore skillful, steady, and meticulous. Indeed it had to be, for Bush to have any chance as the outside challenger in a time of peace and general prosperity. A majority of Americans were satisfied with the Clinton administration's handling of the economy, as with its centrist policies, but uneasy about the nation's moral direction and disgusted by the memory of a 1998 sex scandal that occurred directly in the White House. Bush played on these mixed feelings to effect, promising moral traditionalism and a dignified presidency without a slash-and burn-approach to popular government programs. That November, Gore won a narrow plurality of the popular vote but failed to break through in the Electoral College owing to a number of contested ballots in the state of Florida. In the end, the Supreme Court ruled in Bush's favor, leaving him as the forty-third president. Foreign policy was not a top priority for the American electorate during the 2000 campaign, but with the outcome so painfully close almost anything might have made the difference, and there is considerable evidence from exit polls that voters gave Bush the edge over Gore on international affairs as well as national defense. This edge was based not on any pretense that Bush himself was a foreign policy expert but rather on the impression that he was a strong, sincere leader surrounded by a team of heavyweights who would restore U.S. military capabilities and bring a more tough-minded approach to international problems.[5]

The initial shift in emphasis from Clinton to Bush was certainly toward American nationalism as well as hard-nosed realism in foreign affairs, but not toward increased interventionism abroad. On the contrary, the new president appeared even less interested than Clinton in expanding U.S. military deployments overseas. Bush's foreign policy team reflected and followed his approach. He appointed Colin Powell secretary of state, Donald Rumsfeld secretary of defense, and Condoleezza Rice national security adviser. Vice President Dick Cheney would also play a central role in shaping U.S. foreign policy under Bush. Powell was known to be more open than Cheney or Rumsfeld to the use of alli-

ances, diplomacy, and international institutions in promoting U.S. interests, and was therefore represented in the press as a kind of liberal
multilateralist. In fact, the secretary of state was simply a traditional Republican realist and internationalist in the mold of Bush's own father,
and above all a dutiful soldier. On certain foreign policy issues Bush did
institute important changes early on. He clarified that the United States
under his administration would abstain from membership in the International Criminal Court, and indicated a desire to withdraw soon from
the ABM Treaty in order to freely pursue a program of national missile
defense. On numerous other issues, however, once in office Bush made
no radically hawkish revisions in America's foreign policy stance. In
April 2001, for example, the Chinese capture of a U.S. spy plane created
an incident which Bush handled in a firm but sensible and even conciliatory manner. When expectations for sweeping increases in defense
spending collided with other fiscal priorities—in particular, the president's desire for new tax cuts—then defense gave way, and dramatic
spending increases were postponed. Nor did Bush actually institute a
policy of "rogue state rollback" in the first half of 2001. Instead, the new
administration pursued strategies of hardened containment in relation
to North Korea and Iran, while unsuccessfully urging the UN to authorize targeted, "smart sanctions" against Saddam Hussein's Iraq. Bush's
main priority in the spring and summer of 2001 was domestic rather
than international affairs, and there is no evidence that he sought revolutionary changes in U.S. foreign policy prior to September of that year.
If anything, he was rather a disappointment to the GOP's most fervent
national security hawks.[6]

The terrorist attacks of September 11, 2001, had the effect of transforming Bush's presidency. As the American public rallied to him, Bush
soon responded with clarity, decision, and even eloquence. On September 20, he announced in a stirring address that he would hold any
nation-state directly responsible for supporting or harboring terrorists.
Specifically, he called on the Taliban of Afghanistan to surrender the
leaders of al Qaeda to America. When this demand was refused, Bush
authorized a U.S.-led war against the Taliban that gathered the cooperation not only of traditional American allies but also of Russia, Pakistan,
and the UN. U.S. airpower, special operations forces, and precision

guided munitions were used in support of Afghanistan's Northern Alliance to drive the Taliban from power. The refusal to employ American ground forces directly in greater numbers allowed leading members of both al Qaeda and the Taliban to escape and regroup along the Pakistan border. Nevertheless, the Afghan warfare of late 2001 was a devastating blow to al Qaeda, depriving it of its major territorial base. Bush's "war on terror" had begun with a striking military advance.[7]

With the Taliban apparently toppled, the question arose in Washington of what to do next. Bush and most of his leading advisers, particularly Cheney, did not believe that tightened homeland security would be sufficient. They looked to take the fight to the enemy. They also searched for another opportunity to demonstrate that the United States would not be coerced by any of its adversaries abroad. On this point, Saddam Hussein's Iraq was a special concern. UN sanctions against that country were obviously eroding, and despite great uncertainty over the specifics, it was widely believed that Saddam might be building further weapons of mass destruction. If he were to use such weapons to coerce the United States and its allies—or worse, hand them over to terrorists—then the losses of 9/11 could pale by comparison. This at least was the president's concern. There was also the argument, which Bush found very appealing, that the United States would undercut support for terrorism in countries such as Saudi Arabia by occupying Iraq, encouraging democratization throughout the Middle East, and shaking up the region's sclerotic autocracies. Altogether, Bush was convinced that the United States could no longer rely on deterrence or containment against "rogue states" like Iraq. In his National Security Strategy of 2002, as well as in a series of major public addresses that year, he clarified that the United States reserved the right to take unilateral, preventive military action against regimes that might hand over unconventional weapons to terrorists—a strategy that became known as the Bush doctrine. More generally, he declared that America looked to cooperate with other powers such as Russia and China in affirming a worldwide trend toward democracy and open markets. Indeed, democratic freedoms internationally were now described by the president as "nonnegotiable demands" that were "right and true and unchanging for all people everywhere." The tone of the new strategy was therefore remarkably sweeping, ambitious, and idealistic, in contrast to Bush's approach before 9/11.[8]

The Bush administration's revised foreign policy was often described as "neoconservative." If this means a firm belief in American primacy, democracy promotion, and rogue state rollback, then the new approach was certainly neoconservative. Numerous authors and observers tried to dig deeper for clues to its origins. It was suggested, for example, that the arguments for war in Iraq owed their ultimate ancestry to the philosopher Leo Strauss or perhaps even to Leon Trotsky —something that would no doubt have come as a surprise to either of those individuals. It was also suggested that the central force behind war was the pro-Israel lobby in the United States, an argument for which there was remarkably little hard evidence, especially since that lobby viewed Iran and not Iraq as the greater threat to Israel. In some circles, the word neoconservative was simply used as synonymous with either "American foreign policy hawk," "former Marxist," or "Jewish." Here, the search for origins entered onto even swampier ground. In reality, most of the people described as neoconservative by this time were neither former Marxists nor Jewish nor especially distinct from other U.S. foreign policy hawks. None of the top-ranked figures in the Bush administration, including Dick Cheney, Donald Rumsfeld, and the president himself, could be described as following neoconservative thinking before 9/11. Instead, they were assertive American nationalists and hawks who were convinced of the need for a new, more aggressive foreign policy approach in the days and months after the terrorist attacks of 2001. Neoconservative commentators at venues like *The Weekly Standard* offered such a new approach. In fact they had been making the case for it, publicly, over a period of several years. In this sense, the origins of the Bush doctrine and of the war in Iraq were hidden in plain sight. The president was instinctively drawn toward bold, morally inspired, legacy-making policy departures that ran against established opinion. He was shocked by the terrorist attacks of 9/11; he was open to and inclined toward a highly ambitious new national security strategy; and neoconservative ideas regarding preventive warfare were clear, vigorously argued, and there for the taking. The moment, the individual leader, and the ideas all matched up with one another, even as the president came to his own conclusions. In the absence of 9/11, there is little reason to believe the same ideas would have won out. Still, the president's role was crucial in that another leader might have reacted very differently. And when neoconservative ideas did not serve Bush's purposes, he ignored them.[9]

If Bush's war against the Taliban was politically uncontroversial, his decision to invade Iraq was not. On the left wing of the Democratic Party at least, the war was extremely unpopular from the start. Pockets of doubt and opposition even developed over 2002 among conservatives and within the Republican Party. The first source of such skepticism was a number of leading GOP foreign policy realists. Here, Brent Scowcroft—former national security adviser to Bush's own father—made the clearest case against the war, arguing that containment could continue to work and that an invasion of Iraq would distract the United States from the larger struggle with al Qaeda. Other eminent realists such as Henry Kissinger and James Baker made more nuanced arguments, saying only that international support for any such war was essential. A second source of outright opposition was libertarians like those at the Cato Institute, who viewed the Iraq War as entirely unnecessary and likely to further aggrandize the scope of federal government powers. A third source of opposition was paleoconservatives such as Pat Buchanan, who saw the war as part of a broader, fundamentally unwelcome trend toward American empire overseas. Buchanan took the opportunity to help found a new magazine, the *American Conservative*, based on a right-of-center but anti-interventionist perspective. Moreover, many traditional conservatives such as William F. Buckley and a few senior neoconservatives such as Jeane Kirkpatrick were deeply uneasy about the logic behind the war, even if they did not come out openly against it.[10]

The most striking fact, however, in a practical sense was not conservative opposition but rather how united most Republicans were behind Bush as he led the United States into Iraq. GOP conservatives in particular had long been comfortable with an unyielding, forceful approach toward America's international adversaries. The concept of a war on terror was therefore quite popular among conservatives, in some ways a natural fit temperamentally, and in large part a source of unity rather than of discord among Republicans. It was not only neoconservatives but more traditional right-of-center venues like the *National Review* and the *Wall Street Journal* that came out in favor of the war. Congressional Republicans also lined up behind the president with almost complete unanimity. Bush had succeeded not only in defining the war on terror as the central mission of his presidency but in redefining Republican foreign policy in a remarkably high-risk, assertive, and Wilsonian direction. The sense of uncompromising American nationalism at the heart of the modern conservative movement inclined the political right toward war after 9/11. Nor was initial support for the invasion of Iraq limited to Republican conservatives. A number of leading liberal commentators came out in favor of the war as the only answer to the terrorism emanating from the Middle East. Politically liberal editors of publications such as the *Washington Post* and the *New Republic* also supported the invasion, and twenty-nine Democratic senators—including Hilary Clinton, John Kerry, and John Edwards—voted in October 2002 to authorize the use of force against Saddam Hussein. In other words, in practical political terms, it was Democrats rather than Republicans who were initially deeply divided over the prospect of war in Iraq. The Bush administration undoubtedly grasped this political reality and was content to emphasize an issue going into the 2002 midterm elections that rallied Republicans and won over swing voters while splitting apart the Democrats. Bush threw himself into GOP midterm election efforts, campaigning energetically on behalf of his party. When Democrats called for the creation of a Department of Homeland Security, he resisted, but then reversed himself while branding his opponents as soft on defense. Predictably, national security turned out to be a central issue that November. Voters were not necessarily enthusiastic about the prospect of war but admired Bush for his leadership in the struggle against terrorism, and rewarded his party with modest gains in both houses of Congress. With the midterms complete, the administration turned back to Iraq.[11]

Bush was aware that the American effort would be on more solid ground, both politically and internationally, with allied support. He therefore went to the UN in September 2002 and secured the passage of Resolution 1441, stating that Iraq was already in material breach of prior resolutions dating back to 1990. UN weapons inspectors entered Iraq soon afterward, but Saddam continued to play his usual cat-and-mouse-game with them. In the absence of full Iraqi compliance, Bush went back to the UN a second time for explicit approval by the Security Council of an American invasion. This was something that neither France nor China nor Russia was willing to give. The United States still had some thirty allies that supported the war, including Britain and about half the members of the European Union. With the diplomatic game played out, Bush issued a final ultimatum to Saddam Hussein on March 17, 2003, and authorized an American invasion that began two days later. The initial phase of the war went in some ways better than expected, in large part owing to the excellence of U.S. armed forces in conventional warfare. American troops advanced to Baghdad and overthrew Saddam Hussein within a few weeks and with relatively few casualties on either side. In May, Bush announced "mission accomplished." Then things began to turn sour.

The Bush administration had occupied Iraq with an appalling lack of preparation for postwar stability efforts. Secretary of Defense Rumsfeld in particular saw the war as one to be fought with light, high-technology forces, bound to leave as quickly as they came. Leading career army officers favored a larger number of troops in the invasion, but for the most part they shared Rumsfeld's desire to avoid messy reconstruction efforts or planning for counterinsurgency. Nor was Bush, as an ongoing skeptic of "nation-building" missions, likely to impose such responsibilities on the Pentagon. The postwar planning therefore ended up in the form of the lowest common denominator: invasion without nation building. Interestingly, leading neoconservatives at the Project for the New American Century issued a statement in March 2003 saying that the United States would have to engage in major, costly postwar stability efforts to make the occupation succeed. Many other less hawkish yet expert observers offered similar warnings, but the president went ahead as planned. U.S. occupying forces and agencies were seriously prepared for neither constabulary duties, nor postwar reconstruction efforts, nor the possible need for counterinsurgency operations. Within the White House, there never seems to have been a moment where Bush presided over or insisted on a truly searching analysis among his leading advisors over how to successfully occupy Iraq, much less whether or not to invade. Serious doubts in both cases were dismissed as hand-wringing on the part of a weak-kneed Washington establishment. Instead, postwar planning proceeded on the most unrealistically rosy assumptions, including the notion that a major Arab nation would welcome a Western occupying army, that Iraq was a prime candidate for democratization, and that the postwar reconstruction of that country would essentially pay for itself. The fact that the multiple sects and ethnicities of Iraq had historically been held together primarily by force was dismissed, in a strained usage of liberal pieties, as ethnocentric and culturally biased. The result was one that first-generation neoconservatives such as Jeane Kirkpatrick could have predicted: once the authoritarian order imposed by Saddam Hussein was shattered, without putting anything viable in its place, the result was not democracy but chaos. Widespread looting, insecurity, and disorder followed, permitting the development of a low-level insurgency led by Saddam's former loyalists. Since Iraq's Sunni Arab minority realized that their privileged position under Saddam was over, many of them lent their support to this insurgency, targeting both Shiite civilians and American forces.

By the autumn of 2003, it was obvious that the U.S. occupation had not gone as expected. Bush responded with an overdue effort to secure congressional funding for Iraq's reconstruction and to bring in the UN more directly. Yet the violence, stalemate, and confusion continued into 2004. Iraq's suspected weapons of mass destruction were never discovered, undermining the original case for war. Revelations emerged regarding abuse of prisoners at Abu Ghraib. Foreign jihadists flooded into Iraq, viewing it as a useful testing ground against the United States. Shiite militias and paramilitaries proliferated in response to the disorder. Some traditional American conservatives such as veteran columnist George Will responded by pointing out the inherent difficulties in speedily and forcibly democratizing a country that lacked the cultural prerequisites for it. Even a number of the war's staunchest supporters admitted that the initial dream of an easily democratized Iraq now seemed painfully naive. Still, in looking to the future, both they and Bush were able to make the all too plausible argument that a precipitous U.S. withdrawal would simply make things worse, not only for America's international reputation but for the Iraqi people themselves.[12]

If the American public was of two minds about Iraq by 2004, the base of the Democratic Party was not. Democratic presidential candidates going into that year included General Wesley Clark, Vermont's former governor Howard Dean, Senator John Edwards (D-NC), House Representative Richard Gephardt (D-MO), Senator John Kerry (D-MA), and Senator Joseph Lieberman (D-CT). Kerry campaigned as a mainstream liberal, Lieberman as a culturally conservative pro-war candidate, Gephardt as a traditional New Deal Democrat with hawkish leanings on national security, Edwards as a cheerful southern populist, Clark as a military man, and Dean as an outraged antiwar candidate representing what he called the "Democratic wing of the Democratic Party." As even moderate Democrats turned against Bush and the Iraq War by the fall of 2003, Dean proved to be the candidate with the strongest initial appeal to the Democratic base. Hawks such as Lieberman and Gephardt were complete nonstarters in a party that was now distinctly dovish. But Kerry fought back successfully by nudging to the left on Iraq and by using the argument that he would be the most plausible, electable candidate, particularly in light of his military service in Vietnam. After defeating Dean and the others in Iowa and New Hampshire, Kerry went on to sweep most of the remaining primaries. Of the losing candidates, only Edwards came out looking better than before, which led to his selection as Kerry's running mate.

The fall campaign between Bush and Kerry was hard-fought and intense. The president was a polarizing figure who by this time excited both strong admiration and real hatred, mostly along predictable party lines. Kerry presented himself as a dignified, intelligent, credible alternative, capable of managing the struggle against terrorism. His persona was presidential but unexciting, and he never managed to convincingly finesse the question of exactly where he stood on Iraq. In spite of occasional stumbles, Bush fought back as if he were the challenger. The president and his supporters accused Kerry of waffling on the issues and of being a conventional liberal who would raise taxes and undermine America's efforts in the war on terrorism. The charges were sufficiently plausible that they had an impact. That November, Bush defeated Kerry by a narrow but clear margin of 51 to 48 in the popular vote and 286 to 251 in the Electoral College. The president improved on his performance

from 2000 in several respects. He cut into Democratic-leaning constituencies, including Jewish Americans, urbanites, and Hispanics. He edged
out Kerry among key swing groups such as Catholics, suburbanites, and
married women. He rallied the GOP's conservative base—particularly
evangelical Protestants—enthusiastically to his side. Bush's appeal to
both Republicans and swing voters was based partly on his socially conservative stance on social issues such as same-sex marriage. But his single greatest asset at the time was the impression that whatever his flaws,
he was a strong, straightforward, principled leader who would keep
America safe from terrorism. Exit polls from the day of the election revealed that Bush's advantages over Kerry on the issues of terrorism and
leadership were crucial and overwhelming. The political effects of Iraq
on the election were much more complicated and ambiguous. Americans tend not to turn out incumbent presidents in time of war, and Kerry
did not offer an especially compelling or distinctive prescription about
what to do next. Yet by November 2004, a narrow majority of the electorate had already reached the conclusion that the war was "not worth
the cost." For those voters who considered Iraq the most important issue
in the election, almost three-quarters went for Kerry. As usual, popular
dissatisfaction with a stalemated military conflict hurt the incumbent
and helped the challenger. This raises the intriguing possibility, supported by numerous scholarly studies, that in the absence of the Iraq
War, Bush would have won reelection by an even bigger margin.[13]

As 2005 began, observers from both parties commented on the GOP's
apparent ability to squeeze out closely won but decisive victories in election after election and over issue after issue. It seemed as though Bush
had further solidified the political reconstruction begun by Reagan, toward a lasting conservative Republican dominance in American politics. Bush's efforts at coalition building worked on several key principles.
He began by working from his conservative base, both in Congress and
among the electorate. He gave something substantive to each major element in the Republican Party. For economic conservatives, there were
tax cuts and proposals for the partial privatization of Social Security.
For social and religious conservatives, there was the administration's
support on issues such as abortion, stem cell research, same-sex marriage, and new judicial appointments. For conservative national security

hawks, there was support for missile defense, increased defense spending, the Bush doctrine, and Iraq. Moreover, each major element of the
coalition was not unalterably opposed to the concessions given the
other. On the contrary, GOP conservatives as a whole showed remarkable discipline, especially in the House of Representatives, in agreeing
uon a set list of domestic and international priorities. Of course, conservative cohesion by itself was not sufficient to secure majority status in
the nation at large, so Bush supplemented that cohesion with carefully
selected, cross-partisan appeals to Congress and the country on selected
issues such as prescription drugs and education. The Bush team believed
that such ideologically unconventional appeals would help win over
moderates, independents, and swing voters to the overall Republican
agenda. Bush's stands on foreign policy, counterterrorism, and national
defense also played a crucial role in cementing the GOP coalition and
expanding its support, in ways unanticipated before 9/11. The combination of increased government spending, moral traditionalism, and an
interventionist foreign policy was a striking one. The best phrase to describe it was coined by Fred Barnes, who called this combination "big
government conservatism." While big government conservatism was
not invented by Bush, he certainly took it to new heights, for example
with dramatic increases in domestic discretionary spending. Economic
conservatives, in particular, grumbled that this was hardly what they
expected from a Republican president, but for the most part the GOP
coalition held together during Bush's first term. The president's own
supporters celebrated his military and diplomatic innovations as "radical" and "revolutionary." In fact, Bush was building on longstanding
conservative and American foreign policy ideas. Still, his sweeping international ambitions were palpable. In January 2005, with his second
inaugural address, Bush spoke in the most breath-taking, universalistic
terms about what he now considered the defining mission of his presidency: the "expansion of freedom in all the world." He announced that
America's "interests and beliefs are now one," as "every nation and culture" would welcome democratic human rights, making the United
States safer and more secure. By his own choice, Iraq was now the main
testing ground of that theory. The following month, in an address to the
Conservative Political Action Committee, Karl Rove applauded Bush

for helping to positively transform the Republican Party's appeal by turning it in an optimistic, forward-leaning, confident, and visionary direction. It seemed even to critics as though Bush, conservatives, and the GOP might go on winning elections indefinitely. But as often happens in American politics, the moment of triumph faded with stunning rapidity. Bush had already overreached in Iraq, and now the consequences would come back to haunt him and his party.[14]

National elections in Iraq in 2005 produced a new, representative government. This in itself was something remarkable, given that country's history. Yet the overall trend of the Iraq War in 2005–6 was one of persistent deterioration and violence. Iraq's central government had little control of the country outside of Baghdad's fortified Green Zone. Insurgents and jihadists continued to inflict American casualties, while rampant insecurity dominated the nation's streets. Indeed, the violence took on an increasingly sectarian quality, as Shiite militias lost patience with Sunni jihadist attacks on civilians and began fighting back aggressively. Brutal efforts at "ethnic cleansing" spread throughout Baghdad. Hundreds of thousands of refugees fled the country altogether. Iraq was essentially a failed state. It seemed as though the country might devolve into full-scale civil war along ethnic and religious lines, pulling in neighbors such as Saudi Arabia and Iran. Bush's response to all of this was painfully inadequate. Despite the time he devoted to Iraq, for the most part he refused even to admit in public the reality of the situation and instead simply called for continued support of a war that he claimed was on track to victory. By 2006 the American public had lost patience with both Iraq and the Bush administration's handling of it. This frustration extended well into the Republican Party. The *National Review*'s editor Rich Lowry noted the rise of what he called the "to hell with them hawks"—staunch conservatives fed up with Iraq. The same magazine's founding editor, William F. Buckley, now described the war as a "failed mission." Some moderate Republicans, such as Representative Christopher Shays (R-CT), joined congressional Democrats in supporting a timetable for U.S. disengagement. Even party stalwarts such as Senator John Warner (R-VA) recommended a "change of course." Still, by this point there was little to be gained politically for GOP conservatives and much to be lost in Iraq by coming out for immediate American withdrawal. Most congressional Republicans had no better option than to stick with the overarching war effort, even as electoral defeat loomed large. In the November 2006 midterm elections, the GOP lost control of both houses of Congress. Moderate and independent voters turned decisively against the war, the president, and the Republican Party. A series of congressional scandals, together with the perception of Bush's insufficient response to Hurricane Katrina the previous year, were also important in leading to the GOP's sweeping midterm losses, but popular frustration over Iraq was absolutely central to this defeat.[15]

Bush now faced a difficult choice in the winter of 2006–7. The first option was to follow what by this time had become the conventional wisdom regarding Iraq in centrist political circles and to begin a gradual withdrawal of U.S. forces. This was the recommendation, for example, of the bipartisan Iraq Study Group, led by respected Washington elders James Baker and Lee Hamilton. In some ways this would have been the easier approach, in domestic political terms, since a majority of Americans now clearly favored U.S. disengagement from the Iraq War. The second option was to finally get serious about population security, counterinsurgency, and the imposition of order in Iraq through a more aggressive and sophisticated operational approach. This was the recommendation of Senator John McCain, and of an influential report authored by General Jack Keane and Frederick Kagan of the American Enterprise Institute. Bush chose the second option. No doubt its recommendations suited his pugnacious temperament, as well as his genuine belief that the United States simply could not admit failure in the ongoing war. In January 2007, Bush announced that several additional U.S. Army brigades would be sent to Baghdad and other parts of Iraq in a new, fast troop mobilization known as the "surge," under the command of General David Petraeus. The surge was very unpopular at the time, opposed by Democrats, some GOP moderates, and a majority of the American public. Bush tried to buy time in the first half of 2007 by defying congressional Democrats to defund the war. This they either would not or could not do, since the president retained veto power and a conservative Republican phalanx supportive of Bush still held over a third of the seats in each house of Congress. Instead, Democrats were forced to settle for a report due back from Petraeus in September, in the expectation that this would constitute the climactic moment of the antiwar movement. Everything therefore hinged on actual progress in Iraq. Petraeus had earlier achieved considerable success using counterinsurgency techniques in the northern part of the country. He now applied similar techniques to the broader U.S. war effort. As it happened, Sunni Arab tribal leaders in Anbar province were already coming out in open rebellion against extreme jihadist groups such as al Qaeda in Mesopotamia, appalled by their heavy-handed and brutal behavior against the population. As Sunni Arabs joined with American forces to fight the jihadists, Petraeus saw the opportunity for similar localized security bargains across the country. Using an adept combination of bold military strikes, special operations, improved intelligence, financial payouts, and local diplomacy, U.S. forces were finally able after some hard fighting to reverse the spiraling violence and bring a degree of order to Baghdad as well as other parts of Iraq. When Petraeus testified before Congress in September 2007, he was careful to note that existing military progress was still fragile, incomplete, and ultimately dependent on a process of political reconciliation among Iraq's own embittered sectarian factions. But he also pointed to dramatic reductions in wartime casualties among Iraqi civilians as well as U.S. forces, and to devastating blows struck against al Qaeda in Mesopotamia. On this basis Petraeus was able to recommend some modest and flexible troop withdrawals from Iraq in the coming months. His report was sufficiently credible that it undercut the antiwar movement and allowed Bush to postpone any precipitous U.S. disengagement. For the moment, congressional Democrats stopped trying to tie wartime funding to specific timetables for American withdrawal from Iraq.[16]

The military success of the surge was closely tied to the outcome of the GOP primaries in 2008, and especially to the candidacy of John McCain, since he was most closely associated with the new strategy. The slate of Republican presidential candidates that year indicated both the range of possible issue stands inside the GOP and also the limits of that range in a party still devoted to the legacy of Ronald Reagan. Leading potential candidates included Senator Sam Brownback (R-KS), former New York City mayor Rudy Giuliani, Senator Chuck Hagel (R-NE), former Arkansas governor Mike Huckabee, Representative Ron Paul

(R-TX), former Massachusetts governor Mitt Romney, and Senator Fred Thompson (R-TN). Brownback and Huckabee ran primarily as Christian populists, Giuliani and McCain as national security hawks, and Thompson and Romney as consistent conservatives. Most of the candidates found that opposition to the war in Iraq was not a winning stance in the Republican primaries. Brownback and Hagel in particular had been opposed to the surge, and by the end of 2007 they had dropped out of the race for lack of support. Ron Paul was the one candidate who managed to carve out a small but highly distinct and enduring niche as a strict libertarian and anti-interventionist opposed not only to the Iraq War but to America's global military presence. The race for the 2008 Republican nomination was highly unstable. Support for various candidates in national polling fluctuated, with dramatic highs and lows. Great expectations for Giuliani and Thompson in particular were quickly shattered after the primaries began. Governor Romney seemed to many insiders the most likely nominee, running a steady, well-organized campaign that reached out to all party constituencies. McCain's campaign virtually collapsed in the summer of 2007, and he was always suspect to portions of the GOP's conservative base. But McCain fought back to win in New Hampshire primarily on the basis of his own personal appeal and unyielding stance on the war, while the folksy Huckabee rather than Romney became a favorite of evangelical Protestant voters in Iowa and the South. As conservatives split their vote among several candidates, McCain sailed to victory in South Carolina and Florida, effectively wrapping up the nomination.[17]

The Democratic candidate for president in 2008, Senator Barack Obama (D-IL), was, as he himself noted, an unconventional prospect for the White House. It was not initially obvious that a young, liberal, relatively inexperienced African American with an exotic-sounding name would be the most electable national candidate, but Obama ran an exceptionally meticulous, well-financed, and exciting campaign for the Democratic nomination. During the primary season he quickly became the favorite candidate not only of African Americans but also of college-educated white liberals, not least because of his early public stance against the Iraq War, and in the end he narrowly edged out Senator Hilary Clinton (D-NY) and captured the majority of party delegates. The fall campaign was fought amid an unusually favorable environment for the Democrats; McCain faced a steep uphill climb from the very beginning. Popular approval of George W. Bush had continued to sink toward disastrously low numbers in 2007–8, and as the Republican Party's presidential candidate, McCain could not escape Bush's shadow, no matter how much he tried. Obama, furthermore, continued to wage a very steady, shrewd, and well-organized bid for the White House, capitalizing on popular desire for "change," his own charismatic personality, and strikingly favorable media coverage. McCain energized grassroots conservatives with the selection of Alaska governor Sarah Palin as his vice-presidential running mate, but once a severe financial crisis hit the nation in September, the election was all but over. The final November outcome of a solid electoral and popular majority for Obama was no surprise to serious analysts on either side. McCain retained the support of his party's conservative and evangelical core but otherwise lost to Obama among a wide variety of voting groups. The Democrat won the strong support not only of core constituencies such as liberals, lower-income voters, African Americans, and organized labor but also moderates, young voters, and Latinos. Obama was further unusually competitive among college-educated white professional and upper-income voters. Foreign and defense policy entered into the campaign in a number of subtle ways. Americans respected McCain for his heroic Vietnam War record and gave him the edge against Obama on international and military affairs overall. Indeed, on the specific issue of terrorism McCain's advantage was overwhelming. But terrorism was not the leading issue by 2008, and neither was foreign policy generally. Moreover, Obama offered a credible, intelligent demeanor and a plausible case on foreign policy, in favor of U.S. diplomatic outreach together with retrenchment in Iraq, which resonated considerably with the popular mood. The American people certainly appreciated the reduction of violence associated with the surge inside Iraq, but above all else they were simply tired of the war and refocused on domestic economic issues. Actually, insofar as the Iraq War specifically played into the 2008 election, it hurt McCain in two respects. First, as in 2004 and 2006, those voters most concerned about Iraq voted Democrat. Second, and even more important, the long-term political impact of Iraq over the course of the previous four to five years had been to dramatically undercut popular support for both President Bush and the Republican Party, well before the fall 2008 financial crisis hit—a pattern from which the GOP never recovered while Bush remained in office. The autumn economic crisis was therefore simply the nail in the coffin for Republicans. Under the circumstances, McCain did well to win twenty-one states and 46 percent of the popular vote.[18]

Bush's domestic political legacy to Republicans was obviously deeply problematic. During his last three years in office, the GOP lost control of both houses of Congress as well as the presidency, and slid well behind the Democrats in terms of voter identification nationwide. Bush did manage to secure some crucial conservative judicial appointments, along with a series of tax cuts. Yet he also presided over dramatic expansions of executive authority and government spending, leaving Republicans rather disoriented as the ostensible party of limited government. These were Bush's most striking domestic legacies. During his first term in the White House, he showed considerable skill in securing legislative victories. He alternated adeptly between partisan and cross-partisan initiatives to encourage coalitional support for his overall agenda. He acted with unprecedented energy to personally build up his party in congressional, financial, and organizational terms. The result was that by the end of 2004, many observers saw the GOP as enduringly dominant in American politics. Yet this dominance quickly unraveled, and the predominant tone of Bush's second term was one of failure and unpopularity. He failed to secure passage of major proposed reforms on Social Security and immigration. He failed to respond to Hurricane Katrina with sufficient public attention. He failed to adjust his Iraq policy for the longest time, despite agonizing years of frustration. And while elements of these failures were beyond his control, there was also a sense in which he himself contributed to them. Bush's very qualities of unflinching conviction, idealistic ambition, decisiveness, and indifference to popular opinion carried within them the potential for running off the rails if left unchecked by other virtues. He often seemed frustrated by the simple fact of having to explain or answer questions regarding his chosen policies. He was far from unintelligent, despite cartoon images to the contrary, and in fact he was voluminously curious when he wanted to be. But on important matters that failed to capture his interest, he was not sufficiently curious, probing, tactful, or flexible when he needed to be. He was generally a shrewd and principled politician but not a particularly effective public administrator or communicator, and he appears to have been regularly tempted to overreach in search of sweeping policy legacies. On crucial issues such as Iraq, the seeds of second-term failures and unpopularity were therefore planted during Bush's first term in office.[19]

Given that Bush left the presidency with extraordinarily high disapproval ratings and was conventionally considered by that time to have been a poor steward of America's foreign relations, it is worth noting that his administration could point to a number of genuine international and security policy accomplishments as it exited from office. The Bush administration stabilized and improved U.S. relations with all three of Asia's major powers, China, Japan, and India. Strategic ties to Tokyo and New Delhi were deepened, while Sino-American relations were managed with reassuring steadiness and competence. The administration concluded a wide range of bilateral and regional trade agreements with allies such as Australia, Morocco, and Singapore. It also increased U.S. aid to Africa to combat AIDS and malaria, and conditioned elements of American aid on African economic and political reforms. Regarding nonproliferation, the Bush administration achieved some notable successes. It signed a major arms control agreement with Russia in 2002 leading to the deactivation of thousands of nuclear weapons. It created a new international Proliferation Security Initiative that allowed participants to inspect vessels carrying suspicious cargoes by sea. It helped uncover and shut down an extensive illicit weapons network headed by the father of Pakistan's nuclear program, A. Q. Khan. It won an agreement with Libya in 2003 that led to the dismantling of Tripoli's weapons of mass destruction. It ultimately pursued and signed a similar nuclear agreement with North Korea, complicated mainly by that country's amazingly uncooperative government. Even in relation to Iran, the Bush administration eventually came out in support of European negotiations over Tehran's nuclear program. Washington's cooperation with its allies over tracking, arresting, and breaking up terrorist networks also improved dramatically after 9/11. This was no less true with regard to allies such as France and Germany that opposed the war in Iraq. Indeed, the tone of U.S. relations with Paris and Berlin improved significantly during Bush's second term, aided in part by friendly new governments in both those countries. And in an outcome that would have been viewed as surprising during the winter of 2001–2, no second terrorist attack on American soil occurred on Bush's watch. While numerous observers have attempted to come up with any other conceivable explanation for this outcome, a sensible judgment is that it probably had something to do with the administration's policies on counterterrorism. So if one surveys the Bush record on foreign policy outside of Iraq, on the whole it was better than commonly regarded. Still, most Americans, and Bush himself, viewed Iraq as his single most important foreign policy legacy, and it is on Iraq above all that he must be judged.[20]

The arc of Bush's entanglement in Iraq reads like something out of classical tragedy in which the princely protagonist is brought low by a crucial mistake. In the first act of this drama, the prince responds to an attack on his country with impressive clarity, resolution, and decision. In the second act, these same admirable qualities, taken to their extreme, lead him into a new and misconceived war conducted in a reckless, unwise, and stubborn manner. In the third act, both the prince and his kingdom are endangered because of this costly mistake. In the fourth act, the prince faces up to prior errors and commits himself to correcting them and redoubling his efforts. The fourth act concludes with the kingdom embattled and the prince exiting from power. The fifth act has yet to end.

Bush showed a clear understanding after 9/11 of al Qaeda's implacable and deadly nature. He rallied domestic and international support, initially, for a genuinely necessary "long war" against a worldwide network of jihadist terrorists. Then he overextended himself. The invasion and occupation of Iraq was ill-considered not only in terms of implementation but also of conception. The problem was not one of malicious intent, or criminality, or deliberate lies, as many critics suggested. Indeed, some left-liberal criticisms of Bush were so hysterical and wrongheaded that they made him look sympathetic by comparison. The problem, on the contrary, was the one identified by thoughtful conservatives such as William F. Buckley, Jeane Kirkpatrick, and George Will, namely, that to engineer the creation of an entirely new democracy, by force, in a foreign land, amid historically and culturally inhospitable conditions, is among the most difficult things that any government could possibly undertake, and breath-taking in its sweeping, idealistic ambition. To do so with a careless inattention to the facts on the ground is even worse. That such a policy became known as "conservative" is astonishing and testifies to the ability of strong-willed presidents to reshape party coalitions in their own image. At this point, the Iraq War is still ongoing, and the United States can hardly afford to lose it. In 2006–7, Bush's qualities of combative persistence and determination once again became useful as he insisted on an unpopular but effective correction of counterinsurgency efforts in Iraq. If years from now Iraq is a stable democracy friendly to the United States, then Bush may yet be vindicated, but his initial manner of handling and deciding on the war cannot be a model for Republicans in any case. Not only did he badly mismanage the occupation, he eventually brought his own party to electoral disaster by association. The final, unintended consequence of Bush's early decisions on Iraq is that they ultimately helped permit liberal Democrats to capture unified control of Congress and the White House—no great legacy, from a conservative point of view.

Conclusion

REPUBLICANS AND U.S. FOREIGN POLICY IN THE AGE OF OBAMA

Summary and Findings

The evolution of Republican foreign policy since the 1930s is commonly misunderstood. The traditional storyline is that of a progress from isolationism to internationalism, but as we saw, this is not especially helpful analytically, and it begs more questions than it answers. Prior to World War II, even Republicans like Robert Taft did not call for the strict isolation of the United States from world affairs, any more than later Republicans embraced every form of international commitment. The real story is not progress to internationalism but rather the transition to interventionism from anti-intervention. Republicans have become much more willing over time to embrace U.S. military intervention overseas—a development that had already begun in the 1940s and that has continued throughout the years. Eisenhower, for example, was considerably more comfortable than Taft with American military commitments abroad. The two Bushes, for their part, were the first Republican presidents over the last century to initiate major foreign wars, both of them in Iraq. The trajectory has therefore been one of escalating U.S. military intervention abroad. A close complement to this rising interventionism was an increased Republican hawkishness over the long term with regard to foreign policy. That is, Republicans became increasingly comfortable with a national security policy relying on the accumulation of American military power, and confident in the utility of armed force to address international challenges. Eisenhower, for example, was hardly a pacifist, but he had certain doubts about the wisdom of major military interventions in the developing world. Even Reagan showed considerable practical caution with regard to such interventions. By the time of George W. Bush's invasion of Iraq, however, that caution had given way to confident optimism and an embrace of preventive warfare as a centerpiece of U.S. national security policy. Yet it would be wrong to ascribe this long-term development simply to recent GOP leaders or ideas, since the trend toward increased Republican hawkishness began much earlier. Taft himself by the early 1950s had undergone a striking change of heart, criticizing the Democrats for doing too little to roll back communism overseas, and accepting a much larger role for the U.S. military abroad than he ever would have envisioned in the 1930s. Barry Goldwater, for his part, never had a chance to put his foreign policy ideas into practice, but he was far more hawkish and interventionist than Eisenhower, Kennedy, or LBJ. It would consequently be a stretch to suggest that the long-term Republican trend toward hawkish foreign policies is due, for example, to neoconservative ideas that became influential only in the 1970s.

The continuities in Republican foreign policy are as striking as the changes. The most important such continuity is a consistent, hard-line American nationalism. Republicans believe in American exceptionalism, have sought to preserve their country's freedom of action in world affairs, and have tried to avoid what they view as excessive accommodation toward hostile or threatening nations. Even those GOP leaders who negotiated with adversaries, such as Richard Nixon, have done so with an underlying assumption of continued strategic competition. Republicans have rarely been accommodationist or truly dovish when it comes to foreign policy. Even GOP anti-interventionists such as Taft and his successors have usually been quite nationalistic in their foreign policy approach, jealous of American sovereignty and looking to promote concrete U.S. interests relative to other nations. This sense of American nationalism constitutes a connecting point between Republicans of almost every variety and explains variations that may otherwise be puzzling to outside observers. Whether the GOP pursues foreign policies characterized as isolationist or internationalist, there is always a strong impulse of American nationalism that never wavers.

The tension or oscillation between realism and idealism is also a consistent theme in Republican foreign policy, although one without any obvious one-way progression. A common interpretation is to describe Eisenhower, Nixon, and George H. W. Bush as foreign policy realists, in contrast to Reagan and George W. Bush, who are described as hawkish idealists. If this were true, then the long-term trend would be toward a kind of muscular idealism in Republican foreign policy since the 1980s, away from the realism of an earlier era. While there is certainly something to this, it is also an oversimplification. Eisenhower, for example, believed that the United States should promote a more democratic and interdependent world order, as did the elder Bush. Put at that level of abstraction, virtually every Republican leader since 1945, like virtually every Democrat, has been an "idealist." Furthermore, some undoubted idealists, like Reagan, were capable in the final analysis of managing U.S. foreign policy with considerable care, prudence, and restraint. The relevant contrast, then, is not so much between philosophical realists and philosophical idealists as between those who implemented traditional American foreign policy ideals successfully and pragmatically and those who did not. Eisenhower, Reagan, and George H. W. Bush all fall into the former category, while George W. Bush falls into the latter in important respects. In this sense the younger Bush has more in common with Democratic presidents like Woodrow Wilson or Lyndon Johnson: ambitious and idealistic leaders who reached out for great policy legacies but overextended in their signature foreign policy initiative as a result of an excessive and tragic disconnection from realities on the ground. Richard Nixon, for his part, was highly successful and pragmatic when it came to foreign policy but created a broader impression of disjunction from traditional American ideals through his conduct over the Watergate scandal and for this reason will always be a suspect model to many, even where he is worth emulating.

Divisions within the Republican Party over foreign policy have narrowed over the long term, even as the GOP has become more hawkish. The intraparty divisions from 1939 to the early 1950s between interventionists and anti-interventionists, moderates and conservatives, Northeast and Midwest, were monumental. While there have been important disagreements over a variety of foreign policy issues in more recent years, there has never been anything like the fundamental division of that earlier era. Indeed, in practical terms Republicans have usually been relatively united on foreign policy since the late 1950s, compared, for example, to Democrats. Those divisions that have existed in the GOP over foreign policy have tended to correlate with the intraparty division between moderates and conservatives, but since party moderates have been disempowered over the years, such divisions have become less and less important. Interestingly, however, it is the conservatives and the moderates who have flipped places in important respects since the great party struggles of the Taft era. In the 1940s it was GOP moderates who favored increased defense spending and military intervention overseas and GOP conservatives who resisted. Today the conservatives tend to be the most hawkish, with moderates less so. Again, the one continuity is that conservatives have been more nationalistic than moderates: more reluctant to cede any degree of U.S. sovereignty, more skeptical of international organizations, and more unyielding regarding diplomatic accommodations abroad. The right wing of the Republican Party has never been particularly attracted to what international relations scholars call "realism." On the contrary, the constant touchstone for GOP conservatives has been an intense American nationalism that is in many ways quite idealistic.

Short- and medium-term changes in Republican foreign policy are also striking in their significance and variety. At a number of points over the course of the 1940s the GOP, including its conservative anti-interventionist wing, began to adapt to a new era of American globalism. Under Eisenhower, most Republicans eventually lined up behind a policy of cold war internationalism. In 1964, the GOP embraced the very hawkish foreign policy stance of Barry Goldwater. Only a few years later, most Republicans supported Richard Nixon as he improved relations with Moscow and Beijing. By 1980 the GOP had rediscovered its identity in Ronald Reagan's muscular idealism. After the collapse of the Soviet Union, many Republicans were skeptical of new international commitments. Yet after 9/11, the GOP became the party of the war on terrorism, preventive strikes, a Middle East freedom agenda, and the Bush doctrine.

How to explain the above patterns and permutations in Republican foreign policy? If we return to the explanatory models laid out in this book's first chapter, recall the five factors discussed: economic interests, partisan politics, international pressures, policy ideas, and political leadership. Economic interests provide some explanatory purchase over certain long-term trends. It is probably no coincidence that the GOP abandoned its earlier anti-interventionism and protectionism as the party's regional core shifted from the Midwest to the Sun Belt. Whereas the old Republican Midwest was import-competing in commercial terms, the new Republican Sun Belt was both export-oriented and more dependent on defense spending. Indeed, even the traditional GOP core constituency of midwestern farmers underwent a shift of economic interest as they began to produce increasingly for export. Yet this sort of economic explanation is still of only limited use. For one thing, intra-party differences over foreign policy have not always correlated very strongly with regional economic differences. In the 1940s, for example, there existed large numbers of both midwestern interventionists and northeastern anti-interventionists in the GOP. A more consistent explanation for those divisions would lie in ideological differences over foreign policy between various Republicans, apart from supposed economic interest. Furthermore, while there are obviously powerful economic interests at the base of the GOP, most of them are focused on domestic rather than foreign policy issues. Nor does an increased material interest in defense spending among Republicans really explain very much in terms of specific foreign policy decisions. There is precious little evidence, for example, that any decision over military intervention on the part of presidents from Eisenhower to Bush depended on pressure from the defense industry. Trade policy always looks a little more like pork barrel politics, and if crucial sectors of the GOP were to develop an interest in protectionism, we can safely predict that protectionist ideas would make headway among Republican leaders. But on most foreign policy decisions and tendencies, the evidence of the previous chapters is that vested economic interests explain surprisingly little.

Partisan politics explain more of Republican foreign policy tendencies than do economic interests. In every chapter we saw multiple examples of specific GOP foreign policy stands presented in ways so as to maximize domestic political support, unify the party, and divide the opposition. There is no reason to believe that the Democratic Party operates any differently. Yet it would be excessively and unrealistically cynical to suggest that foreign policy positions are chosen purely for domestic political reasons. Party officials consider both political incentives and sincere convictions when putting forward such positions. Sometimes they even present unpopular stands, either out of strict belief or because they convince themselves that such stands are in fact politically popular. Republicans began in the 1940s as the less hawkish party on foreign policy issues. Their inability to make headway with that stance eventually encouraged them, by the time of the Korean War, to become more hawkish than the Democrats—a position they have never relinquished. On occasion, as in 1964, American voters have punished Republicans for being too hawkish. At other times, as in the 1990s, voters have been largely indifferent to foreign affairs, negating any GOP advantage. In 2006–8, Republicans were punished for having initiated a mismanaged war in Iraq. Yet more often than not, the GOP's long-term reputation as the party of strength on national security has helped it rather than hurt it politically, especially with key constituencies such as white working-class voters, and Republican strategists understand this.

International pressures help explain both short-term and long-term foreign policy trends. Over the long run, the shift from a multipolar to a bipolar world in the 1940s, and then to something like a unipolar world in the 1990s, left the United States with more opportunity to play an active global role diplomatically and militarily. It is therefore hardly surprising that American political parties, including the Republican Party, shifted to a more interventionist foreign policy stance during this long period of time. Short-term international pressures also explain a great deal. When external threats loom large, as they did in the late 1940s, in 1979–80, and after 9/11, Republicans and Democrats alike move to a more aggressive national security stance. Yet the undeniable weight of broad international pressures still leaves considerable room for political parties and their leaders to differ on how exactly to respond. For example, the same external trigger of 9/11 left most conservative Republicans calling for the invasion of Iraq and many liberal Democrats arguing against it. This difference can only be explained by distinct interests or ideologies between these two political factions, since the international pressures operating on both were precisely the same. Similar differences can be found in other cases. Mainstream Democrats adapted fairly quickly to the notion that the United States would play an active role internationally right after World War II; many GOP conservatives fought

most conservative nationalists could embrace. Nor did the ideological permutations end there. First-generation neoconservatives had little use for arguments regarding democracy promotion overseas; later neoconservatives adopted the reverse position. In the 1970s, neoconservatives criticized Democrats for being insufficiently realistic on foreign policy. By the mid-1990s, leading neoconservatives were criticizing Democrats for being insufficiently idealistic. Each of these ideological developments had an important impact on Republican Party foreign policy tendencies. Still, given the range of foreign policy ideas available even within the GOP at any given time, we might ask, why does one particular idea win out, and not another?

The answer to that question, in each of the preceding chapters, is that specific foreign policy ideas are selected because of political leadership and coalition building across multiple policy dimensions. Such forms of coalition building can be highly contingent. In 1952, Eisenhower attracted millions of voters who appreciated his personality and were fed up with Korea. Many of these voters did not necessarily share his distinct combination of fiscal conservatism and internationalism, yet they voted for him regardless, allowing him to pursue his preferred foreign policy stance. In 1968, Richard Nixon won over millions of voters who were disgusted by the social disorder of the previous few years but had little idea of the sweeping foreign policy innovations he would pursue with regard to Moscow and Beijing. In 1992, voters appreciated the foreign policy success of George H. W. Bush but turned against him anyway. Electoral coalitions in the United States come together across a broad range of issues, many of which have nothing to do with international relations at all. For this very reason, party leaders—especially presidents—have some leeway as to the precise foreign policy positions they take. Political leadership is therefore crucial in determining the precise outlines of any party's foreign policy stance. However, one of the other findings of this book is that party issue stands over time are less arbitrary and unstable than might be suggested by formal models. Parties do not flip-flop all over the ideological map in an entirely random fashion. On foreign policy, the Republicans were less hawkish than the Democrats around 1940, and generally more hawkish than the

Democrats from about 1964 on. This long-term tendency was fairly stable and no doubt due to the underlying ideological preferences of core party constituencies on each side. Political leaders can determine exactly how such tendencies are interpreted or implemented in specific cases; they cannot deny the tendencies themselves.

Running through the five explanatory factors outlined above also helps to provide a better understanding of Republican foreign policy under George W. Bush, particularly the invasion of Iraq. There is no evidence to suggest that narrow economic interests dictated that invasion. In terms of partisan politics, the Bush administration undoubtedly hoped to gain rather than lose politically through an aggressive national security policy, but again, there is simply no compelling evidence that the Iraq War was launched primarily to boost GOP electoral fortunes. The attacks of 9/11 created both an incentive and an opportunity to attack Saddam Hussein. Yet the 9/11 attacks also left room for judgment as to how exactly to respond. Neoconservative ideas were certainly important, in that they provided a bold, articulate argument in favor of war, but these ideas were hardly determinate in and of themselves. For one thing, as we have seen, arguments for a relatively aggressive, idealistic, or nationalist foreign policy were not exactly new to Republicans or Americans generally. Even more important, the precise policy choice was up to the president. Bush himself was obviously convinced after 9/11 of both the geopolitical and the idealistic arguments for war against Iraq. Another president might not have been. Bush made war, and he made it in his own manner, sometimes to the great frustration of neoconservatives. To put it another way, neither the external shock of 9/11, nor neoconservative ideas, nor the fact of American power were sufficient to explain war in 2003. Presidential leadership is the crucial ingredient that in combination with these other factors was sufficient to explain the decision for war.

The evidence of the preceding chapters allows for a number of additional generalizations about the relationship between party politics and foreign policy. First, a party's foreign policy stand is often the result of intraparty coalition building. The ways in which parties try to reach out to swing voters with specific foreign policy stands is fairly obvious. Less obvious is the extent to which foreign policy positions often represent a kind of implicit negotiated bargain between various factions in the same party. Such bargains can take two forms. Either each faction can be given something with regard to their foreign policy preferences, or foreign policy preferences can be traded off in relation to policy rewards on domestic policy issues. Indifference toward certain policy decisions or dimensions on the part of important party factions is crucial in allowing broad coalitions to come together. If major coalition partners bitterly object to policy concessions offered to other factions, coalition building becomes much more difficult.

Second, parties are most likely to come up with fresh foreign policy ideas when they are out of power. The incentives to do so are strongest in such cases, as are the opportunities. When a new president first takes control of the White House, having turned out the opposing party, new ideas are put into practice. Then the realities of government take over, and fresh ideas are unlikely to flourish in the absence of dramatic external shock. To a large extent, the basic foreign policy agenda of any new administration is based on ideas developed in opposition, as a critique of the previous president. This means that opposition can be an unusually fertile time for the development of fresh foreign policy ideas, as the out-of-power party struggles to redefine its identity and win back office.

Third, elections shape foreign policy, but elections are not primarily about foreign policy. To be sure, voters reward or punish presidents for their perceived success or failure with regard to international affairs, but so many other factors go into the election of a presidential candidate that one can hardly view elections as a straightforward mandate on foreign policy issues. For example, presidents can lose reelection in spite of foreign policy success, or win in spite of foreign policy failure, because of domestic or personal factors. The notion that elections represent clear popular approval of one specific foreign policy stance over another is even more problematic since voters necessarily bundle all their foreign policy preferences together with myriad other concerns in casting a single ballot. Most elections are more about domestic than international affairs. Yet election results sometimes lead to dramatic changes in U.S.

foreign policy, even when the voters' foreign policy preferences are unclear or cannot be disentangled. It could hardly be otherwise, unless we move to a system of regular, fine-tuned plebiscites on each and every foreign policy issue, and there is little evidence that such a system would be better than the one we have now.

Fourth, a party's political success on foreign policy issues depends heavily on the actions and the record of the other major party. One party can advocate, for example, a certain politically advantageous policy position, but if the other party takes that same position, and does so credibly, then any comparative advantage is lost. On the other hand, if one party takes a position perceived by the general public as politically extreme, or if it presides over unhappy circumstances, then the opposing party will naturally benefit so long as the opportunity is seized. In 1972, for example, by taking a clear dovish stance on Vietnam, Democrats effectively ceded the center of American political opinion to Richard Nixon and the Republicans on foreign policy issues—a maneuver that Democrats have tried to make up for ever since. Yet such maneuvering goes both ways. When Democrats have moved back to the center on foreign policy and defense, when Republicans have been excessively hawkish for the public's taste, or when Republicans have botched their opportunities in power, Democrats have usually taken advantage. In other words, Republican political success on foreign policy issues depends very much on what Democrats do, and vice versa. A useful and related rule of thumb is that nobody likes failure, and in the context of American politics, prolonged and stalemated military engagements are considered failure. Consequently, voters punished the incumbent president's party in 1950–52, 1966–68, and 2006–8, whether Democrat or Republican, and turned it out of the White House.

Fifth, with regard to a political party's foreign policy stance, we found that presidents— not senators, cabinet members, businessmen, bureaucrats, think tanks, or journalists—in the final analysis make foreign policy. There is no other individual even comparable to the president in his ability to shape foreign policy when he sets his mind to it, a fact frequently forgotten in both academic and popular commentary. The president determines the precise outlines of his party's foreign policy stance, and ultimately acts as the focal point for coalition building related to that stance. When a party controls the White House, its foreign policy position and reputation are basically a reflection of the president.

Conservative Foreign Policy Alternatives in the Age of Obama

The preceding analysis ought to shed some light on where conservatives and Republicans are likely headed, as well as where they should be headed, on foreign policy issues. We saw several distinct, overarching patterns in previous chapters, each of which can be projected forward. Broadly speaking, Republicans have been the party of a hawkish American nationalism in foreign affairs, a trend that has if anything only increased over time. Yet there has still been lively intraparty debate over international affairs, and a variety of specific foreign policy tendencies have been evinced by Republicans. Presidents in particular have had considerable freedom to determine precise foreign policy approaches, and Republican presidents have been most successful, both politically and internationally, when they have implemented a conservative, hawkish nationalism with practical discretion, prudence, and care.

What does this mean for the present and future? Let us start with an assessment of the existing administration. The current U.S. president, Barack Obama, pursues a foreign policy shaped by several broad considerations. To begin with, despite a genuine intellectual interest in foreign relations, his greatest policy ambitions are clearly domestic rather than international. On the home front, he looks to pass sweeping liberal reforms in areas such as health care and energy, to rearrange the social compact between government and citizens, and to create a new center-left political coalition of enduring strength. His foreign policy is constrained by these domestic ambitions, as well as by the international conditions he inherited. In a sense, the Obama White House views foreign policy as an exercise in damage control, especially with regard to the aftermath of the war in Iraq. International retrenchment and peaceful diplomacy are consequently stressed not only for principled reasons but because there are limited policy options remaining, and because at the end of the day, domestic priorities are uppermost. Still, like any winning Democrat, Obama cannot be seen as too dovish on foreign policy. A minimum level of perceived strength and competence on national security issues will be requisite to the possibility of his reelection, just as it was requisite to his election in 2008. Afghanistan is therefore crucial to this administration, both politically and on its own merits.

Obama called early on for a new, comprehensive counterinsurgency effort against al Qaeda and the Taliban and for more American troops in Afghanistan, together with an increased U.S. civilian presence. By the end of 2009 he appeared to be living up to that call. Otherwise his emphasis in foreign relations tended to be on consolidation and peacemaking. He looked to withdraw American troops from combat in Iraq, one of his central platforms in 2008. He reversed several Bush-era policies on prisoner detention and interrogation, although to a lesser extent than might have been expected from statements made during the 2008 campaign. Obama offered to pursue far-reaching, direct negotiations with Iran over that country's nuclear program. With this in mind, he refused to take an especially hard stand against Iran's postelection crackdown in the summer of 2009. He showed similar forbearance as North Korea engaged in customarily bad behavior, testing various weapons and backtracking on its earlier commitments. In a striking speech in Prague, Obama laid out the goal of a nuclear-free world, promising to take the lead by, among other things, resubmitting the Comprehensive Test Ban Treaty to the U.S. Senate. With regard to Russia, he concluded negotiations over a new arms control treaty designed to further limit the number of nuclear weapons on both sides.

To some extent, Obama seems to view each of these initiatives as part of an interlocking strategy. For example, if the United States could negotiate an end to Iran's nuclear weapons program, with Russian help, then there would be less need for the United States to deploy missile defenses in Central Europe—a deployment that angers Moscow, and about which Obama is unenthusiastic in any case. In this way, America's relations could be improved with Russia and Iran at the same time, reducing the nuclear threat as well as the strategic burden weighing on the United States. Numerous experts commented on Obama's willingness to downplay democracy promotion as a centerpiece of American foreign policy. Whether in regard to China, Afghanistan, or the Middle East, Obama made it clear that the United States under his administration would be less assertive in calling for domestic changes in other countries. This development led many observers to describe Obama's foreign policies as more realist than idealist—an interesting deviation from the usual inter-party tendencies of the past. Yet while the inclination to downplay democracy promotion in itself certainly aligns with foreign policy realism, Obama's most fundamental instincts seem to be not so much realist as accommodationist. This is in keeping with broad ideological and partisan trends since the Vietnam War, as most liberal Democrats abandoned hard-line foreign policy views and embraced a more accommodationist approach. Obama and his supporters appear to view the president as someone uniquely qualified to bridge divides over cultural, economic, and political lines, an approach he first developed during his days as a community organizer in Chicago. This bridge-building approach is applied abroad as well as domestically. Tremendous emphasis is laid on the importance of conciliatory language, style, and personality. The president's instinct in many cases, internationally, is not so much to think in geopolitical terms as to try to lay out a multifaceted understanding of points of views on every side, recognizing some validity in each perspective. These efforts to split international differences are matched by an assumption of the powerful potentialities of unilateral diplomatic outreach. Obama has suggested repeatedly that if the United States takes the lead by making important concessions on global issues—for example, climate change or arms control—then other countries will follow. Open hands have been extended, diplomatically, to virtually every international competitor or adversary of the United States. These particular elements of Obama's foreign policy approach, which emphasize the transformative possibilities of conciliation, style, and international bridge building as an end in themselves, may be inspiring to many, but they do not exactly constitute realism.

Republicans face a choice as to how to respond to Obama's foreign policy approach, just as they did during previous periods in exile from the White House. We saw similar intraparty debates and reformulations in this book, during the FDR-Truman, Kennedy-Johnson, Carter, and Clinton eras. Now, as before, the GOP might take any of four basic directions, or some new combination of them, as it reformulates its own approach to international affairs. First, Republicans might adopt a policy of strict nonintervention overseas, especially with regard to the U.S. armed forces, while dismantling America's existing military commitments abroad. Second, Republicans might adopt a realist foreign policy that emphasizes great power politics, concrete national interests, alliances, and the prudent coordination of diplomacy and force. Third, Republicans might adopt a hawkish foreign policy that stresses American supremacy, a strong military, and the constant possibility of U.S. intervention overseas, not only to further narrow material interests but also to promote democracy and liberty abroad. Fourth, Republicans might adopt a nationalist foreign policy that focuses on the preservation of American sovereignty and freedom of action, avoiding multilateral commitments on the one hand and diplomatic concessions on the other. A brief survey of the current strengths and weaknesses of each school of thought, in political terms, sheds some light on which directions the Republicans are likely to take.

Republican and conservative anti-interventionists were galvanized into fierce and occasionally eloquent opposition to the war in Iraq. Congressman Ron Paul (R-TX) waged a spirited effort for the 2008 Republican presidential nomination on a pure noninterventionist platform, and gathered a band of dedicated followers in doing so. Conservative anti-interventionists have no doubt become a more visible national presence in recent years, producing some writing of high quality in venues such as *Reason* and the *American Conservative*. Libertarian and paleoconservative factions possess their own intellectual and institutional networks, journals, and, in the case of libertarians, leading think tanks such as the Cato Institute. Conservative anti-interventionist authors such as Ted Galen Carpenter, Christopher Layne, and Christopher Preble have important arguments to make, in the tradition of Senator Robert Taft, about the risks of strategic overextension by the United States.[1] Yet the very extremity of their overarching vision—that is, to largely dismantle America's strategic commitments overseas—leaves anti-interventionists with limited influence on U.S. party politics today. Whatever doubts Americans have about specific military interventions such as in Iraq, there is really no mass movement in the United States for pulling up stakes and bringing the troops home altogether. If there were, one of the two major parties would have embraced that position by now. Moreover, there is already one major political party in the United States inclined since the 1970s to be a little more dovish and less interventionist regarding military matters, the Democrats. Conservatives such as Pat Buchanan and Ron Paul therefore run against the party grain in arguing that Republicans should be the ones to adopt a strictly noninterventionist approach. Anti-interventionists may have more of an impact on Republican Party politics down the road, but they are very unlikely to become a dominant influence inside the GOP in the foreseeable future.

Republican and conservative realists were frequently uncomfortable with the initial arguments for war in Iraq, but formed no coordinated opposition to it. In a way, that lack of opposition captures a central fact about Republican foreign policy realists today: they simply do not have the organization that other conservative foreign policy factions possess.[2] Journalists regularly refer to respected elder statesman such as Henry Kissinger, James Baker, and Brent Scowcroft as if they headed a coherent party faction, but in truth they do not. Instead, they speak for a tendency, they speak for themselves, and sometimes they do not even agree with one another. For example, in December 2006, Baker's position favoring U.S. disengagement from Iraq was commonly taken as the "realist" position, yet Kissinger urged Bush to persist and fight it out. Republican realists have their own think tank, the Nixon Center, and their own journal, the *National Interest*, but they do not carry a political weight in GOP or conservative circles comparable to that of more influential journals and think tanks such as the *Weekly Standard*, the *National Review*, the Heritage Foundation, or the American Enterprise Institute. The leading lights of Republican realism mentioned above are all in their eighties. Few prominent young foreign policy realists have surfaced or been cultivated in the Republican Party. GOP politicians with strong realist leanings, such as Senator Richard Lugar (R-IN), have offered worthy public service but have not found national electoral success, and have tended to retire in recent years. Nor have the conceptual bases of Republican realism been especially well thought out or presented within the political arena. All too often, in popular commentary, foreign policy realism is simply taken as a lack of concern for morality, or a directionless pragmatism. There certainly exists a well-established school of realism in the scholarly study of international relations, offering rich insights into the nature of world politics, but most such work today is either too abstract to be of much interest to policymakers or is done without any clear connection to conservative thought.

Still, even with all of the above disadvantages, Republican realists possess a few crucial and perennial strengths. The first is simply the merits of their arguments. Republican realist analyses and recommendations regarding U.S. foreign policy are sufficiently well attuned to actual international conditions, often enough, that presidents of either party end up being forced to take their advice, if only out of sheer necessity. Second, many of the Republican civil servants who carry the responsibility of real-world expertise and implementation—whether in America's armed forces, the State Department, or U.S. intelligence services—incline toward realism in international affairs. Third, the general American public appreciates and rewards practical success in foreign affairs, and is less messianic or moralistic in this regard than is commonly suggested. Foreign policy "idealism" is to some extent a special preoccupation of party elites and party activists. We will have more to say about this a little later; for the moment, the point is that foreign policy realists do have certain built-in advantages, if they can get past the filtration effect of the nation's chattering classes.

By the process of elimination, we are left to consider the influence of Republican and conservative hawks and nationalists. One of the most striking developments of the Bush years was the way in which hawks and nationalists came together after 9/11 to support the war on terrorism and the invasion of Iraq. This hawk-nationalist alliance was eased by neoconservatives but cemented by President Bush. Numerous observers subsequently declared that wartime frustrations and Republican political defeats indicated the death of the neoconservatives. Yet the hawk-nationalist alliance in the GOP persists, and it constitutes a vocal and formidable bloc that has yet to lose its dominance over the foreign policy tendencies of the Republican Party. If one considers the arguments made today by leading conservative voices on foreign policy, voices such as John Bolton, Max Boot, Dick Cheney, Victor Davis Hanson, Robert Kagan, Charles Krauthammer, William Kristol, or John McCain, there is not much disagreement between them. They tend to be highly skeptical regarding arms control agreements, the efficacy of the UN, or the possibility of fruitful negotiations with U.S. adversaries such as North Korea, Cuba, and Iran. They vigorously support Israel, Taiwan, NATO expansion, increased U.S. military spending, missile defense, and the most aggressive measures against terrorists. They see China and Russia as strategic competitors rather than partners of the United States. They believe in a global mission for the United States, and they view Obama as disturbingly weak and apologetic regarding America's role in the world. Nor is this cluster of views unique to a few public spokesmen. On the contrary, it is common among congressional Republicans, leading GOP politicians, conservative interest groups, and grassroots Republican conservatives nationwide. GOP foreign policy hawks and nationalists argue their case with the help of a well-established network of sympathetic journals, think tanks, foundations, and sounding boards, extending into radio and TV. They have multiple other persistent advantages. They offer clear, bold arguments that resonate with popular feeling regarding American exceptionalism and a strong national defense. They believe in what they are doing. Finally, they operate within a party that is basically hawkish and nationalistic, as they are, on foreign policy matters, and has been for several decades. This gives them a natural influence and a natural audience, regardless of temporary setbacks. Whether or not one calls all such foreign policy hawks or nationalists "neoconservative" hardly matters. The important point is that the hawkish and nationalist tendencies of the GOP obviously predate the neoconservatives and go well beyond their limited demographics. Today as before, a hawkish American nationalism forms the center of gravity of the Republican Party, especially in its conservative base, when it comes to foreign policy issues.

If the basic tendency of Republicans and especially conservatives is toward a hawkish American nationalism, that still leaves some room for choice over specific foreign policy questions. The precise direction taken in the coming years by the GOP on international affairs, the exact criticisms made and recommendations offered, will certainly lean heavily on a number of contingent developments. Much will depend on the exact decisions made by Obama, and on whether he succeeds in foreign as in domestic policy matters. Unexpected international events will no doubt continue to occur, challenging his mastery of U.S. foreign relations. Republicans will have to determine how far they wish to oppose him on international and military affairs, depending on their own convictions and the political circumstances of the time. Republicans will also have to make up their own minds about the specific message and identity of their own party going into upcoming elections. At some time in the future, there will be another GOP president. At that point, he or she will be able to exercise considerable influence over what it means to be a Republican when it comes to foreign policy. As we saw throughout this book, the nomination and election of presidents, and the consequent changes they bring to U.S. foreign relations, often depend on political alliances and events that have little to do with foreign policy per se. This makes it all the more important that conservatives and Republicans think beyond the exigencies of the moment, constructively, to what kind of foreign policy they would like to pursue if given the chance.

The most pressing need right now is for Republicans to find a new balance or fusion of the various foreign policy tendencies in their own party, one that adjusts for some of the political and policy failings of the Bush years and is in a sense more conservative rather than less. A greater emphasis on conservative realism in international affairs would represent such a rebalancing adjustment for the GOP, and it should be clear from the preceding chapters that such an adjustment would be entirely consistent with the actual practices of successful Republican presidents such as Ronald Reagan, Dwight Eisenhower, and Theodore Roosevelt. The new conservative realism would begin from a principled and genuinely rightward philosophical basis. It would start by recognizing that the international political arena is in important respects a perennially anarchic and dangerous place, unlikely to ever be entirely transformed by visionary schemes for international law, world disarmament, or global governance. Under such circumstances, the possibility of the use of force always looms in the background. The freedom, safety, and position of any one nation-state are never entirely secure. This is all the more reason to approach transformational or revolutionary foreign policy proposals with a skeptical mindset, which is to say, the traditional conservative mindset. Conservatism has sometimes been described as the politics of reality. Conservatives pride themselves on their gritty resistance to sweeping, messianic promises of guaranteed progress from politicians when it comes to domestic and socioeconomic matters. That very same tough-mindedness must be applied to foreign policy. There are no permanent solutions to the problems of international security, just as there are no permanent solutions to problems relating to the balancing of freedom, authority, and justice in domestic politics. The preservation of a viable, ordered liberty in even one country is not a foregone conclusion; it requires constant vigilance and care. Conservatives should therefore approach universalistic or perfectionist ideas regarding perpetual peace in world affairs with the same skepticism that they rightly apply to such ideas in domestic affairs: they should consider the risk of unintended consequences, and think, like Hippocrates, to first do no harm.

A new conservative realism in foreign policy would lead to several broad guidelines. The first of these guidelines is offered in the spirit of getting our priorities straight. For the past twenty years, American attention in foreign affairs has tended to focus on the internal politics of smaller countries such as Yugoslavia, Somalia, and Iraq. Debates over U.S. intervention in such cases are then wrongly conflated with broader and more fundamental questions. The truly fundamental question about American foreign policy is whether the United States will continue to be predominant internationally, and here the answer must be yes. Contrary to some gloomy prognostications at the moment, and even accounting for the recent economic recession, the United States possesses multiple and enduring advantages that enable it to play a predominant international role. It has the largest gross national product of any country in the world, immense natural resources, and significant technological advantages over major competitors. It has by far the most powerful and advanced armed forces in the world and is unmatched in conventional military capabilities, bolstered by a worldwide system of bases. It has a large, dynamic, well-educated, and growing population, capable of integrating large numbers of immigrants—an unusual combination of qualities among the world's leading powers. It has an exceptionally robust civil society and a basic political stability and cohesion that some major powers lack. It has the most favorable geopolitical location of any great power in modern times, distant from potential major rivals and also less threatening to them. It is at the very center of a global system of international alliances and institutions created in the 1940s with the hope of nurturing a more liberal and prosperous world order outside of America's own borders—a hope that has already been vindicated beyond even the most optimistic expectations of that decade. Altogether, the United States continues to have a wide margin of superiority over any potential rival, to an extent that is historically unique.[3]

The spectacle of war in Iraq distracted many people from this underlying condition in two ways. First, Iraq demonstrated what ought to have been obvious: that even American power has its limits. Second, it led partisans on all sides to confuse arguments for or against the war with arguments for or against American primacy. Antiwar activists played into this confusion by suggesting that arguments for U.S. international primacy were essentially warmongering and sinister. Yet it is precisely American primacy that for more than sixty years has sheltered the right to antiwar dissent in democracies around the world. The reality is that U.S. global predominance has made the world safer, more democratic, and more prosperous than at any time in human history. This condition of predominance serves not only U.S. interests but also international interests in a world order that is astonishingly free, wealthy, and peaceful by historical standards. The first priority of conservative realists should therefore be to safeguard American primacy internationally, and avoid any policies that carry a strong possibility of eroding its basis.

While the United States is and should remain for some time to come the predominant global power, it is hardly omnipotent. There are several other major powers in the world today, including China, Russia, India, Japan, and the three leading nations of the European Union, Germany, France, and Great Britain. The current situation is highly unusual historically in that five of these seven major powers are democracies, with four of them directly tied into a radiating alliance system centered on a superpower that is also democratic. This set of interlocking alliances between powerful democratic nations has reduced the possibility of great power warfare to unprecedentedly low levels. It is appropriate that the United States work outward from this set of core alliances when formulating new diplomatic initiatives, not only to work from greater strength but because of the considerable commonality of values. NATO in particular ought to be central to U.S. foreign policy in this respect. Yet both Japan and the European members of NATO have limited military capabilities, and their declared interests are not always identical to those of the United States. Indeed, in the case of the European Union, there exists little prior internal cohesion on matters of war and peace. India, for its part, has developed into a very useful and compatible U.S. ally on a wide variety of issues, but India also pursues its own interests distinct from those of the United States. Washington will therefore sometimes have to act without the explicit support of its leading democratic allies, however desirable that support may be. The handling of U.S. relations with China and Russia will continue to be even more of a challenge. Each of these powers is an autocracy possessed of great material capabilities, keen national pride, grievances against the United States, and a determination to assert itself regionally and geopolitically. Both powers also help prop up numerous anti-American dictatorships internationally, partly out of a desire to limit U.S. primacy. Russia looks to construct and maintain a sphere of influence where possible in the former Soviet Union, using military pressure and the economic leverage gained from control over vast oil and gas supplies. China pursues a more subtle, low-key strategy, reassuring its neighbors diplomatically but building up its already tremendous national wealth and economic influence worldwide while concealing its growing military capabilities. In the long run the Chinese will accept neither the independence of Taiwan, a key U.S. ally in the region, nor the indefinite strategic primacy of the United States in the East Asian littoral. The management of Sino-American relations will therefore constitute a material and intellectual challenge of the first order to the United States in the coming years. The best way of approaching relations with both Moscow and Beijing is not to pin everything on hopes for their liberalization, nor to lapse into escapism, nor still to confront them as if they were already bitter U.S. enemies, but rather to prepare for steady, persistent strategic competition with both powers alongside limited cooperation in certain areas. Russian and Chinese power can and should be counterbalanced by the United States, through a combination of diplomacy, regional alliances, economic influence, and military presence. On issues such as trade, investment, counterterrorism,

and nonproliferation, there are ample opportunities for American cooperation with both China and Russia, and these opportunities should be
pursued when they serve U.S. interests. This limited cooperation will
also preserve U.S. diplomatic leverage and help avert a Sino-Russian alliance against Washington. Yet such cooperation can hardly conceal the
fact that the United States will continue to compete with the Russians
for political, economic, and military influence in Central Asia, the Caucasus, and Eastern Europe, just as it will compete with China in East
Asia and beyond. Competition need not imply openly violent hostilities,
which would be a disaster all around, but if the U.S. prepares for such
competition, it may actually help deter violence in the long run.

The preservation of American primacy and the effective management
of great power politics ought to come first when thinking about U.S.
foreign policy. Still, the most immediate security threat to the United
States is the possibility that terrorists might acquire and use weapons of
mass destruction against American citizens. Leading members of a transnational, global network of radical Islamist terrorists have openly
declared that their intention is to kill mass numbers of U.S. civilians—
numbers that would make the number of 9/11 deaths pale by comparison.
Americans should obviously take them at their word. Former president
George W. Bush was often accused of exaggerating this particular threat.
If anything, he probably understated it. For example, Bush suggested
publicly that the terrorists had very little popular support in Islam,
which he described as a religion of peace. Yet while a majority of Mus-
lims worldwide may frown on terrorist tactics, millions still sympathize
with and support the actions of groups like al Qaeda. This popular basis
of support is crucial in providing Islamist terrorists with money, refuge,
and recruits on a wide scale. It would be alarmingly easy for such terrorists to build, steal, or buy a primitive nuclear weapon, and, given their
own demonstrated preference for death, there is little reason to think
that suicide bombers can be deterred. The United States and its allies
must therefore use every conceivable policy instrument to hunt down
and destroy terrorist cells before they can threaten civilians. It is also
essential to be clear about the exact nature of the enemy. To describe
terrorist tactics as evil is entirely appropriate; the deliberate killing of
innocent civilians is wicked and morally indefensible. The United States

need hardly be apologetic in confronting this danger, but it should be intelligent in doing so. Not every self-described Islamist group is terroristic; some are apolitical, some political but nonviolent. The specific threat to Americans comes from radical jihadist terrorist groups that look to kill the citizens of the United States and its allies. In this sense, both Bush and Obama were quite right to say that the United States is not at war with Islam, even though Islamists believe the opposite. It is also essential to be clear about the sources of terror. Jihadist terrorism of the type conducted by al Qaeda is not simply or even primarily the result of frustrated nationalism, poverty, or specific U.S. foreign policy decisions. Al Qaeda rejects nationalism altogether, is led by representatives of prosperous, well-educated classes, and would be an implacable enemy of both Israel and the West regardless of any conceivable policy concessions. The stated goal of al Qaeda is to topple existing regimes in the Muslim world, eject Western influence, establish strict Islamic law, and rebuild the historic power and unity of Islam. This overarching ideological and millenarian vision, while immensely distant from realization, nevertheless really animates its adherents: it is itself a "root cause" of terror, and for all we know is nonamenable to adjustment except by forcible defeat. Americans should therefore expect to be engaged in a long war against Islamist terrorists for years to come, a war that was first declared by the terrorists themselves. Whether or not Iraq was initially a front in that war, it is now. U.S. defeat and humiliation in either Iraq or Afghanistan would certainly be taken by jihadist terrorists as a great victory for their cause. For this reason, the United States cannot afford to fail in either case. Fortunately, jihadist militants have undermined their own appeal in recent years, through murderous attacks on Muslim civilians and brutal misrule whenever they take power. The consequent backlash of opinion in the Muslim world will continue to be as useful to U.S. counterterrorism efforts as anything Washington does.

The proliferation of weapons of mass destruction will persist as a great concern to American officials, and it is imperative that we get the specific policy responses right. The United States should certainly work with its allies to strengthen compliance with the Nuclear Non-Proliferation Treaty, but it is also important to be realistic about what such regimes can accomplish. Dozens of nation-states have the ability to develop well-hidden nuclear weapons programs, and if they choose to cheat, there are limits to what the rest of the world can do about it short of armed occupation. The United States must therefore maintain its own military advantages against proliferators, out of simple prudence, since nonproliferation regimes in themselves have limited impact when nations elect to defy them. Similarly with regard to Russian-American arms control negotiations: there is little argument against continued modest reductions in both U.S. and Russian nuclear arsenals, but the Obama administration should remember that a primary Russian goal in such negotiations is to constrain U.S. conventional military capabilities as well, in the form of American launchers. It is not as if Moscow were somehow doing Americans a great favor simply through the existence of such negotiations. The greatest fantasy of all would be to imagine that the world's nuclear powers will universally divest themselves of their most imposing strategic asset. Obama's declared goal of a nuclear-free world is inspiring but completely unrealistic, and to pretend otherwise could have harmful effects on U.S. national security. For one thing, the United States is not actually going to surrender its nuclear arsenal, and everyone knows it. Consequently, Obama's declaration only invites the usual charges of hypocrisy. A "nuclear-free" world would still be a world of breakout nuclear capacities and clandestine nuclear stockpiles, very likely more unsettling than the one we live in now. Technologically speaking, the genie cannot be put back in the bottle. The United States should therefore maintain a safe, reliable nuclear deterrent—through testing, if necessary—to reassure its allies and deter its foes. At the same time, it should continue to develop ballistic missile defenses as a backup measure, to improve the odds of dealing with contingencies such as an accidental launch.

Within the American political context, diplomacy of any kind with international adversaries is often looked upon as either inherently good, by the left, or necessarily akin to appeasement, by the right. Conservative realists take a different point of view. In itself, diplomacy is neither desirable nor undesirable, but is instead only one tool among several in the nation's foreign policy toolkit. The notion that diplomatic contact or unilateral concessions on their own can transform hostile regimes is not well supported by historical experience, to say the least. Diplomatic promises and warnings must be supported by other forms of power, including military power, or else they are meaningless in practical terms. At the same time, there is no compelling moral or practical reason for conservatives to oppose the use of diplomacy altogether, so long as it is used in a shrewd manner: to do so would be to surrender a form of power that the United States possesses in the world. Once stripped of its rhetorical finery, diplomacy is essentially bargaining over mutual concessions. The key is to ensure that the United States negotiates from strength and gets something sufficiently worthwhile in return for whatever it gives. Diplomatic negotiations with adversarial states can sometimes achieve outcomes that favor U.S. interests, as for example the Bush administration did in 2003 with Libya. Verifiable denuclearization in exchange for normalization is not a bad bargain for the United States. In cases where such outcomes are beyond reach, negotiations need not be pursued for their own sake. But even in cases where America's potential negotiating partners are highly obstreperous, as with Iran and North Korea, the pursuit of negotiations can at the very least help pave the way for later punitive actions in cooperation with U.S. allies. The irony of Obama's diplomatic overtures toward Iran is that they may well reveal, more fully than Bush's approach ever could, the underlying intransigence of Iranian foreign policy. Whether or not this result is intentional, it will have the effect of hardening opinion against Tehran inside the United States and perhaps even among America's leading allies. In the meantime, the tried-and-true method for managing hostile states such as Iran and North Korea is a baseline strategy of containment. Those countries' leaders are no doubt ideologically aggressive and duplicitous toward the United States, but unlike suicide bombers, they do not seek their own destruction. Containment is therefore not a strategic impossibility any more than it was with regard to the bitterly hostile and ideologically minded leaders of the Soviet Union. More to the point, the alternatives to containment are even worse. While preventive military strikes against North Korea or Iran cannot be ruled out categorically, such strikes would carry grave risks for the United States and its allies. The concept of regime change, as it stands, is an aspiration, not a strategy. If either Iran or North Korea can truly be divested of its nuclear weapons program through peaceful negotiations, such an outcome

Picking fights in highly unpromising locations only encourages the impression of weakness when these fights go badly. Having said that, if the United States is going to intervene militarily abroad, which it no doubt will do again in the future, it is absolutely vital that it have the ability and determination to do so in decisive fashion. This means intervening in a manner that is overwhelming and fully capable rather than half-hearted or unconvincing. It also means continuing to develop the capacities within both the U.S. armed forces and other agencies to handle constabulary, reconstruction, and counterinsurgency duties—capacities that have already improved considerably in recent years through hard-won experience. The United States is not culturally or politically especially well suited to sustained "nation-building" operations overseas, and should be much more skeptical about undertaking them, but if it is going to engage in such operations—which necessarily follow most military interventions—then it has to get them right. America must win the wars that it is actually fighting, and at the moment, these are largely unconventional wars. Beyond these current struggles, U.S. leadership in conventional military capabilities undergirds the larger operation of a peaceful and prosperous international system, and cannot be taken for granted. The United States must maintain the ability to deter, dissuade, and if necessary defeat any realistic combination of enemies. Specific weapons systems such as the F-22 are certainly not exempt from considerations of fiscal responsibility or budgetary trade-offs. Yet the best guarantee of both long-term American security and international peace is not military parity but U.S. military superiority wherever possible.

The term "multilateralism" has been offered as a kind of silver bullet to all foreign policy problems in recent years. Liberals constantly argue that only a multilateral approach to world affairs, working through international institutions, can solve global collective action problems. In fact the very use of the word international as an adjective is assumed to lend moral superiority to any noun: international law, international institutions, and international organizations are all commonly taken to be somehow better and nobler than their domestic versions. The evidence for such assumptions is thin indeed. Many leading international organizations such as the UN include among their membership numerous brutal and corrupt dictatorships. Why exactly their voice lends greater moral authority to a given decision is not exactly clear. Nor is it obvious why policy recommendations made by unelected international authorities are necessarily more legitimate and well-informed than decisions taken by local or national elected officials representing genuine democracies. In truth, most international organizations such as the UN are neither especially sinister nor especially helpful but simply powerless in most circumstances to effect major foreign policy decisions on the part of any country. The UN is not an independent actor in world politics; on the contrary, it is an arena in itself for the continued clash or mediation of conflicting national interests. American foreign policy officials should therefore work through such organizations where possible but hold no dogmatic commitment to their supposedly immense significance. Particularly disturbing are current efforts by prominent legal authorities at home and abroad to adjudicate American domestic reforms through international or transnational methods. Whatever one thinks of past and present U.S. law on issues such as abortion, capital punishment, or counterterrorism, these are matters for American themselves to decide through democratic means. To put it bluntly, the U.S. founders did not create a republican and constitutional order inside the United States only to see it dissolved into a mishmash system of global governance. If Americans choose to give up major elements of their nation's sovereignty, then that is certainly their right, but let the debate occur openly and democratically rather than through unelected officials and undemocratic means.

The promotion of a more open and prosperous economic order internationally has been one of the great success stories of American diplomacy since World War II, and should remain a central plank in a conservative realist foreign policy approach. Free trade not only provides economic benefits to American exporters and consumers; to a greater extent than any foreign aid program, it also provides economic opportunities to the poor in developing countries. The Bush administration had a decent record on trade issues, but the Doha round of world trade talks broke down largely owing to the uncompromising negotiating position of other leading governments. The Obama administration and congressional Democratic leaders now threaten to compound these difficulties through a distinctly unenthusiastic approach to free trade. Ideally, the United States should help reinvigorate global trade talks under the auspices of the World Trade Organization. Here is an example of multilateralism that the left disdains, but that conservative realists can support. If open trading arrangements were to break down internationally, it might very well cost more to the average American than all of these other foreign policy problems combined. Failing new global trade talks, the United States should ratify and pursue regional and bilateral trade negotiations with its partners and allies, and avoid the short-term temptation of protectionism. A realistic approach would also remember that an open international economic order by itself is no guarantee of peace.

The fate of free forms of government abroad will always be of great concern to Americans. Stable liberal democracies have rarely, if ever, gone to war with one another, and the United States therefore has a strategic as well as a moral interest in a more democratic world. Yet the concept of democracy promotion divorced from all local political and cultural realities can hardly be a practical central guideline—much less a truly conservative one—for the conduct of U.S. foreign policy. Not every country that has the right to a democratic form of government has the capacity to reach it today. In some nations, such as Russia, a majority of the public actually prefers a strongman like Vladimir Putin to impose order and national pride regardless of democratic niceties. Nationalism is a genuinely popular force in the world. Many countries currently ruled by autocrats—including, for example, Egypt, Saudi Arabia, and China—would probably be even more nationalistic and anti-American if ruled by popularly elected governments. To declare that democracy promotion is the answer to all U.S. security problems is therefore seriously naive. Building patterns of responsible self-government is extremely difficult, as America's founders understood. It is one thing to defend an established, allied democracy from external aggression; it is quite another to try to create a friendly, stable new democracy where none previously existed. The U.S. government has limited ability to engineer reliably positive social change even within its own borders. Conservatives are the first to recognize this truth. Why would this be any less true overseas, with regard to foreign cultures and nations? Americans are not about to abandon their long-term aspirations for the global spread of democracy, nor should they, but the United States must be far more modest than it has been since the end of the cold war about its ability to fine-tune political reforms in distant countries all the way from Washington.

Critics of realism are right to say that power and self-interest cannot be the final end of American foreign policy, but they often draw the wrong conclusions from this insight, assuming that the only idealistic alternative is to focus on the aggressive expansion of democracy overseas. The proper and true end of American foreign policy is neither gross international power, nor the export of democracy, but rather the preservation of a republican and constitutional system of government inside the United States. Both the nation's international power and its promotion of democracy abroad are ultimately means to that end. The GOP during the Bush years embraced a foreign policy approach in invading Iraq that, whatever its merits, deviated from that understanding in important respects, and led to a series of electoral and policy failures. While many Republicans have yet to admit it, the initial years of frustration in Iraq did much to hurt the GOP's reputation for competence on matters of war and peace. Still, this does not mean that a majority of Americans suddenly trust the Democrats on such matters. Democrats have been given a chance to showcase their approach toward world affairs and national security, nothing more. It is not yet clear whether defense and foreign policy issues will have a central role in the 2012 presidential elections, but as Republicans build their central message, national security will no doubt play a part. The political possibilities for conservative foreign policy realism are intriguing. A wide array of swing voting groups, including moderates, independents, Midwesterners, married women, Latinos, and college-educated suburbanites, tend to appreciate the GOP's traditional reputation for vigilance on national security, especially with regard to terrorism, but such swing voters also look for peace through strength and not bungled or reckless interventions abroad. The Republican Party must convince these voters that it values peace as well as strength, and that it is willing to use careful diplomacy as well as military action to that end. Playing down revolutionary visions abroad will not hurt the GOP politically. The general public is actually more realistic about foreign policy than is commonly believed. Most Americans, for example, rank the prevention of terrorism and proliferation as significantly higher priorities than the promotion of democracy overseas.[4] To a much greater extent than the country's intellectual elite, the public instinctively understands that other countries look out for their own interests and that the United States should do the same. The general public also tends to be rather skeptical about arguments for U.S. military intervention, and prefers working with allies not so much for idealistic reasons as to limit the burden on Americans. To be sure, the U.S. public wants a foreign policy that does not violate core national values, but it also prefers practical strength and success in foreign relations over philosophical debates. Barack Obama appealed to this popular sense of pragmatism by claiming to be the true foreign policy realist in 2008, one who would keep the country strong while pursuing responsible diplomacy. But the jury is out as to whether Obama's foreign policy approach in office is actually realistic, and so far the signs are mixed, to say the least. Conservative realism is thus quite distinct from Obama's own approach, as well as from the approach taken by George W. Bush in going to war with Iraq.

On balance, Republicans and conservatives can be proud of the role they have played in the making of U.S. foreign policy since World War II. Indeed, that role has been sufficiently rich and diverse that they have numerous models of successful foreign policy presidents from which to draw positive example today. In particular, there is no longer any need for conservatives to defend every major international decision of George W. Bush, a president whose chief legacies were not conservative. Bush led the GOP away from its central ideal, namely, limited government in domestic affairs. This ideological transformation went hand in hand with an embrace of idealistic overstretch in foreign affairs. There were clear signs in 2009–10 that Republicans had rediscovered their core identity as the party of limited government in opposition to the endless spending, regulation, and domestic economic experiments of the Obama administration. If so, this would be an entirely healthy develop-

NOTES

Introduction
Conservative Traditions in U.S. Foreign Policy

1. David Brooks, "The Republican Divide," *New York Times*, November 11, 2008; David Frum, *Comeback: Conservatism That Can Win Again* (New York: Broadway Books, 2009).

2. For a good, recent exposition of the traditional conservative perspective, see Matthew Spalding, *We Still Hold These Truths* (Wilmington, DE: ISI Books, 2009). Some notable contributions since 2006 to the ongoing debate over the state of American conservatism include Ross Douthat and Reihan Salam, *Grand New Party* (New York: Doubleday, 2008); Charles Dunn, ed., *The Future of Conservatism* (Wilmington, DE: ISI Books, 2007); Michael Gerson, *Heroic Conservatism* (New York: HarperCollins, 2007); Paul Gottfried, *Conservatism in America* (New York: Palgrave Macmillan, 2009); Theodore Lowi, *The End of the Republican Era* (Norman: University of Oklahoma Press, 2006); George Nash, *Reappraising the Right* (Wilmington, DE: ISI Books, 2009); Ron Paul, *The Revolution* (New York: Grand Central, 2008); Ryan Sager, *The Elephant in the Room* (Hoboken, NJ: Wiley, 2006); Andrew Sullivan, *The Conservative Soul* (New York: Harper Perennial, 2007); Sam Tanenhaus, *The Death of Conservatism* (New York: Random House, 2009); Michael Tanner, *Leviathan on the Right* (Washington, DC: Cato Institute, 2007); and Paul Weyrich and Michael Lind, *The Next Conservatism* (South Bend, IN: St. Augustine's Press, 2009). For a mordant, entertaining take on the same issue, see John Derbyshire, *We Are Doomed* (New York: Crown Forum, 2009).

3. See, e.g., J. Peter Scoblic, *U.S. vs. Them: How a Half Century of Conservatism Has Undermined America's Security* (New York: Viking, 2008), and Tanenhaus, *Death of Conservatism*.

4. Stefan Harper and Jonathan Clarke, *America Alone: The Neo-Conservatives and the Global Order* (New York: Cambridge University Press, 2004).

5. Frum, *Comeback*, 184–86.

6. Leading examples published since 2001 include Patrick Allitt, *The Conservatives* (New Haven, CT: Yale University Press, 2009); Peter Berkowitz, ed., *Varieties of Conservatism in America* (Stanford, CA: Hoover Institution Press, 2004); Donald Critchlow, *The Conservative Ascendency* (Cambridge, MA: Harvard University Press, 2007); Brian Glenn and Steven Teles, eds., *Conservatism and American Political Development* (New York: Oxford University Press, 2009); Lisa McGirr, *Suburban Warriors* (Princeton, NJ: Princeton University Press, 2001); Gregory Schneider, *The Conservative Century* (Lanham, MD: Rowman and Littlefield, 2009); Jonathan Schoenwald, *A Time for Choosing* (New York: Oxford University Press, 2001); Bruce Schulman and Julian Zelizer, *Rightward Bound* (Cambridge, MA: Harvard University Press, 2008); and Steven Teles, *The*

Rise of the Conservative Legal Movement (Princeton, NJ: Princeton University Press, 2008).

7. Edward Carmines and Michael Wagner, "Political Issues and Party Alignments," *Annual Review of Political Science* 9 (2006): 67–81; David Leege et al., *The Politics of Cultural Differences: Social Change and Voter Mobilization Strategies in the Post–New Deal Period* (Princeton, NJ: Princeton University Press, 2002), 27–28, 254–58.

8. Seymour Martin Lispet, *American Exceptionalism: A Double-Edged Sword* (New York: W. W. Norton, 1996).

Chapter One
Republicans, Conservatives, and U.S. Foreign Policy

1. On Republican foreign policy under McKinley, see Lewis Gould, *The Spanish-American War and President McKinley* (Lawrence: University Press of Kansas, 1982); Richard Hamilton, *President McKinley, War and Empire*, 2 vols. (New Brunswick, NJ: Transaction Publishers, 2006); Stanley Jones, *The Presidential Election of 1896* (Madison: University of Wisconsin Press, 1964); Walter LaFeber, "Election of 1900," in *History of American Presidential Elections 1789–1968*, ed. Arthur Schlesinger (New York: Chelsea House, 1985), 5:1877–1968; Ernest May, *American Imperialism* (New York: Atheneum, 1968); John Offner, *An Unwanted War: The Diplomacy of the United States and Spain over Cuba, 1895–1898* (Chapel Hill: University of North Carolina Press, 1992); and Richard Welch, *Response to Imperialism: The United States and the Philippine-American War, 1899–1902* (Chapel Hill: University of North Carolina Press, 1979).

2. Howard Beale, *Theodore Roosevelt and the Rise of America to World Power* (Baltimore, MD: Johns Hopkins University Press, 1956); Barton Bernstein and Franklin Leib, "Progressive Republican Senators and American Imperialism, 1898–1916: A Reappraisal," in *To Advise and Consent: The United States Congress and Foreign Policy in the Twentieth Century*, ed. Joel Silbey (Brooklyn, NY: Carlson, 1991), 1–15; Richard Collin, *Theodore Roosevelt's Caribbean* (Baton Rouge: Louisiana State University Press, 1990); Raymond Esthus, *Theodore Roosevelt and the International Rivalries* (Waltham, MA: Ginn-Blaisdell, 1970); James Holmes, *Theodore Roosevelt and World Order* (Washington, DC: Potomac Books, 2006); Frederick Marks, *Velvet on Iron: The Diplomacy of Theodore Roosevelt* (Lincoln: University of Nebraska Press, 1979); Frank Ninkovich, "Theodore Roosevelt: Civilization as Ideology," *Diplomatic History* 10, no. 3 (Summer 1986): 221–45.

3. David Burton, *William Howard Taft: Confident Peacemaker* (Philadelphia, PA: St. Joseph's University Press, 2004); Paolo Coletta, *The Presidency of William Howard Taft* (Lawrence: University Press of Kansas, 1973); Walter Scholes and Marie Scholes, *The Foreign Policies of the Taft Administration* (Columbia: University of Missouri Press, 1970); Norman Wilensky, *Conservatives in the Progressive Era: The Taft Republicans of 1912* (Gainesville: University of Florida Press, 1965).

4. Lloyd Ambrosius, *Woodrow Wilson and the American Diplomatic Tradition: The Treaty Fight in Perspective* (New York: Cambridge University Press, 1990); Robert D. Johnson, *The Peace Progressives and American Foreign Relations* (Cambridge, MA: Harvard University Press, 1995); Arthur Link, *Wilson: Campaigns for Progressivism and*

Peace, 1916–1917 (Princeton, NJ: Princeton University Press, 1965); Herbert Margulies, *The Mild Reservationists and the League of Nations Controversy in the Senate* (Columbia: University of Missouri Press, 1989); Ralph Stone, *The Irreconcilables: The Fight Against the League of Nations* (Lexington: University Press of Kentucky, 1970); William Widenor, *Henry Cabot Lodge and the Search for an American Foreign Policy* (Berkeley and Los Angeles: University of California Press, 1980).

5. Warren Cohen, *Empire Without Tears: America's Foreign Relations, 1921–1933* (New York: Knopf, 1987); Alexander DeConde, *Herbert Hoover's Latin American Policy* (New York: Octagon, 1970); Melvyn Leffler, *The Elusive Quest: America's Pursuit of European Stability and French Security, 1919–1933* (Chapel Hill: University of North Carolina Press, 1979); Christopher Thorne, *The Limits of Foreign Policy: The West, the League, and the Far Eastern Crisis of 1931–1933* (New York: Putnam, 1973); Joan Hoff Wilson, *Herbert Hoover: Forgotten Progressive* (Prospect Heights, IL: Waveland Press, 1992).

6. John Aldrich, *Why Parties?* (Chicago: University of Chicago Press, 1995), 7–14, 284–86; John Gerring, *Party Ideologies in America, 1828–1996* (New York: Cambridge University Press, 1998), 6; E. E. Schattschneider, *Party Government* (New York: Rinehart and Co., 1942), 35–38, 50–53.

7. Edward Carmines and Michael Wagner, "Political Issues and Party Alignments," *Annual Review of Political Science* 9 (2006): 67–81; David Leege et al., *The Politics of Cultural Differences* (Princeton, NJ: Princeton University Press, 2002), 27–28, 254–58; David Mayhew, *Electoral Realignments* (New Haven, CT: Yale University Press, 2002), 8–32; James Sundquist, *Dynamics of the Party System* (Washington, DC: Brookings Institution Press, 1983), 6, 19–47, 298–321.

8. Edmund Burke, *Reflections on the Revolution in France* (New Haven, CT: Yale University Press, 2003); Albert Hirschman, *The Rhetoric of Reaction* (Cambridge, MA: Belknap Press, 1991), 6–13, 43–48, 81–83; Samuel Huntington, "Conservatism as an Ideology," *American Political Science Review* 51, no. 2 (June 1957): 454–73; Robert Nisbet, *Conservatism* (Buckingham, UK: Open University Press, 1986), 21–74; Michael Oakeshott, "On Being Conservative," in Oakeshott, *Rationalism in Politics and Other Essays* (Indianapolis, IN: Liberty Fund, 1991), 407–37; Thomas Sowell, *A Conflict of Visions* (New York: Basic Books, 2007), 9–35.

9. Louis Hartz, *The Liberal Tradition in America* (New York: Harvest, 1991), 4–11, 47–50, 59–62, 147–58; Russell Kirk, *The Roots of American Order* (Wilmington, DE: ISI Books, 2003), 301–44, 393–439; Frank Meyer, *The Conservative Mainstream* (New Rochelle, NY: Arlington House, 1969), 14–15, 25, 38–43; Clinton Rossiter, *Conservatism in America* (Cambridge, MA: Harvard University Press, 1982), 67–96, 198–201. Louis Hartz took the position that America's classically liberal political culture made impossible any genuine conservatism in the United States. For more on the various ideological components of the American founding, see Bernard Bailyn, *The Ideological Origins of the American Revolution* (Cambridge, MA: Belknap Press, 1967); Gordon Wood, *The Creation of the American Republic* (Chapel Hill: University of North Carolina Press, 1969); and Michael Zuckert, *The Natural Rights Republic* (Notre Dame, IN: University of Notre Dame Press, 1996).

10. Ian Clark, *Reform and Resistance in the International Order* (New York: Cambridge University Press, 1980), 1–10; Brian Rathbun, *Partisan Interventions* (Ithaca, NY: Cornell University Press, 2004), 2–3, 14–26. Some authors have suggested that conservatives'

readiness to support hard-line policies in foreign affairs corresponds to and flows from their readiness to support hard-line policies on domestic matters such as crime and welfare. See Rathbun, *Partisan Interventions*, 22.

11. Seymour Martin Lipset, *American Exceptionalism: A Double-Edged Sword* (New York: W. W. Norton, 1996).

12. On the remarkably sweeping, overarching goals of U.S. foreign policymakers, rooted in classical liberal assumptions and dating back to the nation's founding, see Felix Gilbert, *To the Farewell Address* (Princeton, NJ: Princeton University Press, 1961); Robert Kagan, *Dangerous Nation* (New York: Vintage, 2006); Frank Ninkovich, *The Wilsonian Century* (Chicago: University of Chicago Press, 1999); Tony Smith, *America's Mission* (Princeton, NJ: Princeton University Press, 1994); and William Appleman Williams, *The Tragedy of American Diplomacy* (New York: Dell, 1962).

13. Benjamin Fordham, *Building the Cold War Consensus* (Ann Arbor: University of Michigan Press, 1998); Michael Hiscox, *International Trade and Political Conflict* (Princeton, NJ: Princeton University Press, 2002); Helen Milner, *Resisting Protectionism* (Princeton, NJ: Princeton University Press, 1988); Kevin Narizny, *The Political Economy of Grand Strategy* (Ithaca, NY: Cornell University Press, 2007); Peter Trubowitz, *Defining the National Interest* (Chicago: University of Chicago Press, 1998).

14. Miroslav Nincic, *Democracy and Foreign Policy* (New York: Columbia University Press, 1992), 100–107; Charles Ostrom and Brian Job, "The President and the Political Use of Force," *American Political Science Review* 80, no. 2 (June 1986): 541–66. The thesis that political parties are primarily office-seeking is laid out in Anthony Downs, *An Economic Theory of Democracy* (New York: Harper, 1957), 24.

15. The most explicit statement of this argument is Joanne Gowa, "Parties, Voters, and the Use of Force Abroad," *International Organization* 52, no. 2 (Spring 1998): 307–24. It is also implicit in the work of leading realists such as Colin Elman, "Why Not Neorealist Theories of Foreign Policy," *Security Studies* 6, no. 1 (Autumn 1996): 7–53; John Mearsheimer, *The Tragedy of Great Power Politics* (New York: W. W. Norton, 2001); Barry Posen, *The Sources of Military Doctrine* (Ithaca, NY: Cornell University Press, 1984), 7–8, 239; Kenneth Waltz, *Theory of International Politics* (Reading, MA: Addison-Wesley, 1979), 110, 127, 165–66, 174; and Fareed Zakaria, "Realism and Domestic Politics," *International Security* 17, no. 1 (Summer 1992): 177–98.

16. Judith Goldstein, *Ideas, Interests, and American Trade Policy* (Ithaca, NY: Cornell University Press, 1993); Kathleen McNamara, *The Currency of Ideas* (Ithaca, NY: Cornell University Press, 1998); Edward Rhodes, "Sea Change: Interest-Based versus Cultural-Cognitive Accounts of Strategic Choice in the 1890s," *Security Studies* 5, no. 4 (Summer 1996): 73–124; Jerel Rosati, "The Power of Human Cognition in the Study of World Politics," *International Studies Review* 2, no. 3 (Fall 2000): 45–75.

17. On the question of voting determinants, see, e.g., Richard Niemi and Herbert Weisberg, "Vote Determinants: What Determines the Vote?" in *Classics in Voting Behavior*, ed. Richard Niemi and Herbert Weisberg (Washington, DC: Congressional Quarterly Press, 1993), 93–104.

18. Randall Calvert, "Robustness of the Multidimensional Voting Model: Candidate Motivations, Uncertainty, and Convergence," *American Journal of Political Science* 29, no. 1 (February 1985): 69–95; Dennis Mueller, *Public Choice III* (New York: Cam-

bridge University Press, 2003), 84–85, 98–103, 120–26, 249–52; Donald Stokes, "Spatial Models of Party Competition," *American Political Science Review* 57, no. 2 (June 1963): 368–77.

19. Aldrich, *Why Parties*, 18–61.

20. Thomas Preston, *The President and His Inner Circle* (New York: Columbia University Press, 2001), 8–31; Robert Putnam, "Diplomacy and Domestic Politics: The Logic of Two-Level Games," *International Organization* 42, no. 3 (June 1988), 427–60; William Riker, *The Art of Political Manipulation* (New Haven, CT: Yale University Press, 1986), 147, 150–51.

Chapter Two
Robert Taft

1. Robert Dallek, *Franklin D. Roosevelt and American Foreign Policy, 1932–1945* (New York: Oxford University Press, 1981), 70–71; Robert Divine, *The Illusion of Neutrality* (Chicago: University of Chicago Press, 1962), 165–66; Justus Doenecke and John Wilz, *From Isolation to War, 1931–1941* (Wheeling, IL: Harlan Davidson, 2003), 4–16; Manfred Jonas, *Isolationism in America, 1935–1941* (Ithaca, NY: Cornell University Press, 1966), 70–166; Arnold Offner, "Appeasement Revisited: The United States, Great Britain, and Germany, 1933–1940," *Journal of American History* 64 (September 1977): 373–93; Julius Turner, *Party and Constituency: Pressures on Congress*, rev. ed., ed. Edward Schneier (Baltimore, MD: Johns Hopkins University Press, 1970), 63, 69, 71–72.

2. Kristi Andersen, *The Creation of a Democratic Majority, 1928–1936* (Chicago: University of Chicago Press, 1979), 18, 26–38, 69–72; William Leuchtenburg, *Franklin D. Roosevelt and the New Deal* (New York: Harper and Row, 1963), 8–13, 175–76, 184–99; James Sundquist, *Dynamics of the Party System* (Washington, DC: Brookings Institution Press, 1983), 198–239; Clyde Weed, *The Nemesis of Reform: The Republican Party During the New Deal* (New York: Columbia University Press, 1994), 73–96, 109–13, 169–70, 185–90.

3. John Malsberger, *From Obstruction to Moderation: The Transformation of Senate Conservatism, 1938–1952* (London: Associated University Presses, 2000), 33–42, 52–53; Leroy Rieselbach, *The Roots of Isolationism: Congressional Voting and Presidential Leadership in Foreign Policy* (Indianapolis, IN: Bobbs-Merrill, 1966), 80, 106–20.

4. James Patterson, *Mr. Republican: A Biography of Robert A. Taft* (Boston: Houghton Mifflin, 1972), 95, 131, 166–67, 176, 192, 204, 213–16; Robert Taft, "The New Deal: Recovery, Reform, and Revolution," April 9, 1935, in *The Papers of Robert A. Taft*, ed. Clarence Wunderlin (Kent: Kent State University Press, 1997), 1:483 (hereafter *Papers of RAT*).

5. Robert Taft, "Shall the President Make War without the Approval of Congress?" in *We Testify*, ed. N. Schoonemaker and D. Reid (New York: Smith and Durrell, 1941), 215.

6. Geoffrey Matthews, "Robert A. Taft, the Constitution and American Foreign Policy, 1939–1953," *Journal of Contemporary History* 17 (July 1982): 507–22; Clarence Wunderlin, *Robert A. Taft: Ideas, Tradition, and Party in U.S. Foreign Policy* (Lanham, MD: Rowman and Littlefield, 2005), 2–6, 9–31, 36–38.

7. Robert Divine, *The Reluctant Belligerent* (New York: Wiley, 1965), 68; George Gallup, *The Gallup Poll: Public Opinion, 1935-1971* (New York: Random House, 1972), 179–93; Thomas Guinsburg, *The Pursuit of Isolationism in the United States Senate from Versailles to Pearl Harbor* (New York: Garland Publishing, 1982), 206–40; address by Robert Taft, September 6, 1939, in *Papers of RAT*, 2:69–72.

8. Wayne Cole, *America First: The Battle Against Intervention, 1940-1941* (Madison: University of Wisconsin Press, 1953), 10–30; Gallup, *Public Opinion*, 231; Malsberger, *Senate Conservatism*, 52–58, 67–72; Rieselbach, *Roots of Isolationism*, 35–49, 62–67, 80, 106–26, 143–50.

9. A. Scott Berg, *Lindbergh* (New York: Berkley Books, 1999), 427; Cole, *America First*, 35–36, 118, 122–39; idem, *Roosevelt and the Isolationists, 1932-1945* (Lincoln: University of Nebraska Press, 1983), 397, 400, 411–13, 430–31; Justus Doenecke, *Storm on the Horizon: The Challenge to American Intervention, 1939-1941* (Lanham, MD: Rowman and Littlefield, 2000), 3–8; Roland Stromberg, "American Business and the Approach of War, 1935–1941," *Journal of Economic History* 13 (Winter 1953): 58–78.

10. Justus Doenecke, "Power, Markets and Ideology: The Isolationist Response to Roosevelt Policy, 1940–1941," in *Watershed of Empire: Essays on New Deal Foreign Policy*, ed. Leonard Liggio and James Martin (Colorado Springs, CO: Ralph Myles, 1976), 132–61; Patterson, *Mr. Republican*, 217–18; Robert Taft, statement on Lend-Lease, February 26, 1941, *Papers of RAT*, 2:229.

11. Mark Lincoln Chadwin, *The Hawks of World War II* (Chapel Hill: University of North Carolina Press, 1968), 16–22, 44–45, 66–72, 159–66; Divine, *Reluctant Belligerent*, 10–12; Walter Johnson, *The Battle Against Isolation* (Chicago: University of Chicago Press, 1944), 63–64, 246.

12. Hadley Cantril, "America Faces the War," *Public Opinion Quarterly* 4 (July 1940): 387–407; Chadwin, *Hawks of World War II*, 271–77; Gallup, *Public Opinion*, 233, 240; William Langer and S. Everett Gleason, *The Challenge to Isolation: The World Crisis of 1937-1940 and American Foreign Policy* (New York: Harper and Brothers, 1952), 231, 486, 504–5; Stromberg, "American Business and the Approach of War," 72–75.

13. Gallup, *Public Opinion*, 229–33; Donald Bruce Johnson, *The Republican Party and Wendell Willkie* (Urbana: University of Illinois Press, 1960), 63–73, 87–108; Steve Neal, *Dark Horse: A Biography of Wendell Willkie* (Lawrence: University Press of Kansas, 1989), 12, 38–42, 57, 66–121; Patterson, *Mr. Republican*, 213–18; Kirk Porter and Donald Bruce Johnson, eds., *National Party Platforms, 1840-1956* (Urbana: University of Illinois Press, 1956), 389–90; Richard Norton Smith, *Thomas E. Dewey and His Times* (New York: Simon and Schuster, 1982), 18–21, 302–9; C. David Tompkins, *Senator Arthur H. Vandenberg: The Evolution of a Modern Republican, 1884-1945* (East Lansing: Michigan State University Press, 1970), 45–46, 170–85. For an engaging description of the 1940 Republican Convention, although simplistic regarding its consequences, see Charles Peters, *Five Days in Philadelphia* (New York: Public Affairs, 2005).

14. Johnson, *The Republican Party and Willkie*, 84–85, 102; Langer and Gleason, *The Challenge to Isolation*, 504–13, 670; Michael Leigh, *Mobilizing Consent: Public Opinion and American Foreign Policy, 1937-1947* (Westport, CT: Greenwood Press, 1976), 29–51; Henry Stimson and McGeorge Bundy, *On Active Service in Peace and War* (New York: Harper, 1948), 323–26.

15. Cole, *Roosevelt and the Isolationists*, 397; Dallek, *FDR and American Foreign Policy*, 247–49; Gallup, *Public Opinion*, 237–40; Johnson, *Battle Against Isolation*, 84–122; Robert Taft to George F. Stanley, September 8, 1944, in *Papers of RAT*, 2:577.

16. Robert Divine, *Foreign Policy and U.S. Presidential Elections, 1940–1948* (New York: New Viewpoints, 1974), 33–35, 54–59, 81–83; Gallup, *Public Opinion*, 239–40, 247, 250; Leuchtenberg, *FDR and the New Deal*, 321–23; Neal, *Dark Horse*, 159, 167–68, 176–79.

17. Doenecke, *Storm on the Horizon*, 175–76; Franklin Roosevelt, *Public Papers and Addresses of Franklin D. Roosevelt, 1940* (New York: Random House, 1941), 604–8, 633–44; Robert Taft to Gladys Appel, to Scandrett, and Statement on Lend-Lease, December 26, 1940, January 29, February 26, 1941, *Papers of RAT*, 2:211, 218, 226–29; Wunderlin, *Taft*, 59.

18. Cole, *Roosevelt and the Isolationists*, 411–13; Guinsburg, *The Pursuit of Isolationism*, 241–74; Johnson, *Battle Against Isolation*, 170ff.; Neal, *Dark Horse*, 179–206; Arthur Vandenberg, *The Private Papers of Senator Vandenberg* (Boston: Houghton Mifflin, 1952), 10.

19. Sir John Rupert Colville, *The Fringes of Power: 10 Downing Street Diaries, 1939–1945* (New York: Norton, 1985), 428; Gallup, *Public Opinion*, 274–75, 280, 299; William Langer and S. Everett Gleason, *The Undeclared War, 1940–1941* (New York: Harper and Brothers, 1953), 520, 577, 748–58; Roosevelt, *Public Papers and Addresses, 1940* (1941), 384–92, and *1941* (1950), 384–92. Some historians of the period, such as Warren Kimball, argue that Churchill misread FDR's flippant comments at the Atlantic Conference and overestimated the president's readiness to entangle the United States directly in war against Germany. See Warren Kimball, *Forged in War* (New York: William Morrow, 1997), 100–103.

20. Chadwin, *Hawks of World War II*, 235–41; Dallek, *FDR and American Foreign Policy*, 276–78; Gallup, *Public Opinion*, 273, 276–77, 286, 298; Robert Taft to Hulbert Taft, radio address by Robert Taft, and address by Robert Taft, "Shall the United States Enter the European War?," August 26, 29, 1941, *Papers of RAT*, 2:244, 281–83.

21. Cole, *Roosevelt and the Isolationists*, 346–58, 488–507; Gallup, *Public Opinion*, 246, 296; Vandenberg, *Papers*, 18. For two excellent treatments of the Pearl Harbor attack, see Gordon Prange, *At Dawn We Slept: The Untold Story of Pearl Harbor* (New York: Penguin, 1982), and Roberta Wohlstetter, *Pearl Harbor: Warning and Decision* (Stanford, CA: Stanford University Press, 1962).

22. John Morton Blum, *V Was for Victory: Politics and American Culture during World War II* (San Diego, CA: Harcourt Brace, 1976), 220–21, 231–34; Richard Darilek, *A Loyal Opposition in Time of War: The Republican Party and the Politics of Foreign Policy from Pearl Harbor to Yalta* (Westport, CT: Greenwood Press, 1976), 53–57; Robert Divine, *Second Chance: The Triumph of Internationalism in America During World War II* (New York: Atheneum, 1967), 73–74; Ronald Radosh, *Prophets on the Right: Profiles of Conservative Critics of American Globalism* (New York: Simon and Schuster, 1975), 137; Wunderlin, *Taft*, 72–74, 91–94.

23. Dallek, *FDR and American Foreign Policy*, 419; Divine, *Second Chance*, 55–60, 98–99; H. Schuyler Foster, *Activism Replaces Isolationism: U.S. Public Attitudes, 1940–1975* (Washington, DC: Foxhall Press, 1983), 20–22; Gallup, *Public Opinion*, 377; Benjamin

Page and Robert Shapiro, *The Rational Public: Fifty Years of Trends in Americans' Policy Preferences* (Chicago: University of Chicago Press, 1992), 176–77.

24. Divine, *Second Chance*, 70–71, 74, 78, 120–22; Henry Luce, "The American Century," *Life*, February 17, 1941, 61–65.

25. Blum, *V Was for Victory*, 265; Neal, *Dark Horse*, 231–66, 277–92; Wendell Willkie, *One World* (New York: Simon and Schuster, 1943), 2, 69–102, 133–77, 192–203.

26. Walter Lippmann, *U.S. Foreign Policy: Shield of the Republic* (Boston: Little, Brown, 1943), 7, 25–26, 47–77, 100–107, 136, 146, 164–73; Ronald Steel, *Walter Lippmann and the American Century* (Boston: Little, Brown, 1980), 404–12.

27. Patterson, *Mr. Republican*, 248–291; address by Robert Taft at Grove City College, Taft to James H. Crummey, and address by Taft: "Peace or Politics," May 22, July 22, August 26, 1943, in *Papers of RAT*, 2:385, 446–49, 468, 476–80; Wunderlin, *Taft*, 77–90.

28. Darilek, *Loyal Opposition*, 59–74, 120–127, 139–140; Malsberger, *Senate Conservatism*, 100–126; Tompkins, *Vandenberg*, 191–218; Vandenberg, *Papers*, 1:30, 53–60, 69; Wunderlin, *Taft*, 82.

29. Darilek, *Loyal Opposition*, 144–49; Richard Davies, *Defender of the Old Guard: John Bricker and American Politics* (Columbus: Ohio State University Press, 1993), 77–82, 94; Divine, *Second Chance*, 186–89; Johnson, *Republican Party and Willkie*, 268–82; Michael Schaller, *Douglas MacArthur: Far Eastern General* (New York: Oxford University Press, 1989), 78–84; Smith, *Dewey*, 263–65, 334, 338, 344–45, 382–400.

30. Blum, *V Was for Victory*, 254, 294–99; Divine, *Elections*, 130–37, 147; idem, *Second Chance*, 209–10, 216–17, 241–42; Leon Friedman, "Election of 1944," in *History of American Presidential Elections*, ed. Arthus Schlesinger (New York: Chelsea House, 1971), 4:3015–35; Gallup, *Public Opinion*, 470; Porter and Johnson, *National Party Platforms*, 407–12; Smith, *Dewey*, 401–38.

31. Darilek, *Loyal Opposition*, 67; Malsberger, *Senate Conservatism*, 127–42; Smith, *Dewey*, 439–42; Robert Taft to Vanderpoel, address by Taft at Grove City College, address by Taft: "What Foreign Policy Will Promote Peace?," May 6 and May 22, 1943, June 8, 1944, in *Papers of RAT*, 2:360, 449–50, 557; Tompkins, *Vandenberg*, 196–97.

32. Diane Clemens, *Yalta* (New York: Oxford University Press, 1970), 247–55, 287–89; Dallek, *Loyal Opposition*, 342, 389–90, 434, 507–8; Justus Doenecke, *Not to the Swift: The Old Isolationists in the Cold War Era* (Lewisburg, PA: Bucknell University Press, 1979), 39; *Foreign Relations of the United States: The Conferences at Malta and Yalta, 1945* (Washington, DC: Government Printing Office, 1955), 668–69, 677–78, 788, 846, 848, 872, 898, 975–82; Warren Kimball, *The Juggler: Franklin Roosevelt as Wartime Statesman* (Princeton, NJ: Princeton University Press, 1991), 83–125; Eduard Mark, "American Policy Toward Eastern Europe and the Origins of the Cold War: An Alternative Interpretation," *Journal of American History* 68 (September 1981): 313–36; Tompkins, *Vandenberg*, 238–40; Vandenberg, *Papers*, 97–98, 126–56, 176–80.

33. Dallek, *FDR and American Foreign Policy*, 522; Divine, *Second Chance*, 270–71, 313; Doenecke, *Not to the Swift*, 46; Foster, *Activism Replaces Isolationism*, 28–31; Patterson, *Mr. Republican*, 296–97; Radosh, *Prophets on the Right*, 144; Vandenberg, *Papers*, 95–96, 200.

34. James MacGregor Burns, *The Deadlock of Democracy: Four-Party Politics in America* (Englewood Cliffs, NJ: Prentice-Hall, 1963), 196–202; Doenecke, *Not to the*

Swift, 7–13, 22–26, 55–58, 74–75; Malsberger, *Senate Conservatism*, 127–42; Page and Shapiro, *The Rational Public*, 175; Rieselbach, *Roots of Isolationism*, 37, 49–52, 106–22, 150–56.

35. John Gaddis, *Strategies of Containment: A Critical Appraisal of American National Security Policy during the Cold War* (New York: Oxford University Press, 2005), 57–63, 71–74; Alonzo Hamby, *Man of the People: A Life of Harry S. Truman* (New York: Oxford University Press, 1995), 313–14, 359; David Kepley, *The Collapse of the Middle Way: Senate Republicans and the Bipartisan Foreign Policy, 1948–1952* (New York: Greenwood Press, 1988), 3–4; Melvyn Leffler, *A Preponderance of Power: National Security, the Truman Administration, and the Cold War* (Stanford, CA: Stanford University Press, 1992), 8–9, 14–18, 34–36, 53, 100; Harry Truman, *Memoirs: Vol. 1, Year of Decisions* (Garden City, NY: Doubleday, 1955), 552; Vandenberg, *Papers*, 225–51, 373–412.

36. Henry Berger, "Senator Robert A. Taft Dissents from Military Escalation," in *Cold War Critics: Alternatives to American Foreign Policy in the Truman Years*, ed. Thomas Paterson (Chicago: Quadrangle Books, 1971), 177; Aaron Friedberg, *In the Shadow of the Garrison State: America's Anti-Statism and Its Cold War Grand Strategy* (Princeton, NJ: Princeton University Press, 2000), 40–61, 83–97, 155–75; Michael Hogan, *A Cross of Iron: Harry S. Truman and the Origins of the National Security State, 1945–1954* (New York: Cambridge University Press, 1998), 20–21, 70–71, 115–18, 120–21, 157–58; Patterson, *Mr. Republican*, 372–88; Taft, "Inflation and the Marshall Plan," December 30, 1947, in *Papers of RAT*, 3:355–59; Wunderlin, *Taft*, 112–132. Yugoslavia of course was under Communist but not Russian domination, contrary to Taft's statement.

37. Divine, *Elections*, 173, 180–90, 200, 205, 262, 274–76; Gary Donaldson, *Truman Defeats Dewey* (Lexington: University Press of Kentucky, 1998), 131, 167–69, 204–20; Gallup, *Public Opinion*, 721, 759; Hamby, *Man of the People*, 401, 421–22, 454, 460–66; Zachary Karabell, *The Last Campaign: How Harry Truman Won the 1948 Election* (New York: Knopf, 2000), 191–94, 207–11, 257–60; Sean Savage, *Truman and the Democratic Party* (Lexington: University Press of Kentucky, 1997), 81, 137; Smith, *Dewey*, 469–70, 479–539.

38. Doenecke, *Not to the Swift*, 179–84; Kepley, *Collapse of the Middle Way*, 53–61; Ross Koen, *The China Lobby in American Politics* (New York: Harper and Row, 1974), 27–55, 95–99; Patterson, *Mr. Republican*, 313, 425, 437–46; Vandenberg, *Papers*, 530–36; Wunderlin, *Taft*, 145–53.

39. Alan Harper, *The Politics of Loyalty: The White House and the Communist Issue, 1946–1952* (Westport, CT: Greenwood Press, 1969), 126–28, 232; John Earl Haynes and Harvey Klehr, *Venona: Decoding Soviet Espionage in America* (New Haven, CT: Yale Nota Bene, 2000), 8–22, 331–37, 353, 363; David Oshinsky, *A Conspiracy So Immense: The World of Joe McCarthy* (New York: Oxford University Press, 2005 edition), 53–84, 95–114.

40. Harper, *The Politics of Loyalty*, 134, 250; Alfred Hero, *American Religious Groups View Foreign Policy* (Durham, NC: Duke University Press, 1973), 45–46; Oshinsky, *A Conspiracy So Immense*, 115–38, 163–65; Patterson, *Mr. Republican*, 444–49; Richard Gid Powers, *Not Without Honor: The History of American Anti-Communism* (New York: Free Press, 1995), 272.

41. Ronald Caridi, *The Korean War and American Politics* (Philadelphia: University of Pennsylvania Press, 1968), 33–38, 75, 84, 93–102, 116–19, 131–37; Herbert Hoover, "Our National Policies in This Crisis," December 20, 1950, in Herbert Hoover, *Addresses Upon the American Road, 1950–1955* (Stanford, CA: Stanford University Press, 1955), 8–9; Daniel Kelly, *James Burnham and the Struggle for the World* (Wilmington, DE: ISI Books, 2002), 140–47; Leffler, *A Preponderance of Power*, 361–404; Page and Shapiro, *The Rational Public*, 212, 244; Schaller, *MacArthur*, 223–27.

42. Robert Taft, *A Foreign Policy for Americans* (Garden City, NY: Doubleday, 1951), 11–23, 39, 47–66, 73–87, 100–120.

43. Caridi, *Korean War and American Politics*, 145–47, 154–57; Ted Galen Carpenter, "United States NATO Policy at the Crossroads: The Great Debate of 1950–51," *International History Review* 8 (August 1986): 389–414; Rosemary Foot, *The Wrong War: American Policy and the Dimensions of the Korean Conflict* (Ithaca, NY: Cornell University Press, 1985), 117–21, 128–39; Friedberg, *In the Shadow of the Garrison State*, 115–25; Hogan, *A Cross of Iron*, 266, 313, 335–44, 364–65; Schaller, *MacArthur*, 230–50.

44. Stephen Ambrose, *Eisenhower: Soldier and President* (New York: Simon and Schuster, 1990), 245–87; Doenecke, *Not to the Swift*, 211, 217, 222; Patterson, *Mr. Republican*, 499–516, 560; Smith, *Dewey*, 553–57, 577–604; Wunderlin, *Taft*, 177–205.

45. Doenecke, *Not to the Swift*, 247.

Chapter Three
Dwight Eisenhower

1. The best survey of Eisenhower's pre-presidential years is Stephen Ambrose, *Eisenhower: Soldier, General, President-Elect, 1890–1952* (New York: Simon and Schuster, 1983).

2. Barton Bernstein, "Election of 1952," in *The Coming to Power: Critical Presidential Elections in American History*, ed. Arthur Schlesinger (New York: Chelsea House Publishers, 1971), 385–436; Angus Campbell et al, *The American Voter* (Chicago: University of Chicago Press, 1976), 49–51, 526–27, 537–38, 546, 551; Robert Divine, *Foreign Policy and U.S. Presidential Elections, 1952–1960* (New York: New Viewpoints, 1974), 25–36, 50–56, 82–85; George Gallup, *The Gallup Poll: Public Opinion, 1935–1971* (New York: Random House, 1972), 2:1101; Kirk H. Porter and Donald B. Johnson, eds., *National Party Platforms, 1840–1956* (Urbana: University of Illinois Press, 1956), 497–99.

3. Robert F. Burk, *The Eisenhower Administration and Black Civil Rights* (Knoxville: University of Tennessee Press, 1984), 6; Fred Greenstein, *The Hidden-Hand Presidency: Eisenhower as Leader* (New York: Basic Books, 1982), 50; Robert Griffith, "Dwight D. Eisenhower and the Corporate Commonwealth," *American Historical Review* 87 (February 1982), 87–122; Gary Reichard, *The Reaffirmation of Republicanism: Eisenhower and the Eighty-Third Congress* (Knoxville: University of Tennessee Press, 1975), 9–14; Steven Wagner, *Eisenhower Republicanism: Pursuing the Middle Way* (DeKalb: Northern Illinois University Press, 2006), 7.

4. Robert Bowie and Richard Immerman, *Waging Peace: How Eisenhower Shaped an Enduring Cold War Strategy* (New York: Oxford University Press, 1998), 43–48, 249–52;

Blanche W. Cook, *The Declassified Eisenhower* (Garden City, NY: Doubleday, 1981), 183; Eisenhower inaugural address, January 20, 1953, *Public Papers of the Presidents of the United States: Dwight D. Eisenhower* [hereafter *EPP*], *1953* (Washington, DC: Government Printing Office, 1960), 1:1–8; Eisenhower press conferences, November 11, 1953, *EPP: 1953*, 760, and August 4, 1954, *EPP: 1954*, 684; Aaron Friedberg, *In the Shadow of the Garrison State: America's Anti-Statism and Its Cold War Grand Strategy* (Princeton, NJ: Princeton University Press, 2000), 94–95, 127–28.

5. Caroline Pruden, *Conditional Partners: Eisenhower, the United Nations, and the Search for a Permanent Peace* (Baton Rouge: Louisiana State University, 1998), 306, 310.

6. Greenstein, *The Hidden-Hand Presidency*, 19–30, 38–47, 58–151; Richard Immerman, *John Foster Dulles: Piety, Pragmatism, and Power in US Foreign Policy* (Wilmington, DE: Scholarly Resources, 1999), 17–55; Anna Kasten Nelson, "'The Top of the Policy Hill': President Eisenhower and the National Security Council," *Diplomatic History* 7, no. 4 (Fall 1983): 307–26.

7. Justus Doenecke, *Not to the Swift: The Old Isolationists in the Cold War Era* (Lewisburg, PA: Bucknell University Press, 1979), 232–37; Reichard, *The Reaffirmation of Republicanism*, 28–49; David Reinhard, *The Republican Right since 1945* (Lexington: University Press of Kentucky, 1983), 102–28.

8. Robert Dallek, *Lone Star Rising: Lyndon Johnson and His Times, 1908–1960* (New York: Oxford University Press, 1991), 464, 478–81, 511–16; Charles Lerche, "Southern Congressmen and the 'New Isolationism,'" *Political Science Quarterly* 75, no. 3 (September 1960): 321–37; and on the previous two paragraphs, see Anna K. Nelson, "John Foster Dulles and the Bipartisan Congress," *Political Science Quarterly* 102, no. 1 (Spring 1987): 43–64; Leroy Rieselbach, *The Roots of Isolationism: Congressional Voting and Presidential Leadership in Foreign Policy* (Indianapolis, IN: Bobbs-Merrill, 1966), 44, 49, 51–53, 56, 108–9, 150; Barbara Sinclair, *Congressional Realignment, 1925–1978* (Austin: University of Texas Press, 1982), 75–77, 83–88; and Julius Turner, *Party and Constituency: Pressures on Congress*, rev. ed. Edward Schneier (Baltimore, MD: Johns Hopkins University Press, 1970), 64–66, 69, 72, 202.

9. Roger Dingman, "Atomic Diplomacy during the Korean War," *International Security* 13, no. 3 (Winter 1988–89): 61–91; Rosemary Foot, *A Substitute for Victory: The Politics of Peacemaking at the Korean Armistice Talks* (Ithaca, NY: Cornell University Press, 1990), 130–89; Edward Keefer, "President Dwight D. Eisenhower and the End of the Korean War," *Diplomatic History* 10, no. 3 (Summer 1986): 267–89; William Stueck, *The Korean War: An International History* (Princeton, NJ: Princeton University Press, 1995), 326–30.

10. Reichard, *The Reaffirmation of Republicanism*, 51–68, 87–96, 227–28; Duane Tananbaum, "The Bricker Amendment Controversy: Its Origins and Eisenhower's Role," *Diplomatic History* 9, no. 1 (Winter 1985): 73–93; Athan Theoharis, *The Yalta Myths: An Issue in U.S. Politics, 1945–1955* (Columbia: University of Missouri Press, 1970), 180–217.

11. Robert Ferrell, ed., *The Diary of James C. Hagerty: Eisenhower in Mid-Course, 1954–1955* (Bloomington: Indiana University Press, 1983), 129; Greenstein, *The Hidden-Hand Presidency*, 155–227; Byron Hulsey, *Everett Dirksen and His Presidents: How a Senate Giant Shaped American Politics* (Lawrence: University Press of Kansas, 2000),

4–5, 82–83; Ross Koen, *The China Lobby in American Politics* (New York: Harper and Row, 1974), 190–92, 204–11; David Oshinsky, *A Conspiracy So Immense: The World of Joe McCarthy* (New York: Oxford University Press, 2005), 258–60, 299–300, 352–59, 387–93, 416–45, 492–94; Benjamin Page and Robert Shapiro, *The Rational Public: Fifty Years of Trends in Americans' Policy Preferences* (Chicago: University of Chicago Press, 1992), 182.

12. Bowie and Immerman, *Waging Peace*, 47, 96–108, 139–46; John Foster Dulles, "A Policy of Boldness," *Life*, May 19, 1952, 146–60; Ferrell, *Diary of James Hagerty*, 102, 202; Friedberg, *In the Shadow of the Garrison State*, 130–33; John L. Gaddis, *Strategies of Containment: A Critical Appraisal of American National Security Policy during the Cold War* (New York: Oxford University Press, 2005), 393; National Security Council [hereafter NSC] 162/2, October 30, 1953, *Foreign Relations of the United States* [hereafter *FRUS*]: *1952–1954* (Washington, DC: Government Printing Office, 1984), 2:593.

13. Raymond Bauer, Ithiel de Sola Pool, and Lewis A. Dexter, *American Business and Public Policy* (New York: Atheneum, 1964), 23–73, 152–53, 465–90; Dwight Eisenhower, *Mandate for Change, 1953–1956* (Garden City, NY: Doubleday, 1963), 194–95, 292–94; Douglas Irwin and Randall S. Kroszner, "Interests, Institutions, and Ideology in Securing Policy Change: The Republican Conversion to Trade Liberalization after Smoot-Hawley," *Journal of Law and Economics* 42, no. 2 (October 1999): 643–73; Burton Kaufman, *Trade and Aid: Eisenhower's Foreign Economic Policy, 1953–1961* (Baltimore, MD: Johns Hopkins University Press, 1982), 7–9; Reichard, *The Reaffirmation of Republicanism*, 71–84.

14. Eisenhower to Bermingham, February 28, 1951, *The Papers of Dwight David Eisenhower* [hereafter *Eisenhower Papers*] (Baltimore, MD: Johns Hopkins University Press), 12:76–77; Eisenhower to Alfred Gruenther, December 2, 1955, *Eisenhower Papers*, 16:1919–20; James Hershberg, "'Explosion in the Offing': German Rearmament and American Diplomacy, 1953–1955," *Diplomatic History* 16, no. 4 (Fall 1992): 511–49; NSC 162/2, October 30, 1953, *FRUS: 1952–1954*, 2:583, 585; Marc Trachtenberg, *A Constructed Peace: The Making of the European Settlement, 1945–1963* (Princeton, NJ: Princeton University Press, 1999), 122–200.

15. Eisenhower, February 17, 1955, *FRUS: 1955–1957*, 6:4f.; NSC 144/1, *FRUS: 1952–1954*, 4:6–10; Stephen Rabe, *Eisenhower and Latin America: The Foreign Policy of Anti-Communism* (Chapel Hill: University of North Carolina Press, 1988), 33–42, 84–92, 177. On Eisenhower and U.S. cold war dilemmas over allies and intervention, see H. W. Brands, *The Specter of Neutralism: The United States and the Emergence of the Third World, 1947–1960* (New York: Columbia University Press, 1989), 312–21; Zachary Karabell, *Architects of Intervention: The United States, the Third World, and the Cold War, 1946–1962* (Baton Rouge: Louisiana State University Press, 1999), 5–10, 225–26; and Douglas Macdonald, *Adventures in Chaos: American Intervention for Reform in the Third World* (Cambridge, MA: Harvard University Press, 1992), 35–36, 250–51.

16. NSC, *FRUS: 1952–1954*, 4:1064–65, 1096; Piero Gleijeses, *Shattered Hope: The Guatemalan Revolution and the United States, 1944–1954* (Princeton, NJ: Princeton University Press, 1991), 140–48, 283, 295–304, 361–63, 380–81; Richard Immerman, *The CIA in Guatemala: The Foreign Policy of Intervention* (Austin: University of Texas Press, 1982), 14–19, 155–58, 161–86, 194–98.

17. Stanley Bachrach, *The Committee of One Million* (New York: Columbia University Press, 1976), 41–102; Chen Jian, *Mao's China and the Cold War* (Chapel Hill: University of North Carolina Press, 2001), 38–48, 163–204; David Allen Mayers, *Cracking the Monolith: U.S. Policy against the Sino-Soviet Alliance, 1949–1955* (Baton Rouge: Louisiana State University Press, 1986), 6, 142–49; NSC 166/1, November 6, 1953, *FRUS: 1952–1954*, 14:278–306; Bennett Rushkoff, "Eisenhower, Dulles, and the Quemoy-Matsu Crisis, 1954–1955," *Political Science Quarterly* 96, no. 3 (Fall 1981): 465–80.

18. Memorandum by the assistant secretary of state for Far Eastern affairs to the secretary of state, January 6, 1954, *FRUS 1952–1954*, vol. 13, *Indochina*: pt. 1, 944, n.2, and memorandum of discussion at the 179th meeting of the National Security Council, January 8, 1954, ibid., pt. 1, 949; *FRUS 1952–1954*, vol. 13, *Indochina*: pt. 2, 1224–25, 1238–40; Melanie Billings-Yun, *Decision against War: Eisenhower and Dien Bien Phu, 1954* (New York: Columbia University Press, 1988), 92, 109, 132, 159–60; Gallup, *Public Opinion*, 2:1146, 1170–71; George Herring and Richard Immerman, "Eisenhower, Dulles, and Dien Bien Phu: 'The Day We Didn't Go to War' Revisited," *Journal of American History* 71, no. 2 (September 1984): 343–63; *EPP: 1954*, 381–90; Qiang Zhai, *China and the Vietnam Wars, 1950–1975* (Chapel Hill: University of North Carolina Press, 2000).

19. Mark Gasiorowski, "The 1953 Coup d'Etat in Iran," *International Journal of Middle East Studies* 19, no. 3 (August 1987): 261–86; Kermit Roosevelt, *Countercoup* (New York: McGraw Hill, 1979), 120–24, 147–49, 156–57, 176–97; Barry Rubin, *Paved with Good Intentions: The American Experience and Iran* (New York: Oxford University Press, 1980), 54–90; Kuross Samii, *Involvement by Invitation: American Strategies of Containment in Iran* (University Park: Pennsylvania State University Press, 1987), 141–43; Vladislav Zubok, "Soviet Intelligence and the Cold War: The 'Small' Committee of Information, 1952–53," *Diplomatic History* 19, no. 3 (Summer 1995): 466–68.

20. NSC, *FRUS, 1952–1954*, 2:397; Memorandum, NSC meeting, June 24, 1954, *FRUS 1952–1954*, 2:696; Memorandum, Eisenhower conversation with Sherman Adams and Herbert Hoover, Jr., November 5, 1956, *FRUS 1955–1957*, 26:1000–1001; Memorandum of telephone conversations with the president, November 9, 1956, *FRUS 1955–1957*, 25:425; Dwight Eisenhower, *Waging Peace, 1956–1961* (Garden City, NY: Doubleday, 1965), 95; Johanna Granville, "'Caught with Jam on Our Fingers': Radio Free Europe and the Hungarian Revolution of 1956," *Diplomatic History* 29, no. 5 (November 2005): 811–39; Peter Grose, *Operation Rollback: America's Secret War Behind the Iron Curtain* (Boston: Houghton Mifflin, 2000), 164–89, 206–19; Ronald Krebs, *Dueling Visions: U.S. Strategy toward Eastern Europe under Eisenhower* (College Station: Texas A&M University Press, 2001), 28–45, 100–107; Gregory Mitrovich, *Undermining the Kremlin: America's Strategy to Subvert the Soviet Bloc, 1947–1956* (Ithaca, NY: Cornell University Press, 2000), 158–65, 175–76.

21. Bowie and Immerman, *Waging Peace*, 109–122, 222–41; Robert Divine, *Blowing on the Wind: The Nuclear Test Ban Debate, 1954–1960* (New York: Oxford University Press, 1978), 3–35; Eisenhower speech to American Society of Newspaper Editors, April 16, 1953, *EPP: 1953*, 179–88; Andrew Erdmann, "War No Longer Has Any Logic Whatever: Dwight D. Eisenhower and the Thermonuclear Revolution," in John L. Gaddis et al., *Cold War Statesmen Confront the Bomb: Nuclear Diplomacy since 1945* (New York:

Oxford University Press, 1999), 101–9; Richard Hewlett and Jack Holl, *Atoms for Peace and War* (Berkeley and Los Angeles: University of California Press, 1989), 1–16; Vladislav Zubok and Konstantin Pleshakov, *Inside the Kremlin's Cold War* (Cambridge, MA: Harvard University Press, 1996), 184–85, 193–94.

22. Jeff Broadwater, *Eisenhower and the Anti-Communist Crusade* (Chapel Hill: University of North Carolina Press, 1992), 207; Campbell et al., *The American Voter*, 45–61, 75, 198–200, 526–27; Divine, *Elections*, 98–99, 136–39, 160; Gallup, *Public Opinion*, 2:1457–58; Sinclair, *Congressional Realignment*, 86–88; John Sloan, *Eisenhower and the Management of Prosperity* (Lawrence: University Press of Kansas, 1991), 10.

23. Michael Bishku, "The 1958 American Intervention in Lebanon: A Historical Assessment," *American-Arab Affairs* 31 (Winter 1989–90): 106–19; Fawaz Gerges, *The Superpowers and the Middle East: Regional and International Politics, 1955–1967* (Boulder, CO: Westview Press, 1994), 25, 34, 54–55, 65–66, 79–81, 102–22; Robert Murphy, *Diplomat Among Warriors* (Garden City, NY: Doubleday, 1964), 407–8, 450; Salim Yaqub, *Containing Arab Nationalism: The Eisenhower Doctrine and the Middle East* (Chapel Hill: University of North Carolina Press, 2004), 178, 269–271; *EPP: 1957*, 6–16; Minutes, NSC meeting, July 31, 1958, *FRUS: 1958–1960*, 12:129, 132.

24. Trumbull Higgins, *The Perfect Failure: Kennedy, Eisenhower, and the CIA at the Bay of Pigs* (New York: Norton, 1989), 57, 78; Kaufman, *Trade and Aid*, 58–73, 193; Rabe, *Eisenhower and Latin America*, 100, 124–30, 157, 175.

25. William Burr, "Avoiding the Slippery Slope: The Eisenhower Administration and the Berlin Crisis, November 1958–January 1959," *Diplomatic History* 18, no. 2 (Spring 1994): 177–205; Campbell Craig, *Destroying the Village: Eisenhower and Thermonuclear War* (New York: Columbia University Press, 1994), 94; Eisenhower, *Waging Peace*, 340–47; John S. D. Eisenhower notes, Eisenhower-Dulles conversation, January 29, 1959, *FRUS: 1958–1960*, 8:303; Hope Harrison, "New Evidence on Khrushchev's 1958 Berlin Ultimatum," *Cold War International History Project Bulletin* 4 (Fall 1994): 35–39; Trachtenberg, *A Constructed Peace*, 248–82.

26. Craig, *Destroying the Village*, 50–52; Robert Divine, *The Sputnik Challenge* (New York: Oxford University Press, 1993), 19, 41–44, 172–77, 191–96; Eisenhower press conference, March 2, 1955, *EPP: 1955*, 303; Friedberg, *In the Shadow of the Garrison State*, 137–39; Peter Roman, *Eisenhower and the Missile Gap* (Ithaca, NY: Cornell University Press, 1996), 30–62, 118–21, 175–92, 207; David A. Rosenberg, "The Origins of Overkill: Nuclear Weapons and American Strategy, 1945–1960," *International Security* 7, no. 4 (Spring 1983): 3–8, 44–71.

27. Michael Beschloss, *Mayday: Eisenhower, Khrushchev, and the U-2 Affair* (New York: Harper and Row, 1986), 14–66; Divine, *Blowing on the Wind*, 152, 213–40; George Kistiakowsky, *A Scientist at the White House* (Cambridge, MA: Harvard University Press, 1976), 375; Roman, *Eisenhower and the Missile Gap*, 104, 193.

28. Divine, *Elections*, 286–87; Gaddis, *Strategies of Containment*, 163, 175, 181–82, 197–234; Michael Latham, "Ideology, Social Science, and Destiny: Modernization and the Kennedy-Era Alliance for Progress," *Diplomatic History* 22, no. 2 (Spring 1998): 199–229; Iwan Morgan, *Eisenhower versus the Spenders* (New York: St. Martin's Press), 34–35; Theodore Sorenson, "Election of 1960," in Schlesinger, *The Coming to Power*, 437–57.

29. Regarding contemporary orbital photographs of Soviet missile sites, see John Gaddis, *We Now Know: Rethinking Cold War History* (New York: Oxford University Press, 1997), 247–48.

30. Eisenhower, *Waging Peace*, 652; Robert Ferrell, *The Eisenhower Diaries* (New York: W. W. Norton, 1981), 288–89; Nicol Rae, *The Decline and Fall of the Liberal Republicans: From 1952 to the Present* (New York: Oxford University Press, 1989), 40, 45, 163; Reichard, *The Reaffirmation of Republicanism*, 228–37; Reinhard, *The Republican Right*, 134–58; Wagner, *Eisenhower Republicanism*, 7–42, 114–32.

31. Charles Alexander, *Holding the Line: The Eisenhower Era, 1952–1961* (Bloomington: Indiana University Press, 1975), 158; Campbell et al., *The American Voter*, 45–47, 537–38; Samuel Lubell, *The Future of American Politics* (New York: Harper and Row, 1965), 191–93, 223–24; Stephen Skowronek, *The Politics Presidents Make: Leadership from John Adams to Bill Clinton* (Cambridge, MA: Belknap Press of Harvard University Press, 1997), 46; James Sundquist, *Dynamics of the Party System* (Washington, DC: Brookings Institution Press, 1983), 256–68, 287–90, 334–37.

Chapter Four

Barry Goldwater

1. The Editors, "The Magazine's Credenda," *National Review*, November 19, 1955, 6; Daniel Kelly, *James Burnham and the Struggle for the World* (Wilmington, DE: ISI Books, 2002), 115–237; George Nash, *The Conservative Intellectual Movement in America Since 1945* (Wilmington, DE: ISI Books, 2006); Murray Rothbard, "The Transformation of the American Right," *Continuum* 2 (Summer 1964): 220–31; William Rusher, *The Rise of the Right* (New York: William Morrow, 1984), 33–85.

2. Robert Goldberg, *Barry Goldwater* (New Haven, CT: Yale University Press, 1995), 3–139.

3. Goldberg, *Goldwater*, 62, 89–90, 121, 154; Barry Goldwater, *The Conscience of a Conservative* (Princeton, NJ: Princeton University Press, 2007), 6–19, 27–31, 37, 53–65.

4. Goldwater, *The Conscience of a Conservative*, 82–84, 89–90, 105–120.

5. Daniel Bell, ed., *The Radical Right* (Garden City, NY: Doubleday, 1963); William Hixson, *The Search for the American Right Wing: An Analysis of the Social Science Record, 1955–1987* (Princeton, NJ: Princeton University Press, 1992), 107; Lisa McGirr, *Suburban Warriors: The Origins of the New American Right* (Princeton, NJ: Princeton University Press, 2001), 4–5, 8–10; Kirkpatrick Sale, *Power Shift: The Rise of the Southern Rim and Its Challenges to the Eastern Establishment* (New York: Vintage, 1976), 17–53; Gregory Schneider, *Cadres for Conservatism: Young Americans for Freedom and the Rise of the Contemporary Right* (New York: New York University Press, 1999), 31–54; Jonathan Schoenwald, *A Time for Choosing* (New York: Oxford University Press, 2001), 62–99.

6. James MacGregor Burns, *The Deadlock of Democracy: Four-Party Politics in America*, (Englewood Cliffs, NJ: Prentice-Hall, 1963), 196–202; Michael Kramer and Sam Roberts, *"I Never Wanted to Be Vice-President of Anything!": An Investigative Biography of Nelson Rockefeller* (New York: Basic Books, 1976), 81–85, 266; Nicol Rae, *The Decline and Fall of the Liberal Republicans* (New York: Oxford University Press, 1989),

163–67; Barbara Sinclair, *Congressional Realignment, 1925–1978* (Austin: University of Texas Press, 1982), 83–88, 91–113.

7. Byron Hulsey, *Everett Dirksen and his Presidents: How a Senate Giant Shaped American Politics* (Lawrence: University Press of Kansas, 2000), 4–5, 82–83.

8. Barry Goldwater, *With No Apologies* (New York: William Morrow, 1979), 101–4, 109–17; Kramer and Roberts, *"I Never Wanted to be Vice-President of Anything!,"* 230–42; Rick Perlstein, *Before the Storm: Barry Goldwater and the Unmaking of the American Consensus* (New York: Hill and Wang, 2001), 76–99; Theodore White, *The Making of the President: 1960* (New York: Atheneum, 1961), 66–77, 183–93, 204, 215–20.

9. Edward Carmines and James Stimson, *Issue Evolution: Race and the Transformation of American Politics* (Princeton, NJ: Princeton University Press, 1989), 38–39; Philip Converse, Angus Campbell, Warren Miller, and Donald Stokes, "Stability and Change in 1960: A Reinstating Election," *American Political Science Review* 55, no. 2 (June 1961): 269–80; Robert Divine, *Foreign Policy and U.S. Presidential Elections, 1952–1960* (New York: New Viewpoints, 1974), 286–87; George Gallup, *The Gallup Poll: Public Opinion, 1935–1971* (New York: Random House, 1972), 3:1669–70, 1672, 1676, 1683, 1689; Theodore Sorensen, "Election of 1960," in *The Coming to Power: Critical Presidential Elections in American History,* ed. Arthur Schlesinger (New York: Chelsea House, 1971), 437–57.

10. Goldberg, *Goldwater,* 155–57; Barry Goldwater, *Why Not Victory?* (New York: McGraw-Hill, 1962), 29–30, 44–45, 84–89, 162–63; Hulsey, *Everett Dirksen,* 143–56, 168; David Reinhard, *The Republican Right Since 1945* (Lexington: University Press of Kentucky, 1983), 164–67.

11. Ernest May and Philip Zelikow, *The Kennedy Tapes* (Cambridge, MA: Harvard University Press, 1997), 65, 127, 133, 200, 203, 342–43, 557; Timothy McKeown, "The Cuban Missile Crisis and Politics as Usual," *Journal of Politics* 62, no. 1 (February 2000): 70–87; Thomas Paterson and William Brophy, "October Missiles and November Elections: The Cuban Missile Crisis and American Politics, 1962," *Journal of American History* 73, no. 1 (June 1986): 87–119; James Sundquist, *Politics and Policy: The Eisenhower, Kennedy, and Johnson Years* (Washington, DC: Brookings Institution Press, 1968), 481–83.

12. Goldberg, *Goldwater,* 149–194; John Kessel, *The Goldwater Coalition: Republican Strategies in 1964* (Indianapolis, IN: Bobbs-Merrill, 1968), 25–28, 39–45, 60, 87–88; Rae, *Liberal Republicans;* 53–70; Rusher, *Rise of the Right,* 69, 87–127; F. Clifton White, *Suite 3505: The Story of the Draft Goldwater Movement* (New Rochelle, NY: Arlington House, 1967), 20–98, 121–22.

13. Carmines and Stimson, *Issue Evolution,* 44–47, 117–18; Mary Dudziak, *Cold War Civil Rights* (Princeton, NJ: Princeton University Press), 115–202, 208–13.

14. Mary Brennan, *Turning Right in the Sixties: The Conservative Capture of the GOP* (Chapel Hill: University of North Carolina Press, 1995), 50–55, 75–81; Goldberg, *Goldwater,* 191, 197–209; Perlstein, *Before the Storm,* 151–52, 366–93; Kirk Porter and Donald Bruce Johnson, eds., *National Party Platforms, 1840–1968* (Urbana: University of Illinois Press, 1972), 683–89; Schoenwald, *A Time for Choosing,* 93–146; White, *Suite 3505,* 11–18, 199–213, 377–408.

15. Earl Black and Merle Black, *The Rise of Southern Republicans* (Cambridge, MA: Belknap Press, 2002), 28–29, 150; Angus Campbell, "Interpreting the Presidential Victory," in *The National Election of 1964*, ed. Paul Tillet et al. (Washington, DC: Brookings Institution Press, 1966), 259–68, 278; Robert Erikson, "The Influence of Newspaper Endorsements in Presidential Elections: The Case of 1964," *American Journal of Political Science* 20, no. 2 (May 1976): 207–33; Goldberg, *Goldwater*, 210–37; Rae, *Liberal Republicans*, 75.

16. Larry Berman, *Planning a Tragedy: The Americanization of the War in Vietnam* (New York: W. W. Norton, 1982), 123–28, 149–50; Terry Dietz, *Republicans and Vietnam, 1961–1968* (New York: Greenwood Press, 1986), 61, 64–101; Gallup, *Public Opinion*, vol. 3, 1934; William Conrad Gibbons, *The U.S. Government and the Vietnam War: Executive and Legislative Roles and Relationships* (Princeton, NJ: Princeton University Press, 1986–1995), pt. II: 141, 252, 301–30, 337, 357–58, and pt. IV: 165–66; H. R. McMaster, *Dereliction of Duty* (New York: Harper Perennial, 1997), 324–33.

17. Brennan, *Turning Right in the Sixties*, 104–16; The Editors, "The John Birch Society and the Conservative Movement," *National Review*, October 19, 1965, 914–20, 925–29; Jacob Javits, *Order of Battle: A Republican's Call to Reason* (New York: Pocket Books, 1966), 63; James Sundquist, *Dynamics of the Party System* (Washington, DC: Brookings Institution Press, 1983), 376–77, 382–85.

18. Dietz, *Republicans and Vietnam*, 102–3; Gibbons, *The U.S. Government and the Vietnam War*, pt. IV, 139, 376; Stephen Hess and David Broder, *The Republican Establishment: The Present and Future of the GOP* (New York: Harper and Row, 1967), 1–11, 397–416; John Mueller, *War, Presidents, and Public Opinion* (New York: Wiley, 1973), 53–57, 82–89, 164–65; Melvin Small, *At the Water's Edge: American Politics and the Vietnam War* (Chicago: Ivan R. Dee, 2005), 74.

19. John Ehrman, *The Rise of Neoconservatism* (New Haven, CT: Yale University Press, 1995), 34–40, 64–72 ; Murray Friedman, *The Neoconservative Revolution: Jewish Intellectuals and the Shaping of Public Policy* (New York: Cambridge University Press, 2005), 28–36, 100–125; Irving Kristol, *Neoconservatism: The Autobiography of an Idea* (New York: Free Press, 1995), x–xi, 75–91.

Chapter Five
Richard Nixon and Henry Kissinger

1. Leading examples of the now conventional and very critical view of Nixon's foreign policy approach are Robert Dallek's *Nixon and Kissinger: Partners in Power* (New York: HarperCollins, 2007); Joan Hoff, *Nixon Reconsidered* (New York: Basic Books, 1994), chaps. 5–8; and Melvin Small, *The Presidency of Richard Nixon* (Lawrence: University Press of Kansas, 1999), chaps. 3–5.

2. Useful biographical works on Richard Nixon include Jonathan Aitken, *Nixon: A Life* (Washington, DC: Regnery Publishing, 1993); Stephen Ambrose, *Nixon*, 3 vols. (New York: Simon and Schuster, 1987–1991); Roger Morris, *Richard Milhous Nixon: The Rise of an American Politician* (New York: Henry Holt, 1990); Herbert Parmet, *Richard*

Nixon and His America (Boston: Little, Brown, 1990); Tom Wicker, *One of Us: Richard Nixon and the American Dream* (New York: Random House, 1991); and Gary Wills, *Nixon Agonistes* (Boston: Houghton Mifflin, 1970). Nixon's own memoirs are strikingly candid in places. He describes his background and career up until 1967 in *RN: The Memoirs of Richard Nixon* (New York: Simon and Schuster, 1990).

3. Lewis Chester, Godfrey Hodgson, and Bruce Page, *An American Melodrama: The Presidential Campaign of 1968* (New York: Viking Press, 1969), 100, 113, 190–208, 217–23, 433–75, 484–89, 516–17; Nixon, *Memoirs,* 264, 304–5; William Rusher, *The Rise of the Right* (New York: William Morrow, 1984), 194–217.

4. Dan Carter, *The Politics of Rage: George Wallace, the Origins of the New Conservatism, and the Transformation of American Politics* (New York: Simon and Schuster, 1995), 324–70; Chester, Hodgson, and Page, *American Melodrama,* 280, 503–610, 652–58, 680–84; Philip Converse et al., "Continuity and Change in American Politics: Parties and Issues in the 1968 Election," *American Political Science Review* 63, no. 4 (December 1969): 1083–1105; Walter LaFeber, *The Deadly Bet: LBJ, Vietnam, and the 1968 Election* (Lanham, MD: Rowman and Littlefield, 2005), 99–113, 151–65; Kevin Phillips, *The Emerging Republican Majority* (New Rochelle, NY: Arlington House, 1969), 166–75, 181, 274–78, 462.

5. Hoff, *Nixon Reconsidered,* 19–49, 115–44; Robert Mason, *Richard Nixon and the Quest for a New Majority* (Chapel Hill: University of North Carolina Press, 2004), 26–28; Nixon, *Memoirs,* 354, 414; James Reichley, *Conservatives in an Age of Change: The Nixon and Ford Administrations* (Washington, DC: Brookings Institution Press, 1982), 59–78; Small, *Presidency of Richard Nixon,* 153–54, 162–82.

6. National Security Council [hereafter NSC], *Foreign Relations of the United States* [hereafter *FRUS*]: *Vietnam, September 1968–January 1969* (Washington, DC: Government Printing Office, 2003), 609–15; Terry Dietz, *The Republicans and Vietnam, 1961–1968* (New York: Greenwood Press, 1986), 137–39; H. R. Haldeman, *The Ends of Power* (New York: Times Books, 1978), 81; Richard Nixon, "Asia after Vietnam," *Foreign Affairs,* October 1967, 111–25; idem, *Memoirs,* 51, 344–50; Small, *Presidency of Richard Nixon,* 28, 35, 52, 65–67, 98–99.

7. Walter Isaacson, *Kissinger: A Biography* (New York: Simon and Schuster, 1992), 17–128; Henry Kissinger, *A World Restored: Metternich, Castlereagh and the Problems of Peace 1812–1822* (Boston: Houghton Mifflin, 1957), 1–3, 144–45, 172–73, 329; idem, *American Foreign Policy* (New York: W. W. Norton, 1969), 11–12, 46–47, 56, 94, 128–35; idem, *White House Years* (Boston: Little, Brown and Co., 1979), 55–61, 69, 195; idem, "The White Revolutionary: Reflections on Bismarck," *Daedalus* 97 (Summer 1968): 888–924; Harvey Starr, *Henry Kissinger: Perceptions of International Politics* (Lexington: University Press of Kentucky, 1984), 44–73; Jeremi Suri, *Henry Kissinger and the American Century* (Cambridge, MA: Belknap Press, 2007), 7–15.

8. Hoff, *Nixon Reconsidered,* 153; Isaacson, *Kissinger,* 129–39, 151–56, 202–5; Kissinger, *White House Years,* 9–48; Nixon, *Memoirs,* 340–41.

9. Ole Holsti and James Rosenau, *American Leadership in World Affairs: Vietnam and the Breakdown of Consensus* (Boston: Allen and Unwin, 1982), 108–33; John Mueller, *War, Presidents and Public Opinion* (New York: Wiley, 1973), 92, 119, 164–65; Robert Tucker, *A New Isolationism: Threat or Promise?* (Washington, DC: Potomac Associ-

ates, 1972), 37, 96–109; Eugene Wittkopf, *Faces of Internationalism: Public Opinion and American Foreign Policy* (Durham, NC: Duke University Press, 1990), 23–26, 34–49, 118–19, 125.

10. Joseph Fry, *Dixie Looks Abroad: The South and U.S. Foreign Relations, 1789–1973* (Baton Rouge: Louisiana State University Press, 2002), 269–70, 288; Nixon, *Memoirs*, 350–51; Nicol Rae, *The Decline and Fall of the Liberal Republicans* (New York: Oxford University Press, 1989), 106; William Shaffer, *Party and Ideology in the United States Congress* (Washington, DC: University Press of America, 1980), 72, 77–82, 126, 137, 342–43; Barbara Sinclair, *Congressional Realignment, 1925–1978* (Austin: University of Texas Press, 1982), 117–19.

11. Kissinger, *White House Years*, 66–69, 192; Nixon, Kansas City speech, July 6, 1971, *Public Papers of the Presidents: Richard Nixon* [hereafter *NPP*]: *1971* (Washington, DC: Government Printing Office), 806; Starr, *Kissinger*, 105.

12. Memorandum, Nixon to Kissinger, February 1, 1969, President/Kissinger memos, Box 341, National Security Council [NSC] Files; National Security Decision Memorandum 17, "Relaxation of Economic Controls Against China," June 26, 1969, Policy Papers, Box H-210, NSC Institutional Files; and Memo, Kissinger to Nixon, "The U.S. Role in Soviet Maneuvering Against Peking," September 10, 1969, Country Files—Europe: USSR, vol. V, Box 710, NSC Files, Nixon Presidential Materials Staff, National Archives II (College Park, MD). See also Robert Bernstein and William Anthony, "The ABM Issue in the Senate, 1968–1970: The Importance of Ideology," in *To Advise and Consent: The United States Congress and Foreign Policy in the Twentieth Century*, ed. Joel Silbey (Brooklyn, NY: Carlson Publishing, 1991), 2:465–73; William Burr, "Sino-American Relations, 1969: The Sino-Soviet Border War and Steps Toward Rapprochement," *Cold War History* 1, no. 3 (April 2001): 73–112; Kissinger, *White House Years*, 165–70, 182–87; William Safire, *Before the Fall: An Inside View of the Pre-Watergate White House* (Garden City, NY: Doubleday, 1975), 370. All further archival references for this chapter are from the Nixon Presidential Materials Staff at National Archives II, College Park, Maryland, unless otherwise specified.

13. Nixon and Dobrynin, Memorandum of conversation, February 17, 1969, copy in President's Trip Files, Box 489, NSC Files; Raymond Garthoff, *Détente and Confrontation: American-Soviet Relations from Nixon to Reagan* (Washington, DC: The Brookings Institution, 1994 edition), 77–87, 135–39; Kissinger, *White House Years*, 135–144.

14. Nixon press briefing, Guam, July 25, 1969, *NPP*: *1969*, 544–45; Nixon radio-television address, November 3, 1969, *NPP*: *1969*, 905–6; Annual foreign policy report, February 18, 1970, *NPP*: *1970*, 118–19; Kissinger, *White House Years*, 32, 662–64, 672, 914–15, 1264; Robert Litwak, *Détente and the Nixon Doctrine* (New York: Cambridge University Press, 1984), 2, 120; Barry Rubin, *Paved with Good Intentions: The American Experience and Iran* (New York: Oxford University Press, 1980), 124–39; Lewis Sorley, *Arms Transfers under Nixon* (Lexington: University Press of Kentucky, 1983), 173.

15. Memo, Nixon to Ho Chi Minh, July 15, 1969, Henry A. Kissinger Office Files [hereafter HKOF], Country Files—Vietnam, Box 106, NSC Files; Memo, Kissinger to Nixon, September 10, 1969, "Special NSC Meeting 9/12/69—Vietnam," Meeting Files (1969–1974), Box H-024, NSC Institutional ("H") Files; *NPP*: *1969*, 901–9; Pierre Asselin, *A Bitter Peace: Washington, Hanoi, and the Making of the Paris Agreement* (Chapel

Hill: University of North Carolina Press, 2002), 13–26; William Burr and Jeffrey Kimball, "Nixon's Secret Nuclear Alert: Vietnam War Diplomacy and the Joint Chief of Staff Readiness Test, October 1969," *Cold War History* 3, no. 2 (January 2003): 113–49; Charles DeBenedetti, *An American Ordeal: The Antiwar Movement of the Vietnam Era* (Syracuse, NY: Syracuse University Press, 1990), 248–68; Jeffrey Kimball, *Nixon's Vietnam War* (Lawrence: University Press of Kansas, 1998), 158–70; Mueller, *War, Presidents and Public Opinion*, 92, 94; Nixon, *Memoirs*, 393–394, 397–399, 403–5; James Sundquist, *The Decline and Resurgence of Congress* (Washington, DC: Brookings Institution Press, 1981), 248–49.

16. "NSC Cambodia," April 22, 1970, NSC Meetings, President's Speech File, Box 57, President's Personal Files [hereafter PPF]; *NPP: 1970*, 404–10, 529–41; Phillip Davidson, *Vietnam at War* (New York: Oxford University Press, 1991), 624–29; H. R. Haldeman, *The Haldeman Diaries* (New York: G. P. Putnam's Sons, 1994), 159–63, 172; Kissinger, *White House Years*, 449, 495, 969; David Levy, *The Debate over Vietnam* (Baltimore, MD: Johns Hopkins University Press, 1995), 159–60; Small, *Presidency of Richard Nixon*, 78; Sundquist, *Decline and Resurgence of Congress*, 250–52.

17. Memo, Staff Secretary John Brown to Ehrlichman, Finch, and Haldeman, September 8, 1970, Haldeman Staff Memos, Box 66, Staff Member and Office Files: H. R. Haldeman, White House Special Files; H. R. Haldeman, *The Complete Multimedia Edition of the Haldeman Diaries* [CD-ROM Diaries] (Santa Monica, CA: Sony Electronic Publishing Co., 1994), July 11, August 31, 1970; John Coyne, *The Impudent Snobs: Agnew vs. the Intellectual Establishment* (New Rochelle, NY: Arlington House, 1972), 360–427; Mason, *New Majority*, 77–112; Nixon, *Memoirs*, 490–95; Safire, *Before the Fall*, 316–40.

18. Joanne Gowa, *Closing the Gold Window: Domestic Politics and the End of Bretton Woods* (Ithaca, NY: Cornell University Press, 1983), 13–32, 136, 165; Robert Keller and Ann Mari May, "The Presidential Political Business Cycle of 1972," *Journal of Economic History* 44 (June 1984): 265–71; Allen Matusow, *Nixon's Economy: Booms, Busts, Dollars, and Votes* (Lawrence: University Press of Kansas, 1998), 84, 87–106, 126–55; Nixon, *Memoirs*, 497, 515–22; Safire, *Before the Fall*, 509–28.

19. Memorandum of conversation, Henry Kissinger and Chou En-lai, October 21, 1971, "For the President's File—China Trip," Box 846, NSC Files; Nixon-Mao conversation, Beijing, February 21, 1972, in *The Kissinger Transcripts: The Top Secret Talks with Beijing and Moscow*, ed. William Burr (New York: New Press, 1998), 61, 64; *FRUS: United Nations, 1969–1972*, 838–58; Chen Jian, *Mao's China and the Cold War* (Chapel Hill: University of North Carolina Press, 2001), 235–72; Evelyn Goh, "Nixon, Kissinger, and the 'Soviet Card' in the U.S. Opening to China, 1971–1974," *Diplomatic History* 29, no. 3 (June 2005): 475–502; Kissinger, *White House Years*, 726–727, 741–765, 781–84, 1057–87, 1490–92; Leonard Kusnitz, *Public Opinion and Foreign Policy: America's China Policy, 1949–1979* (Westport, CT: Greenwood Press, 1984), 138–41; Nixon, *Memoirs*, 551–80; Memo, Kissinger to Nixon, "China," February 24, 1973, Box 6, PPF.

20. Memoranda of conversations, Nixon and Brezhnev, May 22, 26, 1972, President's Trip Files, Box 487, NSC Files; *Department of State Bulletin* 66 (June 26, 1972): 898–99; McGeorge Bundy, *Danger and Survival: Choices About the Bomb in the First Fifty Years* (New York: Random House, 1988), 553–56; Anatoly Dobrynin, *In Confidence: Moscow's Ambassador to America's Six Cold War Presidents* (New York: Random House, 1995),

274; Haldeman, *Diaries,* 445–46, 451–55, 462–65; Kissinger, *White House Years,* 1222–29; Keith Nelson, *The Making of Détente: Soviet-American Relations in the Shadow of Vietnam* (Baltimore, MD: Johns Hopkins University Press, 1995), 102–3, 145–46.

21. Annual foreign policy report, February 9, 1972, *NPP: 1972,* 204–7, 211; Coral Bell, *The Diplomacy of Détente* (New York: St Martin's Press, 1977), 3, 222; John Gaddis, *Strategies of Containment: A Critical Appraisal of American National Security Policy During the Cold War* (New York: Oxford University Press, 2005), 287–92, 295, 305; Kissinger, *White House Years,* 116–19, 127–30, 265–69, 535, 765, 1089, 1132–34, 1250–55; Nixon, *Memoirs,* 618; Kissinger statement to the Senate Foreign Relations Committee, September 19, 1974, in *American Foreign Policy* (New York: W. W. Norton, 1977), 145–73.

22. Memo, Nixon to Kissinger, October 19, 1972, HKOF, Country Files—Vietnam, Box 104, NSC Files; Memo, Alexander Haig to Kissinger, October 23, 1972, Alexander Haig Chronological Files, Box 996, NSC Files; Asselin, *A Bitter Peace,* 27–101; Haldeman, *Diaries,* 451–55, 510, 515–24; Kissinger, *White House Years,* 1017–20, 1200–1201, 1304, 1345–46, 1361, 1380, 1400; Robert Mann, *A Grand Delusion: America's Descent Into Vietnam* (New York: Basic Books, 2001), 678; Ngo Quang Troung, *The Easter Offensive of 1972* (Washington, DC: U.S. Army Center of Military History, 1980), 64, 123, 158, 172; Nixon, *Memoirs,* 697, 701–2; Qiang Zhai, *China and the Vietnam Wars, 1950–1975* (Chapel Hill: University of North Carolina Press), 202–6.

23. Mason, *New Majority,* 137–72; Benjamin Page and Robert Shapiro, *The Rational Public* (Chicago: University of Chicago Press, 1992), 239, 250, 262, 265; Rae, *Liberal Republicans,* 107–108; Rusher, *Rise of the Right,* 239–46.

24. Earl Black and Merle Black, *The Rise of Southern Republicans* (Cambridge, MA: Belknap Press, 2002), 25, 211, 230; Carter, *Politics of Rage,* 415–50; Everett Ladd, *Transformations of the American Party System* (New York: W. W. Norton, 1978), 26–27, 153–61, 240, 333–58; Mason, *New Majority,* 172–91; Arthur Miller et al., "A Majority Party in Disarray: Policy Polarization in the 1972 Election," *APSR* 70, no. 3 (September 1976): 753–78; George Nash, *The Conservative Intellectual Movement in America Since 1945* (Wilmington, DE: ISI Books, 2006), 513.

25. Memorandum of conversation, Kissinger and Tho, January 8, 1973, "For the President's File—Vietnam Negotiations," vol. XXIII, Box 860, NSC Files; Asselin, *A Bitter Peace,* 109–80; Larry Berman, *No Peace, No Honor: Nixon, Kissinger, and Betrayal in Vietnam* (New York: Free Press, 2001), 185–94, 212–21; Iliya Gaiduk, *The Soviet Union and the Vietnam War* (Chicago: Ivan R. Dee, 1996), 244–45; Haldeman, CD Rom Diaries, December 7, 10, 20, 1972; Nguyen Tien Hung and Jerrold Schecter, *The Palace File* (New York: Harper and Row, 1986), 73–74, 376–96; Kissinger, *White House Years,* 1361–80, 1442–47; Nixon, *Memoirs,* 718, 725–26, 733, 743; Qiang Zhai, *China and the Vietnam Wars,* 202–5; Norman Thorpe and James Miles, "Comments on Air Warfare—Christmas 1972," in *Law and Responsibility in Warfare: The Vietnam Experience,* ed. Peter Trooboff (Chapel Hill: University of North Carolina Press, 1975), 145.

26. The first critique is best articulated in Kimball, *Nixon's Vietnam War,* 260; the second critique, in Berman, *No Peace, No Honor,* 9. For evidence of counterinsurgent success, see Phillip Davidson, *Vietnam at War* (New York: Oxford University Press, 1991), 615, 634, 661; and Lewis Sorley, *A Better War: The Unexamined Victories and Final Tragedy of America's Last Years in Vietnam* (New York: Harcourt Brace, 1999), 274.

For an example of one of Kissinger's gloomier assessments regarding Saigon's ultimate capacity to survive, see John Ehrlichman, *Witness to Power: The Nixon Years* (New York: Simon and Schuster, 1982), 316. In negotiations with Moscow and Beijing, characteristically playing to his audience in order to secure his diplomatic objective, Kissinger held out the suggestion that the United States would not block purely internal political changes in South Vietnam after the signing of a peace agreement, but he never suggested that the United States would stand by and allow a North Vietnamese invasion. See Memorandum of conversation, Kissinger and Zhou En-lai, June 21, 1972, "China, Dr. Kissinger's Visit June 1972," HKOF, Country Files—Far East, Box 97, NSC Files; and Memorandum of conversation, Kissinger, Brezhnev, Gromyko, et al., September 13, 1972, "HAK Trip to Moscow September 1972," HKOF, Box 74, NSC Files.

27. Christopher Andrew and Vasili Mitrokhin, *The World Was Going Our Way: The KGB and the Battle for the Third World* (New York: Basic Books, 2005), 69–87; Alistair Horne, *A Small Earthquake in Chile* (New York: Viking Press, 1973), 25–26, 32, 131–49, 347–55; Kissinger, *White House Years*, 653–83, and *Years of Upheaval* (Boston: Little, Brown, 1982), 374–413; Peter Kornbluh, *The Pinochet File: A Declassified Dossier on Atrocity and Accountability* (New York: New Press, 2003), 3–18, 22–29, 36–78, 97–120, 146–60, 242–44; David Rockefeller, *Memoirs* (New York: Random House, 2002), 432; Paul Sigmund, *The Overthrow of Allende and the Politics of Chile, 1964–1976* (Pittsburgh, PA: University of Pittsburgh Press, 1978), 3–8, 48, 103, 133, 227, 283–84, 291; U.S. Senate, *Covert Action in Chile, 1963–1973*, 94th Cong., 1st sess. (Washington, DC: Government Printing Office, 1975), 19–35.

28. "Cabinet Meeting," October 18, 1973, Box 92, President's Office Files, White House Special Files; telephone conversation, Kissinger and Haig, October 24, 1973, Chronological File, Box 23, Henry A. Kissinger Telephone Conversation Transcripts; Barry Blechman and Douglas Hart, "The Political Utility of Nuclear Weapons: The 1973 Middle East Crisis," *International Security* 7, no. 1 (Summer 1982): 132–56; Dobrynin, *In Confidence*, 321–23; Kissinger, *Years of Upheaval*, 481–82, 575–53, 615–38, 777–86, 947, 1052–1110; William Quandt, *Peace Process: American Diplomacy and the Arab-Israeli Conflict Since 1967* (Washington, DC: Brookings Institution Press, 2005), 55–97, 104–173; Edward Sheehan, "How Kissinger Did It: Step by Step in the Middle East," *Foreign Policy*, Spring 1976, 3–70.

29. Robert Brigham, *Guerrilla Diplomacy: The NLF's Foreign Relations and the Viet Nam War* (Ithaca, NY: Cornell University Press, 1999), 118–19; William Duiker, *The Communist Road to Power in Vietnam* (Boulder, CO: Westview Press, 1996), 329–36; Kissinger, *Years of Upheaval*, 324–27; Sundquist, *Decline and Resurgence of Congress*, 254–60, 277.

30. Gerald Ford, *A Time to Heal* (New York: Harper and Row, 1979), 138–39, 180; Robert Kaufman, *Henry M. Jackson: A Life in Politics* (Seattle: University of Washington Press, 2000), 266–81; Kissinger, *Years of Renewal* (New York: Simon and Schuster, 1999), 112–15, 128–35, 255–60, 302–9; idem, *Years of Upheaval*, 985–98; Noam Kochavi, "Insights Abandoned, Flexibility Lost: Kissinger, Soviet Jewish Emigration, and the Demise of Détente," *Diplomatic History* 29, no. 3 (June 2005): 503–30; Paula Stern, *Water's Edge: Domestic Politics and the Making of American Foreign Policy* (Westport, CT: Greenwood Press, 1979), 10–15, 23, 145–69, 173–98, 212.

31. Memoranda of conversations between Brezhnev and Ford, November 23, November 24, 1974, National Security Archive, George Washington University, Washing-

ton, DC; Ford, *A Time to Heal*, 129, 133, 183, 218–19, 263–64, 306; Garthoff, *Détente and Confrontation*, 489–505; John Robert Greene, *The Presidency of Gerald R. Ford* (Lawrence: University Press of Kansas, 1995), 11–13, 67–72, 124–26, 161; Kaufman, *Jackson*, 256–57, 288–89; Kissinger, *Years of Renewal*, 169–91, 243–55, 286–302; Nixon, *Memoirs*, 1023–1026.

32. Burr, *Kissinger Transcripts*, 326; Ford, *A Time to Heal*, 298–304; Garthoff, *Détente and Confrontation*, 526–33; Robert Gates, *From the Shadows: The Ultimate Insider's Story of Five Presidents and How They Won the Cold War* (New York: Simon and Schuster, 1996), 85–88; Kissinger, *Years of Renewal*, 635–664; Daniel Thomas, *The Helsinki Effect: International Norms, Human Rights, and the Demise of Communism* (Princeton, NJ: Princeton University Press, 2001), 91–121, 285–86.

33. Duiker, *Communist Road to Power*, 336–50; Ford, *A Time to Heal*, 253–54; Hung and Schecter, *Palace File*, 156–57, 286–87, 296–98, 354–55, 434; Christopher Jespersen, "Kissinger, Ford, and Congress: The Very Bitter End in Vietnam," *Pacific Historical Review* 71, no. 3 (August 2002): 439–73; Kissinger, *Years of Renewal*, 463–95, 520–46; Gunter Lewy, *America in Vietnam* (New York: Oxford University Press, 1978), 205–10.

34. Ford, *A Time to Heal*, 276–84; Richard Head et al, *Crisis Resolution: Presidential Decision Making in the Mayaguez and Korean Confrontations* (Boulder, CO: Westview Press, 1978), 109–18, 131; Kissinger, *Years of Renewal*, 547–75; Christopher Jon Lamb, *Belief Systems and Decision Making in the Mayaguez Crisis* (Gainesville: University of Florida Press, 1988), 9, 21–31, 81, 91–93.

35. Piero Gleijeses, "Moscow's Proxy? Cuba and Africa, 1975–1988," *Journal of Cold War Studies* 8, no. 2 (Spring 2006): 3–51; Greene, *Presidency of Gerald R. Ford*, 102–15; Kissinger, *Years of Renewal*, 791–833, 903–1016; John Marcum, *The Angolan Revolution, Vol. 2, Exile Politics and Guerrilla Warfare, 1962–1976* (Cambridge, MA: MIT Press, 1978), 245–258; Sundquist, *Decline and Resurgence of Congress*, 286–89; Odd A. Westad, "Moscow and the Angolan Crisis, 1974–1976: A New Pattern of Intervention," *Cold War International History Project Bulletin* 8–9 (Winter 1996–97): 21–32.

36. Lloyd Bitzer and Theodore Rueter, *Carter vs. Ford* (Madison: University of Wisconsin Press, 1980), 33–34, 100–101, 174–76, 298–300; Ford, *A Time to Heal*, 385, 398, 422–25; *The Gallup Poll: Public Opinion, 1972–1977* (Wilmington, DE: Scholarly Resources,1978), 2:881–82, 887–88, 902–11; Greene, *Presidency of Gerald R. Ford*, 30–31, 58–59, 126, 163–87; Kissinger, *Years of Renewal*, 861–67; Leo Ribuffo, "Is Poland a Soviet Satellite? Gerald Ford, the Sonnenfeldt Doctrine, and the Election of 1976," *Diplomatic History* 14, no. 3 (Summer 1990): 385–403; Jules Witcover, *Marathon: The Pursuit of the Presidency, 1972–1976* (New York: Viking Press, 1977), 373–432, 456–71, 485–86, 545–51, 657.

Chapter Six

Ronald Reagan

1. Patrick Buchanan, *Conservative Votes, Liberal Victories* (New York: Quadrangle Press, 1975), 8, 170–77; Donald Critchlow, *The Conservative Ascendency* (Cambridge, MA: Harvard University Press, 2007), 123, 151; Everett C. Ladd, *Transformations of the American Party System* (New York: W. W. Norton, 1978), 292–97; Michael Mandlebaum and William Schneider, "The New Internationalisms," in *Eagle Entangled*, ed. Kenneth

Oye, Donald Rothchild, and Robert Lieber (New York: Longman, 1979), 38–40, 44; William Rusher, *The Rise of the Right* (New York: William Morrow, 1984), 263–94; William Shaffer, *Party and Ideology in the United States Congress* (Lanham, MD: University Press of America, 1980), 72, 95, 137.

2. Thomas Evans, *The Education of Ronald Reagan* (New York: Columbia University Press, 2006), 57–80, 111–53; Ronald Reagan, *An American Life* (New York: Simon and Schuster, 1990), 19–143; Kurt Ritter and David Henry, *Ronald Reagan: The Great Communicator* (New York: Greenwood Press), 11–28, 135–43; Stephen Vaughn, *Ronald Reagan in Hollywood: Movies and Politics* (New York: Cambridge University Press, 1994), 37, 63–66, 124–26.

3. Lou Cannon, *Governor Reagan* (New York: Public Affairs, 2003), 197–99, 213, 348–62; Matthew Dallek, *The Right Moment* (New York: Free Press, 2000), 240–42; Jonathan Schoenwald, *A Time for Choosing: The Rise of Modern American Conservatism* (New York: Oxford University Press, 2001), 190–220.

4. Adam Clymer, *Drawing the Line at the Big Ditch: The Panama Canal Treaties and the Rise of the Right* (Lawrence: University Press of Kansas, 2008), 25–39; Critchlow, *The Conservative Ascendancy*, 123–24; Reagan, *An American Life*, 178; Jules Witcover, *Marathon* (New York: Viking Press, 1977), 70, 398–402, 408–14, 485–86.

5. On Carter's foreign policy, see Jerel Rosati, *The Carter Administration's Quest for Global Community* (Columbia: University of South Carolina Press, 1987); David Skidmore, *Reversing Course: Carter's Foreign Policy, Domestic Politics, and the Failure of Reform* (Nashville, TN: Vanderbilt University Press, 1996); and Gaddis Smith, *Morality, Reason, and Power: American Diplomacy in the Carter Years* (New York: Hill and Wang, 1986).

6. Clymer, *Drawing the Line at the Big Ditch*, 40–81, 90–163; Alan Crawford, *Thunder on the Right: The "New Right" and the Politics of Resentment* (New York: Pantheon Books, 1980), 51; George Moffett, *The Limits of Victory: The Ratification of the Panama Canal Treaties* (Ithaca, NY: Cornell University Press, 1985), 82–107, 171–76, 207–12; Richard Viguerie, *The New Right—We're Ready to Lead* (Falls Church, VA: Viguerie Co., 1980), 19–81, 87; Philip Williams, "The American Mid-Term Elections," *Political Studies* 27 (December 1979): 608.

7. Dan Caldwell, *The Dynamics of Domestic Politics and SALT: The SALT II Treaty Ratification Debate* (Columbia: University of South Caroline Press, 1991), 102–5, 181–82; John Ehrman, *The Rise of Neoconservatism* (New Haven, CT: Yale University Press), 97–135; Jeane Kirkpatrick, "Dictatorships and Double Standards," *Commentary*, November 1979, 35–45; Paul Nitze, *From Hiroshima to Glasnost: At the Center of Decision* (New York: G. Weidenfeld, 1989), 352–54; Charles Tyroler, ed., *Alerting America: The Papers of the Committee on the Present Danger* (Washington, DC: Pergamon-Brassey's, 1984), 3–15, 42, 162, 179.

8. Paul Kengor, *The Crusader: Ronald Reagan and the Fall of Communism* (New York: Regan Books, 2006), 53–54, 64–65; Paul Lettow, *Ronald Reagan and His Quest to Abolish Nuclear Weapons* (New York: Random House, 2005), 16, 22–27; Kiron Skinner, Annelise Anderson, and Martin Anderson, eds., *Reagan: In His Own Hand* (New York: Free Press, 2001), 10–12, 33–35, 60–63, 84–85, 99–102, 109–13, 118, 147–50, 480–87.

9. Thomas Edsall, *Chain Reaction: The Impact of Race, Rights, and Taxes on American Politics* (New York: Norton, 1991), 129–31; Bruce Nesmith, *The New Republican Coalition: The Reagan Campaigns and White Evangelicals* (New York: Peter Lang, 1994),

17–69; Rusher, *The Rise of the Right*, 252–58, 296–97; James Allen Smith, *The Idea Brokers: Think Tanks and the Rise of the New Policy Elite* (New York: Free Press, 1993), 174–83, 194–205; Viguerie, *The New Right*, 123–26.

10. Reagan, "Address to the Conservative Political Action Conference," Washington, DC, February 6, 1977, in *A City Upon a Hill: Speeches by Ronald Reagan Before the Conservative Political Action Conference*, ed. James Roberts (Washington, DC: American Studies Center, 1989), 31–37.

11. Christopher Bailey, *The Republican Party in the U.S. Senate, 1974–1984* (New York: St. Martin's Press, 1987), 54, 65, 69–70, 92, 123; Nicol Rae, *The Decline and Fall of the Liberal Republicans* (New York: Oxford University Press, 1989), 114, 118–21, 136–37, 158–62, 168; David Reinhard, *The Republican Right since 1945* (Lexington: University Press of Kentucky, 1983), 234, 240; Shaffer, *Party and Ideology*, 331–34; Barbara Sinclair, *Congressional Realignment, 1925–1978* (Austin: University of Texas Press, 1982), 154, 157, 159, 163–68.

12. Larry Bartels, *Presidential Primaries and the Dynamics of Public Choice* (Princeton, NJ: Princeton University Press, 1988), 219–47, 267–69; Rae, *Liberal Republicans*, 139, 143–44; Reinhard, *Republican Right*, 240–42, 247–49.

13. Paul Abramson, John Aldrich, and David Rohde, *Change and Continuity in the 1980 Elections* (Washington, DC: Congressional Quarterly Press, 1982), 45–46, 98–99, 121–53, 169–82; Andrew Busch, *Reagan's Victory: The Presidential Election of 1980 and the Rise of the Right* (Lawrence: University Press of Kansas, 2005), 121, 130–44; Jack Germond and Jules Witcover, *Blue Smoke and Mirrors* (New York: Viking Press, 1981), 1–19, 310–21; Nesmith, *The New Republican Coalition*, 73–78; William Schneider, "The November 4 Vote for President: What Did It Mean?" in *The American Elections of 1980*, ed. Austin Ranney (Washington, DC: American Enterprise Institute for Public Policy Research, 1981), 212–62.

14. Lou Cannon, *President Reagan* (New York: Public Affairs, 2000), 196–239; Paul Gottfried and Thomas Fleming, *The Conservative Movement* (Boston: Twayne Publishers, 1988), 96–97, 104; Steven Hayward, *The Age of Reagan: The Conservative Counterrevolution, 1980–1989* (New York: Crown Forum, 2009), 57–95; Ole Holsti, *Public Opinion and American Foreign Policy* (Ann Arbor: University of Michigan Press, 2004), 155, 184–85; Rae, *Liberal Republicans*, 145, 168–95, 205, 208–14; James Reichley, "The Reagan Coalition," *Brookings Review* 1 (Winter 1982): 6–9; David Stockman, *The Triumph of Politics* (New York: Harper and Row, 1986), 8–14.

15. Martin Anderson, *Revolution* (San Diego, CA: Harcourt Brace Jovanovich, 1988), 284–90; Douglas Brinkley, ed., *The Reagan Diaries* (New York: Harper Perennial, 2007), 90–91; Lou Cannon, *President Reagan*, 153, 172–81, 263–65, 293–95, 375–76, 630; Richard Darman, *Who's in Control?* (New York: Simon and Schuster, 1996), 39–40; Anatoliy Dobrynin, *In Confidence* (New York: Random House, 1995), 477, 521; Alexander Haig, *Caveat* (New York: Macmillan, 1984), 77, 80–86, 355–56; Hayward, *The Age of Reagan*, 96–134; George Shultz, *Turmoil and Triumph* (New York: Scribner's, 1993), 1135–36. For Reagan's letters, see, e.g., Kiron Skinner, Annelise Anderson, and Martin Anderson, *Reagan: A Life in Letters* (New York: Free Press, 2003).

16. Christopher Simpson, *National Security Directives of the Reagan and Bush Administrations* (Boulder, CO: Westview Press, 1995), 46–49; Stockman, *The Triumph of Politics*, 107–9, 269–99.

17. Cannon, *President Reagan*, 163, 291; Robert Gates, *From the Shadows* (New York: Simon and Schuster, 1996), 245, 256, 346–356; Haig, *Caveat*, 118, 125–130; Mark Lagon, *The Reagan Doctrine* (Westport, CT: Praeger, 1994), 78–82; James Scott, *Deciding to Intervene* (Durham, NC: Duke University Press, 1996), 25–27, 34–35.

18. Dobrynin, *In Confidence*, 563; Adam Garfinkle, *The Politics of the Nuclear Freeze* (Philadelphia, PA: Foreign Policy Research Institute, 1984), 234–38; Reagan, "Arms Reduction and Nuclear Weapons," November 18, 1981, *Weekly Compilation of Presidential Documents* 17: 1273; Skinner, Anderson, and Anderson, *A Life in Letters*, 402, 407; Strobe Talbott, *Deadly Gambits* (London: Picador, 1985), 116–51.

19. Reagan to Leonid Brezhnev, December 23, 1981, ES, NSC, HSF: Records, USSR: GSB (8190210), Box 38, Ronald Reagan Library [hereafter RRL], Simi Valley, CA; Laurence Barrett, *Gambling with History* (New York: Penguin, 1984), 298; Carl Bernstein and Marco Politi, *His Holiness: John Paul II and the Hidden History of Our Time* (New York: Doubleday, 1996), 12, 260–69, 357; Haig, *Caveat*, 104, 240–42, 303–16; Reagan, *An American Life*, 301–4; Caspar Weinberger, *In the Arena* (Washington, DC: Regnery, 2001), 280.

20. NSDD-24, and NSDD-41, February 9 and June 2, 1982, RRL; Richard Pipes, *Vixi: Memoirs of a Non-Belonger* (New Haven, CT: Yale University Press, 2003), 170–73, 179–80; Alan Dobson, "The Reagan Administration, Economic Warfare, and Starting to Close Down the Cold War," *Diplomatic History* 29, no. 3 (June 2005): 531–56; Reagan, *An American Life*, 237–38, 316, 320, 552, 558; Thomas Reed, *At the Abyss* (New York: Presidio Press, 2004), 226–28, 239, 266–70; Shultz, *Turmoil and Triumph*, 135–45.

21. Reagan address at Notre Dame University, address to members of the British Parliament, and remarks to the National Association of Evangelicals, May 17, 1981, June 8, 1982, and March 8, 1983, *Public Papers of the Presidents: Ronald Reagan* [hereafter RPP], *1981*, 434, *RPP: 1982*, 743–47, and *RPP: 1983*, 359–64; John Arquilla, *The Reagan Imprint* (Chicago: Ivan R. Dee, 2006), 149–54; Skinner, Anderson, and Anderson, *A Life in Letters*, 376.

22. Reagan radio-television address, March 23, 1983, *RPP: 1983*, 442–43; Derek Leebaert, *The Fifty-Year Wound* (Boston: Little, Brown, 2002), 451, 528–29; Lettow, *Ronald Reagan and His Quest to Abolish Nuclear Weapons*, 19–42, 81–121, 214–15; Reagan, *An American Life*, 257–258, 547–50, 608–9; Shultz, *Turmoil and Triumph*, 189, 246–64, 466, 509; Skinner, Anderson, and Anderson, *A Life in Letters*, 427.

23. NSDD-32, "U.S. National Security Strategy," May 20, 1982, and NSDD-75, "U.S. Relations with the USSR," January 17, 1983, RRL. For useful commentary, see Martin Anderson and Annelise Anderson, *Reagan's Secret War* (New York: Crown Publishers, 2009); Arquilla, *The Reagan Imprint*, 38–43, 51–53, 227–35; John Gaddis, *Strategies of Containment* (New York: Oxford University Press, 2005), 353–56, 369–77; Lettow, *Ronald Reagan and His Quest to Abolish Nuclear Weapons*, 61–72, 75–82; and Pipes, *Vixi*, 188–202.

24. Robert Beck, *The Grenada Invasion* (Boulder, CO: Westview Press, 1993), 57–58, 106–13, 138; Robert McFarlane, *Special Trust* (New York: Cadell and Davies, 1994), 257–67; Colin Powell, *My American Journey* (New York: Random House, 1995), 292; Paul Seabury and Walter McDougall, *The Grenada Papers* (San Francisco, CA: Institute for Contemporary Studies, 1984), 190–91, 207–8; Shultz, *Turmoil and Triumph*, 323–45; Weinberger, *Fighting for Peace*, 101–33.

25. Brinkley, *Reagan Diaries*, 184; Cannon, *President Reagan*, 339–401; Ralph Hallenbeck, *Military Force as an Instrument of U.S. Foreign Policy: Intervention in Lebanon, August 1982–February 1984* (New York: Praeger, 1991), 8–10, 131, 138–53; Benjamin Page and Robert Shapiro, *The Rational Public* (Chicago: University of Chicago Press, 1992), 259–60; Shultz, *Turmoil and Triumph*, 101–14, 220–32; Weinberger, *Fighting for Peace*, 135–74.

26. Christopher Andrew and Oleg Gordievsky, *KGB: The Inside Story* (New York: HarperCollins, 1990), 488–507, 583–601; Brinkley, *Reagan Diaries*, 199; Kengor, *The Crusader*, 188; Don Oberdorfer, *From the Cold War to a New Era* (Baltimore, MD: Johns Hopkins University Press, 1998), 65–71; Nancy Reagan, *My Turn* (New York: Random House, 1989), 336–37; Ronald Reagan, *An American Life*, 584–89, 595, 602; Reagan, "Address to the Nation and Other Countries," January 16, 1984, *RPP: 1984*, 40–45. Beth Fischer rightly argues that the KAL 007 and Able Archer incidents led Reagan to personally take the initiative—and not primarily for political reasons—to reduce the dangers of nuclear war, but she overstates the other changes in his anti-Soviet policies during the winter of 1983–84. See Fischer, *The Reagan Reversal* (Columbia: University of Missouri Press, 1997), 18, 49, 122–31.

27. Paul Abramson, John Aldrich, and David Rohde, *Change and Continuity in the 1984 Elections* (Washington, DC: Congressional Quarterly Press, 1986), 50–63, 70–79, 134–42, 163–204; William Schneider, "The November 6 Vote for President: What Did It Mean?," in *The American Elections of 1984*, ed. Austin Ranney (Durham, NC: Duke University Press, 1985), 203–44.

28. Memoranda of conversations, November 19, 20, 1985, and October 10, 11, 12, 1986, Box 2, End of Cold War Collection, National Security Archive [hereafter NSA], George Washington University, Washington DC; "Joint Statement," November 25, 1985, *Department of State Bulletin* 86 (January 1986): 8–9; Mikhail Gorbachev, *Memoirs* (New York: Doubleday, 1996), 165–68, 405–8, 419, 444; Jack Matlock, *Reagan and Gorbachev* (New York: Random House, 2004), xi, 215–37; Oberdorfer, *From the Cold War to a New Era*, 189–209; Reagan, *An American Life*, 11–14, 567, 611–15, 628, 634–39, 675–83, 707–8; Shultz, *Turmoil and Triumph*, 531–33, 599–607, 699–702, 718–27, 751–80.

29. NSDD-166, "Expanded U.S. Aid to Afghan Guerrillas," [April 1985?], RRL; Steve Coll, *Ghost Wars* (New York: Penguin, 2004), 125–69; Charles Krauthammer, "The Reagan Doctrine," *Time*, April 1, 1985, 54–55; Lagon, *The Reagan Doctrine*, 91–100; Peter Rodman, *More Precious Than Peace* (New York: Charles Scribner's Sons, 1994), 220, 248–250, 259–288, 336–40; Scott, *Deciding to Intervene*, 24–25, 28, 31–38, 59.

30. Theodore Draper, *A Very Thin Line* (New York: Hill and Wang, 1991), 30–40, 61–85, 120–201, 249–63, 541–70; McFarlane, *Special Trust*, 17–35, 40–68, 105; Edwin Meese, *With Reagan* (Washington, DC: Regnery Gateway, 1992), 242–56, 288–302; Reagan, *An American Life*, 484–527, 536–38; Shultz, *Turmoil and Triumph*, 285–87, 793–804, 827–83, 857; Lawrence Walsh, *Final Report of the Independent Counsel for Iran/Contra Matters* (Washington, DC: U.S. Government Printing Office, 1993), 1:xiv–xvii, 119, 204, 445, 466–67, 520–23; 2:673–74, 686–87.

31. Reagan to Gorbachev, April 10, 1987, Executive Secretariat, NSC, Heads of State, USSR, Box 41, RRL; Memoranda of conversations, December 8 and 9, 1987, May 29, 1988, Box 3, End of the Cold War Collection, NSA; Reagan address at Moscow State University, May 31, 1988, *RPP: 1988*, 684; Cannon, *President Reagan*, 265, 698–700,

706–7; Raymond Garthoff, *The Great Transition* (Washington, DC: Brookings Institution Press, 1994), 291–99, 307–38, 351–58; Janne Nolan, "The INF Treaty," in *The Politics of Arms Control Treaty Ratification,* ed. Michael Krepon and Dan Caldwell (New York: St. Martin's Press, 1991), 355–97; Page and Shapiro, *The Rational Public,* 280–81; Reagan, *An American Life,* 683–91, 698–701, 711; Shultz, *Turmoil and Triumph,* 863–86, 989–1014, 1101–6, 1131.

32. Haig, *Caveat,* 90; William Kline et al., "The Philippines, 1983–1986: Arranging a Divorce," in *Dealing with Dictators,* ed. Ernest May and Philip Zelikow (Cambridge, MA: MIT Press, 2006), 137–65; Shultz, *Turmoil and Triumph,* 636, 970; Tony Smith, *America's Mission* (Princeton, NJ: Princeton University Press, 1994), 268–71, 287–95, 300, 303–4.

33. Thomas Carothers, *In the Name of Democracy: U.S. Policy Toward Latin America in the Reagan Years* (Berkeley and Los Angeles: University of California Press, 1991), 153; Gary Dorrien, *The Neoconservative Mind* (Philadelphia, PA: Temple University Press, 1993), 10–11; Ehrman, *The Rise of Neoconservatism,* 135–72; Francis Fukuyama, *America at the Crossroads* (New Haven, CT: Yale University Press, 2006), 38, 45; Jeane Kirkpatrick, *The Reagan Phenomenon* (Washington, DC: American Enterprise Institute, 1983), 54, 61; Irving Kristol, *Neoconservatism: The Autobiography of an Idea* (New York: Free Press, 1995), xi; Norman Podhoretz, "Appeasement by Any Other Name," *Commentary,* July 1983, 25–38.

34. Arquilla, *The Reagan Imprint,* 227–35; Coral Bell, *The Reagan Paradox* (Aldershot, UK: Edward Elgar, 1989), 16–21; Melvyn Leffler, *For the Soul of Mankind* (New York: Hill and Wang, 2007), 448, 462–65; Jack Matlock, *Autopsy on an Empire* (New York: Random House, 1995), 77, 590–91, 667–72; Rodman, *More Precious Than Peace,* 197, 317–23, 477; Fareed Zakaria, "The Reagan Strategy of Containment," *Political Science Quarterly* 105, no. 3 (Autumn 1990): 373–95. The literature on the causes of the cold war's end, including its relationship to U.S. foreign policy, is voluminous and growing. For a good introduction embodying a range of perspectives, see Stephen Brooks and William Wohlforth, "Power, Globalization, and the End of the Cold War," *International Security* 25, no. 3 (Winter 2000–2001): 5–53; Garthoff, *The Great Transition;* Stephen Kotkin, *Armageddon Averted* (New York: Oxford University Press, 2001); Richard Hermann and Richard Ned Lebow, *Ending the Cold War* (New York: Palgrave Macmillan, 2004); Jeremi Suri, "Explaining the End of the Cold War: A New Historical Consensus?," *Journal of Cold War Studies* 4 (Fall 2002): 60–92; and William Wohlforth, ed., *Cold War Endgame* (University Park, PA: Philadelphia State University Press, 2003).

35. Andrew Busch, *Ronald Reagan and the Politics of Freedom* (Lanham, MD: Rowman and Littlefield, 2001): 2–16, 128, 140; Cannon, *President Reagan,* 755–56; Robert Collins, *Transforming America* (New York: Columbia University Press, 2007), 93–115, 235–55; John P. Diggins, *Ronald Reagan: Fate, Freedom, and the Making of History* (New York: W. W. Norton, 2007), 37–54; Hayward, *The Age of Reagan,* 632–39; Thomas Mann, "Thinking about the Reagan Years," in *Looking Back on the Reagan Presidency,* ed. Larry Berman (Baltimore, MD: Johns Hopkins University Press, 1990), 18–29; William Pemberton, *Exit with Honor* (Armonk, NY: M. E. Sharpe, 1997), 201–14; John Sloan, *The Reagan Effect* (Lawrence: University Press of Kansas, 1999), 269; Sean Wilentz, *The Age of Reagan* (New York: Harper, 2008), 281–87.

Chapter Seven
George H. W. Bush

1. A useful guide to Bush's early life is Herbert Parmet, *George Bush: The Life of a Lone Star Yankee* (New York: Scribner, 1997).

2. Paul Abramson, John Aldrich, and David Rohde, *Change and Continuity in the 1988 Elections* (Washington, DC: Congressional Quarterly Press, 1991), 124–25, 173–98; Barbara Farah and Ethel Klein, "Public Opinion Trends," in *The Election of 1988*, ed. Gerald Pomper et al. (Chatham, NJ: Chatham House, 1989), 110–27; and Paul Quirk, "The Election," in *The Elections of 1988*, ed. Michael Nelson (Washington, DC: Congressional Quarterly Press, 1989), 63–92.

3. James A. Baker III, *The Politics of Diplomacy* (New York: G. P. Putnam's Sons, 1995), 19–20, 32; Ryan Barilleaux and Mark Rozell, *Power and Prudence* (College Station: Texas A&M University Press, 2004), 5–12, 117–22; George Bush and Brent Scowcroft, *A World Transformed* (New York: Vintage, 1998), 18–19, 60; John Robert Greene, *The Presidency of George Bush* (Lawrence: University Press of Kansas, 2000), 45, 91, 99–100, 144; Steven Hurst, *The Foreign Policy of the Bush Administration* (London: Paul Cassell, 1999), 2–14; David Mervin, *George Bush and the Guardianship Presidency* (New York: St. Martin's Press, 1996), 15–37.

4. George H. W. Bush, "Remarks at the Texas A&M University Commencement Ceremony," May 12, 1989, *Public Papers of the President: George H.W. Bush* [hereafter *BPP*], *1989*, 540–43; Baker, *Politics of Diplomacy*, 45, 67–72, 82, 94, 150–57, 168–71, 238–43; Bush and Scowcroft, *A World Transformed*, 7–16, 40–45, 54, 59, 73, 79–85, 114–17, 141–43, 148–49, 154–55, 162–74, 207, 215, 228–29; Raymond Garthoff, *The Great Transition: American-Soviet Relations and the End of the Cold War* (Washington, DC: Brookings Institution Press, 1994), 375–89, 404–18, 424–28; Don Oberdorfer, *From the Cold War to a New Era: The United States and the Soviet Union, 1983–1991* (Baltimore, MD: Johns Hopkins University Press, 1998), 328–34, 366–86, 410–30.

5. Baker, *Politics of Diplomacy*, 149, 158–68, 198, 204, 208, 234–39, 250–52, 257–59; Bush and Scowcroft, *A World Transformed*, 150, 164–72, 182–203, 234–35, 279–289, 299; Garthoff, *The Great Transition*, 411–18, 432–37; Mikhail Gorbachev, *Memoirs* (New York: Doubleday, 1996), 510–15, 529, 533–34; Philip Zelikow and Condoleezza Rice, *Germany Unified and Europe Transformed: A Study in Statecraft* (Cambridge, MA: Harvard University Press, 1997), 26–28, 93–98, 103, 113, 127, 137, 152, 167–68, 182–84, 204–7, 215–17, 266, 341–42.

6. Baker, *Politics of Diplomacy*, 104–5, 109–12, 308–9, 589–94; Bush and Scowcroft, *A World Transformed*, 89, 97–110, 156–58, 174–78; Robert Ross, "National Security, Human Rights, and Domestic Politics: The Bush Administration and China," in *Eagle in a New World*, ed. Kenneth Oye, Robert Lieber, and Donald Rothchild (New York: Harper Collins, 1992), 281–313.

7. Baker, *Politics of Diplomacy*, 181–89; Kevin Buckley, *Panama: The Whole Story* (New York: Simon and Schuster, 1991), 222–54; Eytan Gilboa, "The Panama Invasion Revisited," *Political Science Quarterly* 110, no. 4 (Winter 1995–96): 539–62; Parmet, *Lone Star Yankee*, 202–5, 412–14; Colin Powell, *My American Journey* (New York: Bal-

lantine Books, 1996), 401–21; Bob Woodward, *The Commanders* (New York: Simon and Schuster, 1991), 83–195.

8. On this and subsequent paragraphs relating to the Gulf War, see Baker, *Politics of Diplomacy*, 1–16, 268, 276–77, 336, 362; Bush and Scowcroft, *A World Transformed*, 306–82, 441–43, 460–61, 486; Lawrence Freedman and Efraim Karsh, *The Gulf Conflict* (Princeton, NJ: Princeton University Press, 1993), 25–27, 35–39, 59, 98, 183, 206–8, 216–21, 246, 266–73, 300, 409; Richard Haass, *War of Necessity, War of Choice* (New York: Simon and Schuster, 2009), 26–152; Powell, *My American Journey*, 446–517; Woodward, *The Commanders*, 199–376; and Steve Yetiv, *Explaining Foreign Policy: U.S. Decision-Making and the Persian Gulf War* (Baltimore, MD: Johns Hopkins University Press, 2004), 61–81, 154–84. Bush's reference to the new world order is from his "Address Before a Joint Session of Congress on the Crisis in the Persian Gulf and the Federal Budget Deficit," September 11, 1990, *BPP: 1990*.

9. Bush and Scowcroft, *A World Transformed*, 363, 380, 388; Greene, *Presidency of George Bush*, 79–88, 124, 151; Parmet, *Lone Star Yankee*, 367, 430, 470; Yetiv, *Explaining Foreign Policy*, 85–103; John Zaller, "Strategic Politicians, Public Opinion, and the Gulf Crisis," in *Taken By Storm: The Media, Public Opinion, and U.S. Foreign Policy in the Gulf War*, ed. W. Lance Bennett and David Paletz (Chicago: University of Chicago Press, 1994), 250–74.

10. Bush, "Remarks to the Supreme Soviet of the Republic of the Ukraine in Kiev, Soviet Union," August 1, 1991, *BPP: 1991*; Baker, *Politics of Diplomacy*, 472–75, 519, 525–28; Bush and Scowcroft, *A World Transformed*, 283–85, 325–26, 494–505, 510–20, 536–40; Garthoff, *The Great Transition*, 435–37, 446–49, 461–72, 487–99; Celeste Wallander, "Western Policy and the Demise of the Soviet Union," *Journal of Cold War Studies* 5, no. 4 (Fall 2003): 137–77.

11. Baker, *Politics of Diplomacy*, 636–40, 648–50; John Hirsch and Robert Oakley, *Somalia and Operation Restore Hope* (Washington, DC: United States Institute of Peace, 1995), 12–32, 37, 41–46, 54–58, 81; Jessica Lee, "Bush Defends Gulf War Decisions," *USA Today*, August 5, 1992, A2; Powell, *My American Journey*, 562; Warren Strobel, *Late-Breaking Foreign Policy: The News Media's Influence on Peace Operations* (Washington, DC: United States Institute of Peace, 1997), 132–34, 143–52; Jon Western, "Sources of Humanitarian Intervention: Beliefs, Information, and Advocacy in the U.S. Decisions on Somalia and Bosnia," *International Security*, 26, no. 4 (Spring 2002): 112–42.

12. Baker, *Politics of Diplomacy*, 606–11; Hurst, *Foreign Policy of the Bush Administration*, 170–93.

13. Paul Abramson, John Aldrich, and David Rohde, *Change and Continuity in the 1992 Elections* (Washington, DC: Congressional Quarterly Press, 1994), 26–30, 43–44, 131–220, 247; Ross Baker, "Sorting Out and Suiting Up: The Presidential Nominations," in *The Election of 1992*, ed. Gerald Pomper et al. (Chatham, NJ: Chatham House, 1993), 48; Barilleaux and Rozell, *Power and Prudence*, 40–41; Greene, *Presidency of George Bush*, 74–78, 151–55, 161–79.

14. Douglas Brinkley, "Democratic Enlargement: The Clinton Doctrine," *Foreign Policy*, Spring 1997, 117, 120–21, 125; Elizabeth Drew, *On the Edge: The Clinton Presidency* (New York: Simon and Schuster, 1994), 112, 138; David Halberstam, *War in a*

Time of Peace (New York: Scribner, 2001), 23, 167–68; William Hyland, *Clinton's World: Remaking American Foreign Policy* (Westport, CT: Praeger, 1999), 12, 16–26; Stephen J. Stedman, "The New Interventionists," *Foreign Affairs*, Spring 1993, 4–5; Karin von Hippel, *Democracy by Force: U.S. Military Intervention in the Post–Cold War World* (New York: Cambridge University Press, 2000), 64, 73, 77.

15. David Frum, *Dead Right* (New York: Basic Books, 1994), 124–58; Richard Haass, "Paradigm Lost," *Foreign Affairs*, January–February 1995, 43–58; Kenneth Waltz, "Structural Realism After the Cold War," *International Security* 25, no. 1 (Summer 2000): 5–41; Eugene Wittkopf and James McCormick, "Congress, the President, and the End of the Cold War: Has Anything Changed?" *Journal of Conflict Resolution* 42, no. 4 (August 1998): 440–66.

16. Derek Chollet and James Goldgeier, *America Between the Wars: From 11/9 to 9/11* (New York: Public Affairs, 2008), 20–21, 110–11; Terry Deibel, *Clinton and Congress: The Politics of Foreign Policy* (New York: Foreign Policy Association, 2000), 19–20, 59–62; Henry Kissinger, *Diplomacy* (New York: Simon and Schuster, 1994), 808–36; Irving Kristol, "Defining Our National Interest," *National Interest* 21 (Fall 1990): 16–25.

17. Deibel, *Clinton and Congress*, 17–18, 44–56, 64; Ole Holsti, *Public Opinion and American Foreign Policy* (Ann Arbor: University of Michigan Press, 2004), 155, 195, 263; William Link, *Righteous Warrior: Jesse Helms and the Rise of Modern Conservatism* (New York: St. Martin's Press, 2008), 421–26, 455–57; Peter Spiro, "The New Sovereigntists," *Foreign Affairs*, November–December 2000, 9–15.

18. Jacob Heilbrunn, *They Knew They Were Right: The Rise of the Neocons* (New York: Doubleday, 2008), 201–17; Jeane Kirkpatrick, "A Normal Country in a Normal Time," *National Interest* 21 (Fall 1990): 40–45; William Kristol and Robert Kagan, "Toward a Neo-Reaganite Foreign Policy," *Foreign Affairs*, July–August 1996, 18–32; Joshua Muravchik, "Lament of a Clinton Supporter," *Commentary*, August 1993, 15–22.

19. Patrick Buchanan, "America First—and Second, and Third," *National Interest* 19 (Spring 1990): 77–82; Samuel Francis, *Beautiful Losers: Essays on the Failure of American Conservatism* (Columbia: University of Missouri Press, 1993), 222–31; Justin Raimondo, *Reclaiming the American Right* (Wilmington, DE: ISI Books, 2008), 263–83.

20. Deibel, *Clinton and Congress*, 31, 47, 50.

21. Gary Jacobson, "The 1994 House Elections in Perspective," *Political Science Quarterly* 111, no. 2 (Summer 1996): 203–23; James Kitfield, "The Folk Who Live on the Hill," *National Interest* 58 (Winter 1999–2000): 48–55.

22. Derek Chollet and Ivo Daalder, *Getting to Dayton: The Making of America's Bosnia Policy* (Washington, DC: Brookings Institution Press, 2000), 17–19, 31–32, 61–64; Deibel, *Clinton and Congress*, 18, 36–41, 48; Elizabeth Drew, *Showdown: The Struggle Between the Gingrich Congress and the Clinton White House* (New York: Simon and Schuster, 1996), 243–55, 346–47; Link, *Righteous Warrior*, 426–35, 456–58.

23. James Ceaser and Andrew Busch, *Losing to Win: The 1996 Elections and American Politics* (Lanham, MD: Rowman and Littlefield, 1997), 3–7, 60–83, 165; Chollet and Goldgeier, *America Between the Wars*, 140, 143–44; Jonathan Clarke, "Gone to the Lake: The Republicans and Foreign Policy," *National Interest* 44 (Summer 1996): 34–45; Everett C. Ladd, "1996 Vote: The 'No Majority' Realignment Continues," *Political Science Quarterly* 112, no. 1 (Spring 1997): 1–28.

24. Deibel, *Clinton and Congress*, 37–44, 73; Link, *Righteous Warrior*, 444–65; James Traub, *The Best Intentions: Kofi Annan and the UN in the Era of American World Power* (New York: Farrar, Straus and Giroux, 2006), 140–41.

25. Ivo Daalder and Michael O'Hanlon, *Winning Ugly: NATO's War to Save Kosovo* (Washington, DC: Brookings Institution Press, 2000), 132–34, 161–62.

26. Chollet and Goldgeier, *America Between the Wars*, 145, 172–74, 187–204; Francis Fukuyama, *America at the Crossroads: Democracy, Power, and the Neoconservative Legacy* (New Haven, CT: Yale University Press, 2006), 40–43, 48–49, 56; Robert Kagan and William Kristol, eds., *Present Dangers: Crisis and Opportunity in American Foreign and Defense Policy* (San Francisco: Encounter Books, 2000); Norman Podhoretz, "Strange Bedfellows: A Guide to the New Foreign Policy Debates," *Commentary*, December 1999, 19–31.

Chapter Eight
George W. Bush

1. The best pre-presidential biography of George W. Bush is Bill Minutaglio, *First Son* (New York: Times Books, 1999). See also Bush's own campaign autobiography, *A Charge to Keep* (New York: HarperCollins, 1999). For useful insights into Bush's character, see the essays by Fred Greenstein and Hugh Heclo in *The George W. Bush Presidency: An Early Assessment*, ed. Fred Greenstein (Baltimore, MD: Johns Hopkins University Press, 2003).

2. Daniel Casse, "Is Bush a Conservative?" *Commentary*, February 2004, 19–26; David Grann, "Where W. Got Compassion," *New York Times Magazine*, September 12, 1999; Stephen Skowronek, *Presidential Leadership in Political Time: Reprise and Reappraisal* (Lawrence: University Press of Kansas, 2008), 117–49. See also Marvin Olasky, *Compassionate Conservatism* (New York: Free Press, 2000).

3. George W. Bush, "A Distinctly American Internationalism" and "A Period of Consequences," in *The George W. Bush Foreign Policy Reader*, ed. John Dietrich (Armonk, NY: M. E. Sharpe, 2005), 22–31; James Mann, *Rise of the Vulcans: The History of Bush's War Cabinet* (New York: Viking, 2004), 244–60; Condoleezza Rice, "Promoting the National Interest," *Foreign Affairs*, January–February 2000, 45–62.

4. James Ceaser and Andrew Busch, *The Perfect Tie* (Lanham, MD: Rowman and Littlefield, 2001), 63–72, 77–102.

5. Paul Abramson, David W. Rohde, and John H. Aldrich, *Change and Continuity in the 2000 Elections* (Washington, DC: Congressional Quarterly Press, 2002), 131–37, 149–67; Andrew Bennett and Troy White, "Foreign Policy in the Presidential Campaign," in *The Election of the Century*, ed. Stephen Wayne and Clyde Wilcox (Armonk, NY: M. E. Sharpe, 2002), 19–44; Ceaser and Busch, *The Perfect Tie*, 27–46, 134–67; Gerald Pomper, "The 2000 Presidential Election: Why Gore Lost," *Political Science Quarterly* 116, no. 2 (Summer 2001): 201–23.

6. Richard Haass, *War of Necessity, War of Choice* (New York: Simon and Schuster, 2009), 168–86; Lawrence Kaplan and William Kristol, *The War Over Iraq* (San Francisco: Encounter Books, 2003), 68–71; Alexander Moens, *The Foreign Policy of George*

W. Bush (Burlington, VT: Ashgate, 2004), 60–68, 87–117; Steven Lee Myers and James Dao, "Bush Plans Modest Increase for the Pentagon," *New York Times*, February 1, 2001; Colin Powell, *My American Journey* (New York: Ballantine, 1996), 143–45, 242–43, 328–29, 438, 474, 562; David Sanger, "Collision with China: The Overview," *New York Times*, April 10, 2001.

7. Frederick Kagan, *Finding the Target: The Transformation of American Military Policy* (San Francisco: Encounter Books, 2006), 287–310; Michael Noonan and John Hillen, "The Promise of Decisive Action," *Orbis* 46, no. 2 (Spring 2002): 229–46.

8. George W. Bush, *National Security Strategy of the United States* (Washington, DC: Government Printing Office, 2002); Douglas Feith, *War and Decision* (New York: Harper, 2008), 514–15; Philip Gordon, "Bush's Middle East Vision," *Survival* 45, no. 1 (Spring 2003): 155–64; Haass, *War of Necessity*, 192–246; Nicholas Lemann, "How It Came to War," *New Yorker*, March 31, 2003, 36–40; Steven Metz, *Iraq and the Evolution of American Strategy* (Washington, DC: Potomac Books, 2008), 76–84, 102–3; Bob Woodward, *Plan of Attack* (New York: Simon and Schuster, 2004), 1–9, 29–66, 72–136.

9. Frank Bruni, "For President, A Mission and a Role in History," *New York Times*, September 22, 2001; Ivo Daalder and James Lindsay, *America Unbound: The Bush Revolution in Foreign Policy* (Washington, DC: Brookings Institution Press, 2003), 15–16, 46–49, 62–71; Jacob Heilbrunn, *They Knew They Were Right: The Rise of the Neocons* (New York: Doubleday, 2008), 227–52; Joshua Muravchik, "The Neoconservative Cabal," *Commentary*, 116, no. 2 (September 2003): 26–34.

10. Linda Bridges and John Coyne, *Strictly Right: William F. Buckley and the American Conservative Movement* (Hoboken, NJ: John Wiley and Sons, 2007), 311–12; Pat Buchanan, *A Republic, Not an Empire* (Washington, DC: Regnery, 2002), 46, 369–89; James Dao and Eric Schmitt, "Rift Over Plans to Impose Rule on Iraq," *New York Times*, October 10, 2002; Brian Doherty, *Radicals for Capitalism* (New York: Public Affairs, 2007), 608–12; Henry Kissinger, *Does America Need a Foreign Policy?* (New York: Touchstone Books, 2002), 293–302; Brent Scowcroft, "Don't Attack Saddam," *Wall Street Journal*, August 15, 2002.

11. Gary Jacobson, "Terror, Terrain, and Turnout: Explaining the 2002 Midterm Elections," *Political Science Quarterly* 118, no. 1 (Spring 2003): 1–22; Nicholas Lemann, "Without a Doubt," *New Yorker*, October 14 and 21, 2002, 173–79; Robert Novak, *The Prince of Darkness: 50 Years Reporting in Washington* (New York: Three Rivers Press, 2007), 587–94; Leon Wieseltier, "Against Innocence," *New Republic*, March 3, 2003, 26–28; Woodward, *Plan of Attack*, 168.

12. Anthony Cordesman, *The Iraq War: Strategy, Tactics, and Military Lessons* (Washington, DC: Center for Strategic and International Studies Press, 2003), 497–557; The Editors, "An End to Illusion," *National Review*, May 3, 2004; James Fallows, *Blind Into Baghdad: America's War in Iraq* (New York: Vintage, 2006), 43–106; Kagan, *Finding the Target*, 323–59; Jeane Kirkpatrick, *Making War to Keep Peace* (New York: Harper Perennial, 2007), 272, 279–83, 290–93, 300; Michael O'Hanlon, "Iraq Without a Plan," *Policy Review* 128 (January 2005); Project for the New American Century, "Statement on Post-War Iraq," March 19, 2003; George Will, "Time for Bush to See the Realities of Iraq," *Washington Post*, May 4, 2004. Leading early accounts of the Iraq war also include Michael Gordon and Bernard Trainor, *Cobra II* (New York: Pantheon Books, 2006); George

Packer, *The Assassins' Gate* (New York: Farrar, Straus and Giroux, 2005); and Thomas Ricks, *Fiasco: The American Military Adventure in Iraq* (New York: Penguin, 2006). The most careful counterargument in defense of the Pentagon's postwar planning is Feith, *War and Decision*.

13. James Ceaser and Andrew Busch, *Red Over Blue: The 2004 Elections and American Politics* (Lanham, MD: Rowman and Littlefield, 2005), 2–30, 97–99, 107–40; James Campbell, "Why Bush Won the Presidential Election of 2004," *Political Science Quarterly* 120, no. 2 (Summer 2005); John Green et al, "Agents of Value," in *The Values Campaign? The Christian Right and the 2004 Elections*, ed. John Green, Mark Rozell, and Clyde Wilcox (Washington, DC: Georgetown University Press, 2006), 22–55; Philip Klinkner, "Mr. Bush's War: Foreign Policy in the 2004 Election," *Presidential Studies Quarterly* 36, no. 2 (June 2006): 281–96.

14. Fred Barnes, "A Big Government Conservatism," *Wall Street Journal*, August 15, 2003; idem, *Rebel in Chief: Inside the Bold and Controversial Presidency of George W. Bush* (New York: Crown Forum, 2006), 17–32, 61, 117–18, 157–98; James Ceaser and Daniel DiSalvo, "A New GOP?" *Public Interest* 157 (Fall 2004): 3–17; John Micklethwait and Adrian Wooldridge, *The Right Nation: Conservative Power in America* (New York: Penguin Books, 2005); Andrew Taylor, *Elephant's Edge: The Republicans as a Ruling Party* (Westport, CT: Praeger, 2005).

15. On the course of the Iraq war in 2005–6, see Metz, *Iraq*, 169–81; Ricks, *Fiasco*, 398–433; and Bob Woodward, *State of Denial* (New York: Simon and Schuster, 2006), 367–491. On domestic criticisms and ramifications of Iraq, see Bridges and Coyne, *Strictly Right*, 326–27; Gary Jacobson, "Referendum: The 2006 Midterm Congressional Elections," *Political Science Quarterly* 122, no. 1 (Spring 2007): 1–24; Rich Lowry, "The 'To Hell With Them' Hawks," *National Review*, March 27, 2006; and John Mueller, "The Iraq Syndrome," *Foreign Affairs*, November–December 2005, 44–54.

16. James Baker and Lee Hamilton, *Iraq Study Group Report* (New York: Vintage Books, 2006); International Institute for Strategic Studies, *Strategic Survey 2008* (London: Routledge, 2008), 205–15; Metz, *Iraq*, 182–90; Thomas Ricks, *The Gamble: General David Petraeus and the American Military Adventure in Iraq, 2006–2008* (New York: Penguin Press, 2009); Linda Robinson, *Tell Me How This Ends* (New York: Public Affairs, 2008).

17. James Ceaser, Andrew Busch, and John Pitney, *Epic Journey: The 2008 Elections and American Politics* (Lanham, MD: Rowman and Littlefield, 2009), 53–88.

18. David Brady et al, "The 2008 Democratic Shift," *Policy Review* 152 (December 2008 and January 2009); Ceaser, Busch, and Pitney, *Epic Journey*, 131–62; Gary Jacobson, "The 2008 Presidential and Congressional Elections," *Political Science Quarterly* 124, no. 1 (Spring 2009): 1–30.

19. Sidney Milkis and Jesse Rhodes, "George W. Bush, the Republican Party, and the 'New' American Party System," *Perspectives on Politics* 5, no. 3 (September 2007): 461–88; Grover Norquist and Dov Zakheim, "Dollars and Sense," *National Interest* 96 (July–August 2008): 4–7; James Pfiffner, "The First MBA President," *Public Administration Review* 67, no. 1 (January–February 2007): 6–20; Andrew Rudalevige, "The Decider," in *The George W. Bush Legacy*, ed. Colin Campbell et al. (Washington, DC: Congressional Quarterly Press, 2008), 135–63.

20. Robert Lieber, *The American Era: Power and Strategy for the 21st Century* (New York: Cambridge University Press, 2007), 79–94, 158–75, 204–6; Fareed Zakaria, "What Bush Got Right," *Newsweek*, August 18 and 25, 2008, 22–27.

Conclusion

Republicans and U.S. Foreign Policy in the Age of Obama

1. Ted Galen Carpenter, *Smart Power* (Washington, DC: Cato Institute, 2008); Christopher Layne, *The Peace of Illusions* (Ithaca, NY: Cornell University Press, 2007); Christopher Preble, *The Power Problem* (Ithaca, NY: Cornell University Press, 2009).

2. Jacob Heilbrunn, *They Knew They Were Right* (New York: Doubleday, 2008), 273–79.

3. Stephen Brooks and William Wohlforth, *World Out of Balance* (Princeton, NJ: Princeton University Press, 2008).

4. Daniel Drezner, "The Realist Tradition in American Public Opinion," *Perspectives on Politics* 6, no. 1 (March 2008): 51–70.

INDEX

abortion, 168, 190, 192, 200, 205, 235, 249, 279
Abrams, Elliot, 227, 228, 256, 264
Abu Ghraib, 277
accommodationism, 291; and Carter, 196; and
    Democratic Party, 303; and Eisenhower,
    119; and neoconservatives, 296; and
    Obama, 9, 303; and Republican Party, 8,
    291; and Soviet Union, 228, 245–46; tenets
    of, 29, 30, 33
Acheson, Dean, 78, 84, 87
affirmative action, 149, 204
Afghanistan: and Carter, 202; and George W.
    Bush, 271–72; Northern Alliance, 272; and
    Obama, 302; and Reagan, 209, 214, 219, 221,
    222–23; and Soviet Union, 221, 222–23, 228;
    and terrorism, 313
Africa, 181–82, 262, 287
African Americans, 41; and black nationalism,
    137; and Dukakis, 234; and Eisenhower, 89;
    and election of 1948, 75; and election of
    1960, 127; and election of 1984, 220; and
    election of 2008, 285; and Goldwater, 135;
    and Johnson, 132, 137; and militancy, 192;
    and Obama, 284; and Republican Party,
    124–25, 137; and Vietnam, 146
Agnew, Spiro, 145, 160, 176
AIDS, 287
Aiken, George, 64, 92, 136
Albanians, 262
Alexander, Lamar, 260, 261
Algeciras Conference, 15
Allen, Richard, 199
Allende, Salvador, 172, 173
Alliance for Progress, 109
al Qaeda, 271, 272, 274, 283, 288, 302, 312, 313
America First Committee, 45–46, 47, 54–55
American Communist Party, 78
American Conservative, 274, 304
American Enterprise Institute, 201, 256, 282, 305
American exceptionalism, 5, 11, 22, 27–28, 227,
    291, 307, 322

American Revolution, 5, 25
Anderson, John, 203, 205
Andropov, Yuri, 218
Angola, 181, 182, 182, 183, 185, 186, 187, 223, 228,
    244
anti-ballistic missiles, 145, 157, 197. *See also* mis-
    sile defense
Anti-Ballistic Missile Treaty, 164, 214, 268, 271
anti-interventionism, 35, 38; and Buchanan,
    274; and Clinton, 232; and conservatism,
    30, 31, 304–5; and Democratic Party, 46;
    and election of 1944, 68; and election of
    1948, 75; and election of 2000, 269; and
    election of 2008, 284; and Franklin Roos-
    evelt, 47, 54, 56, 58; and Hoover, 20, 22; and
    Mackinac declaration, 66; and neoconser-
    vatives, 140; and Neutrality Acts, 44; and
    overseas commitments, 6; and Republican
    Party, 8, 31, 34, 40, 42, 45, 46, 47, 49, 51, 254,
    257–58, 259, 290, 292, 293, 294, 304–5; and
    Robert Taft, 21, 39, 43–44, 50, 52, 53, 57,
    64, 72, 83, 291; tenets of, 30; and United
    Nations, 71; and Vandenberg, 65; view
    of, 30
anti-Vietnam War movement, 138, 150, 153, 158,
    159, 160, 166, 167, 171, 192
apartheid, 226
Arab-Israeli war of 1967, 174
Arabs, 108, 217; and oil embargo, 174, 175
Arbenz, Jacobo, 99–100
Arizona, 123
arms control, 143, 308; and Carter, 195, 196; and
    Clinton, 232, 262; and Congress, 185; and
    conservatives, 177; and Eisenhower, 105–6,
    111, 115; and election of 1984, 219, 220; and
    Ford, 177, 178; and George H. W. Bush, 8,
    232, 236, 237, 244, 245–46, 251; and George
    W. Bush, 287; and Helms, 256; and Hoover,
    20; and Kissinger, 186; and national secu-
    rity hawks, 177; and Nixon, 156–57, 163–64,
    186; and Obama, 302, 303, 314; and Reagan,

arms control (*continued*)
   206, 207, 210–11, 213, 218, 219, 221–22, 224,
   228, 229; and Republican Party, 262. *See
   also* nuclear policy
Ashbrook, John, 167
Asia, 14–15
Atlantic alliance, 125
Atlantic Charter, 57, 60, 63
Atlantic community, 62
atoms for peace, 105, 106
Austin, Warren, 64
Australia, 100, 287
Austria, 236
autocrats/authoritarian rule, 182, 319; and
   Carter, 198; and Eisenhower, 99; and
   George W. Bush, 272; and Nixon, 157, 158;
   and Reagan, 226, 227; and Republican
   Party, 255
Azores, 56

B-1 bomber, 208
B-2 bomber, 208
Baker, Howard, 139, 196, 198, 203
Baker, James, 235, 238, 243, 254, 274, 282, 305
Balkans, 247, 256, 258, 260
ballistic missiles, 110, 111, 113, 156, 164, 208, 210,
   211, 221, 314
Baltic states, 237, 244, 245
banks, 16, 17, 18, 20, 59
Barnes, Fred, 280
Batista, Fulgencio, 109
Bauer, Gary, 264, 269
Bay of Pigs, 128, 129
Beirut Marine barracks bombing, 217
Bell, Daniel, 139, 140
Berlin, 107, 109–10, 114, 156, 163. *See also* East
   Germany
Berlin Wall, 128, 129, 236, 237
Beveridge, Albert, 14
Bishop, Maurice, 215
Bismarck, Otto von, 151
Black Power, 192
Bohlen, Charles, 94
Boland amendment, 210, 223
Bolton, John, 306
Boot, Max, 306
Borah, William, 18, 19, 42
Bosnia, 246–48, 251, 252, 253, 255, 258, 260, 261
Bosnian Moslems, 258, 260
Bozell, L. Brent, 120

Bretton Woods system, 68–69, 161, 162
Brezhnev, Leonid, 163, 177, 179, 221
Bricker, John, 66, 91, 94
Bricker amendment, 94–95
Bridges, Styles, 91
Brooke, Edward, 139, 154
Brooks, David, 1
Browder, Earl, 67
Brown, Pat, 192
Brownback, Sam, 283, 284
Bryan, William Jennings, 11, 12, 13
Brzezinski, Zbigniew, 195
Buchanan, Pat, 160, 232, 248–49, 258, 260–61,
   263, 274, 305
Buckley, James, 161
Buckley, William F., Jr., 119, 124, 137, 196, 225,
   274, 281, 288
Buckleyites, 145
Bulgaria, 73
Burke, Edmund, 5; *Reflections on the Revolu-
   tion in France,* 25
Burnham, James, 80, 118
Bush, George H. W., 38, 232–52, 254, 297;
   and arms control, 8; background of, 233;
   "Chicken Kiev" speech, 245; and Clinton,
   252, 253; and Congress, 242; and conservatism, 8, 233, 234, 235, 236, 237, 239, 242,
   245, 248–49, 252; convictions of, 235; and
   democracy, 8, 292; and election of 1980,
   203; and George W. Bush, 266; and great
   power relations, 244; and Intermediate
   Nuclear Forces Treaty, 225; and interventionism, 290; and Iraq, 241–44, 290; and
   Malta summit, 237; manner of, 250–51; and
   military, 235, 243, 246, 247; and Panama,
   240–41; and Powell, 271; prudence of, 7–8;
   and Reagan, 233, 236; and realism, 292;
   and Republican Party, 242–43; and Soviet
   Union, 8, 232, 234, 235, 236–37, 244–46, 251;
   and Strategic Arms Reduction Treaty, 244–
   45; Ukraine speech (1991), 245, 246
Bush, George W., 38, 265–89, 316; and Afghanistan, 271–72; and Africa, 287; and Anti-
   Ballistic Missile Treaty, 268; and arms control, 287; and autocracies, 272; background
   of, 266–67; and Bush doctrine, 1–2, 3, 9,
   272, 273, 280, 293; and Catholics, 279; character of, 286–87; and China, 268, 271, 272,
   276, 287; and Clinton administration, 268;
   and coalition building, 279–80; and Con-

gress, 275, 279, 280, 282; and conservatism, 8, 265, 267–68, 269, 274, 275, 277, 279, 281, 289, 321; and defense spending, 268, 271, 280; and democracy, 1, 8, 265, 268, 272, 273, 277, 288–89; and Democratic Party, 267, 274, 275; and domestic policy, 265, 271, 280, 286; and economy, 279, 280, 298; and education, 267, 280; and election of 2000, 265, 267–70; and election of 2004, 278–79; and France, 276, 287–88; and free trade, 268, 272; and George H. W. Bush, 252; and Germany, 287–88; and government, 265, 267, 268, 270; as governor of Texas, 267; and Great Britain, 276; and hawk-nationalist alliance, 306; and hawks, 271, 273, 292; and health care, 267; and Hispanics, 279; and humanitarian missions, 268; and Hurricane Katrina, 282, 286; as idealist, 292; and India, 287; and International Criminal Court, 268; and interventionism, 270, 280, 290, 291; and Iran, 271, 287; and Iraq, 2, 3, 8–9, 265, 268, 271, 272, 273, 274, 279, 280, 281–84, 286, 287, 288–89, 290, 291, 298, 321; and Islamist terrorism, 312; and Japan, 287; and Jewish Americans, 279; and Johnson, 292; and judiciary, 279, 286; and Kosovo, 269; and Kyoto Protocol, 268; and libertarianism, 267; and Middle East, 8, 265, 272, 275; and military, 265, 268, 270, 271–72; and missile defense, 268, 271, 280; and morality, 265, 270, 273, 280; and multilateral agreements, 268; and nationalism, 265, 270, 273; and national security, 1, 265, 268, 270, 273, 275, 279–80, 291, 298; and nation-building, 265, 268, 276; and neoconservatism, 273–75, 276, 277, 298; and North Korea, 268, 271, 287; and nuclear weapons, 287; and oil, 266; as orthodox innovator, 267; and Pakistan, 271, 272, 287; political legacy of, 286–87; and prescription drugs, 280; and preventive war, 1, 8, 265, 272, 291; and Project for the New American Century, 264; and public opinion, 275, 282, 285, 286, 287; and Reagan, 267, 268, 279; and realism, 8–9, 270, 292, 321; and regime change, 1, 265; and regulation, 267; and religion, 266, 268, 269, 279; and Republican Party, 8, 268, 274, 275, 279–81, 282; and rogue states, 1, 271, 272, 273; and Russia, 271, 272, 276, 287; and Saddam Hussein, 271, 272, 275, 276, 277;

and same-sex marriage, 279; second inaugural address, 280; and September 11 terrorist attacks, 1; and spending, 265, 267, 280; and stem cell research, 279; and suburbanites, 279; and taxes, 267, 271, 279, 286; and terrorism, 271–72, 274, 275, 279, 280, 288, 312; and trade, 287, 318; and unilateralism, 272; and United Nations, 271, 272, 275, 276, 277; and urbanites, 279; and Wilson, 292; and women, 279

Bush, Jeb, 264
Bush, Laura Walker, 266
Bush, Prescott, 92, 115, 124
Bush doctrine, 1–2, 3, 9, 272, 273, 280, 293
business: and Bricker amendment, 95; and conservatism, 18, 200; and Eisenhower, 97, 99, 100; and Franklin Roosevelt, 41, 47; and Goldwater, 124; and Hoover, 20; and LaFollette, 18; and Reagan, 189, 191, 192, 205; and Republican Party, 190, 294; and Robert Taft, 21; and Sun Belt, 123; and Theodore Roosevelt, 14; and William Howard Taft, 16, 22; and World War II, 46, 47. *See also* corporations

California, 123
Cambodia, 158, 159–60, 170, 171, 180, 222
Camp David Accords, 175, 194
Canada, 248
Capehart, Homer, 91
Caribbean, 12, 13, 15
Carnegie Endowment, 49
Carpenter, Ted Galen, 304
Carter, Jimmy, 175, 183, 188, 219; and accommodationism, 196; and cold war, 194, 196, 202; and conservatism, 195, 196; and election of 1980, 203–4; and evangelical Protestants, 200; as failed president, 204; and human rights, 183, 184–185, 194, 195, 198; and Iran, 195, 198, 202, 204; and Kissinger, 183; and Reagan, 194, 198–99; and Republican Party, 303; and Soviet Union, 183, 194, 195, 196, 198, 202
Carter Doctrine, 202
Case, Clifford, 124
Casey, William, 209
Castlereagh, Lord, 151
Castro, Fidel, 109, 113, 127, 128, 129, 130, 172, 173, 259–60
Catholic Church, 211

Catholics, 41, 46, 124, 146; and Dukakis, 234; and Eisenhower, 88; and election of 1896, 11; and election of 1948, 75; and election of 1960, 128; and election of 1968, 147; and election of 1984, 220; and George H. W. Bush, 234, 250; and George W. Bush, 279; and Nixon, 168; and Reagan, 189, 205, 220; and Republican Party, 79; and World War II, 46

Cato Institute, 257, 274, 304

Caucasus, 312

Central America, 14, 209, 219

Central Asia, 312

Central Europe, 238, 302

Century Group, 48

Chamber of Commerce, 200

Chambers, Whittaker, 78, 118, 144

Chamoun, Camille, 108

Chemical Weapons Convention, 262

Cheney, Richard, 235, 264, 270, 272, 273, 306

Chiang Kai-shek, 74, 76, 84, 101

Chile, 172, 173, 173, 227, 228

China, 76, 77, 81, 310; and Angola, 181; autocracy of, 319; and Clinton, 252, 253; and democracy, 239; and Eisenhower, 87, 93, 100, 101–2; and election of 1960, 127; and Ford, 184; future challenges from, 311–12; and George H. W. Bush, 239–40, 251; and George W. Bush, 268, 271, 272, 276, 287; and hawk-nationalist alliance, 307; and Hoover, 21; and Kissinger, 152, 155–56, 162, 163, 184, 186; and Korean War, 79, 80; and Marxism, 239; and McKinley, 12, 13; most-favorednation trade status of, 240; and Nixon, 142, 150, 155–56, 162–63, 165, 166, 169, 185, 186, 187, 293, 297; and Obama, 302; and post–cold war internationalism, 153; repression in, 245; and Republican Party, 76, 255, 256, 259; and Robert Taft, 81; and Russia, 312; and Soviet Union, 101, 155–56, 162, 163, 165; and Taiwan, 311; and Tiananmen Square massacre, 239, 251; and Viet Minh, 103; and William Howard Taft, 17. See also East Asia

Chinese Communists, 61

Chinese Nationalists, 61, 74, 76, 81, 84, 101, 122

Church, Frank, 154

Churchill, Winston, 48, 56, 69–70

CIA, 100, 104, 172, 181, 209, 226, 233

civil rights: and conservatism, 24–25; and Democratic Party, 75; and Eisenhower, 88–89, 106; and election of 1960, 128; and election of 1988, 234; and Goldwater, 121, 132, 135; and Johnson, 132, 135, 137; and McGovern, 168; and Nixon, 126; partisan disagreement over, 23; and Republican National Convention of 1964, 133; and Republican Party, 4, 124–25, 132, 133; and Rockefeller, 124; and Southern Democrats, 92; and Sun Belt, 123; and Wallace, 147

Civil Rights Acts of 1957 and 1960, 121

Civil Rights Acts of 1964–65, 140

Clark, Bennett, 46

Clark, Wesley, 278

class. See middle class; upper class voters; working class

Clifford, Clark, 207

Clinton, Hilary, 275, 284–85

Clinton, William Jefferson, 252–64; as centrist "New Democrat," 252; character of, 249, 261; and conservatism, 232, 253, 261, 263–64; and economy, 249, 252, 261, 270; election of, 232; and election of 1992, 249–50; and election of 1996, 260, 261; and election of 2000, 270; and George H. W. Bush, 247; and George W. Bush, 268; and Helms, 256; and Reagan, 253; and Republican Party, 252, 253, 254, 255, 258–259, 262, 303

cold war, 33, 74, 250, 293; and Carter, 194, 196, 202; and Congress, 187; and Eisenhower, 7, 85, 89, 92, 93, 96, 99, 105, 115; and election of 1948, 75; and election of 1960, 127; end of, 253, 254, 255, 316; and Ford, 177, 179; and George H. W. Bush, 232, 237; and Goldwater, 121; and Irving Kristol, 141; and Johnson, 132, 135; and Kennedy, 113, 128; and Kissinger, 165, 186; and nationalism, 92; and Nixon, 153, 172, 186; and Reagan, 7, 189, 199, 207, 213, 214, 215, 218, 222, 228, 229; and Robert Taft, 81; and Vietnam, 184

collective security, 19, 89, 242

college-educated voters, 285, 320

Colombia, 15

colonialism, 108, 112

Commentary, 256

Committee for the Survival of a Free Congress, 195

Committee on the Present Danger (CPD), 196–97

Committee to Defend America by Aiding the Allies, 48, 51, 54–55

communism, 33; and 1974 midterm elections, 178; and Arab world, 108; and Buckley, 119; and Carter, 194; collapse of, 246, 253, 257; and Committee on the Present Danger, 197; and conservatism, 118, 254, 296; and Democratic Party, 77; and domino theory, 102; and Eisenhower, 83, 85, 87–88, 89, 93, 95, 96, 97, 99–100, 101, 102, 103, 104, 107, 108, 112, 113, 114, 115; and election of 1960, 127; and election of 1972, 168; fall of, 239; and Ford, 178, 182; and George H. W. Bush, 236–37; and Goldwater, 117, 121–22, 126, 129; and Helsinki agreement, 179; and internationalism, 92; and Johnson, 135; and Kennedy, 128; and nationalism, 92; and neoconservatives, 140, 198; and Nixon, 143, 150, 155, 159, 168, 175; and post–cold war internationalism, 153; and postwar foreign aid, 73; and postwar settlement, 70; and Reagan, 7, 189, 191–92, 199, 201, 202, 208, 209, 211, 212, 213, 215, 218, 219, 221, 222, 223, 224, 226, 227, 229; and Republican Party, 39, 47, 91, 93, 94, 119, 133, 190, 254, 296; and Robert Taft, 39, 74, 77, 81, 83, 291; and Sun Belt voters, 123; and Truman, 72, 75, 76–77, 78, 81, 84. *See also* Marxism

Communist Party of the United States, 46, 67

Comprehensive Test Ban Treaty, 262, 302

Congress, 190; and 1962 midterm elections, 131; and arms control, 185; and Balkans, 260; and civil rights, 132; and Clinton, 258–59; and conservatism, 201; and Contras, 224; and Cuban Missile Crisis, 129–30; and destroyers for bases deal, 52; and détente, 185; and Dirksen, 126; and Eisenhower, 91, 92, 93, 94, 97–98, 101, 102, 103, 111; and election of 1956, 107; and election of 1964, 135; and election of 1972, 168–69; and election of 1980, 205; and election of 1992, 250; and election of 2008, 286; and executive agreements with other countries, 94; and first Iraq War, 243; and Franklin Roosevelt, 46, 57; and George H. W. Bush, 237, 239, 240, 241, 242, 243, 246, 248; and George W. Bush, 275, 279, 280, 282; and Grenada, 216; and Iraq Liberation Act, 264; and Japan, 58; and Kosovo, 263; and Lend-Lease program, 55; and Mackinac declaration, 65; and Mayaguez, 180; and Neutrality Acts, 56; and New Right, 196; and Nicaragua, 209–10; and Nixon, 144, 150, 153–54, 159, 160–61, 164, 165–66, 168, 169, 175, 176, 187; and Pearl Harbor attack, 58; and postwar foreign aid, 73; and postwar settlement, 70; and presidency, 94; and Reagan, 206, 208, 223, 230; and Republican Party, 125, 255; and Robert Taft, 57, 81; and Selective Service Act, 52, 57; and Soviet Union, 185; and term limits, 259; and Theodore Roosevelt, 14, 15, 16; and trade agreements, 185; and Truman, 82; and union of nations, 68; and United Nations, 71; and Vietnam, 136, 154, 175, 179; and War Powers Act, 175; and World War II, 49

Connally, John, 162, 203

conscription, 51, 52, 57

conservatism, 31; and accommodation, 30; alternative schools of, 6; and American exceptionalism, 22; and American Revolution, 25; and anti-interventionism, 30, 31, 304–5; and arms control, 177; big government, 280; and Buchanan, 248–49, 261; and Buckley, 119; and Bush doctrine, 2; and business, 18, 200; and capitalism, 118; and Carter, 195, 196; classical, 25, 26–27; and Clinton, 232, 253, 261, 263–64; and communism, 254, 296; compassionate, 8, 265, 267–68; and Congress, 201; and Democratic Party, 168, 190; and détente, 187–88; diversity of, 22; and domestic policy, 22, 119; and economy, 35, 200, 201; and Eisenhower, 82, 83, 88, 111, 115, 116; and election of 1964, 133, 134, 135; and election of 1968, 193; and election of 1984, 220–21; and election of 2008, 284, 285; and evangelical Protestants, 200; and extreme right, 132–33; fiscal, 15, 73, 82, 111; and Ford, 177, 178, 182; and George H. W. Bush, 233, 234, 235, 236, 237, 239, 242, 245, 248–49, 252; and George W. Bush, 2, 8, 265, 267–68, 269, 274, 275, 277, 279, 281, 289, 321; and Goldwater, 117, 124, 132, 133; and government, 24, 26; and government spending, 200; and hawk-nationalist alliance, 307; and Helsinki

conservatism (*continued*)
agreement, 179; and Hoover, 20; and idealism, 29, 30; ideological tensions in, 28–29;
ideology of, 24–25; and internationalism,
296; and Iraq War, 274, 305; and Irving
Kristol, 141; and John Birch Society, 123;
and justice, 24; and liberalism, 5–6; and
limited government, 322; and McCain, 284;
and McKinley, 22; midwestern, 125; and
nationalism, 30, 296; and national security,
4; and Nixon, 142, 145, 149, 153, 157, 159, 160,
162, 167, 176, 187, 188; and party politics,
22–38; and postwar foreign aid, 73; and
presidential leadership, 3; and Reagan, 7,
182, 189, 190, 191, 192, 193, 199, 200–201,
203, 205, 206, 207, 220–21, 225, 227, 229,
230, 231; and realism, 29, 30, 308–9, 321,
322; and reforms, 24, 26; and regulation,
200; and Republican Party, 1, 4–5, 17, 18, 23,
24, 41–42, 124, 125, 133, 134, 137, 141, 154,
190, 194, 201–2, 231, 253, 255, 292, 293; and
Robert Taft, 50; and Rusher, 190; social, 35,
117, 201, 261; Sun Belt, 123; and taxes, 200;
and Theodore Roosevelt, 14, 15; and think
tanks, 201; and traditionalism, 118; and
transformational and perfectionist political
visions, 5; and Vietnam, 136–37, 138, 179;
and William Howard Taft, 17; and World
War II, 46
Conservative Caucus, 195
Conservative Political Action Committee, 280
Conservative Political Action Conference, 201
constitutionalism, 118, 322
consumer safety, 149, 167
containment: and Committee on the Present
Danger, 197; conservative rejection of, 119;
and Eisenhower, 87, 113; and George H. W.
Bush, 236; and Goldwater, 121, 129; and Iraq
War, 274; and Kennedy, 128; and Kissinger,
152, 185, 186; and Korean War, 80; and
Nixon, 164, 185, 186; of North Korea and
Iran, 315; and Reagan, 208, 214; and Robert
Taft, 39, 80; strategy of, 72–73; and Tru-
man, 81
continentalism, 48
Contract with America, 259, 260
Contras, 208, 209, 210, 219, 223, 226
Conventional Armed Forces in Europe (CFE)
Treaty, 237
Cooper, John Sherman, 154

Coors, Joseph, 201
corporations: and Reagan, 205, 212; and Republican Party, 125; and Robert LaFollette, 18;
and Theodore Roosevelt, 14; and William
Howard Taft, 16; and World War II, 49. *See
also* business
Council on Foreign Relations, 49
counterculture, 138, 192
covert action: and Angola, 181; and Eisenhower, 89, 100, 103, 104, 109; and election
of 1960, 127; and election of 1984, 219; and
Kissinger, 186; and Nixon, 172, 173, 186; and
Reagan, 212, 229
crime, 146; and election of 1988, 234; and Mc-
Govern, 168; and Nixon, 145, 160, 167; and
Reagan, 192; and Republican Party, 137, 259;
and Supreme Court, 138; and Wallace, 147
criminal justice, 4, 23
Croatians, 246, 260
Crocker, Chester, 226
Cuba: and Angola, 181, 228; and Eisenhower,
107, 109, 115; and Goldwater, 129, 130, 135;
and Grenada, 215–16; and hawk-nationalist
alliance, 307; and Kennedy, 113, 128; and
McKinley, 12; and Reagan, 209, 222, 223;
and Republican National Convention of
1964, 133; and Republican Party, 255; and
Soviet Union, 129–30; and Spain, 11–12;
and Theodore Roosevelt, 15
Cuban Missile Crisis, 129–30
culture, 25, 34–35, 249
Czech crisis (1938), 40
Czechoslovakia, 100, 178

Daley, Richard, 167
Dallas, 123
Davis, James, 64
Dawes Plan, 21
Dayton Accords, 260
Dean, Howard, 278
death penalty, 204, 234
defense industry, 123, 294
defense spending, 234; and Carter, 183, 194,
202, 204; and Committee on the Present
Danger, 197; and Congress, 185; and
Eisenhower, 83, 89, 96, 97, 105, 110–11, 112,
113–14, 115; and election of 1984, 219; and
George W. Bush, 268, 271, 280; and Gold-
water, 117, 122; and Hoover, 21; and Ken-
nedy, 128; and Lodge, 18; and Nixon, 126;

and post–cold war internationalism, 153;
and Reagan, 193, 199, 206, 208–9, 214, 219;
and Republican Party, 256, 293, 294; and
Robert Taft, 74, 82, 83, 84; and Rockefeller,
124; and Truman, 79. *See also* national
security; spending
democracy: and American exceptionalism, 5;
and Carter, 195, 198; and China, 239; and
Clinton, 252; and conservatism, 24, 27; and
Eisenhower, 99, 292; and founders, 27–28;
and George H. W. Bush, 8, 232, 235, 240,
242, 251, 292; and George W. Bush, 1, 8, 265,
268, 272, 273, 277, 288–89; and idealists, 29;
and Irving Kristol, 255; and Kissinger, 152;
and local political and cultural realities,
319–20; Luce on, 61; and neoconservatism,
297; and Nixon, 157, 158; and Obama, 302,
303; and party politics, 23; and Project for
the New American Century, 264; and public opinion, 321; and Reagan, 213, 225–26,
227, 228; and realists, 254; and Republican
Party, 256, 304; and Robert Taft, 44; and
Wilson, 19
Democratic National Convention of 1968,
146–47
Democratic National Convention of 1972,
167–68
Democratic Party: and accommodationism,
303; and civil rights, 75, 132; and Clinton,
249; and Committee on the Present Danger, 197; and communism, 77; constituency
of, 41, 42; and Contras, 224; and doves, 153,
154, 305; and economy, 4–5; and Eisenhower, 87, 91, 92–93, 96, 102, 106, 107, 112,
116; and election of 1896, 11; and election of
1900, 12; and election of 1940, 52–53; and
election of 1956, 107; and election of 1960,
127, 128; and election of 1968, 148; and election of 1972, 167; and election of 1976, 184;
and election of 1980, 204; and election of
1984, 219–21; and election of 1988, 234; and
election of 2000, 269–70; and election of
2004, 278–79; and election of 2008, 284–85,
286; and elections of 1962, 130–31; and elections of 1966, 138; and elections of 1968,
146–47; and elections of 1974, 178; and elections of 2002, 275; and first Iraq War, 243;
and Franklin Roosevelt, 46; and George H.
W. Bush, 239, 240, 243, 248; and George W.
Bush, 267, 274, 275; and Goldwater, 168;

and Gulf of Tonkin Resolution, 136; and
hawks, 154, 295; and idealism, 297; and
interventionism, 11, 295; and Iraq War,
295; and Korean War, 80; and Lend-Lease
program, 55; and liberalism, 3, 4–5, 24, 138,
153, 168; as majority party, 116; and Mayaguez, 180; and McCarthy, 79; and McKinley, 12, 13; and national security, 154, 269,
295, 320; and neoconservatism, 140, 297;
and New Deal, 42, 59; and 1930's international disengagement, 41; and Nixon, 154,
157, 161, 167, 168; post–cold war internationalism in, 168; and Reagan, 189, 192,
201, 205, 208, 227, 231; and Republican
Party, 4, 91, 125, 300; and segregation, 116;
and 60s social upheaval, 138; and social
issues, 190; and social liberals, 23; Southern, 41, 42, 92, 95, 116, 128, 132, 146, 154, 175,
189, 190, 243; and Spanish American War,
12; and trade, 98; and Truman administration, 72; and United Nations, 71; and Vietnam, 3, 138, 154, 300, 303; and Wallace, 147;
and wartime cash and carry policy, 44; and
Wilsonian foreign policy, 60; and working
class, 204
Department of Homeland Security, 275
desegregation, 88–89, 121, 145, 149. *See also*
race; segregation
détente, 143; and Carter, 194, 195; and Congress, 185; and conservatism, 187–88; and
Eisenhower, 106, 115; and Ford, 177, 178, 182,
185, 193; and George H. W. Bush, 236; and
Kissinger, 164–65, 182, 186, 187, 193; and
Nixon, 164–65, 166, 176, 185, 186, 187; and
Reagan, 183, 193, 199; and Republican Party,
187–88, 190
developing world, 316, 318; and Carter, 194;
and Eisenhower, 99, 106; and Kissinger,
186; and Nixon, 157, 186; and post–cold war
internationalism, 153; radical nationalists
in, 99; and William Howard Taft, 16
Dewey, Thomas: and Bretton Woods, 69; and
Eisenhower, 82, 86, 87; and election of 1944,
66–67, 68; and election of 1948, 75, 76; and
Republican Party, 50; and Robert Taft, 67
Diem, Ngo Dinh, 103
Dien Bien Phu, 102, 103, 114
Dillon, Douglas, 128
Dirksen, Everett, 91, 95–96, 125–26, 128, 132,
136, 137

Disraeli, Benjamin, 149–50
Dixiecrats, 75
Dobrynin, Anatoly, 156
Dolan, Terry, 195
Dole, Robert, 233, 256, 258, 260, 261
domestic policy, 35; and Clinton, 252; and conservatism, 22, 119; and Eisenhower, 85, 87, 89, 115; and Ford, 177; of Franklin Roosevelt, 40, 41, 58–59; and George H. W. Bush, 232, 235, 242, 243, 248, 249, 250; and George W. Bush, 265, 271, 280, 286; and Goldwater, 117, 120–21; and health care, 135, 149, 167, 267, 301; and international issues, 34–35; and Johnson, 135, 136; and McGovern, 168; and Nixon, 126, 149–50, 167; and Obama, 301; and Reagan, 200, 229–30; and Republican Party, 125, 259, 294; and Robert Taft, 74; and Rockefeller, 124
domestic spending: and election of 1960, 128; and George W. Bush, 265; and Republican National Convention of 1964, 133; and Robert Taft, 82. See also spending
Dominican Republic, 15
doves: and accommodationists, 30; beliefs of, 29; and Committee on the Present Danger, 197; and Democratic Party, 153, 154, 168, 300, 305; and election of 1968, 148; and Ford, 185; and idealists, 29; and Nixon, 153, 157, 159, 164, 166, 169, 175, 185; and Obama, 302; and Republican Party, 8, 291
Duff, James, 92
Dukakis, Michael, 234
Dulles, Allen, 104
Dulles, John Foster, 105; and Bretton Woods, 69; and China, 101; and Congress, 93; and Dewey, 67; and Eisenhower, 91; and European defense, 98; and Guatemala, 99; and internationalism, 92; and Iran, 103; and nuclear weapons policy, 96; and Soviet Union, 104

Eagle Forum, 200
Eagleton, Thomas, 168
East Asia, 312; and Eisenhower, 89, 100–104; and Reagan, 227; and Theodore Roosevelt, 15; and William Howard Taft, 16, 17. See also China; Japan; Korean War; North Korea; South Korea; Taiwan
East Berlin, 163
East Coast, 48

Eastern Europe, 228, 257, 312; collapse of communism in, 246; and Eisenhower, 87, 94, 96, 104, 105, 107; and Ford, 178, 183–84; and George H. W. Bush, 232, 236, 245, 251; and Goldwater, 122; and Helsinki agreement, 178, 179; and Lippmann, 62; and Nixon, 156; and postwar settlement, 70; and Reagan, 193, 211, 213; and Republican Party, 255; and Sonnenfeldt Doctrine, 183; and Soviet Union, 70, 72
East Germany, 104, 109, 129, 237, 238. See also Berlin
economy, 34–35; and Buchanan, 249; and budget deficits, 74, 88, 219, 242, 243; and Carter, 204; and Clinton, 249, 252, 261, 270; and conservatism, 200; and Democratic Party, 4–5; and Dirksen, 125–26; and Eisenhower, 83, 85, 87, 88, 89, 96, 106, 111, 116, 297; and election of 1896, 11; and election of 1900, 13; and election of 1956, 107; and election of 1976, 184; and election of 1984, 219; and election of 1988, 234; and election of 1992, 249; and election of 1996, 260; and election of 2008, 285, 286; and elections of 1974, 178; and Ford, 177; and Franklin Roosevelt, 41; and George H. W. Bush, 235, 239, 242, 243, 248, 250; and George W. Bush, 279, 280, 298; and Goldwater, 120, 123; and Hoover, 20; and internationalism, 92; of Iraq, 241; and moderates, 125; and nationalism, 92; and Nixon, 126, 142, 149, 155, 161, 162, 165, 167, 187; and policy considerations, 34; and Reagan, 192, 199, 205, 206, 208–9, 211–12, 215, 220, 230, 231; and Republican Party, 1, 4, 23, 31–32, 92, 125, 202, 259, 293–94; and Robert Taft, 69, 74; and Theodore Roosevelt, 14; and William Howard Taft, 16. See also inflation
education: and conservatism, 25; and George W. Bush, 267, 280; and Goldwater, 120, 121; and Nixon, 167
Edwards, John, 275, 278
Egypt: autocracy of, 319; and Carter, 194; and Eisenhower, 103, 107–8; and George H. W. Bush, 241; and Yom Kippur War, 173, 174, 175. See also Suez crisis (1956)
Eisenhower, Dwight, 38, 85–116; and accommodationism, 119; and African Americans, 89; and arms control, 105–6, 111, 115; and autocratic regimes, 99; background of, 86;

and Berlin, 107, 109–10, 114; and budget deficits, 88; and business, 99, 100; character of, 107; and China, 87, 93, 100, 101–2; and civil rights, 88–89, 106; and cold war, 7, 85, 89, 92, 93, 96, 99, 105, 115; and collective security, 89; and colonialism, 112; and commerce, 97; and communism, 83, 85, 87–88, 89, 93, 95, 96, 97, 99–100, 101, 102, 103, 104, 107, 108, 112, 113, 114, 115; and Congress, 91, 92, 93, 94, 97–98, 101, 102, 103, 111; and conservatism, 88, 115, 116; and containment, 87, 113; and covert action, 89, 100, 103, 104, 104, 109; and Cuba, 107, 109, 115; and defense spending, 83, 89, 96, 97, 105, 110–11, 112, 113–14, 115; and democracy, 99, 292; and Democratic Party, 87, 91, 92–93, 96, 102, 106, 107, 112, 116; and détente, 106, 115; and developing world, 99, 106; and Dewey, 82, 86, 87; and diplomacy, 92; and domestic policy, 85, 87, 89, 115; and East Asia, 89, 100–104; and Eastern Europe, 87, 94, 96, 104, 105, 107; and East Germany, 104, 109; and economic aid, 103, 104, 108; and economy, 83, 85, 87, 88, 89, 96, 106, 111, 116, 297; and Egypt, 103, 107–8; and election of 1952, 82–83, 85, 86–87; and election of 1956, 106–7; and election of 1960, 127; and farm programs, 88; and fiscal conservatism, 82, 111; and fiscal responsibility, 89; and foreign aid, 83, 89, 92, 97, 98, 98, 109, 112, 115; and Franklin Roosevelt, 97; and free trade, 92, 114; and Goldwater, 120, 121, 122; and government, 88, 106, 114; and Great Britain, 102, 103, 104; and hawks, 112, 115; and Hungary, 104–5, 107, 114, 115; and ICBMs, 113; and Indochina, 101, 102–3, 107; and inflation, 88, 106; and international commerce, 89; and internationalism, 7, 82, 85, 89–90, 92, 96, 115, 293, 297; and interventionism, 290–91; and Iran, 103–4; and Irish Catholics, 88; and Johnson, 93; and Kennedy administration, 109; and Korean War, 87, 88, 93–94, 97, 107, 297; and labor laws, 88; and Latin America, 99–100, 108–9; and Lebanon, 108; and liberals, 112; manner of, 90; and Marshall, 86; and McCarthy, 87, 95, 96; and Middle East, 103, 107–8; and Midwest, 97; and military, 2, 83, 86, 89, 98, 99, 101, 102, 104, 108, 110, 112, 114; and military aid, 100, 103, 104, 108; military career of, 86;

and moderates, 85, 115; and multilateralism, 90; and nationalism, 85, 92, 94, 115; and national security, 96–97, 114; and National Security Council, 102; and NATO, 86, 89, 98, 110, 111; and New Deal, 88, 106, 115, 116, 119; and nuclear test ban, 107, 111–12; and nuclear weapons policy, 89, 96–97, 98, 99, 101, 102, 104, 105–6, 107, 109, 110, 111, 113; and oil, 103; and Old Guard, 87, 88, 92, 93, 94, 95, 96, 97, 101, 114; and partisan politics, 90, 116; personality of, 85–86, 297; and Polish Catholics, 88; and presidency, 95, 96; and protectionism, 97; and psychological warfare, 89; and public opinion, 90; and racial desegregation, 88–89; and realism, 292, 308; and regulation, 88; and Republican Party, 7, 85, 88, 91, 92, 93, 95, 96, 97–98, 101, 102, 107, 111, 114, 115–16; and Robert Taft, 82–83, 86; and Rockefeller, 124; and socialism, 87; and social security, 88; and South, 116; and Southern Democrats, 92; and Soviet Union, 7, 87, 89, 94, 96–97, 98, 99, 100, 101, 103, 104–6, 107, 108, 109–12, 113; and spending, 87; and Suez Canal, 103, 107; and Taiwan, 96, 101–2; and tariffs, 98; and taxes, 83, 87, 88, 106; and Third World, 89, 99, 108, 112, 113; and trade, 98; and Truman, 86, 87, 89, 94, 95, 97, 104; and unilateralism, 90; and United Nations, 90, 101; and upper- and middle-income voters, 87; and urban and suburban voters, 87; and Vietnam, 137; and war, 104, 114; and welfare state, 88; and West Berlin, 110; and Western Europe, 89, 98–99, 104; and West Germany, 109; and white southerners, 87; and Yalta agreements, 94

election of 1896, 11
election of 1900, 12–13
election of 1912, 17
election of 1916, 19
election of 1940, 49–50, 52, 53
election of 1944, 66–68
election of 1948, 75, 76
election of 1952, 82–83, 85, 86–87
election of 1956, 106–7
election of 1960, 126–28, 144
election of 1964, 117, 131–35, 137, 141
election of 1968, 139, 141, 144–48, 193
election of 1972, 161, 162, 167–69
election of 1976, 182–83, 184, 190, 193–94

election of 1980, 203–5
election of 1984, 219–21
election of 1988, 233–34
election of 1992, 246, 248–52, 258
election of 1996, 258, 260–61
election of 2000, 265, 267–70
election of 2004, 278–79
election of 2006, 1
election of 2008, 1, 283–86, 304
elections, as shaping foreign policy, 299–300
elections of 1938, 42
elections of 1942, 59
elections of 1946, 73
elections of 1958, 116
elections of 1962, 129, 130–31
elections of 1966, 138–39
elections of 1970, 160–61
elections of 1974, 178
elections of 1978, 196
elections of 1986, 224
elections of 1990, 241, 242–43
elections of 1994, 259
elections of 2002, 275
elections of 2006, 282
El Salvador, 209, 210, 226
environment, 167, 219, 252, 303
Environmental Protection Agency, 149
equal rights amendment, 149, 200
Ethiopia, 222
ethnic conflict, 246, 251, 252
Europe, 14–15, 18, 61, 181
European Economic Community, 99
European Union, 276, 310, 311
evangelicalism: and Bryan, 11; and conservatism, 200; and election of 1980, 205; and election of 1984, 220; and election of 2008, 284, 285; and George H. W. Bush, 234, 250; and George W. Bush, 279; and Reagan, 7, 189, 205

Falwell, Jerry, 200
Farabundo Marti National Liberation Front (FMLN), 209, 210
farmers/agriculture, 20, 59, 75, 88, 120, 121, 135, 205, 241, 294
fascism, 40, 43, 75, 77. See also Nazis
FBI, 47
Fight for Freedom Committee, 48
Finland, 105
Florida, 123, 147

Forbes, Steve, 260, 261, 264, 269
Ford, Gerald, 137, 176–77, 190, 202; and Africa, 181–82; and Angola, 181, 182; and Carter, 183; and détente, 182; and election of 1976, 193–94; and election of 1980, 203; and Kissinger, 177; and Mayaguez, 180–81; and Reagan, 182, 193; and Sonnenfeldt Doctrine, 183–84; and Soviet Union, 177
foreign aid, 318; and Clinton, 232, 253; and Eisenhower, 83, 89, 92, 97, 98, 98, 103, 104, 108, 109, 112, 115; and George H. W. Bush, 244; and Goldwater, 122; to Great Britain, 46, 48, 49, 51, 53–54, 55–56; and Helms, 256, 262; and Kennedy, 112–13; and Nixon, 157, 169, 170, 175; and northeastern Republicans, 125; and Republican Party, 91, 97, 98, 254, 255, 259; and Robert Taft, 73–74, 83; and Southern Democrats, 92; and Truman, 73
foreign economic aid: and Eisenhower, 103, 104, 108, 115; and Franklin Roosevelt, 48; and George H. W. Bush, 237; and Hoover, 20; and Nixon, 157, 169, 175. See also foreign aid
foreign military aid: and Eisenhower, 100, 103, 104, 108; and Ford, 179; and Franklin Roosevelt, 48; and Nixon, 153, 157, 169, 174, 175; and Reagan, 209, 222–23
Foreign Policy Association, 49
Formosa, 81
founders, 5, 26, 27, 120, 318, 319, 322
France, 100, 156, 310; and cash and carry policy, 44; collapse of, 45; and Franklin Roosevelt, 40; and George H. W. Bush, 241; and George W. Bush, 276, 287–88; and German reunification, 237, 238; and Germany, 50, 52, 98–99; and Harding, 20; and Indochina, 102, 103; and Locarno Conference, 21; and Lodge, 19; and SALT I, 164; and Theodore Roosevelt, 15
Francis, Samuel, 258
Friedman, Milton, 118, 200
Frum, David, 1
Fuchs, Klaus, 77
Fukuyama, Francis, 350n33, 354n26

Gaither Committee Report, 110–11
Geneva intermediate-range nuclear forces talks, 211
Geneva summit, 1955, 106
Geneva summit, 1985, 221
geopolitics, 7, 142, 155, 164

Gephardt, Richard, 278

German Americans, 46, 53, 72

Germany, 310; and France, 50, 52; and Franklin Roosevelt, 40, 56; and George H. W. Bush, 232, 237–39, 246, 251; and George W. Bush, 287–88; illiberal forces in, 21; and Locarno Conference, 21; and Lodge, 18; reunification of, 237–39; and Robert Taft, 83; and submarines, 55, 56; and Theodore Roosevelt, 15; war against, 47, 48–49; and William Howard Taft, 18; and Wilson, 19; and World War II, 45. *See also* Berlin; East Germany; Nazis; West Germany

Gingrich, Newt, 256, 259, 260

Giuliani, Rudy, 283, 284

globalism, 69, 252, 258, 293

Goldwater, Barry, 38, 291, 293; and African Americans, 135; and agriculture, 121; and American sovereignty, 122; and authors and intellectuals, 123; background of, 119; and Berlin Wall, 129; and business, 124; and Castro, 129, 130; and civil rights, 121, 132, 135; and cold war, 121; and communism, 117, 121–22, 126, 129; *The Conscience of a Conservative*, 120; and conservatism, 124, 132, 133; and containment, 121, 129; and Cuba, 129, 130, 135; and defense spending, 117, 122; and Democratic Party, 168; and desegregation, 121; and domestic policy, 117, 120–21; and East Germany, 129; and economy, 120, 123; and education, 120, 121; and Eisenhower, 120, 121, 122; and election of 1960, 126, 127; and election of 1964, 117, 131–35, 141; and election of 1968, 141; and executive branch, 120; and farmers, 135; and farm subsidies, 120; and federal government, 120; and foreign aid, 122; and founders, 120; and government, 117; and hawks, 117, 291; and Hungary, 122; and independents, 135; and internationalism, 135; and intervention, 117; and Iron Curtain, 122; and Johnson, 135, 136; and Kennedy, 129; and Laos, 129; and libertarians, 117, 124; and local self-government, 121; and Lodge, 132; manner of, 120, 134; and Midwest, 123; and military, 117, 122; and moderates, 132, 135; and NAACP, 121; and national defense, 126; and nationalism, 121; and national press corps, 134; and New Deal, 135; and Nixon, 144, 145, 149, 160; and nuclear policy, 122, 133, 134, 135; and nuclear test ban, 122, 129; and professionals, 124; and public housing, 121; and public power, 121; and race, 135; and racial conservatives, 117; and Reagan, 189, 191; and Republican Party, 117, 122–23, 135; and Rockefeller, 126, 132, 133; and social conservatism, 117; and Social Security, 134; and social welfare, 121; and South, 121, 131, 132, 135; and South Korea, 122; and South Vietnam, 122; and Soviet Union, 117, 121, 122, 129; and spending, 120; and students, 123; and suburban conservatives, 117; and Sun Belt, 117, 123; and taxes, 120–21, 122; and United Nations, 122; and urban renewal, 121; and Vietnam, 133, 135, 136; and voting rights, 121; and war, 135; and West, 131, 132; and white segregationist voters, 135; and white suburbanites, 135

Goodell, Charles, 154, 161

Good Neighbor Policy, 21, 40

Gorbachev, Mikhail: coup against, 245; and George H. W. Bush, 236, 237, 240, 244, 245–46; and German reunification, 238; and Iraq, 241; and Reagan, 221–22, 224–25, 228

Gore, Albert, Jr., 249, 269–70

Gottfried, Paul, 258

government, 118; centralized, 47, 50, 118; and classical liberals, 118; and conservatism, 24, 26, 322; and Eisenhower, 88, 106, 114; and election of 1960, 128; expanding role for, 26; and founders, 5; and Franklin Roosevelt, 41; and George W. Bush, 265, 267, 268, 270; and Goldwater, 117, 120, 121; and liberalism, 26; limited, 1, 24, 25, 26, 39, 43, 80, 83, 114, 117, 118, 257, 267, 296, 321, 322; and moral norms, 35; and national security state, 118; and Nixon, 142, 146; and Obama, 301; and Reagan, 191; and redistribution of wealth, 35; and Republican Party, 1, 296, 321; and Robert Taft, 39–40, 43, 50, 74, 80, 82, 83. *See also* regulation; spending

Gramm, Phil, 260

Great Britain, 100; and Bretton Woods agreements, 68; and cash and carry policy, 44, 45; and Eisenhower, 102, 103, 104; and Franklin Roosevelt, 40; and George H. W. Bush, 241; and George W. Bush, 276; and German reunification, 237, 238; and Harding, 20; and Hoover, 20; and imperialism,

Great Britain (*continued*)
108; and Lippmann, 62; and Locarno Conference, 21; and Lodge, 19; and NATO, 98; and Robert Taft, 57, 63–64; and SALT I, 164; and Theodore Roosevelt, 15; and Truman, 73; and United States, 310; wartime aid to, 46, 48, 49, 51, 53–54, 55–56; and William Howard Taft, 18
Great Depression, 21, 40
great power relations, 7, 142, 154–55
Great Society, 135, 137, 139, 140
Greece, 73, 74, 74
Greenland, 56
Grenada, 215–16, 218, 220
Guam Doctrine, 157
Guatemala, 99–100
Gulf of Tonkin, 136
Gulf of Tonkin Resolution, 136, 159

Haass, Richard, 352n8, 353n15, 354n6, 355n8
Hagel, Chuck, 254, 283, 284
Hague Conference, second, 15
Haig, Alexander, 208, 209
Haiti, 252, 253, 258
Haldeman, Bob, 160
Hall, Theodore, 77
Halleck, Charles, 128
Hamilton, Lee, 282
Hanson, Victor Davis, 306
Harding, Warren G., 19–20
Hatfield, Mark, 139, 154
hawk(s), 232; and Angola, 181; and anticommunism, 118; and arms control, 177; beliefs of, 29; and Carter, 196; and Clinton, 232, 249, 263; and Committee on the Present Danger, 197; conservative, 31; and Democratic Party, 154, 168, 190, 295, 297–98; and doves, 29, 153–54; and Eisenhower, 112, 115; and election of 1968, 148; and election of 2000, 269; and election of 2008, 284; and Ford, 177, 180; and Franklin Roosevelt, 51; and George H. W. Bush, 247; and George W. Bush, 271, 273, 292; and Goldwater, 117, 121, 126, 291; and internationalism, 92; and intervention, 6, 30; and military power, 6; and nationalism, 30, 92, 257, 306–7; and neoconservatives, 273; and Nixon, 7, 153–54, 164, 165; and Project for the New American Century, 264; and Reagan, 7, 182, 189, 199, 231, 292; and Republican Party, 2, 3, 6,

8, 256–57, 290, 291, 292, 293, 295, 297–98, 301, 304, 306–7; and Sun Belt, 123; and Theodore Roosevelt, 22; and Truman, 75; and World War II, 48, 49
Hayek, Friedrich, 118
health care, 135, 149, 167, 267, 301
Helms, Jesse, 225, 255–56, 259–60, 262
Helms-Burton law, 259–60
Helsinki Conference, 178–79, 182, 183
Heritage Foundation, 201, 305
Hickenlooper, Bourke, 91
Hiroshima, 106
Hispanics, 220, 234, 279. *See also* Latinos
Hiss, Alger, 77, 78, 144
Hitler, Adolf, 44, 47, 52, 56, 58, 133, 151. *See also* Nazis
Ho Chi Minh, 158
Hoover, Herbert, 20, 21, 40, 80
Horn of Africa, 195, 247
Howe, Irving, 139
Huckabee, Mike, 283, 284
Hughes, Charles Evans, 19
humanitarianism, 29, 232, 246–47, 252, 253, 254, 268
human rights, 176, 246; and Carter, 183, 184–85, 194, 195, 198; and Clinton, 252, 253; and Ford, 178; and George H. W. Bush, 239; and Kissinger, 182; and Nixon, 157; and Reagan, 214, 221, 225, 226, 227; and Republican Party, 255
Humphrey, Hubert, 112, 146, 147–48, 167
Hungary, 104–5, 107, 114, 115, 122, 236, 237
Hurricane Katrina, 282, 286
Hussein, Saddam, 251; and George H. W. Bush, 241–44; and George W. Bush, 271, 272, 275, 276, 277; and 9/11 attacks, 298; and Project for the New American Century, 264. *See also* Iraq
Hutchison, Kay Bailey, 263

Iceland, 56
idealism, 256, 257; and Democratic Party, 297; and doves, 29; and internationalism, 61; and liberalism, 26; and Obama, 303; and Reagan, 292, 293; and Republican Party, 291–92
immigrants, 11, 41
immigration, 258, 286
imperialism, 12, 13, 14
independents, 42, 135, 205, 250, 320
India, 287, 310, 311

Indochina, 101, 102–3, 107. *See also* Vietnam/
    Vietnam War
inflation, 74, 88, 106, 162, 204, 220, 230. *See also*
    economy
intercontinental ballistic missiles (ICBMs),
    110, 111, 113, 156, 164, 208. *See also* ballistic
    missiles
Intermediate Nuclear Forces Treaty (INF),
    224–25
intermediate-range ballistic missiles (IRBMs),
    111
intermediate- range nuclear forces (INFs), 210,
    211
Internal Revenue Service, 133
International Atomic Energy Agency, 106
International Criminal Court, 262, 268, 271
international institutions, 253, 317–18
internationalism, 59–66, 293; and Bush doc-
    trine, 2; and Clinton, 249, 250; cold war,
    91; and communism, 92; and conservatism,
    296; and Democratic Party, 295; and Dewey,
    67; and Dirksen, 125; and Dulles, 91; and
    Eisenhower, 7, 82, 85, 89–90, 91, 92, 96, 115,
    293, 297; and election of 1944, 68; and elec-
    tion of 1948, 75; and election of 1960, 127,
    128; and Ford, 177, 184; and George H. W.
    Bush, 242; and Goldwater, 135; and hawks,
    92; and Kissinger, 184; and Lippmann,
    62–63; and neoconservatism, 296–97; and
    Nixon, 144, 184, 296; and Northeast, 125;
    and Reagan, 207; and Republican Party, 42,
    60–65, 66–67, 71, 72, 91–92, 95–96, 125, 154,
    290, 291, 295–96; and Robert Taft, 63–65;
    and Southern Democrats, 92; and United
    Nations, 71; and Vandenberg, 70; of
    Willkie, 61–62
international law, 16, 19, 21, 64, 71, 81, 308
international monetary fund, 68
international organizations, 29, 194, 232, 257,
    293
international system, 28, 37
interventionism, 30, 32, 35; and anticommu-
    nism, 118; and anti-interventionism, 29;
    and Clinton, 232, 253, 263; and Democratic
    Party, 11, 295; and Eisenhower, 290–91; and
    election of 1940, 53; and election of 1996,
    261; and Franklin Roosevelt, 40; and
    George H. W. Bush, 246, 247, 290; and
    George W. Bush, 265, 270, 280, 290, 291;
    and Goldwater, 117; and hawks, 6; and

Kissinger, 186; and Nixon, 186; and periph-
    eral strategic interests, 256; and Reagan,
    207, 215–18, 229; and Republican Party, 6,
    11, 34, 42, 48, 71, 72, 141, 254, 256–57, 258,
    259, 290, 292, 293, 294, 295, 296, 304–5; and
    Robert Taft, 72, 75, 76, 83, 84; and Theo-
    dore Roosevelt, 14, 15; and vital interests,
    316–17; and William Howard Taft, 17; and
    World War II, 44–58. *See also* military
Iran: arms sales to, 223; and Carter, 195, 198,
    202, 204; containment of, 315–16; and
    Eisenhower, 103–4; and George H. W.
    Bush, 241; and George W. Bush, 271, 287;
    and hawk-nationalist alliance, 307; and
    Iraq, 241, 244, 281; negotiation with, 315;
    and neoconservatives, 273; and Nixon, 157,
    173; and Obama, 302, 315; and Reagan, 223;
    and Republican Party, 255, 256; and Soviet
    Union, 72
Iran–Contra arms affair, 223–24
Iran hostage negotiations, 204
Iranian Communist Party (Tudeh), 103
Iraq: economy of, 241; and George H. W. Bush,
    247–48, 251, 290; and George W. Bush,
    2, 3, 8–9, 265, 268, 271, 272, 273, 274, 279,
    280, 281–84, 286, 287, 288–89, 290, 291,
    298, 321; internal politics of, 309; and Iran,
    241, 244; and Kuwait, 241, 242, 243; no-fly
    zones over, 244; and Obama, 8, 302; occu-
    pation of, 8, 276–77; and Reagan, 241; and
    Republican Party, 255, 256; and Saudi Ara-
    bia, 241; and terrorism, 313; and Yom Kip-
    pur War, 173
Iraq Liberation Act, 264
Iraq Study Group, 282
Iraq War, 274–78, 281–84, 286, 287, 288–89,
    298; and American primacy, 310; and
    Anbar province, 283; and conservatism,
    305; and conservatives, 280; and Demo-
    cratic Party, 295; and early occupation, 265;
    and election of 2004, 279; and election of
    2008, 284, 285; and hawk-nationalist alli-
    ance, 306; and Kissinger, 274; mismanage-
    ment of, 2, 3, 276–77; and neoconserva-
    tism, 3, 273; and Obama, 284, 285, 301; and
    Republican Party, 295, 304, 305, 320; surge
    strategy in, 265–66, 282–83, 284, 285; and
    tactical errors thesis, 2; and U. S. invasion,
    1, 2, 30, 265, 276
Irish voters, 46, 79, 88

Islam, 312, 313
isolationism, 2, 65, 70, 72, 92, 160, 290, 291
Israel, 140, 176, 217, 313; and Carter, 194; and
    hawk-nationalist alliance, 307; and John-
    son, 173; and Lebanon, 216, 217; and neo-
    conservatives, 273; and Nixon, 157; and
    Reagan, 223; and Republican Party, 255;
    Yom Kippur War, 173, 174
Italians, 46

Jackson, Henry "Scoop," 154, 164, 167, 176,
    177
Jackson-Vanik amendment, 176, 177, 185–86
Japan, 310; attack on Pearl Harbor, 58; and
    Congress, 58; economic sanctions against,
    57–58; and Franklin Roosevelt, 58; and
    George H. W. Bush, 248; and George W.
    Bush, 287; and Hoover, 20, 21; illiberal
    forces in, 21; invasion of Manchuria, 21;
    and military, 311; and Nixon, 155; secret
    codes of, 68; and Theodore Roosevelt, 15;
    war with, 57; and William Howard Taft, 17.
    See also East Asia
Javits, Jacob, 115, 124, 134, 137, 154
Jenner, William, 91
Jews, 41, 47, 53, 176, 186, 220, 273, 279
John Birch Society, 123, 133, 137, 192
John M. Olin Foundation, 201
John Paul II, 211
Johnson, Hiram, 42
Johnson, Lyndon, 112, 131, 291; and African
    Americans, 132, 137; and civil rights, 132,
    135, 137; and cold war, 132, 135; and commu-
    nism, 135; and domestic policy, 135, 136; and
    Eisenhower, 93; and election of 1960, 127;
    and election of 1964, 134, 135; and election
    of 1968, 148; and George W. Bush, 292; and
    Goldwater, 135, 136; and health care, 135;
    and Israel, 173; and jobs, 137; and national
    security, 93; and neoconservatives, 139;
    and northern cities, 137; and poverty, 135,
    137; and Republican Party, 303; and segre-
    gation, 132; and Vietnam, 135–36, 138, 146,
    147–48, 172
Jordan, 173
judiciary, 145, 167, 230, 279, 286

Kagan, Frederick, 282
Kagan, Robert, 256–57, 263–64, 306
KAL 007, 218

Keane, Jack, 282
Keating, Kenneth, 124, 129
Kellogg-Briand Pact, 21
Kennedy, Edward, 167, 202
Kennedy, John F., 112, 291; assassination of, 131;
    and civil rights, 132; and Cuban Missile
    Crisis, 129–30; and Eisenhower, 109; and
    election of 1960, 127–28; and election of
    1964, 134; and Goldwater, 129; and Khrush-
    chev, 130; and Nixon, 173; and Reagan, 230;
    and Republican Party, 303
Kennedy, Robert, 146
Kent State University, 159
Kerry, John, 275, 278, 279
Keyes, Alan, 269
KGB, 172, 173
Khalilzad, Zalmay, 256
Khan, A. Q., 287
Khmer Rouge, 180
Khrushchev, Nikita, 106, 109, 110, 111, 112, 113,
    128, 130
King, Martin Luther, Jr., 146
Kirk, Russell, 118
Kirkpatrick, Jeane, 197, 198, 226, 227–28, 247,
    257, 264, 274, 277, 288
Kissinger, Henry, 38, 254, 305; and Angola,
    181, 182, 186; and arms control, 186; back-
    ground of, 151; and Carter, 183; and Chile,
    173; and China, 152, 155–56, 162, 163, 184,
    186; and cold war, 165, 186; and contain-
    ment, 152, 185, 186; and covert action, 186;
    and democracy, 152; and détente, 164–65,
    182, 186, 187, 193; and developing world,
    186; and election of 1976, 184; and Ford,
    177; and great power relations, 154–55; and
    Helsinki accords, 178–79; and Hitler, 151;
    and human rights, 182; and ideology,
    186–87; and illiberal regimes, 186; and
    Intermediate Nuclear Forces Treaty, 225;
    and internationalism, 184; and interna-
    tional order, 151; and interventionism, 186;
    and Iraq War, 274; and Mayaguez, 180;
    and Middle East, 185, 186; and Middle East
    peace talks, 186; and military, 151, 186; and
    morality, 185–86; and national security,
    155–56; and Nazis, 151; and Nixon, 152;
    and nuclear policy, 152; and nuclear war,
    185, 186; philosophy of, 151–52; and realism,
    142, 152; and SALT II, 178; and secret diplo-
    macy, 186; and Soviet Union, 142, 156, 176,

178–79, 184, 185, 186; and unilateral action, 186; and Vietnam, 152, 159, 166, 170, 171, 179, 184, 186; and Yom Kippur War, 173–75
Knowland, William, 91
Knox, Frank, 51
Kohl, Helmut, 211, 237, 238
Koh Tang, 180
Korean War, 79–80, 84; and Eisenhower, 87, 88, 93–94, 97, 107, 297; and Republican Party, 295; and Robert Taft, 39, 79. *See also* North Korea; South Korea
Kosovo, 247, 257, 262–63, 269
Krauthammer, Charles, 222, 306
Kristol, Irving, 139, 140, 141, 201, 255, 257, 264
Kristol, William, 256–57, 263–64, 306. *See also* *Weekly Standard*
Kurdish Iraqis, 244
Kuwait, 241, 242, 243, 250
Kyoto Protocol, 262, 268

labor, 75, 88, 176, 220
labor, organized: and Dukakis, 234; and election of 1896, 11; and election of 1968, 147; and election of 1984, 220; and election of 2008, 285; and Franklin Roosevelt, 41; and Hoover, 20; and Nixon, 168, 176; and Reagan, 191
La Follette, Robert, 14, 18
La Follette, Robert, Jr., 42
Laird, Melvin, 157
Langer, William, 71, 91
Laos, 128, 129, 159
Latin America, 8; and Eisenhower, 99–100, 108–9; and Franklin Roosevelt, 40; and George H. W. Bush, 232, 251; and Hoover, 21; and LaFollette, 18; Nazi infiltration of, 48; and Nixon, 172; and Reagan, 227; and Theodore Roosevelt, 15; and William Howard Taft, 16–17
Latinos, 285, 320. *See also* Hispanics
Laxalt, Paul, 139
Layne, Christopher, 304
League of Nations, 19–20, 59, 62, 70–71
Lebanon, 108, 215, 216–18, 220, 223, 224
Le Duc Tho, 170
Lend-Lease program, 54–55, 55
liberalism, 154; and American Revolution, 5; and Carter, 184; classical, 28, 118; in colonial America, 25–26; and conservatism, 5–6; and Democratic Party, 3, 4–5, 23, 24,

168; and doves, 153; and Dukakis, 234; economic, 35; and Eisenhower, 112; and election of 1944, 67; and election of 1948, 75; and election of 1964, 134; and election of 1980, 203; and election of 1984, 220; and election of 2008, 285; and elections of 1978, 196; and Ford, 182; and Franklin Roosevelt, 40; and George H. W. Bush, 234, 242, 246; and government, 26; and Helsinki agreement, 179; and Hoover, 20; and Irving Kristol, 141; and Mondale, 219; and multilateralism, 317; and neoconservatives, 140; and Nixon, 126, 149, 157, 160, 167, 176, 187; and Northeast, 124; and Obama, 284, 301; and paleoconservatism, 258; and promotion of democracy and trade, 28; and race riots, 137; and Reagan, 229, 230; and realism vs. idealism, 29; and Republican Party, 190, 202; and Rockefeller, 124; social, 35; and Supreme Court, 137–38; and United States, 25–26; and Vietnam, 146; and wealth redistribution, 35; and William Howard Taft, 16; and World War II, 46
libertarians, 35, 118, 257; and election of 2008, 284; and George W. Bush, 267; and Goldwater, 117, 124; and Iraq War, 274; and Reagan, 205; and Republican Party, 304; and Robert Taft, 47
Libya, 287, 315
Lieberman, Joseph, 278
Lindbergh, Charles, 47, 54
Lindsay, John, 124
Lippmann, Walter, 62–64
Lithuania, 237
Locarno Conference, 21
Lodge, Henry Cabot, 18, 19, 20
Lodge, Henry Cabot, Jr., 64, 82, 86, 92, 124, 126, 132
Los Angeles, 123
lower-income voters, 285
Lowry, Rich, 281. *See also* *National Review*
Lubell, Samuel, 116
Luce, Henry, 49, 60–61, 63
Lugar, Richard, 254, 263, 305

MacArthur, Douglas, 66, 79, 80, 81, 84
Mackinac declaration, 65–66
Malta summit, December 1989, 237
Manchuria, 15, 17, 21
Mansfield, Michael, 112, 154

Mao Zedong, 76, 101–2, 156, 162, 163
Marcos, Ferdinand, 226
Marshall, George, 68, 78, 84, 86
Marshall Plan, 73, 74, 74, 150
Marxism, 118, 141, 209, 273; in Africa, 181, 182; and China, 239; and Congress, 185; and Granada, 215–16; and Reagan, 212–13, 222. See also communism
Marxist-Leninism, 186, 198
Matsu, 101, 114, 127
Mayaguez incident, 180–81
McCain, John, 258, 263, 269, 282, 283, 284, 285–86, 306
McCarran, Pat, 46
McCarthy, Eugene, 146
McCarthy, Joseph, 77, 78–79, 84, 87, 91, 95, 96
McCarthyism, 106
McCloskey, Pete, 167
McCone, John, 128
McCormick, Robert, 46
McGovern, George, 167, 168, 184
McKinley, William, 11–13, 12, 21, 22
McNamara, Robert, 128
Metternich, Klemens von, 151
Mexico, 18, 248
Meyer, Frank, 26
mid-Atlantic states, 41
middle class, 1, 138, 147, 149, 192, 205, 234, 250
Middle East, 293; and Carter, 194; and Clinton, 261; and Eisenhower, 103, 107–8; and George W. Bush, 8, 265, 272, 275; and Kissinger, 185, 186; and Nixon, 173–75, 186; and Obama, 302; and Soviet Union, 173
Midwest, 32, 39, 46; and Bretton Woods Agreement, 69; and civil rights, 132; and Eisenhower, 97; and election of 1896, 11; and election of 1940, 53; and election of 1968, 147; and election of 1980, 203; and Ford, 183; and Goldwater, 123; and moderates, 125; and Reagan, 205; and Republican Party, 41, 42, 71, 91, 116, 202, 292, 294, 320; and World War II, 46
military, 11, 27; and airpower, 179, 263, 271; and anti-interventionists, 31; and Army-McCarthy hearings, 95; and atomic airpower, 80, 91, 96; and Borah, 18; and Bush doctrine, 2; and Clinton, 252, 253, 263; and conservatism, 27, 31; and democracy promotion, 28; and doves, 29; and Eisenhower, 2, 83, 86, 89, 98, 99, 101, 102, 104, 108, 110,

112, 114; and election of 1996, 261; and Ford, 179; and Franklin Roosevelt, 40, 55–56; and George H. W. Bush, 235, 243, 246, 247; and George W. Bush, 265, 268, 270, 271–72; and Goldwater, 117, 122; and Grenada, 216; and hawk-nationalist alliance, 307; and hawks, 6, 29, 31; and Hoover, 21; and idealism, 29; and Kennedy, 113; and Kissinger, 151, 186; and LaFollette, 18; and McKinley, 12; mutual limitations, 20; and nationalism, 92; and Nixon, 156, 157, 165, 166, 169, 174, 175, 186; and Obama, 302; and partisan politics, 32; and post–cold war internationalism, 153; predominance of American, 309, 317; preventive action by, 256, 316; and public opinion, 321; and Reagan, 189, 204, 207, 208, 215–18, 220, 229; and Republican Party, 2, 3, 74, 82, 141, 254, 255, 256, 257, 259, 290, 304, 320–21; and Robert Taft, 39, 40, 44, 80–81; and Southern Democrats, 92–93; and Stevenson, 107; and Theodore Roosevelt, 13–14, 15, 17; total personnel of, 97; and Truman, 74; and vital interests, 316–17; and Western Europe, 82, 84, 98, 99; and William Howard Taft, 16, 17. See also interventionism; nuclear policy
Milosevic, Slobodan, 246, 247, 262–63
minimum wage laws, 59
missile defense, 213–14, 260, 261–62; and George W. Bush, 268, 271, 280; and hawk-nationalist alliance, 307; and Obama, 302; and Reagan, 208; and Republican Party, 255, 257, 259. See also Strategic Defense Initiative (SDI)
Mitterand, François, 211
moderates: and Eisenhower, 85, 115; and election of 1968, 148; and election of 2008, 285; and Ford, 183; and George H. W. Bush, 250; and Goldwater, 132, 135; and Nicaragua, 210; and Nixon, 145, 159; and Reagan, 192, 203, 205, 221; and Republican National Convention of 1964, 133; and Republican Party, 137, 154, 190, 202, 292, 293, 320
Mondale, Walter, 219–20, 221
monetary policy, 161–62
Monroe Doctrine, 11
morality: and Carter, 183; and conservative traditionalists, 118; and George H. W. Bush, 249, 251; and George W. Bush, 265, 270, 273, 280; and Hoover, 21; and international

institutions, 317–18; and Kissinger, 185–86; and Nixon, 185–86, 187; partisan disagreement over, 23; and Reagan, 183, 205, 230; and realism, 305, 306; and Republican Party, 4; and use of force, 29

Moral Majority, 200

Morocco, 15, 287

Moscow summit (1988), 225

Moslems, in former Yugoslavia, 246, 253

Mossadeq, Mohammed, 103, 104, 113

Moynihan, Daniel Patrick, 139, 149

Mozambique, 222

multilateralism, 317–18; and Clinton, 252; and Eisenhower, 90; and George W. Bush, 268; and Mackinac declaration, 66; and Republican Party, 254, 256, 304; and Southern Democrats, 92; and trade, 97

Multiple Independently Targetable Reentry Vehicles (MIRVs), 164

Munich Agreement, 44

Muravchik, Joshua, 256

Muskie, Edmund, 154, 161, 167

MX intercontinental ballistic missile, 208

NAACP, 121

Nagasaki, 106

Namibia, 182

Nasser, Gamal Abdul, 107–8, 113

National Association of Manufacturers, 200

National Conservative Political Action Committee, 195

National Endowment for Democracy (NED), 226

National Front for the Liberation of Angola (FNLA), 181, 182

National Interest, 305

nationalism, 319; and accommodationism, 29; and Borah, 18; and Buchanan, 249, 261; and Clinton, 232; and cold war, 92; and communism, 92; and conservatism, 31, 296; and Eisenhower, 85, 92, 94, 115; and election of 2000, 269; and George W. Bush, 265, 270, 273; and Goldwater, 121; and hawks, 2, 92, 257, 306–7; and Mackinac declaration, 65; and military, 92; and New Right, 195; and Reagan, 182, 193, 205, 215; and Republican Party, 3, 6, 8, 91, 92, 254, 255–56, 258, 259, 291, 293, 301, 304, 306–7; and Robert Taft, 64, 291; and sovereignty, 6; tenets of, 6, 29–30; and United Nations, 71; and unyielding approach to foreign adversaries, 6

National Republican Senatorial Committee, 120

National Review, 119, 120, 123, 145, 275, 305. See also Lowry, Rich

national security: and Angola, 181; and arms control, 177; and Carter, 196; and Clinton, 252, 263; and Committee on the Present Danger, 197; and conservatism, 4; and Democratic Party, 154, 269, 295, 320; and Eisenhower, 96–97, 114; and election of 2008, 284, 285; and Ford, 177; and Franklin Roosevelt, 53; and George H. W. Bush, 242; and George W. Bush, 1, 265, 268, 270, 273, 275, 279–80, 291, 298; and Goldwater, 126; and hawk-nationalist alliance, 307; and Kissinger, 155–56; and limited government, 118; and Lyndon Johnson, 93; and Nixon, 7, 145, 155; and Obama, 302, 314; and Project for the New American Century, 264; and Reagan, 189, 199, 201, 225; and Republican Party, 2, 254, 259, 290, 295, 320–21; and Robert Taft, 43, 44, 74; and Southern Democrats, 92; and Taft, 74; and Truman, 72, 76. See also defense spending

National Security Council (NSC), 102, 129–30, 223

National Security Council directive No. 162/2, 97

National Security Decisions Directive-32, 214

National Security Decisions Directive-75, 214

National Security Decisions Directive-166, 222

National Security Strategy (2002), 272

National Union for the Total Independence of Angola (UNITA), 181, 182

nation-building, 112–13, 252, 253, 255, 265, 268, 276, 317

NATO, 19, 73, 76; Able Archer exercise, 218; and Eisenhower, 86, 89, 98, 110, 111; and election of 1996, 261; and Ford, 178; and George H. W. Bush, 237; and German reunification, 238; and Great Britain, 98; and hawk-nationalist alliance, 307; and military, 311; and Reagan, 210, 212, 218; and Republican Party, 76, 259; and Republican Party internationalists, 91; and Robert Taft, 76; and Truman administration, 76; and West Germany, 98

Nazis, 45, 53, 54, 133; and Kissinger, 151; and Latin America, 48; and Republican Party, 47–49; and Robert Taft, 47, 83. See also Germany; Hitler, Adolf

neoconservatism, 33; and Bosnia, 256; and Bush doctrine, 2; and Carter, 198; and Clinton, 256; and democracy, 297; and Democratic Party, 140, 297; and George W. Bush, 273–75, 276, 277, 298; and hawk-nationalist alliance, 306, 307; and internationalism, 296–97; and Iraq War, 3; and Johnson, 139; and 9/11 attacks, 298; origins of, 139–40; and presidency, 3; and Project for the New American Century, 264; and Reagan, 205, 227; and realism, 255; and Republican Party, 140, 291

Neutrality Acts (1935-37), 40, 44, 56

New Deal: and Democratic Party, 41, 167–68; and Dewey, 67; and Eisenhower, 88, 106, 115, 116, 119; and election of 1944, 67; and election of 1948, 75; and Goldwater, 135; and moderates, 82; and neoconservatives, 140; and Nixon, 160; and Old Guard conservatives, 77; and Reagan, 191, 227, 230; and Republican Party, 23, 40, 115, 124, 137; and Robert Taft, 42–43, 50, 59, 63, 74; and Wallace, 147

New Economic Policy, 162, 167

New Jewel movement, 215

New Left, 139, 140

New Republic, 275

New Right, 195–96, 200, 201–2, 205

New York, 125

New Zealand, 100

Nicaragua: and Carter, 195, 198, 202; and Congress, 209–10; and election of 1984, 219; and George H. W. Bush, 244; peace agreement in, 228; and Reagan, 208, 209–10, 219, 222, 223, 226; and William Howard Taft, 17

9/11 attacks. *See* September 11, 2001 attacks

Nitze, Paul, 196–97

Nixon, Richard, 38, 109, 254; and allies, 157–58, 173; and Angola, 186, 187; and antiwar protests, 150, 158; and arms control, 156–57, 163–64, 186; and arms sales, 157; and arts, 149; and autocratic regimes, 157, 158; background of, 144, 150; and Berlin, 156, 163; and California governor's race, 131, 144; and Catholics, 168; and centrism, 144, 187; character of, 143; and Chile, 172, 173; and China, 142, 150, 155–56, 162–63, 165, 166, 185, 186, 187, 293, 297; and civil rights, 126; and cold war, 153, 172, 186; and communism, 143, 150, 155, 159, 168, 175; and Congress, 144, 150, 153–54, 159, 160–61, 164, 165–66, 168, 169, 175, 176, 187; and conservatism, 142, 145, 149, 157, 159, 160, 162, 167, 176, 187, 188; and containment, 164, 185, 186; and covert action, 172, 173, 186; and crime, 145, 160, 167; and democracy, 157, 158; and Democratic Party, 154, 157, 161, 167, 168, 300; and desegregation, 145, 149; and détente, 164–65, 166, 176, 185, 186, 187; and developing world, 157, 186; and domestic policy, 126, 149–50, 167; and doves, 153–54, 157, 159, 164, 166, 169, 175, 185; and drugs, 160, 167; and Eastern Europe, 156; and economic aid, 157, 169, 175; and economy, 126, 142, 149, 155, 161, 162, 165, 167, 187; and education, 167; and Eisenhower, 86–87, 144, 149, 173; and election of 1960, 126, 127–28, 144; and election of 1968, 144–48; and election of 1972, 161, 162, 167–69; and elections of 1970, 160–61; and environment, 167; and equal rights amendment, 149; and family, 149; and federal bureaucracy, 149; and foreign aid, 157, 170; and foreign military aid, 157, 169, 174, 175; and geopolitics, 7, 155, 164; and global power relations, 150; and Goldwater, 144, 145, 149, 160; and government, 142, 146; and great power relations, 7, 154–55; and great power relations vs. regional issues, 172; and hawks, 7, 153–54, 157, 164, 165; and health care, 149, 167; and human rights, 157; and Humphrey, 147–48; and ideology, 186–87; and illiberal regimes, 186; and inflation, 162; and integration, 167; and Intermediate Nuclear Forces Treaty, 225; and internationalism, 144, 296; and Iran, 157, 173; and isolationism, 160; and Israel, 157; and Japan, 155; and judiciary, 145, 167; and Kennedy, 173; and Kissinger, 152; and labor organizations, 176; and Latin America, 172; and law and order, 187; and liberalism, 126, 149, 157, 160, 167, 176, 187; and lower-middle class, 149; manner of, 158; and middle-class suburbanites, 147; and Middle East, 173–75, 186; and military, 156, 165, 166, 186; and moderates, 145, 159; and monetary policy, 161–62; and morality, 185–86, 187; and Moynihan, 149; and national security, 7, 145, 155; and New Deal, 160; and Northern voters, 147; and North Vietnam, 158–59, 165, 166; and nuclear policy, 156, 158, 163–64, 174, 185, 186; and obscenity, 160; and patriotism, 149, 160; and power vs. ideology, 155; and public opinion, 158, 159, 160, 164, 165–66, 167, 169, 170, 171; and race, 145, 149; and Reagan, 145, 193, 223; and realism, 142, 187, 292; and regulation, 149, 167; and religion, 149; and Republican Party, 143, 144, 145, 157, 159, 160–61, 163, 165, 167, 168, 169, 175, 187; and Robert Taft, 149; and Rockefeller, 126; and Saudi Arabia, 157, 173; and segregationists, 147; and social and cultural polarization, 160; and social issues, 160; and Social Security, 149; and social unrest, 145; and South, 145, 149, 168; and South Africa, 157; and Southeast Asia, 151; and Southern Democrats, 175; and South Vietnam, 151; and Soviet Union, 142, 150, 155–57, 158, 162, 163–65, 166, 169, 172, 173, 174, 175, 176, 184, 185, 186, 187, 293, 297; and spending, 126, 149, 167; and Statement of Basic Principles with Soviet Union, 164; and strategic competition, 291; and Taiwan, 156, 163; and tariffs, 145; and Third World, 156; and trade, 163, 164, 176; and unilateral action, 186; and United Nations, 162; and Vietnam, 137, 142, 145, 146, 147–48, 150–51, 153, 155, 156, 157, 158–60, 161, 162, 165–66, 169–72, 175–76, 179, 186, 187; and wage and price controls, 162, 167; and Wallace, 147; and Watergate scandal, 173, 174, 175, 187–88, 292; and Western Europe, 155; and white-collar professionals, 147; and whites, 147; and Willkie, 144; and working class, 149; and Yom Kippur War, 173–75

Nixon Center, 305

Nixon Doctrine, 157

Noriega, Manuel, 240–41

Norquist, Grover, 356n19

North, Oliver, 223

North American Free Trade Agreement (NAFTA), 248, 249, 259

Northeasterners, 46, 76; and Bretton Woods Agreement, 69; and civil rights, 132; and election of 1896, 11; and election of 1940, 53; and election of 1964, 134; and election of 1968, 147; and election of 1980, 203; and Ford, 183; and internationalism, 64; and Lend-Lease program, 55; and Reagan, 205–6; and Republican Party, 49, 55, 71,

82, 83, 92, 116, 124, 125, 190, 202, 292, 294; and Sun Belt, 123

Northerners: and election of 1896, 11; and Johnson, 137; and Nixon, 147; and Reagan, 205; and Republican Party, 79

North Korea, 79–80, 262; containment of, 315–16; and George W. Bush, 268, 271, 287; and hawk-nationalist alliance, 307; negotiation with, 315; and Obama, 302; and Republican Party, 255, 256. See also East Asia; Korean War

North Vietnam, 158–59, 160, 165, 166, 169, 170, 171, 176, 179. See also Vietnam/Vietnam War

Notre Dame University, 212

nuclear freeze movement, 210, 211, 213–14

Nuclear Non-Proliferation Treaty, 313

nuclear policy: and Committee on the Present Danger, 197–98; and Dulles, 96; and Eisenhower, 89, 96–97, 98, 99, 101, 102, 104, 105–6, 107, 109, 110, 111–12, 113; and election of 1984, 219–20; and Geneva summit, 221; and George H. W. Bush, 245; and George W. Bush, 287; and German reunification, 238; and Goldwater, 122, 133, 134, 135; and hydrogen bomb, 106; and Kennedy, 113; and Kissinger, 152, 185; and massive retaliation, 96, 114; and mutual assured destruction, 199, 213; and New Look, 97, 114; and Nixon, 156, 158, 163–64, 174, 185; and North Korea and Iran, 315–16; and Obama, 302, 314; and Reagan, 199, 208, 210–11, 213, 218–19, 224–25, 228, 296; and Reykjavik summit, 221–22; and zero option, 210. See also arms control

nuclear proliferation, 1, 112, 252, 256, 311–12, 313–14, 321

nuclear testing: and Eisenhower, 107, 111–12; and Goldwater, 122, 129; and Kennedy, 128; and Republican Party, 262; and Stevenson, 107

Obama, Barack, 301–3; and accommodationism, 9, 303; and election of 2008, 284–85; and hawk-nationalist alliance, 307–8; and Iran, 315; and Iraq, 8; manner of, 303; personality of, 9, 285; and pragmatism, 8–9, 321; and realism, 321; and Republican Party, 303–4

obscenity, 138, 160

oil and gas, 212; and Arab embargo, 174, 175; and Eisenhower, 103; and George H. W. Bush, 251; and George W. Bush, 266; and Iraq, 241; and Russia, 311; and Sun Belt, 123

Old Guard conservatives, 75; and Eisenhower, 94; and United Nations, 71

Old Guard Republicans, 76; and Bricker amendment, 95; decline of, 125; and Eisenhower, 87, 88, 92, 93, 95, 96, 97, 101, 114; and fascism, 77; and McCarthy, 79, 95; and Sun Belt, 123. *See also* Republican Party

Old Right, 118–19

O'Neill, Tip, 216

Open Door policy, 13, 21

open skies, 105, 106

Operation Pluto, 109

Organization of Eastern Caribbean States, 216

Pacific coast, 125

Paine, Thomas, 230

Pakistan, 101, 156, 223, 271, 272, 287

paleoconservatism, 258, 274, 304

Palestinian Liberation Organization (PLO), 216, 217

Palestinians, 140

Palin, Sarah, 285

Palme, Olaf, 169

Panama, 15, 240–41

Panama Canal, 193, 195–96, 216

Panama Canal Zone, 241

Paris Peace Accords, 169–70, 171, 175

Paris peace talks, 166

Paris summit, 112

patriotism, 5, 25, 27, 149, 160, 205, 234

Paul, Ron, 8, 283, 284, 304, 305

Pearl Harbor, attack on, 58, 60, 63, 65, 68, 86

Percy, Charles, 139, 154

Perle, Richard, 176, 225, 227, 247, 256, 264

Perot, Ross, 249, 250

Pershing II intermediate-range missiles, 210

Persian Gulf, 202, 246

Persian Gulf War, 243, 249, 250

Petraeus, David, 282, 283

Philippines, 12–13, 15, 100, 226

Phillips, Howard, 195

Phoenix, 123

Pinochet, Augusto, 173, 228

Pipes, Richard, 197, 227

Podhoretz, Norman, 197, 228, 264

Poland, 67, 70, 72, 73, 211, 214, 228, 236, 238

Polish voters, 53, 88

political party, 3; coalition building in, 298–99; and conservatism, 22–38; and domestic support, 36; and foreign policy, 298–301; ideological traditions of, 23; and individual and group interests, 23; and policy alternatives, 23; and realignment, 23–24

Popular Front for the Liberation of Angola (MPLA), 181, 182

Popular Unity coalition, 172

populism, 11, 13, 205, 233, 249

Portugal, 181

poverty, 135, 137, 209

Powell, Colin, 216, 254–55, 260, 270–71

Powers, Gary, 112

Preble, Christopher, 304

prescription drugs, 280

president: and coalition building, 297; and Congress, 94; and domestic support, 36; and Eisenhower, 95, 96; and international system, 37; latitude in foreign policy, 6–7; leadership of, 3, 6; and out-ofpower party, 299; and political coalitions, 35–36, 37–38, 308; and Republican Party internationalists, 91; and Robert Taft, 50; as shaping foreign policy, 300–301; and war, 298

press/media: and Agnew, 160; doves in, 153; and George H. W. Bush, 239, 246; and Goldwater, 134; and World War II, 46, 49

private property, 24, 118

progress, 5, 25

progressivism, 14, 17–18, 22

Project for the New American Century (PNAC), 263–64, 276

Proliferation Security Initiative, 287

pro-Nazi fringe groups, 46

Proposition No. 13, 200

protectionism: avoidance of, 319; and Buchanan, 249, 261; and Eisenhower, 97; and George H. W. Bush, 239–40, 248; and Republican Party, 11, 71, 97, 294; and Robert Taft, 44

Protestants, 11, 41, 46, 128, 147. *See also* evangelicalism

Public Interest, The, 140

public opinion: and 1942 midterm elections, 59; and Buchanan, 249; and Carter, 184, 204; and Central America, 209; and China, 239, 240; and Clinton, 270; and conscription, 52; and Cuban Missile Crisis, 130; and democracy, 321; and Democratic Party, 190; and destroyers for bases deal, 52; and Eisenhower, 90; and election of 1940, 53; and election of 1980, 204; and election of 1984, 219–20; and election of 1988, 234; and elections, 299; and Ford, 180, 184; and Franklin Roosevelt, 56; and George H. W. Bush, 232, 241–42, 243, 246–47, 248, 250; and George W. Bush, 275, 282, 285, 286, 287; and Grenada, 216, 220; and Helsinki agreement, 179; and Hoover, 21; and internationalism, 59–60; and Korean War, 80, 94; and Lebanon, 217–18, 220; and Lend-Lease program, 55; and McCarthy, 77, 79; and military, 321; and Mondale, 220; and NATO, 76; and Nixon, 158, 159, 160, 164, 165–66, 167, 169, 170, 171; and nuclear proliferation, 321; and Obama, 321; and Panama Canal, 195–96; and Paris peace agreement, 170; and Reagan, 204, 206, 207, 210, 219, 220, 223, 225, 234; and realism, 321; and Republican Party, 189–90, 294, 295; and SALT II, 198; and silent majority, 158, 160; and terrorism, 321; and Theodore Roosevelt, 16; and Tiananmen Square massacre, 239; and United Nations, 71; and Vietnam, 136, 153, 171, 179, 180; and Wilkie's internationalism, 62; and world role of United States, 59, 72; and World War II, 45, 46, 49, 50, 57

Puerto Rico, 12, 63
Putin, Vladimir, 319

Quadripartite Agreement, 163
Quayle, Dan, 234, 264
Quemoy, 101, 114, 127

race, 137, 146; and Agnew, 145; and Bricker amendment, 95; and Goldwater, 117, 135; and Nixon, 145, 149; and Reagan, 192; and Republican Party, 137; and Wallace, 147. See also desegregation; segregation
Radio Free Europe, 105, 213
Reagan, Nancy, 219, and
Reagan, Ronald, 38; and Afghanistan, 209, 214, 219, 221, 222–23; and American exceptionalism, 227; and Angola, 223; and antiwar demonstrations, 192; and arms control, 206, 207, 210–11, 213, 218, 219, 221–22, 224, 228, 229; and arms race, 199; and autocrats,

226, 227; background of, 190–91; and business, 189, 191, 192, 205; and Carter, 194, 198–99; and Catholics, 189, 205, 220; and Central America, 209; character of, 190–91; and Chile, 227, 228; and Clinton, 253; coalition of, 205–6, 207, 227, 231; and cold war, 7, 189, 199, 207, 213, 214, 215, 218, 222, 228, 229; and communism, 7, 189, 191–92, 199, 201, 202, 208, 209, 211, 212, 213, 215, 218, 219, 221, 222, 223, 224, 226, 227, 229; and Congress, 206, 208, 223, 230; and conservatism, 7, 182, 189, 190, 191, 192, 193, 199, 200–201, 203, 205, 206, 207, 220–21, 225, 227, 229, 230, 231; and Conservative Political Action Conference, 201; and containment, 208, 214; convictions of, 207–8, 215; and corporations, 205, 212; and counterculture, 192; and covert action, 212, 229; and crime, 192; and Cuba, 209, 222, 223; and defense spending, 193, 199, 206, 208–9, 214, 219; and democracy, 213, 225–26, 227, 228; and Democratic Party, 189, 192, 201, 205, 208, 227, 231; and détente, 183, 193, 199; and domestic policy, 200, 229–30; and East Asia, 227; and Eastern Europe, 193, 211, 213; and economy, 192, 199, 205, 206, 208–9, 211–12, 215, 220, 230, 231; and election of 1968, 144, 193; and election of 1976, 182, 183, 193–94; and election of 1980, 203–5; and election of 1984, 219–21, 220; and election of 2008, 283; and El Salvador, 226; and evangelicalism, 7, 189, 205; and federal budget, 206; and Ford, 182, 193; and Franklin Roosevelt, 191, 230; and free enterprise, 191, 230; and free market, 199; and Geneva summit of November 1985, 221; and George H. W. Bush, 233, 236; and George W. Bush, 267, 268, 279; and Goldwater, 189, 191; and government planning, 191; as governor, 139; and Grenada, 215–16, 218; gubernatorial campaign of 1966, 192; and hawks, 7, 189, 199, 231, 292; and Helsinki, 183; and human rights, 214, 221, 225, 226, 227; and idealism, 292, 293; and independents, 205; and inflation, 220, 230; and interest rates, 220; and internationalism, 207; and Iran, 223; and Iraq, 241; and Israel, 223; and John Birch Society, 192; and judiciary, 230; and Kennedy, 230; and Latin America, 227; and law and order, 192; and Lebanon, 215, 216–18;

Reagan, Ronald (*continued*)
and liberalism, 229, 230; and libertarians, 205; and lower-middle class, 205; manner of, 192, 199, 204, 206, 207–8, 220; and Marxism, 212–13, 222; and Middle America, 192; and Midwest, 205; and military, 189, 204, 208, 220, 229; and military aid, 209, 222–23; and military intervention, 207, 215–18, 229; and missile defense, 208; and moderates, 192, 203, 205, 221; and morality, 183, 205, 230; and Moscow summit of 1988, 225; and mutual deterrence, 213; and national defense, 201; and nationalism, 182, 193, 205, 215; and national security, 189, 199, 201, 225; and National Security Council (NSC), 223; and NATO, 210, 212, 218; and neoconservatism, 205, 227; and New Deal, 191, 227, 230; and New Right, 200, 205; and Nicaragua, 208, 209–10, 219, 222, 223, 226; and Nixon, 145, 193, 223; and Northeasterners, 205–6; and Northern voters, 205; and nuclear arms reductions, 208; and nuclear policy, 199, 208, 210–11, 213, 218–19, 224–25, 228, 296; and open markets, 213; and Panama Canal, 216; and patriotism, 205; and Philippines, 226; and Poland, 211, 214, 228; and public opinion, 204, 206, 207, 210, 219, 220, 223, 225, 234; and race riots, 192; and realism, 308; and regulation, 191; and Republican Party, 7, 189, 191, 192, 193, 199, 201, 205, 208, 213, 225, 230, 231; and right-wing students, 205; and rollback, 7, 189, 208, 214; and school prayer, 200; and segregationists, 205; and social policy, 206; and social spending, 206, 230; and South, 193, 203, 205, 208; and South Africa, 226; and South Korea, 227; and Soviet Union, 7, 189, 193, 199, 208, 209, 210–16, 218–19, 220, 221, 223, 224, 228–29, 316; speech at Notre Dame University, 212; speech to National Association of Evangelicals, 213; speech to UN General Assembly (1984), 219; and spending, 191, 230; and Strategic Arms Limitation Treaty (SALT II), 198; and suburbanite professionals, 205; and Sun Belt, 7, 189; and taxes, 191, 192, 206, 220, 230; and Third World, 222; and unemployment, 220; as union leader, 191; and Vietnam, 209; and Wall Street, 205; and Washington summit of December 1987, 224; and Watergate, 193; and welfare reform, 192; and West, 193, 203; and Western Europe, 222; and white southerners, 205; and white working-class and middle-class voters, 192; and women, 200; and working class, 205

Reagan Doctrine, 222

realism, 232–33; and Clinton, 232; and conservatism, 26–27, 308–9, 321, 322; and Eisenhower, 292, 308; and election of 2000, 269; and George H. W. Bush, 292; and George W. Bush, 8–9, 270, 292; and idealism, 29; and Kissinger, 142, 152; and Lippmann, 62; and nationalists, 30; and Nixon, 142, 150, 187, 292; and Obama, 8, 9, 303, 321; and Powell, 271; and public opinion, 321; and Reagan, 308; and Republican Party, 31, 254–55, 258, 291–92, 293, 304, 305–6, 308–9; tenets of, 6; and Theodore Roosevelt, 13, 22; and World War II, 48

Reciprocal Trade Act (1934), 40

regime change, 1, 256, 264, 265

regulation: of banks and securities, 59; and Carter, 204; and conservatism, 119, 200; and Eisenhower, 88; and Franklin Roosevelt, 41, 47; and George W. Bush, 267; and Nixon, 149, 167; and Reagan, 191. *See also* government

religion, 24, 25, 118, 149, 153, 184, 266, 268, 269, 279

religious charities, 267, 268

Religious Right, 269

Republicanism, modern, 85, 88, 107, 115, 119, 124, 125

Republican National Convention of 1940, 49–50

Republican National Convention of 1952, 82

Republican National Convention of 1960, 126–27

Republican National Convention of 1964, 133

Republican National Convention of 1976, 183, 194

Republican National Convention of 1980, 203

Republican National Convention of 1992, 249

Republican National Convention of 1996, 261

Republican National Convention of 2000, 269

Republican Party, 76; and accommodationism, 8, 291; and American exceptionalism, 291; and anti-interventionism, 8, 31, 34, 40, 42, 45, 46, 47, 49, 51, 254, 257–258, 259, 290, 292, 293, 294, 304–305; and Bretton Woods

Agreement, 69; and Bricker amendment, 95; and Buchanan, 249; and Buckley, 119; and Bush doctrine, 2, 3; and cash and carry policy, 44; and China, 76; and civil rights, 132, 133; and Clinton, 253, 254, 258–59, 262; and communism, 39, 47, 119; and conservatism, 1, 4–5, 17, 18, 23, 24, 41–42, 124, 125, 133, 134, 137, 141, 154, 190, 194, 201–2, 231, 253, 255, 292, 293; constituency of, 41–42; and Cuban Missile Crisis, 129–30; decline of, 125; and defense spending, 74; and Democratic Party, 4, 300; and détente, 187–88; and Dirksen, 126; diversity of, 22; and doves, 153, 154, 291; and economy, 1, 4, 23, 31–32, 34, 92, 125, 202, 259, 293–94; and Eisenhower, 7, 85, 87, 88, 91, 92, 93, 95, 96, 97–98, 101, 102, 107, 111, 114, 115–16; and election of 1896, 11; and election of 1900, 12–13; and election of 1940, 52–53; and election of 1952, 82; and election of 1956, 107; and election of 1960, 126–27, 128; and election of 1964, 135, 137; and election of 1968, 147, 148; and election of 1976, 184; and election of 1980, 205; and election of 1984, 219–21; and election of 1988, 233–34; and election of 2006, 1; and election of 2008, 1, 283–86; and elections, 2002 midterm, 275; and elections, 2006 midterm, 282; and elections of 1946, 73; and elections of 1962, 130, 131; and elections of 1966, 138–39; and elections of 1968, 146; and elections of 1974, 178; and elections of 1986, 224; and elections of 1990, 242–43; and elections of 1994, 259; and expansionism, 11, 13; and fascism, 77; and Ford, 177, 183; and foreign aid, 73, 97; and foreign economic policy, 97–98; and Franklin Roosevelt, 41, 42, 46, 48, 49, 51, 56, 58–59; and free trade, 41; and George H. W. Bush, 233, 236, 237, 240, 242–43, 248, 250; and George W. Bush, 8, 268, 274, 275, 279–81, 282; and Goldwater, 117, 122–23, 135; and hawks, 2, 3, 6, 8, 31, 154, 256–57, 290, 291, 292, 293, 295, 297–98, 301, 304, 306–7; and Hoover, 20, 21; ideological tensions in, 28–29, 33–34, 125; and internationalism, 42, 60–65, 66–67, 71, 72, 91–92, 95–96, 125, 154, 290, 291, 295–96; and international pressures, 32–33, 34; and interventionism, 6, 11, 34, 42, 48, 71, 72, 141, 254, 256–57, 258, 259, 290, 292, 293, 294, 295, 296, 304–5; and Iraq

War, 266, 305, 320; and isolationism, 291; and Johnson, 303; and Korean War, 79, 80, 93; and liberalism, 124, 125, 153, 202; and limited government, 1, 321; and Mackinac declaration, 65–66; and McCarthy, 78–79, 95; and McKinley, 13; and middle class, 1; and midwesterners, 42; and military, 2, 3, 74, 82, 141, 254, 255, 256, 257, 259, 290, 304, 320–21; as minority party, 116; and moderates, 124–25, 154; and nationalism, 3, 6, 8, 91, 92, 92, 254, 255–56, 258, 259, 291, 293, 301, 304, 306–7; and national security, 2, 254, 259, 290, 295, 320–21; and NATO, 76; and neoconservatives, 140; and New Deal, 59, 115; and new league of nations, 65, 66; and 1930's international disengagement, 40–41; and Nixon, 143, 144, 145, 157, 159, 160–61, 163, 165, 167, 168, 169, 175, 187; and Northeasterners, 49, 55, 71, 82, 83, 92, 116, 124, 125, 190, 202, 292, 294; and Obama, 303–4; and Pearl Harbor attack, 58; and Philippines, 13; and postwar settlement, 70; and progressivism, 17–18, 22; and protectionism, 11, 97; and public opinion, 189–90; and Reagan, 7, 189, 191, 192, 193, 199, 201, 205, 208, 213, 225, 230, 231; and realism, 31, 254–55, 258, 291–92, 293, 304, 305–6, 308–9; and Rockefeller, 126; and Southern Democrats, 92; and Spanish American War, 12; and Sun Belt, 123; and Theodore Roosevelt, 14, 16; and trade, 11; and Truman, 72, 82; and unilateralism, 2; and United Nations, 71; and Vietnam, 136–37, 138, 154, 179; and Watergate, 189–90; and Wilkie, 62; and William Howard Taft, 17; and Wilsonian foreign policy, 60; and World War II, 39, 47, 48, 71–72. *See also* Old Guard Republicans
Reykjavik summit, 221–22
Rhodesia, 182
Rice, Condoleezza, 268, 270
Richards, Ann, 267
Richardson Foundation, 201
Robertson, Pat, 233
Rockefeller, Nelson, 125, 127, 131, 190; and Eisenhower, 124; and election of 1964, 134; and election of 1968, 144, 145; and Ford, 182; and Goldwater, 126, 132, 133; and Nixon, 126; reelected as governor of New York, 139

Rogers, William, 152
rogue states, 1, 256, 271, 272, 273
Romania, 156
Romney, George, 144–45
Romney, Mitt, 284
Roosevelt, Franklin, 47, 94, 146; and aid to
    Great Britain, 53; and Atlantic Charter, 60,
    63; and Atlantic policy, 55–56; and Churchill,
    56; and communism, 76–77; and Congress,
    46, 57, 58–59; and Democratic Party,
    46; and destroyers for bases deal, 51–52;
    domestic policy of, 40, 41, 58–59; and
    Eisenhower, 97; election of, 40; and elec-
    tion of 1940, 53; and election of 1944,
    67–68; and four freedoms, 60, 63; and
    Germany, 55–56; and international mone-
    tary stability, 40; and interventionism, 40;
    and Japan, 58; and Lend-Lease program,
    54–55; and Lippmann, 62; and military, 40;
    and national security, 53; and neoconserva-
    tives, 140; and Neutrality Acts, 40, 44; and
    New Deal, 23; and postwar settlement,
    69–70; and Reagan, 191, 230; and Republi-
    can Party, 42, 46, 48, 49, 51, 303; and Rob-
    ert Taft, 43; and United Nations, 70–71; and
    Western progressives, 42; and Yalta confer-
    ence, 70
Roosevelt, Theodore, 13–16, 17, 18, 22, 48, 308
Rosenberg, Julius, 77
Rostow, Eugene, 197
Rostow, Walt, 113
Rothbard, Murray, 119
Rove, Karl, 280–81
Rumania, 73
Rumsfeld, Donald, 262, 264, 270, 273, 276
rural voters, 41, 46, 53, 71, 123
Rusher, William, 190
Russell, Richard, 154
Russia, 245, 310; and China, 312; and democ-
    racy, 319; future challenges from, 311–12;
    and George W. Bush, 271, 272, 276, 287; and
    hawk-nationalist alliance, 307; and Obama,
    302; and Republican Party, 255, 256; and
    Theodore Roosevelt, 15; and William How-
    ard Taft, 17. See also Soviet Union

Sadat, Anwar, 174, 175
Safire, William, 245
San Diego, 123

Sandinistas, 209, 228
Saudi Arabia, 157, 173, 212, 241, 272, 281, 319
Savimbi, Jonas, 181, 182, 223
Scaife Foundation, 201
Schlafly, Phyllis, 200
Schlesinger, James, 177
school busing, 150, 167, 204
school desegregation, 149
school prayer, 138, 200, 204
Scott, Hugh, 124, 165
Scowcroft, Brent, 235, 254, 274, 305
segregation, 116, 127, 132, 147, 205. See also
    desegregation; race
Selective Service Act, 52, 57
self-determination, 56, 236, 238, 245
September 11, 2001 attacks, 265, 271, 312; allied
    cooperation after, 287; and Democratic
    Party, 295; and George W. Bush, 1, 272, 288,
    298; and hawk-nationalist alliance, 306;
    and nationalism, 275; and neoconserva-
    tives, 273, 274; and Republican Party, 280,
    293, 295. See also terrorism
Serbia, 246
Serbs, 246, 247, 253, 258, 260, 262–63
Shah of Iran, 104
Shanghai Communiqué, 163
Shays, Christopher, 281
Shiites, 216, 244, 277, 281
Shipstead, Henrik, 71
Shultz, George, 207, 217, 224
Siberian pipeline, 212
Singapore, 287
Six Days' War, 140
Skowronek, Stephen, 267
socialism, 87
Social Security, 59, 88, 134, 149, 279, 286
Solidarity union movement, 211, 236
Solzhenitsyn, Alexander, 178, 182
Somalia, 246–47, 252, 253, 258, 309
Sonnenfeldt, Helmut, 183
Sonnenfeldt Doctrine, 183
South Africa, 157, 181, 182, 226
Southeast Asia, 151
Southeast Asian Treaty Organization
    (SEATO), 100–101
Southern Democrats: and Bricker amendment,
    95; and civil rights, 92, 132; and Eisen-
    hower, 92; and election of 1960, 128; and
    first Iraq War, 243; and Franklin Roosevelt,

41, 42; and liberalism, 190; and Nixon, 175; and Reagan, 189; and segregation, 116; and Vietnam, 146, 154

Southerners, 46, 92; and Carter, 196; and Eisenhower, 87, 116; and election of 1956, 107; and election of 1968, 147; and election of 1972, 168–69; and election of 1980, 203; and election of 1984, 220; and George H. W. Bush, 233, 234; and Goldwater, 121, 131, 132, 135; and Nixon, 145, 149, 168; and Reagan, 193, 203, 205, 208; and Republican Party, 137, 141, 202, 253; and segregation, 75, 95, 121; textile industries in, 145; and Wallace, 147

South Korea, 122, 227. *See also* East Asia; Korean War

South Vietnam: and Eisenhower, 103; and Ford, 179, 182; and Goldwater, 122; and Nixon, 151, 157, 159, 160, 165, 166, 169, 170, 171, 175, 176; and Republican National Convention of 1964, 133. *See also* Vietnam/ Vietnam War

sovereignty, 65, 291, 318; and Bricker amendment, 94; cession of, 27; and Goldwater, 122; and nationalism, 6; and Republican Party, 91, 293, 304; and Robert Taft, 64; and United Nations, 71

Soviet Jews, 176, 186

Soviet Union, 67; and accommodationism, 228, 245–46; and Afghanistan, 202, 221, 222–23, 228; and Angola, 181, 182; and arms control, 156–57; and atomic bomb, 76, 77–78; and Baltic states, 244, 245; and Bulgaria, 73; and Carter, 183, 194, 195, 196, 198, 202; and Central Europe, 238; and Chile, 172, 173; and China, 101, 155–56, 162, 163, 165; collapse of, 8, 228–29, 246, 250, 257, 293; and Committee on the Present Danger, 197–98; and Congress, 185; and Cuba, 109, 129–30; and Eastern Europe, 70, 72; economy of, 211–12, 215; and Eisenhower, 7, 87, 89, 94, 96–97, 98, 99, 100, 101, 103, 104–6, 107, 108, 109–12, 113; and election of 1960, 127; espionage by, 76, 77–78, 79; as evil empire, 213; and Ford, 177, 178–79, 183–84; and George H. W. Bush, 8, 232, 234, 235, 236–37, 244–46, 251; and German reunification, 238–39; and Goldwater, 117, 121, 122, 129; and Grenada, 215–16; Hitler's

invasion of, 56; and Horn of Africa, 195; and intercontinental ballistic missiles, 110; and Iran, 72; and Iraq, 241; and Kennedy, 113, 128; and Kissinger, 142, 156, 176, 178–79, 184, 185, 186; and Korean War, 93; and Lebanon, 216; and Lippmann, 62; and Middle East, 173; and most-favored-nation trade status, 176, 245; and neoconservatives, 139; and Nixon, 142, 150, 155–57, 158, 162, 163–65, 166, 169, 172, 173, 174, 175, 176, 184, 185, 186, 187, 293, 297; and Poland, 70, 72, 73; and post–cold war internationalism, 153; and postwar foreign aid, 73; and postwar settlement, 70; and Reagan, 7, 189, 193, 199, 208, 209, 210–16, 218–19, 220, 221, 223, 224, 228–29, 316; and Republican National Convention of 1964, 133; and Robert Taft, 63–64, 77, 81, 84; and Rumania, 73; and Russia, 311; and socialist revolution, 186–87; and SS-20 theater-range missiles, 210; and Third World War, 118; and Truman, 72–73, 77–78, 84; and Turkey, 72; and United States, 33; and Vietnam, 180; Wilkie on, 61; and Yom Kippur War, 173, 174, 175; and Yugoslavia, 73. *See also* Russia

Soviet Union Communist Party, 245

Spain, 11–12, 13

Spanish American War, 12, 13

spending: and Clinton, 253; and conservatism, 119, 200; and Eisenhower, 87, 110; and election of 1996, 261; and Franklin Roosevelt, 41; and George H. W. Bush, 248; and George W. Bush, 267, 280; and Goldwater, 120; and hawk-nationalist alliance, 307; and Nixon, 126, 149, 167; and Reagan, 191, 230; and Republican Party, 141, 257, 259. *See also* defense spending; domestic spending; government

Sputnik, 110, 111, 112

Stalin, Joseph, 69–70, 93, 105, 139

Stassen, Harold, 60, 63, 66

State Department, 91, 255, 262

Stennis, John, 154

Stevenson, Adlai, 87, 107

Stimson, Henry, 21, 51

Strategic Arms Limitation Talks (SALT), 156, 182

Strategic Arms Limitation Treaty (SALT I), 163–64

Strategic Arms Limitation Treaty (SALT II), 177, 178, 194, 197–98, 202

Strategic Arms Reduction Treaty (START I), 244–45

Strategic Defense Initiative (SDI), 213–14, 218, 219, 221, 222, 224. *See also* missile defense

Strauss, Leo, 273

Stuart, R. Douglas, 46

suburban voters, 92, 117, 135, 137, 205, 279, 320

Suez crisis (1956), 103, 107–8. *See also* Egypt

Sun Belt, 7, 32, 117, 123, 139, 189, 194, 202, 294

Sunni Arabs, 277, 283

Sunnis, 216, 281

Supreme Court, 137–38, 270

Symington, Stuart, 112

Syria, 173, 175, 216, 241

Taft, Robert, 38, 39–84, 91, 290, 293, 304; and anti-interventionism, 21, 39, 43–44, 50, 52, 53, 57, 64, 72, 83, 291; and Atlantic Charter, 63; background of, 42; and Bretton Woods Agreement, 69; and budget deficits, 74; and business, 21; and cash and carry, 44–45; and century of common man, 63; and China, 81; as cold warrior, 81; and communism, 39, 74, 77, 81, 83, 291; and Congress, 57, 81; and conscription, 52; as conservative, 50; and containment, 39, 80; death of, 95; and defense spending, 74, 82, 83, 84; and democracy, 44; and Dewey, 67; and domestic legislation, 74; and domestic spending, 82; and Eisenhower, 82–83, 86; and election of 1940, 53; and election of 1944, 66; and election of 1948, 75; and election of 1952, 82, 83; and fascism, 43; and foreign aid, 73–74, 83; *A Foreign Policy for Americans,* 80; and four freedoms, 63; and Franklin Roosevelt, 43; and free trade, 69; and government, 39–40, 43, 50, 74, 80, 82, 83; and Great Britain, 57, 63–64; and Greece, 74; and inflation, 74; and internationalism, 63–65; and international law, 71, 81; and interventionism, 72, 75, 76, 83, 84; and Korean War, 39, 79; and Lend-Lease program, 54, 55; and libertarians, 47; and Lippmann, 63–64; and Luce, 63; and Mackinac declaration, 65; and McCarthy, 78–79; and military, 39, 40, 44, 80–81; and national defense, 43; and nationalism, 64, 291; and national security, 43, 44, 74; and NATO, 76; and Nazis, 83; and New Deal,

42–43, 50, 59, 63, 74; and Nixon, 149; and postwar world role for United States, 64; as presidential contender, 50; and protectionism, 44; and sovereignty, 64; and Soviet Union, 63–64, 77, 81, 84; and tariff policies, 44; and taxes, 74, 82; and trade, 44; and Truman, 74, 81, 84; and Turkey, 74; and United Nations, 71, 81; and united nations organization, 69; and US naval escorts, 57; and Vandenberg, 74; and Western Europe, 81, 82, 83; and Wilkie, 64; and world federalism, 63

Taft, William Howard, 16–18, 22, 42, 64

Taiwan, 81, 91; and China, 311; and Eisenhower, 96, 101–2; and election of 1960, 127; and hawk-nationalist alliance, 307; and Nixon, 156, 163; and Republican Party, 255. *See also* East Asia

Taiwan Strait, 101, 156

Taliban, 271–72, 274, 302

tariffs: and Bretton Woods Agreement, 69; and Eisenhower, 98; and Hoover, 20; and Nixon, 145; and Republican Party, 69; and Robert Taft, 44

taxes, 47; and California tax revolt of 1978, 200; and Carter, 200, 204; and conservatism, 119, 200; and Eisenhower, 83, 87, 88, 106; and election of 1988, 234; and Franklin Roosevelt, 41; and George H. W. Bush, 234, 242, 248; and George W. Bush, 267, 271, 279, 286; and Goldwater, 120–21, 122; and McGovern, 168; and Reagan, 191, 192, 206, 220, 230; and Republican Party, 259; and Robert Taft, 74, 82

terrorism, 266, 306; and election of 2008, 285; and George W. Bush, 271–72, 274, 275, 279, 280, 288, 312; and hawk-nationalist alliance, 307; Islamist, 312–13; military action against, 316; nuclear, 312; and public opinion, 321; and Republican Party, 293; and Russia and China, 311–12; threat from, 312–13. *See also* September 11, 2001 attacks

Tet Offensive, 146

Texas, 123

Thailand, 101

Thatcher, Margaret, 211, 216

Thieu, Nguyen Van, 148, 158, 165, 166, 169, 170, 179

Third World: and Committee on the Present Danger, 197; and Eisenhower, 89, 99, 108, 112, 113; and George H. W. Bush, 237, 246;

and Helms, 262; and Kennedy, 112–13; and
Nixon, 156; and Reagan, 222; and Southern
Democrats, 92
Thomas, Norm, 75
Thompson, Fred, 284
Thurmond, Strom, 75, 145
Tiananmen Square massacre, 239, 251
Tomahawk cruise missiles, 210
Tower, John, 136, 139, 145
trade, 28; and Clinton, 252, 253; and Congress,
185; and Democratic Party, 98; and Eisen-
hower, 98; and founders, 5; and Franklin
Roosevelt, 40–41; and George H. W. Bush,
8, 232, 237, 239–40, 245, 251; and George W.
Bush, 287, 318; and interventionists, 48; and
McKinley, 12, 13; and Nixon, 163, 164, 176;
and Obama, 318–19; reciprocal, 98; and
Republican Party, 11, 41, 294; and Robert
Taft, 44; and Russia and China, 311–12; and
William Howard Taft, 16; and World War
II, 46
trade, free, 318; and classical liberals, 118; and
Eisenhower, 92, 114; and George H. W.
Bush, 235, 242, 248; and George W. Bush,
268, 272; and Hoover, 20; and paleocon-
servatism, 258; and Reagan, 199, 213; and
Republican Party, 91, 259; and Robert Taft,
69; and Southern Democrats, 92; and
Wilson, 19
Trident submarines, 208
Trotsky, Leon, 273
Trotskyism, 139
Trubowitz, Peter, 31–32
Truman, Harry: and communism, 72, 75,
76–77, 78, 81, 84; and Congress, 82; and
containment, 81; and defense spending, 79;
and Eisenhower, 86, 87, 89, 94, 95, 97, 104;
and election of 1948, 75; and foreign aid, 73;
as hawkish, 75, 76; and Korean War, 79–80;
and MacArthur, 81; and national security,
72, 76; and NATO, 76; and Republican
Party, 82, 303; and Robert Taft, 74, 81, 84;
and Soviet Union, 72–73, 77–78, 84; and
universal military training, 74
Turkey, 72, 73, 74, 74, 130

U-2 flights, 111, 112, 126
unilateralism, 9, 90, 186, 253, 272
Union for the Total Independence of Angola
(UNITA), 223
United Fruit Company, 99, 100

United Nations, 61; and Bricker amendment,
95; and China, 162; and Clinton, 252, 253;
and conflict mediation, 318; creation of,
70–71; and Eisenhower, 90, 101; and
George H. W. Bush, 233, 243, 247; and
George W. Bush, 271, 272, 275, 276, 277;
and Goldwater, 122; and hawk-nationalist
alliance, 307; and Helms, 262; and inspections in Iraq, 244; and moral authority,
317–18; and Nixon, 162; and Republican
Party, 91, 125, 255, 259; Resolution 1441, 275;
and Robert Taft, 69, 71, 81; and Yom Kippur War, 174
United Nations Association, 60
United Nations Security Council, 71, 241
United States: and conservatism, 25–26; and
freedom of action, 39; and Hoover, 20; and
liberalism, 25–26; national sovereignty of,
64; and open and liberal international economic order, 61; postwar world role of, 64;
predominance of, 309–10, 312; and Soviet
Union, 33
United States Marines, 108, 217
United States Navy, 15, 17, 55–56, 57
upper class voters, 48, 87, 250, 285
urban voters, 46, 48, 71, 87, 92, 137, 279
U.S.S. *Maine*, 12

Vandenberg, Arthur: and Bretton Woods, 69;
and internationalism, 72; and isolationism,
65; and Japan, 58; and Lend-Lease, 55;
and postwar foreign aid, 73; and postwar
league of nations, 66; and postwar settlement, 70; and presidency, 50; and Robert
Taft, 74, 76
Vanik, Charles, 176
Venezuela, 15, 109
Venona cables, 77, 78
Vienna summit (1961), 128
Viet Minh, 102, 103
Vietnamese Communists, 136
Vietnam/Vietnam War, 146; and Angola, 181;
and Christmas bombings, 169; and Committee on the Present Danger, 197; and
Congress, 154, 185; and conservatism, 138;
and Democratic Party, 3, 138, 154, 300, 303;
and draft deserters, 167; and Duck Hook
campaign, 158, 159; and Easter Offensive,
165–66, 170; and Eisenhower, 137; and elec-
tion of 1968, 147–48; and Ford, 179–80,
184; and Goldwater, 133, 135, 136; and

Vietnam/Vietnam War (*continued*)
Humphrey, 147–48; and Johnson, 135–36, 138, 146, 147–48, 172; and Kennedy, 128; and Kissinger, 152, 159, 166, 170, 171, 179, 184, 186; and McGovern, 168; and Nixon, 137, 142, 145, 146, 147–48, 150–51, 153, 155, 156, 157, 158–60, 161, 162, 165–66, 169–72, 175–76, 179, 184, 186, 187; and Operation Linebacker, 165–66; and Operation Linebacker II, 169; and post–cold war internationalism, 153; and public opinion, 153; and Reagan, 209; and Republican Party, 138, 154; and Vietnamization, 157, 159; and Wallace, 147, 148. *See also* Indochina

Viguerie, Richard, 195
Virginia, 123, 147
Voice of America, 213
voting rights, 121, 137

Wallace, George, 147, 148, 167
Wallace, Henry, 53, 60, 63, 74, 75
Wall Street Journal, 275
Walsh, David, 46
Walsh, Lawrence, 224
war: and Eisenhower, 104, 114; and George W. Bush, 1, 272, 291; and Goldwater, 135; and Kellogg-Briand Pact, 21; and president, 298; preventive, 1, 8, 104, 265, 272, 291, 293; and Republican Party, 293; and Wilson, 19
Warner, John, 281
War on Poverty, 134
War Powers Act, 175
Warren, Earl, 137–38
Warsaw Pact, 110, 211, 237
Washington Conference, 20
Washington Post, 275
Washington summit (1987), 224
Watergate scandal, 143, 178; and election of 1976, 184; and Nixon, 173, 174, 175, 187–88, 292; and Reagan, 193; and Republican Party, 189–90
weapons of mass destruction, 272, 277, 312, 313–14. *See also* nuclear policy
Weaver, Richard, 118
Weekly Standard, The, 256, 273, 305. *See also* Kristol, William
Weinberger, Caspar, 207, 217, 224

Welch, Robert, 123, 124
welfare, 41, 88, 118, 125, 137, 139, 168, 192, 259
West Berlin, 110
Western Europe: and Eisenhower, 89, 98–99, 104; and Lippmann, 62; military deployments to, 82, 84; and Nixon, 155; and Reagan, 222; and Republican Party nationalism, 91; and Robert Taft, 81, 82, 83; and Truman, 79
Western peace movements, 211
Western progressives, 20, 40, 42
Western states, 131; and Carter, 196; and election of 1968, 147; and election of 1980, 203; and Goldwater, 132; and Reagan, 193, 203; and Republican Party, 116, 137, 141, 202
West Germany, 98–99, 109, 163, 237, 238
Weyrich, Paul, 195
Wheeler, Burton, 46, 54
Will, George, 277, 288
Willkie, Wendell, 49–50, 53, 55, 60, 64, 65, 66, 144; *One World*, 61–62, 64
Wilson, James, 139
Wilson, Woodrow, 17, 18, 19–20, 56, 59, 60, 62, 71, 292
Wilsonianism, 60, 275
Wolfowitz, Paul, 256, 264, 268
women, 200, 219, 279, 320
Wood, Robert, 46
working class, 138, 146; and Democratic Party, 204; and Dukakis, 234; and election of 1968, 147; and election of 1984, 220; and George H. W. Bush, 234; and Nixon, 149; and Reagan, 192, 205; and Republican Party, 295
Works Progress Administration, 59
World Trade Organization, 319
World War I, 18, 19, 59
World War II, 39, 51–52, 69, 71–72

Yalta conference, 70, 77, 94
Yeltsin, Boris, 245
Yom Kippur War, 173–75
Young Americans for Freedom, 123, 133
Yugoslavia, 73, 246, 262–63, 309

Zaire, 181